Women in Management

WOMEN
IN MANAGEMENT

BETTE ANN STEAD

University of Houston

PRENTICE-HALL, INC., ENGLEWOOD CLIFFS, N.J. 07632

Library of Congress Cataloging in Publication Data
Main entry under title:

Women in management.

  Bibliography; p.
  1. Women executives — United States — Addresses,
essays, lectures.   2. Women in business — United States —
Addresses, essays, lectures.   3. Sex discrimination
against women — United States — Addresses, essays, lectures.   4. Discrimination in employment — United States —
addresses, essays, lectures.   I. Stead, Bette Ann,
(date)
HF5500.3.U54W648   331.4'81'658400973   77-13982
ISBN 0-13-961730-2
ISBN 0-13-961722-1 pbk.

Printed in the United States of America

10   9   8   7   6   5   4   3

Prentice-Hall International, Inc., *London*
Prentice-Hall of Australia Pty. Limited, *Sydney*
Prentice-Hall of Canada, Ltd., *Toronto*
Prentice-Hall of India Private Limited, *New Delhi*
Prentice-Hall of Japan, Inc., *Tokyo*
Prentice-Hall of Southeast Asia Pte. Ltd., *Singapore*
Whitehall Books Limited, *Wellington, New Zealand*

TO LUCY

Contents

III

GETTING ALONG WITH THE CORPORATE WOMAN 105

IV

IDENTIFYING LANGUAGE BARRIERS AND REMEDIES 159

Preface

Hope — glimmers of hope. Government pressures and legal decisions have given women with a wealth of work experience, a good education, or both, hope that they may reach their long-overdue and appropriate place in the organization hierarchy. Responsible, reasonable women — women who support themselves and their families, and women who work to provide necessary supplements to their husband's income — are hoping finally to reach the organization levels for which they are qualified and also to receive commensurate economic rewards. Many of these women have watched and waited for years as they have trained a procession of incoming bosses and authored important letters, company policies, procedures, speeches, and even legislation that bore their male bosses' names. And sometimes they have quietly looked for another job when they found themselves in the position of covering for incompetence, or alcoholism, or a general lack of initiative.

Many of these women are not connected in any formal way with the feminist movement. When they are not at work, they are busy caring for family members, keeping a household going, doing civic work, pursuing more education, or resting after a hard day's work. But they read and they watch and they listen. They know of the court battles settled in favor of women, they see the government representatives coming in to check their company's affirmative action plan, they see an occasional woman making some progress, and they hope.

Women students are turning to thoughts of careers with aspirations of leadership. Not only are they majoring in professions where few women have ventured before, but they are taking management courses in colleges of business administration. Today's students not only have the natural hope that youth has always had, but today's students also read about court settlements and equal opportunity laws. Faculty members are looking for materials to use in conjunction with social issues or womens' studies courses.

Many personnel managers, training directors, and affirmative action officers are new to their role of implementing equal opportunity for women. Top executives are willing to make the necessary initial verbal and written statement supporting affirmative action and yet wonder how it is ever going to filter through the organization.

All these people have a common goal — a productive environment for people which leads to a productive organization. They look for advice, sources of information, and professional encouragement. This book is intended to help them.

Highly readable articles have been selected for their relevancy. The cases provide insight into the kinds of discriminatory experiences women are having and will be useful for discussion of how to handle these situations appropriately when they arise. The discussion questions should guide the reader into purposeful areas for discussion. Every effort was made to write the annotated bibliography, which contains references to articles based on empirical research, in a concise, simple style. The findings should prove useful to people in many different roles. The glossary should clear up some fuzzy areas. The research tools should aid those interested in furthering equal opportunity through empirically based findings, and the brief section on the laws should provide some basic background and information.

Acknowledgements

Since 1972, I have worked to aid women in gaining equal job opportunities and appropriate pay. The following people and organizations have entered my life in numerous supportive ways to provide the environment which eventually led to this book. I honor them in this acknowledgement section.

A. E. Meissner and Sharon McKinley Bendy, Sun Oil Company; Kathleen Gammill, Houston Natural Gas Corporation; Maxine R. Hacke, Gulf Oil Corporation; William G. Ryan, *Business Horizons*; The U.S. Naval War College; Mary Kerr, Johnson Space Center; Sally Hazen and Diane Barber, Pennzoil Company; Noel B. McClure, Norma F. Schneider, J. H. Wilson, and Robert H. Milsted, University of Houston; Sandra S. Weber and Rebekah Estrada, University of Houston M. D. Anderson Memorial Library; Vivien Simon, Houston Foundation for Continuing Education; Dr. Charles Summer, University of Washington; the Academy of Management; General Jeanne M. Holm; President and Mrs. Gerald R. Ford; Louis Baudean and Earl T. Kivett, Prentice-Hall, Inc.; the faculty and administration of the College of Business Administration, University of Houston; Ethel E. Berry and Charles R. Berry; Morris P. Wolf.

In addition, for their help in reviewing the manuscript, I am grateful to Professor William P. Anthony, College of Business, The Florida State University; Dr. Rowland G. Baughman, Keuka College; Ms. Sandra Ekberg-Jordan, Director of the Graduate Management Program for Women, Pace University; Professor Elizabeth Lanham, College of Business Administration, The University of Texas at Austin; and Professor Patricia Ann Renwick, Graduate School of Administration, University of California at Irvine. And to Linda Siebert and Sonia Meyer of Prentice-Hall, Inc., my thanks for their cooperation in producing this book.

Women in Management

I

Debunking Myths
and Stereotypes

This opening section will lay the foundation for an understanding of why women have problems gaining equal opportunity. The myths, stereotypes, and other barriers are reviewed in the first four articles (Dipboye; Reif, Newstrom, and Monczka; Fenn; Minahan). The remaining articles (Durkin; Women's Bureau; Tharp) give empirical research data to help remove the barriers.

Where have these barriers come from? Who is responsible? They come from centuries of acculturation/socialization brought about by different cultures, societies, and traditions. We are all responsible for accepting and reinforcing them at some time or other during our lives.

Are these myths and stereotypes appropriate today? (It is beyond the scope of this book to determine if they were ever appropriate.) They are certainly inappropriate today for very pragmatic reasons: seven out of ten women work today out of pressing economic need, we are literally wasting the brain power of half our population—women who can make invaluable contributions to business, science, technology, and the arts; and, finally, they are inappropriate because they place grave limitations on the full development of our modern world. The ethical consequences have been staggering. Families supported by women have suffered low standards of living; children supported by women have had little opportunity for top quality university educations; and individual women themselves have been forced into work routines that offer little opportunity for progress, self-direction, or creativity.

Some say, "We are not ready yet; let equal opportunity happen naturally. It will come in time." How sad that this was not solved on the basis of ethics centuries ago. That is why the equal opportunity laws are needed today.

Women as Managers— Stereotypes and Realities

Robert L. Dipboye

In spite of the increasing number of women entering occupations formerly reserved for men, the management field has become one of the last frontiers of female liberation. Indeed, in 1970 less than 5 percent of all managers were women, a remarkably small percentage since women constitute approximately 40 percent of the total work force.

Recent studies reveal that the stereotype of women as lacking the abilities and character traits required of managers is widely held and has contributed to the lack of progress in this area of employment. Virginia Schein, of the Metropolitan Life Insurance Company, asked 300 middle level managers to describe "women in general," "men in general" and "the successful manager." According to her findings, the successful manager was perceived to possess the traits of aggressiveness, emotional stability, vigor and self-reliance. "Men in general" were believed to possess the same attributes ascribed to the successful manager, while women were rated as deficient in most of these characteristics.[1] In another survey of male and female executives conducted by the *Harvard Business Review*, the majority of male respondents believed women to be unsuited for management because of their "unstable temperaments."[2] A more recent survey of executives revealed that females were perceived to be unfit as managers because of their purported lack of dependability.[3]

These findings confirm Douglas McGregor's observation that "the model of the successful manager in our culture is a masculine one. The good manager is aggressive, competitive, firm and just. He is not feminine, he is not soft and yielding, or dependent or intuitive in the womanly sense." The sex-typing of management as a male occupation, requiring male traits, poses a major barrier to women who would otherwise qualify and excel in positions of leadership. Much of this sex-typing is

Robert L. Dipboye, "Women as Managers—Stereotypes and Realities," *Survey of Business* (May/June 1975), pp. 22-26.

based on myths. To be specific, at least five stereotypes, commonly presented as arguments against women in management, appear to be fallacious.

STEREOTYPE 1: MEN ARE INTELLECTUALLY SUPERIOR

One common stereotype holds that men are more intelligent and, in general, more competent than women. However, research comparing men and women on a variety of aptitudes does not support the supposed intellectual superiority of men. On the contrary, the most consistent finding has been that women surpass men on tests of verbal aptitude. Furthermore, women tend to excel in tests of memory and in scholastic achievement.[4]

Although women are not handicapped intellectually, the stereotype of the ideal woman discourages expression of abilities. For instance, Hollander found that as the grade point average of high school males increased, their self-esteem also increased. On the other hand, self-esteem of women *decreased* with increases in their grade point averages, so that women with A averages had lower self-esteem than those with C averages.[5]

Within organizations, many basically intelligent women unfortunately act "empty-headed" in order to fulfill the expectations of male superiors. The woman with enough intellectual talent to be a manager often is torn between the desire for approval by male authorities (for whom she must play the role of the naive, uninformed person) and the need for an outright demonstration of competence (for which she risks ridicule by acting "out-of-role").

STEREOTYPE 2: MEN ARE EMOTIONALLY MORE STABLE THAN WOMEN

Another common belief is that women are more vulnerable to drastic swings of mood than men. Again, research does not support such a general conclusion. One reason for this stereotype of feminine instability may be that traditionally a woman's expression of the emotions of fear, anxiety, grief, disappointment or pain has been more socially acceptable than it has been for men. According to Sidney Jourard, one reason that the average man dies earlier than the average woman is that the "male role, as personally and socially defined, requires man to appear tough, objective, striving, achieving, unsentimental and emotionally unexpressive. But seeming is not being. If a man is tender ... if he weeps, if he shows weakness, he will likely be viewed as unmanly by others, and he will probably regard himself as inferior to other men."[6]

Since women may express a greater variety of emotions than men without fear of disapproval it may be thought incorrectly that they are temperamentally unstable. However, the same range of emotions exists in men even though they are less likely to be expressed.

Misconceptions concerning menstruation have also contributed to the stereotype of feminine instability. Current evidence reveals that women react individually to menstruation and premenstruation. Furthermore, a recent review of the research in this area by Mary Parlee suggests that many popular notions may be incorrect, and on the basis of the research to date, "it is difficult to predict anything about an individual's behavior from the fact [that] she is in the premenstrual or menstrual phase of the cycle."[7]

Of course, biological cycles affect mood and temperament, but an increasing amount of research reveals that these cycles exist in *both* men and women. For example, one researcher found that men also were subject to cycles of emotionality which varied from three and one-half to nine weeks in length and were highly predictable for each individual.[8] There is no evidence to support the contention that the effects of emotional cycles on the performance of women are any greater than the effects of similar cycles on the performance of men.

STEREOTYPE 3: MEN VALUE ACHIEVEMENT, PROMOTION AND MEANINGFUL WORK MORE THAN WOMEN

Women have long been described as interested in what Herzberg has termed the hygiene factors, i.e., money, security, clean working conditions, social relations and other extrinsic factors of work. In comparison, men who aspire to be managers are believed to value intrinsic motivators such as the desire to achieve, to be promoted, to assume responsibility and to perform work which utilizes important abilities. Because of alleged differences in motivation, women are thought less committed to work itself.

Several studies dispute the notion that women are less intrinsically motivated. In a recent survey of male and female employees, both men and women rated the intrinsic factors of their work as more important than the extrinsic factors. There were no differences between the sexes in the expressed importance of the intrinsic factors.[9]

A national survey of employed men and women found that women were as dissatisfied as men with work which failed to utilize their abilities. In the same survey, no difference was found between men and women in terms of the value placed on social relations.[10] Finally, a survey comparing the motivation to manage among male and female managers and educational administrators revealed no consistent differences between men and women in either the desire to manage or the needs related to this desire.[11]

Considerable evidence points out that women are as committed to their jobs as men. Two -thirds of working women are economically independent and over one-third are the sole wage earners, contradicting the myth that women work only for "pin money." Also, data from the U.S. Department of Labor reveal that sex is a poor predictor of turnover and absenteeism, contrary to the popular notion that absenteeism and turnover rates are higher among women than men.

According to this study, women show slightly higher absenteeism than men (5.6 vs. 5.2 days absent due to illness in 1970),[12] and slightly higher turnover (monthly quit rates averaged 2.2 percent for males and 2.4 for females in 1968).[13] However, differences in absenteeism and turnover can be explained by the restriction of women to routine, low-status positions within organizations. If men and women were matched on the type of work performed, it is likely that even these slight differences would be eliminated. Actually, when chances for promotion or utilization of abilities are minimal, commitment to the job decreases for *both men and women.* Given such a situation, an employee is likely to lower his/her aspirations in order to avoid future frustration.

In one national survey, most working women saw promotion as less likely and as less important than the working men in this sample. However, women who faced possible promotions equaled men in their desire for advancement.[14] These and other findings indicate that women, given equal opportunity for self-growth and advancement, are as committed to work and are as intrinsically motivated as men.

STEREOTYPE 4: MEN ARE INHERENTLY MORE ASSERTIVE THAN WOMEN

Men often are described as innately more assertive than women, who are purported to be passive and docile by nature. In general, American women do tend to score lower on personality measures of dominance because of cultural values and not basic biological differences in the sexes. Current research and observation indicate that women can assimilate to roles requiring the assertion of influence and leadership as effectively as men. Fears that women will be passive managers or that they will overreact by being tyrants are not justified.

Jerolyn Lyle and Jane Ross compared the leadership styles of 70 male and 70 female managers matched on occupation level, tenure and other relevant characteristics. Contrary to the stereotypes, most of the women adopted active, effective leadership styles and were actually more diverse in their management styles than the men.[15]

Of course, women managers face certain problems which do not exist for the typical male. A woman attempting to exert leadership in a male environment may be on the "horns of a dilemma." Since a successful manager is seen as assertive and self-reliant, a failure to fulfill this role would cause her subordinates and peers to perceive her as weak and passive, more capable of being led than leading. But if she demonstrates assertiveness, initiative or ambition, many men and women will see her as hostile, maladjusted and overcontrolling. Too often "leadership" qualities for a man are judged as traits of hostility and aggression in a woman.

STEREOTYPE 5: THE SUCCESSFUL MANAGER POSSESSES MASCULINE ATTRIBUTES

Underlying the belief that women are less qualified than men for managerial positions is the assumption that the successful manager possesses most of the traits valued in men, such as assertiveness, emotional stability and ambition, but few of the traits valued in women, such as dependence, passivity and emotionality. This assumption is oversimplified in view of the psychological research on leadership.

Throughout the 1940's and 1950's, psychologists sought to determine the traits distinguishing the effective leader from the ineffective leader. After exhaustive research, no trait, whether a personality characteristic, a physical attribute or an aptitude, was found consistently to distinguish good leaders from bad ones.

An accurate conclusion derived from this research is that the characteristics of a good leader depend on the situation. The most important quality of a good leader may be the ability to change his or her style of management according to the situation. Unfortunately, some managers lack flexibility because they rigidly adhere to the stereotype of the good leader as a tough, unemotional and dominant individual.

Distortion in Perceptions Due to Sex Stereotypes

Psychological research has failed to support many popular notions concerning differences in personality and aptitude between the sexes. Of course, differences do exist to the extent that men tend to surpass women on some specific aptitudes and personality dimensions, while on other specific traits, women tend to surpass men. However, individual differences among men and among women are so great that the stereotype of the typical woman or the typical man is meaningless.

Despite contradictory evidence, stereotypes concerning female inadequacy as managers persist and act to distort perceptions of male and female performance and potential. One obvious consequence of these ideas is that a man is more likely to be selected for a managerial position than is an equally qualified woman. In one study conducted by a university placement center, college recruiters evaluated the employment suitability of male and female candidates for a management position. Although all individuals were identical in experience, grade point averages and other qualifications, men were consistently rated more suitable than female candidates.[16]

Benson Rosen and Thomas Jerdee suggest that once a woman is selected for a managerial position, her superiors will be less committed to her career development than they would be to the career of a man in her position.[17] The authors surveyed 1,500 managers, asking for decisions regarding hypothetical male and female subordinates faced with a variety of conflicts and problems. One such problem involved a conflict between job demands and family obligations. Most of the respondents indicated that, given such a conflict, they would expect the male employee to put his job above his family, but they would expect a woman in the same situation to sacrifice her career.

Another incident judged by the respondents involved a situation in which personal misconduct threatened a valued employee's job. The managers surveyed indicated that they would make more exceptions and go to greater efforts to retain a male employee than they would a woman with equal qualifications. Also, respondents in this study tended to select a male over an equally qualified female when asked to choose a participant in a management development seminar.

Not only can sex stereotypes act to prevent the selection and development of female managerial talent, but they can distort performance evaluation. In one study, raters were asked to evaluate the quality of a professional paper with half believing that the author was male and the other half believing the author was female. Those who thought the author was female judged the paper poorer in its professional quality than those believing the author was male.[18] In another study, raters attributed the good performance of a man in traditionally male tasks to intelligence while the success of a woman on the same tasks was attributed to luck. According to the authors, what is skill for the male is "luck" for the female.[19]

The Self-Fulfilling Nature of Sex Stereotypes

The ultimate consequence of sex stereotypes is that they may become self-fulfilling. Unfortunately, many women believe themselves less capable of managing than men and have become resigned to jobs for which they are overqualified. Too many capable women have given up or avoided career aspirations either to behave consistently with a self-concept or to adjust to a society shaped and dominated by men.

Dramatic proof of this underutilization of talented women was provided in a study of the development of 1,528 gifted children with an average I.Q. of 152.[20] A follow-up survey, conducted when the average age of the group was 35, revealed that virtually all the men were employed — over 70 percent in the professions and the semiprofessions. Outstanding achievement disclosed by the male group included the youngest brigadier general in the Army, a famous plastic surgeon, a motion picture director, famous novelists, scientists, professors, and highly successful entrepreneurs and executives.

Although as many women (67 percent) as men (70 percent) finished college, less than 48 percent of the women were employed full-time. Of those with jobs, almost all were elementary school teachers, secretaries and clerks. Very few were found in law, medicine, the sciences or management. According to the researchers, the most notable achievement of the highly gifted woman in the sample was her selection of a highly gifted mate. Considering the potential contributions to the sciences, to the arts and business which could have been made by these and other equally capable women, one is confronted with what author Caroline Bird has termed the "high cost of keeping women down."

Social and legal forces will eventually bring a more equitable representation of women in management. Although there will be problems, management has much to gain from the integration of women into its ranks. Indeed, the experience of those companies which have women managers and supervisors is generally positive. One Department of Labor study revealed that 75 percent of the male and female employees surveyed had favorable attitudes toward women as managers after working for a woman.[21]

Rather than resisting the inevitable, today's managers can act to ease the transition. A first step in this direction would be the reexamination of stereotypes, which distort perceptions and treatment of women. Most important, managers should be sensitive to the female managerial talent among their employees and should make concerted efforts to encourage and develop this talent.

NOTES

[1] Virginia Schein, "The Relationship Between Sex Role Stereotypes and Requisite Management Characteristics," *Journal of Applied Psychology* 57 (1973), pp. 95-100.

[2] G. W. Bowman, N. B. Worthy and S. A. Greyser, "Are Women Executives People?" *Harvard Business Review* 43 (1965), pp. 14 – 16.

[3] B. M. Bass, J. Krusell and R. H. Alexander, "Male Managers' Attitudes Toward Working Women," *American Behavioral Scientist* 15 (1971), pp. 77 – 83.

[4] A. Anastasi, *Differential Psychology*, 3rd ed. (New York: Macmillan & Co., (1958).

[5] J. Hollander, "Sex Differences in Sources of Social Self-Esteem," *Journal of Consulting and Clinical Psychology* 38 (1972), pp. 343 – 47.

[6] S. M. Jourard, "Some Lethal Aspects of the Male Role," in R. E. Coffey et al., *Behavior in Organizations: A Multidimensional View* (Englewood Cliffs, N.J.: Prentice-Hall, Inc., 1975).

[7] Mary Brown Parlee, "The Premenstrual Syndrome," *Psychological Bulletin* 80 (1973), pp. 454 – 65.

[8] R. B. Hersey, "Emotional Cycles in Man," *Journal of Mental Science* 77 (1931), pp. 151 – 69.

[9] S. D. Saleh and M. Lalljee, "Sex and Job Orientation," *Personnel Psychology* 22, No. 4 (1969), pp. 465 – 71.

[10] J. E. Crowley, T. E. Levitlin and R. P. Quinn, "Seven Deadly Half Truths About Women," *Psychology Today* 6 (March 1973), pp. 94 – 96.

[11] J. B. Miner, "Motivation to Manage Among Women: Studies of Business Managers and Educational Administrators," *Journal of Vocational Behavior* 5 (1974), pp. 197 – 208.

[12] R. Tsuchigane and N. Dodge, *Economic Discrimination Against Women in the United States* (Lexington, Mass.: Toronto, 1974), pp. 40 – 41.

[13] U.S. Department of Labor, Wages and Labor Standards Administration, "Facts About Women's Absenteeism and Labor Turnover," August 1969.

[14] J. Crowley et al., "Half Truths."

[15] Jerolyn Lyle and Jane L. Ross, *Women in Industry* (Lexington, Mass.: Toronto, 1974), pp. 89 – 92.

[16] R. L. Dipboye, H. L. Fromkin, and K. Wiback, "Relative Importance of Applicant Sex, Attractiveness, and Scholastic Standing in Evaluation of Job Applicant Resumes," *Journal of Applied Psychology* 60 (1975), pp. 39 – 44.

[17] B. Rosen and T. Jerdee, "Sex Stereotyping in the Executive Suite," *Harvard Business Review* 52 (March-April 1974), pp. 45 – 58.

[18] G. I. Pheterson, S. B. Kiesler and P. A. Goldberg, "Evaluation of the Performance of Women as a Function of Their Sex, Achievement and Personal History," *Journal of Personality and Social Psychology* 19 (1971), pp. 114 – 18.

[19] K. Deaux and T. Enswiller, "Explanations of Successful Performance on Sex-Linked Tasks: What's Skill for the Male is Luck for the Female," *Journal of Personality and Social Psychology* 29 (1973), pp. 80 – 85.

[20] L. M. Terman and M. Oden, *The Gifted Child Grows Up* (Stanford, California: Stanford University Press (1947).

[21] Report of a Special Task Force to the Secretary of Health, Education and Welfare, *Work in America* (Cambridge, Mass.: MIT Press, 1973), p. 60.

DISCUSSION QUESTIONS

1.   What examples have you seen of highly intelligent women "playing dumb" to gain acceptance?

2.   What examples have you seen of men holding back expression of their emotions because they were afraid of being perceived as "weak"?

3.   What examples have you seen of women hiding behind the myth of monthly emotional cycles to get out of work?

4.   List all the men and women you know who have changed jobs during the last three years. Compare them by job level. Which list is longer?

5.   Do you know any successful women managers? How do they provide leadership?

6.   Do you know any intelligent women who have begun to believe the stereotype that they are less capable? How do they exhibit this belief?

7.   Males should give top priority to their jobs when career and family demands conflict. Why do you agree or disagree with this statement?

8.   Managers make greater efforts to counsel males on their personal conduct when it threatens their careers. Females may get little or no counseling. Why? Would you agree that this is appropriate? Explain.

9.   Females should give priority to their families when career and family demands conflict. Why do you agree or disagree with this statement?

10.   What actions could be taken to insure that the same kind of disciplinary action for the same offense be given both sexes?

11.   What actions could be taken to insure that the same training opportunities be given both sexes?

Exploding Some Myths
About Women Managers

William E. Reif
John W. Newstrom
Robert M. Monczka

Are women managers different from their male counterparts in ways that affect job performance and, therefore, their ability to contribute to the achievement of organizational objectives? Are there substantial reasons for excluding them from managerial positions to the extent that they are excluded today?[1]

The organization's answer to both questions generally has been "yes," largely because of a wide variety of assumptions, or myths, about women managers. Some representative assumptions are:

• Women are more emotional and sensitive to the feelings of others, while men are rational and coolly objective in their relationships with others.

• Women are uncomfortable in a man's world.

• Women work as a hobby or for luxuries and, as a result, lack the ambition, aggressiveness, and dedication necessary to excel in business.

• Women have higher rates of sickness and absenteeism.

• Women do not understand statistics.[2]

On the assumption that women are significantly different from men in important ways, many organizations have taken the position that special training and development programs are required to prepare women for management positions. In an article entitled "Management Development for Women," Brenner presents a set of recommendations for setting up effective programs to prepare women for management. One of his four underlying assumptions is that women require special programs, because "in general, they have different skills and different attitudes toward the managerial role than men do."[3]

William E. Reif, John W. Newstrom, and Robert M. Monezka, "Exploding Some Myths About Women Managers," *California Management Review*, Vol. XVII, no. 4, pp. 72–79. Copyright © 1975 by the Regents of the University of California. Reprinted by permission.

Companies are not alone in establishing separate management training programs for women. Educational institutions, such as the University of Michigan's Division of Management Education, conduct programs that are directed to women, apparently on the assumption that women's needs are different. The brochure for one program, "Management Briefing for Women," states that the three-day seminar has been designed to "meet the needs of women who wish to develop their managerial skills." Great care was taken, however, not to offend any prospective participants by stressing that women are invited and encouraged to participate in all management seminars.

While special treatment appears to be the dominant approach, there are writers and practitioners who believe that women should participate in the same management and supervisory training programs as men, both in and outside the organization. A recent survey of twenty prominent business firms found that although some interest was expressed in special programs for women (on the assumption that inferiorities are commonly found in women), only one firm had what could be classified as a special development program.[4] Interestingly enough, one other company excludes women entirely from its management-development programs. The overall survey report cautions against the use of special programs unless they are open to all persons who need added exposure in a particular discipline. Otherwise, such programs may take on negative connotations and continue to promote the myth that women, along with other minority groups, are innately less capable of performing effectively as managers.

REVIEW OF RELEVANT RESEARCH

Is there evidence that women managers are different—psychologically and socially—from men? If women are different in ways that account for variances in managerial performance, special considerations are probably warranted. If, on the other hand, they are not different in these ways, it is time to engage in more meaningful discussions of the role of women in business. This review of research findings is not intended to be exhaustive but is meant to be representative of what is known about the capabilities of women to manage.

In testing for differences in level of measured ability and knowledge in twenty-two dimensions related to business, the Johnson O'Connor Research Foundation's Human Engineering Laboratory found that there are no differences between men and women in fourteen categories, women excel in six, and men excel in two areas. Women are superior in finger dexterity, graphoria, ideaphoria, observation, silograms, and abstract visualization, while men excel in grip and structural visualization.[5] These results, and others, led to the following observation:

> The aptitudes which seem to underlie successful management are: Objective Personality, Abstract Visualization, and high English Vocabulary. Equal numbers of men and women possess objective personality and high vocabulary. More women have abstract visualization than men. The ratios are three women in four, one man in two. Theoretically at least, there ought to be more women in management than men.[6]

An exhaustive review by Knowles and Moore of the research contributions concerned with female biology and socialization factors by Bennis, McClelland, Maccoby, Gizberg, Hoffman, Rossi, Masters and Johnson, and others, led them to conclude that the one difference that biologists, psychologists, social psychologists, and sociologists all seem to agree on is women's greater concern for relationships among people.

> About the only testable difference between men and women seems to be women's greater ability in interpersonal relationships ... the manager of the future will need to be more people-centered, more able to work with people than to exercise position power.[7]

In his book *Managing Women in Business*, Ellman raised the question, "How different are women?" His research led to the general conclusion that, "From an analysis of the data ... it may be seen that the differences between men and women are far less important than the similarities between them."[8] He suggested that there is some evidence to support the contention that women are more concerned with associates and friends, the quality of supervision, and the surroundings of a job, while men are more interested in the benefits of a job, opportunities for education and advancement, and pay.

The noted Harvard psychologist David McClelland, in trying to synthesize the thousands of psychological studies indicating sex differences, remarked that "the problem is not lack of information, but making sense out of a surfeit of facts."[9] He went on to identify women as more interdependent, more interested in people than things, less analytical, and less manipulative of things than men.

A recent article by Crowley, Levitin, and Quinn attempted to dispel some ill-founded stereotypes of the "average woman."[10] The study found that a significant sex difference does exist in the importance women place on having co-workers who are friendly and helpful. However, women and men attach the same importance to having a competent supervisor rather than having a nice supervisor who is concerned with the welfare of subordinates. The study also provided some support for the proposition that women are more concerned than men with the hygiene aspects of their jobs (such as good hours, pleasant physical surroundings, and convenient travel to and from work).

This study also revealed that women and men are equally concerned that their work is self-actualizing, equally discontented with intellectually undemanding jobs, and equally concerned with opportunities for getting ahead on the job. Overall, these research findings show that there are "more on-the-job similarities between men and women than differences."[11]

Another recent study by Lirtzman and Wahba investigated the capability of women to assume managerial roles, especially aspects related to the decision-making process. The results clearly do not support the contention that women will adopt a sex-role-related strategy in a competitive situation under conditions of uncertainty. In discussing the practical implications of their findings, the authors concluded:

> From a practical point of view these findings raise questions about the traditions of business which bar the accession of women to high organizational positions precisely because it is expected that women will "naturally" act according to sex related roles; that is, noncompetitively.[12]

All of these research findings, although not conclusive, strongly suggest that many of the assumptions that women managers are basically different from men ("different" usually meant as inferior) are not well supported by facts.

A SOCIAL-PSYCHOLOGICAL VIEW OF WOMEN MANAGERS

Most of the research on women managers takes a predominantly psychological approach and is concerned with understanding the attitudes, values, and beliefs women hold about themselves and their work-related roles. Once this psychological make-up is established, strong inferences are made about how women will behave in a business situation. Less attention has been given to understanding how women related to the environment within which they operate, their attitudes about it, and the extent to which the socialization process has affected their view of the managerial role and the congruence between their self-concept and role expectations.

The psychology of women managers cannot be understood outside the social context and social pressures that direct and support their behavior. The purpose of this study is to provide information about women managers' perceptions of their work environment and to see if their views of the formal and informal aspects of organization are significantly different from those of men. If their social perceptions are different, there would be some basis for predicting sex differences in personality and social conduct. This, in turn, would lead one to conclude that women should be treated differently and that certain modifications in organizational climate would be in order. It would also lend credence to the need for special training programs for women so that they could be conditioned to more nearly fit the role expected of them as managers.

One of the most significant features of this study is its concern for how women managers themselves perceive their work environment. Other studies have found it more convenient to ask men, such as a group of personnel directors, what they think women's attitudes are, or to use a sample of women from the general population, most of whom are not managers and have no aspirations to become managers. There is reason to believe that, psychologically and sociologically, there is just as much difference between female managers and nonmanagers as there is between male managers and nonmanagers. One could also expect there to be more commonality among managers, male and female, than between managers and nonmanagers.

Methodology

The semantic differential technique was used to measure men and women managers' perceptions of their formal and informal organizations. The semantic differential was chosen because of its ability to measure perceptions along two independent dimensions, evaluative and potency. The evaluative dimension measures perceptions of the "goodness" or "badness" of organizational concepts. In other words, are they believed to be valuable and beneficial to the individual in satisfying his needs? The potency dimension measures perceptions of the "strength" or "weakness" of particular concepts, or the extent to which they are pervasive in the work environment and influential in affecting individual behavior.

The research instrument was developed by selecting eight concepts to represent the formal organization and eight to represent the informal organization. The concepts are:

Formal Organization Concepts

Authority
Job description
Performance appraisal
Chain of command
Policies
Controls
Organizational objectives
Supervisor

Informal Organization Concepts

Voluntary teamwork
Clique
Personal influence
Co-worker evaluation
Social interaction
Group cohesion
Social group membership
Grapevine

Bipolar adjective pairs were chosen through a judgmental selection process that took into consideration their appropriateness for the concepts being studied and their high factor-loading scores. The bipolar adjective pairs selected to record perceptions of the evaluative dimension were: fair — unfair, good — bad, valuable — worthless, pleasant — unpleasant, and clear — hazy. The potency pairs were: strong — weak, hard — soft, and large — small.[13]

The sixteen-page questionnaire was administered to 286 men and 55 women who were participants in management-development programs. They represented 164 organizations, the majority of which were business and government organizations. The organizations varied in size from less than 50 to more than 20,000 employees and had annual sales or revenues from under $250,000 to over $500 million.

Statistical analyses of the data included (1) calculation of the evaluative and potency means for each of the sixteen concepts and for the formal and the informal organizations overall; and (2) application of the standard "t" test to determine if significant differences exist between male and female perceptions of the formal and the informal organizations.

RESEARCH RESULTS

The individual and overall means of the eight formal and eight informal concepts for the evaluative and potency dimensions are shown in Tables 1 and 2. The relatively high mean scores along the evaluative dimension for both men and women indicate that the concepts representing the formal and informal organizations, with the exception of clique and grapevine, were perceived to be quite good, that is, valuable to the respondents in satisfying their needs (Table 1). The mean scores along the potency dimension, although lower than the evaluative scores, reveal that the organizational variables were generally perceived to be quite strong and influential in affecting behavior (Table 2).

TABLE 1 Formal and Informal Organizational Concepts, Evaluative Means

	Evaluative Means*	
	Women	Men
Formal		
Supervisor	6.22	5.84
Organizational objectives	6.12	5.99
Authority	6.00	5.71
Performance appraisal	5.93	5.48
Job description	5.84	5.44
Policies	5.79	5.69
Chain of command	5.77	5.74
Controls	5.77	5.60
Overall means	5.93	5.69
Informal		
Voluntary teamwork	6.01	5.79
Group cohesion	5.67	5.41
Personal influence	5.56	5.09
Social group membership	5.49	5.12
Social interaction	5.47	5.21
Co-worker evaluation	5.12	4.67
Clique	3.29	3.12
Grapevine	3.06	3.31
Overall means	4.96	4.72

*Minimum score = 1.00; maximum score = 7.00.

Formal Versus Informal Concepts

The data show that the formal organizational concepts were perceived by men and women to be better (more valuable) and stronger (more influential) than the informal ones. Voluntary teamwork and group cohesion were the only informal concepts that compared favorably with the set of formal organization variables. For men and women the evaluative means of all other informal concepts were lower than the lowest of the formal concepts. Along the potency dimension women respondents viewed *all* formal concepts as more influential in affecting behavior than any of the informal concepts. For men all formal concepts except job description and performance appraisal were perceived as stronger and more influential than any informal organization variables.

Clique and grapevine had the lowest composite evaluative and potency means of all sixteen variables, indicating that they were viewed as relatively bad and weak. The fact that they were perceived as weak and having little influence on individual behavior is fortunate. Although the difference is not statistically significant, it is interesting to note that

TABLE 2 Formal and Informal Organizational Concepts, Potency Means

Concept	Potency Means*	
	Women	Men
Formal		
Organizational objectives	5.72	5.35
Authority	5.24	5.33
Policies	5.13	5.05
Performance appraisal	5.12	4.77
Supervisor	5.05	5.15
Controls	5.00	5.12
Chain of command	4.98	5.03
Job description	4.87	4.72
Overall means	5.14	5.07
Informal		
Personal influence	4.86	4.86
Voluntary teamwork	4.85	4.74
Group cohesion	4.82	4.74
Social group membership	4.61	4.38
Grapevine	4.55	4.18
Co-worker evaluation	4.52	4.39
Social interaction	4.45	4.50
Clique	3.85	3.89
Overall Means	4.56	4.46

*Minimum score = 1.00; maximum score = 7.00.

women managers perceive the grapevine to be more influential in affecting behavior than men.

Women's and Men's Perceptions

In order to get a clearer picture of how men and women view the formal and informal aspects of organization the standard "t" test was employed. For men it revealed that along the evaluative dimension there is a statistically significant difference between all formal concepts and six of the eight informal concepts, the exceptions being voluntary teamwork and group cohesion. Along the potency dimension there is a significant difference between six formal concepts (all except performance appraisal and job description) and all informal concepts. Men clearly view the two sets of organizational variables differently. They perceive the formal organizational concepts as being more valuable in satisfying needs (evaluative dimension) and more influential in affecting behavior (potency dimension) than the informal ones.

For women, along the evaluative dimension there is a significant difference between four formal concepts (supervisor, organizational objectives, authority, and performance appraisal) and five informal concepts (social group membership, social interaction, co-worker evaluation, clique, and grapevine). And along the potency dimension there is a significant difference between six formal concepts (all except chain of command and job description) and three informal concepts (co-worker evaluation, social interaction, and clique). Women apparently do not make such a sharp distinction between the formal and informal organizations, and do not have as great a tendency as men to look to the formal organization for the satisfaction of needs and cues for appropriate behavior. The data show, however, that although men perceive concepts relating to the formal organization as significantly more valuable and influential than those of the informal organization, women view the formal organizational aspects even more positively than men.

The standard "t" test also was used to determine if statistically significant differences exist between men and women in the ways they perceive the various components of the formal and informal organizations along the evaluative and potency dimensions. Table 3 lists the differences at the 0.05 significance level for seven of the sixteen organization concepts along the evaluative dimension and two concepts along the potency dimension.

TABLE 3 Significant Differences in Perception of Organizational Concepts Between Men and Women

Concept	Evaluative Dimension Significant Difference at 0.05 Level	Potency Dimension Significant Difference at 0.05 Level
Organizational objectives		X
Supervisor	X	
Authority	X	
Performance appraisal	X	X
Job description	X	
Personal influence	X	
Social group membership	X	
Co-worker evaluation	X	
Overall		
Formal organization	X	
Informal organization	X	

Of the eight formal concepts, women consider four (supervisor, authority, performance appraisal, and job description) to be more valuable in satisfying their needs, and two (organizational objectives and performance appraisal) to be more influential in affecting behavior than men.

The way women responded to performance appraisal is of particular interest. Other research implies that women managers are discriminated against when it comes to promotion.[14] If they really feel this way one would expect them to view performance appraisal negatively. On the contrary, this study found that women view performance appraisal as significantly more valuable and influential than men.

Women perceive three of the eight informal concepts significantly differently from men along the evaluative dimension. They view personal influence, social group membership, and co-worker evaluation as more valuable in satisfying needs. This result is consistent with other research and lends support to the proposition that women place higher value on interpersonal relationships, especially those with peers. It is somewhat surprising that although these three informal concepts are perceived as more valuable by women, they are not perceived as being significantly more influential in affecting behavior.

In all cases the significant differences in perception of the work environment between men and women are a product of the more positive feelings women have about the formal and informal organizations. Along the evaluative dimension women regard the total organization to be significantly more supportive of need satisfaction. This finding does not support the many opinions expressed in the literature that the world of business is foreign to most women and that they do not fit comfortably in managerial roles.

CONCLUSIONS

The results of this research, along with the other reported findings, lead to several conclusions about women managers.

First, men and women managers are more similar than dissimilar in their feelings about the organizational climate within which they work. This conclusion is based upon their perceptions of the sixteen concepts that were chosen to represent the formal and informal organizations. Primary differences were found to exist in the more positive views that women have of the formal organization and its ability to satisfy needs, and the extent to which they value interpersonal relationships as evidenced by higher evaluative mean scores for personal influence, social group membership, and co-worker evaluation. No significant differences exist between men and women that would limit the capacity of women to perform effectively in managerial roles.

Second, women managers tend to view the organization as an integrated whole. Men, on the other hand, differentiate between formal and informal organizational concepts and clearly prefer the formal organization, both in terms of its value in satisfying needs and its influence on individual behavior. One implication of this finding is that women managers may find it more satisfying to work in an organization in which the technical (formal) and social (informal) aspects are compatible and supportive of their needs for affiliation and other socially derived forms of gratification. This kind of work environment would be very consistent with the organization-development (OD) approaches of organizational behaviorists, who contend that the most effective systems are those that are capable of maintaining a climate that allows individuals to experience need satisfaction and at the same time supports the organization's efforts to achieve its objectives.

Third, this study proposes that decisions made about women on the basis of their sex, without considering such individual factors as background, education, experience, personality, and potential, are likely to be wrong. It appears that many of the stereotypes of women are not representative of women who hold or aspire to responsible positions in business. Moreover, the supposed sex differences in personality, abilities, and attitudes about work for the most part have not been based upon empirical observations of women managers but have resulted from judgments about traits that have been rightly or wrongly attributed to women in general.

This conclusion does not imply that women on the average are equal or superior to men in all capacities that are important for managers. It simply argues that women should be considered on the basis of their personal qualifications in the same way that men are. On that basis it is realistic to assume that there are many women who are well qualified for management positions.

Fourth, the need to establish special management-development programs for women is questioned. This is especially true of programs whose purpose it is to "condition" women so that they will feel more at home in business. The results of this study indicate that women managers do not perceive their environment as threatening or dissatisfying but as highly supportive. It is recommended that a more effective change strategy would be to modify the beliefs of those persons who do not think that women are capable of managing, rather than to change the attitudes of women about their roles at work. Special training programs may be in order, but not for the group for which they were originally intended.

In conclusion, there is considerable research evidence to support the fact that women managers psychologically are not significantly different from their male counterparts and that they may possess even superior attributes and skills in some areas related to managerial effectiveness. From a social psychological standpoint — that is, how they view themselves as a part of the environment within which they operate — this study has shown that women managers have much in common with men. Differences do exist, but mostly in ways that would serve to *increase* the probability of women functioning well as managers. It is recommended, therefore, that organizations begin treating women as equals, not because of moral obligations or pressures from outside interest groups to improve female-male ratios, but because they would more effectively utilize valuable human resources.

NOTES

[1] According to the Department of Labor, 40 percent of the work force is women, but only about 3 percent of them are in management or administrative positions. Men outnumber women in management by 5 to 1, and the ratio has changed little since 1950. In top management positions, men outnumber women by a ratio of 600 to 1.

[2] For a comprehensive review of stereotypes of women see Charles D. Orth III and Frederic Jacobs, "Women in Management: Pattern for Change," *Harvard Business Review* (July-August 1971), pp. 139 – 47; Lawrence C. Hackamack and Alan B. Solid, "The Woman Executive," *Business Horizons* (April 1972), pp. 89-93; Jane W. Torrey, "A Psychologist's Look at Women," *Journal of Contemporary Business* (Summer 1973), pp. 25-40; Eleanor Brantley Schwartz and James J. Rago, Jr., "Beyond Tokenism: Women as True Corporate Peers," *Business Horizons* (December 1973); pp. 69-76; and Rosalind Loring and Theodora Wells, *Breakthrough: Women into Management* (New York: Van Nostrand Reinhold Company, 1972).

[3] Marshall H. Brenner, "Management Development for Women," *Personnel Journal* (March 1972), p. 166. For an example of a company operating under the same set of assumptions, see Susan C. Ells, "How Polaroid Gave Women the Kind of Affirmative Action Program They Wanted," *Management Review* (November 1973), pp. 11-15.

[4] *Female Employment... Evaluation and Change* (Towers, Perrin, Forster & Crosby, Inc., 1973).

[5] Jon J. Durkin, "The Potential of Women," (Bulletin 87, The Johnson O'Connor Research Foundation Incorporated, 1971).

[6] *Ibid.*, p. 3.

[7] Olenda S. Knowles and Barbara A. Moore, "Today's Woman Executive," *Business and Public Administration Student Review* (Fall 1970), p. 72.

[8] Edgar S. Ellman, *Managing Women in Business* (Waterford, Conn.: National Foremen's Institute, Bureau of Business Practice, National Sales Development Institute, 1963), p. 23.

[9] David McClelland, "Wanted: A New Self Image for Women," *Dialogue on Women* (Indianapolis: Bobbs-Merrill Company, 1967), p. 37.

[10] Joan E. Crowley; Teresa E. Levitin, and Robert P. Quinn, "Seven Deadly Half-Truths About Women," *Psychology Today* (March 1973).

[11] *Ibid.,* p. 96.

[12] Sidney I. Lirtzman and Mahmoud A. Wahba, "A Managerial Myth: Differences in Coalitional Behavior of Men and Women in Organizations." *Proceedings of the 32nd Annual Meeting of The Academy of Management* (Academy of Management, 1973), p. 194.

[13] For a more detailed account of the research methodology see William E. Reif, Robert M. Monczka, and John W. Newstrom, "Perceptions of the Formal and the Informal Organizations: Objective Measurement Through the Semantic Differential Technique," *Academy of Management Journal* (September 1973), pp. 392 – 94.

[14] Douglas C. Basil, *Women in Management: Promotion and Prejudice* (New York: University of Cambridge Press, 1971).

DISCUSSION QUESTIONS

1.   Why should women have their own management development programs? Why should women participate in the same management development programs as men?

2.   Research has shown that the differences between men and women are far less important than their similarities. List all the similarities you can think of.

3.   List any ways that women seem different from men. How many of these differences might indicate "inferiority" to men?

4.   How have women's socialization processes (the way the total environment affected them as they grew up) influenced their view of management?

5.   Why do you think women have less tendency to look to the formal organization for both need satisfaction and appropriate behavior cues?

6.   What ideas do you have for communicating the fact that "no significant differences exist between men and women that should limit the capacity of women to perform effectively in managerial roles"?

Female Dimension:
Barriers to Effective Utilization
of Women in
the World of Work

Margaret Fenn

Women are under-utilized in the world of work. Today 39% of the total labor force are women, yet only about 1% of them reach the upper levels of management or the top of their profession. The participation rate of women between the ages of 16–65 is a startling 43.4%, but the success measures, when compared to males is less than comforting. The pay gap is more than $3,000 per year on the average, the unemployment rate for women is higher than for men, and the largest percent of working women are found in lower paying jobs.[1] Facts are facts, but the big question is why. We know that we are experiencing a period of awakening. We have passed laws barring discrimination on any basis, and we do know that many organizations have instituted affirmative action programs. Yet women continue to experience real barriers in the world of work.

Rather than merely point a finger and shout male chauvinism, we need to take a hard look at the interplay of a variety of factors which influence women. The interplay of these influences contribute to women's lack of progress in the world of work because of woman's own inability to maximize her contribution.

CULTURAL VIEW OF ROLE OF WOMEN

The societal image of women in our culture seems to be bounded by two dimensions. Women are viewed primarily as sex objects and as servants. As a result of this two dimensional scale, from birth the process of social-

Note: Dr. Margaret Fenn is Associate Professor, Department of Management and Organization at the University of Washington. This paper was presented at the SRA Ninth Annual Meeting in Las Vegas, Nevada on October 7, 1975.

Margaret Fenn, "Female Dimension: Barriers to Effective Utilization of Women in the World of Work," *Journal of the Society of Research Administrators* (Winter 1976), pp. 19–25.

ization for women emphasizes sexism and servitude. A primary example of this can be found in our definition of work. According to Webster, work is described as the exertion of strength or faculties to accomplish something. It is a general term for purposive effort. Yet the Census Bureau and the Bureau of Labor Statistics include payment or reward for that effort and as a result exclude homemakers from the census of workers ..., hence implying serfdom in the definition.

Socialization processes emphasize independence, work, and career orientation for males, and dependency and sex orientation for women. Researchers have repeatedly shown this in a variety of ways ... the way children are responded to by their parents, the kinds of toys that are chosen for them, the role taking within the family in imitative acts, and hundreds of ways of channeling that occur within the family long before the child is of school age. Channelization in terms of sex role differentiation continues throughout the schooling process, and in all public occasions. Children's literature is replete with examples emphasizing dependency and sexism for women, "Sugar and spice and everything nice, that's what little girls are made of."

Based on this cultural view of the role of women, we move easily into a set of basic assumptions differentiating the sexes. Assumptions about the physical and psychological differences are easily formed. For example, "women are weak." This may be true if we are talking about grip, or other forms of muscular exertion. However in a statistical sense, we know that more males than females are born, but that more females survive, and their life expectancy exceeds men's by several years. Males are assumed to be aggressive, thing oriented, and independent; females are assumed to be passive, sensitive, dependent, and people oriented. Acting on the basis of these assumptions, relationships are patterned, and socialization continues. Males are cast in ascendant, independent, forceful, unemotional and cognitive roles. Females are taught to be dependent, unforceful, subordinate, and emotional. The emphasis for women is instinctive, nurturant, and dependent; for males the emphasis tends to be toward intellect, productivity, and independence.

There is evidence to refute these assumptions but we tend to ignore it. Intellectual and cognitive ability inherent differences in the sexes are nonexistent. The Human Engineering Laboratory of the Johnson O'Connor Research Foundation has limited itself to the discovery and measurement of inherent aptitudes and acquired knowledge.[2] They found the following differences in the level of measured ability between men and women:

Thirteen aptitudes including analytical reasoning, foresight, inductive reasoning and number memory, showed no discernible sex difference. There was no discernible difference between men and women in acquired knowledge as measured by tests of English vocabulary. Women did excel in finger dexterity, accounting aptitude, verbal persuasion, and abstract visualization. Men excelled in grip and structural visualization, In summary, out of 22 aptitude and knowledge areas measured, there is no sex difference in 14; women excel in 6 and men excel in 2. The point is simple. There is no field of work which can claim to be the exclusive domain of either sex, based on aptitude.

In spite of this, the cultural concept of women's role continues the circular reasoning which contributes to the inability of women to maximize their potential.

FACTORS WITHIN WOMEN

Women tend to have a negative image of their own self worth. They are constantly reminded that women's role is passive and non-assertive. Physical attractiveness, sensitivity, and service are dominant modes, reflecting the two dimensional axis of sexuality and servitude mentioned earlier. Constant emphasis on dependency, other-directedness, nurturance, sacrifice and caring contribute to feelings of ambivalence about self worth. Parents, teachers, peers, and advertising reiterate the role model constantly. A girl's worth is measured by her attractiveness to the opposite sex. To be popular, she has to be pretty. To be successful she has to have boy friends. To be accepted by boys, she has to subjugate herself. If she has intellectual ability, she has to explain it away, or underutilize it. If she has physical skill and ability she has to challenge, but fail to win.

The behavioral result of this constant process is acquiescence. The intellectual result is increased diagnostic ability, but indecisiveness and inability to make decisions and act. The socialization process for females stresses nurturance and supportiveness of males. Girls are constantly advised against risk taking and urged to take the safe sure ways. Their educational process seldom emphasizes leadership and teamwork roles for women. They are taught individual sports rather than team sports in physical education classes, they play with dolls rather than cowboys and Indians. The individual female who is independent enough to make a decision for herself, to take a risk, or to go contrary to the culture is seldom made to assume the consequences of her decision if they are unpleasant. Someone is always ready to kiss the bumps. It is soothing at the time, but simply contributes to increasing the female's dependency.

Because she lacks conviction of her own ability, she tends to undermine her own self-confidence. Because she fails to expose herself, she develops a pattern of avoidance of risk taking. Because her motivation is other-directed, she fails to set goals for herself and plan how to achieve them. The result is low achievement motivation. Because she fails to set goals and plans, she doesn't seek, and she doesn't prepare. Because she doesn't set goals, plans, seek, prepare, she doesn't achieve. Lack of achievement helps to contribute to her own feeling of inferiority and leads her right back to where she started — dependent, passive, and ambivalent.

FACTORS WITHIN OTHERS

A woman's experience with others reinforces the factors within her which contribute to her negative self-image. Informal attitudes of both sexes play a part. Women are assigned roles in the culture emphasizing dependency. Since I've suggested that primary role expectations for women move around a dual axis, role senders expectation for satisfactory performance reflect these base parameters. Mass media, radio, TV, movies, periodicals, and popular literature reflect the generalized framework. Immediate participants in the role set (relatives, friends, and children) help to define the specific parameters to the dual axis of sexuality and servitude.

Mothers provide a role image primarily of the servant model. They also encourage participation and imitation in this model; they cook, bake, clean, chauffer, nurse, garden, and shop. All these activities include an element of service to others. At the same time mothers begin the process of emphasis in the sexual role. They emphasize personal appearance and posture, and behavior intended to attract interest and attention.

The role models continue through the school years, teachers are women, administrators are men; boys are athletes, girls are cheerleaders; boys take shop, girls take home economics. As career choice time approaches girls are channeled into nursing, boys into medicine; girls to dental hygiene, boys to dentistry; girls to service industries, boys to skill trades and on and on.

What happens when females approach the boundaries of expected behavior for their roles? First they are censured — "nice girls don't do that." Then they are ridiculed — "our tomboy daughter, she prefers footballs to dolls." Then they are discouraged — "go into nursing, the training is shorter and girls will never succeed in medical school." Then she is denied — "we can't afford college for you since your brother will be away at engineering school; why not take typing and get a job?" Her need to achieve is gently sublimated to a need to nurture and serve. She is discouraged and protected from taking risks by her parents. At the same time she is subjected to peer pressure to fit the mold. "If you take chemistry you won't have time to date" — "If you get good grades you're a drag" — "If you always win at tennis no one will want to play with you"—"If you really swim your hair will look a fright and your muscles will bulge"—and on and on. So she doesn't plan for the long range, and doesn't recognize choice points, but begins to back into or avoid decision making. She becomes more dependent on others because it is easy and comfortable. She ceases her formal education, takes a job, finds a man and becomes the role model. More than half of the high school graduates are women, but the percent receiving degrees for advanced study drops sharply as the degree level progresses (41% Bachelor Degrees, 37% Master's Degrees, and 11% of Doctoral Degrees) [3]

In the workplace most women's job opportunities are clearly female-role oriented. The surprising thing is that the socialization process toward female roles is so complete that there is little support from either males or females for the uncommon woman who is willing to challenge, to take risks, to make decisions, and strive for achievement.

Women lack acquaintance with leader roles, and teamwork. Given a choice between equally qualified female and male bosses the usual choice is male. Sex may be part of the choice, but the actual fact is that many women do not know how to lead effectively; do not know how to plan, organize, and control; do not know how to use their analytical ability to pinpoint problem areas and screen alternatives; do not know how to make decisions; and do not know how to activate after decisions.

Both men and women are suspicious, intolerant, and unsupportive of women who challenge the sex and servant role in the work place. These attitudes in others are a reflection of the individual attitudes that have been socialized and contribute in large measure to the final set of factors I'd like to mention.

FACTORS WITHIN THE ORGANIZATION

The total staffing process within an organization is a reflection of the individual and combined assumptions of female roles. Recruitment and selection practices tend to favor males. Many decisions are based on myths that continue to exist and which reflect the sex and service axis. Examples are: women don't need to work; women are temporary when they do work; women can be paid less because they are supported by husbands and fathers. Each of the myths has been disproved by research and statistical evidence, yet they fit the social role ascribed to women so they persist.

Selection, placement, training, and reward reflect these assumptions. A job description may be stated in objective terms. It describes a job to be accomplished. The specification of qualities and skills necessary to successfully perform the job often are also objectively stated. However, objective statements may be interpreted subjectively during the recruitment and selection process. Recruitment may center in predominantly male colleges for managerial trainees. Selection may be based on the assumption of permanence or impermanence of the prospective candidate. These practices are not deliberate and intentionally sexist, but are often inadvertant reflections of the attitudinal beliefs of the employer.

Once an individual has been hired, the question of placement becomes paramount. Surveys have shown that women tend to be channeled into dead end jobs. They are not often found in positions that have direct lines of progression to top management jobs. Again these practices are a reflection of the myths that surround women in business. A woman is not expected to be a long time employee. She is not thought of as career oriented. Women help contribute to this myth in two ways. They themselves are not achievement oriented, and they do not have the confidence in themselves to aggressively seek recognition and promotion. Women also fail to support one another in the sense of pulling together as a team. So competent females are steered into jobs of servitude and fail to recognize or accept that fact. The bosses "girl Friday," "the strong right arm," are usual roles for women in industry.

Salary scales are notably less for women than men. Again a reflection assumption of women's worth by men, and acceptance of lack of worth on women's part. In countless organizations, women are placed in assistant *to* categories rather than assistant status. The inclusion of the word *to* in a title is a clear indication of two things; poor pay, and lack of independency in decision making and action. The assistant *to* never makes decisions or takes action in her own right, but always as a representative of her boss. The assistant acts in his own right.

Training and development opportunities are an almost exclusive male prerogative in organizations. Women contribute to this phenomena by not actively seeking opportunities to increase their ability and status. They emphasize the supportive and acquiesant rather than the self-expressive, confident, aggressive characteristics. They do not expect to and are not expected to strive for leadership.

Promotional opportunities are often overlooked by females. They do not plan their career pattern, they do not prepare for advancement, and they do not approve of other women breaking the role parameters. One way to promotion resides in the sponsorship of one higher in the organization. It is difficult for both the sponsor and the woman he is sponsoring for a variety of reasons. The foremost one is the sexual connotation implied by others. Another strong one is the servant one; if the sponsor supports his "strong right arm," he'll lose her services and deprive himself. It is also difficult for a woman to get tapped into the informal communication and power structure of the organization. A key to the men's wash room doesn't do her much good. She seldom gets to play golf, sail, or drink with the "boys" after work. They may learn to accept and appreciate her, but there are also wives and other women who present barriers to these informal opportunities.

A final area of leadership in organizations that mitigates against women is the area of decision making and action. Most decision making involves some risk taking. Women have not been taught the skills necessary to state problems, consider alternatives, and make decisions. They have been taught skills in diagnosing, but lack the emphasis on skill pattern of decision. They do not command respect, and they do not understand or exercise leadership qualities. They are not independent enough to exercise choice and assume the responsibilities that result from action.

WHAT CAN WE DO TO HELP WOMEN?

Obviously we in organizations cannot start the socialization process for all or even some females. We have to work with what we have. We can understand and appreciate the impact that women's opinions and attitudes about themselves have on their leadership potential. We can recognize the fact that attitudes, opinions, and actions of others have a great bearing on a woman's ability to perform, but we would be hard pressed to be able to deal with those attitudes. So what can we do?

Organizations must start with themselves. They must examine in depth each practice which has an effect on the career of its women. They will probably have to start the process of attitude change and organizational practice with emphasis on orders, rules and legal practice which are explicit and enforceable. Changed behavior will lead to changed attitudes. They probably will have to legislate fair practices, and accomplish their enforcement by stringent penalties for violations. Awareness and action have to precede attitudinal changes.

Women must be helped to understand that they can afford to be independent. They must be assigned duties that entail some risk taking. They must be encouraged and forced to make decisions and to live with the consequences. A supportive climate is necessary for this learning process. The female learning to express her independence must be allowed to make mistakes, must be helped to recognize and learn from those mistakes, and must be forced to live with the consequences. Hopefully with strong mentors and guides, the costliness (not only in terms of dollars, but in terms of emotion and physical stress) can be kept at a minimum during this transition process.

Women must be encouraged and helped to understand that they must set goals for their careers, they must plan and prepare to meet those goals and they must evaluate the results. Long-range rather than short-term planning is a new concept for most women — it is a step away from dependency and toward independence.

Women must be helped to recognize sex as one of the givens in their lives, but to accept the fact that they also have a variety of other givens including a brain. The dimensions of servitude and sexuality must be expanded if women are to maximize their potential.

Difficult as it seems, organizations can and must set specific quotas and goals for women as employees. Numbers and target dates must be publicly committed, and periodically evaluated. Commitment and public exposure are strong spurs to action. Recruitment sources, selection practices, must emphasize the commitment to fulfill the quotas. Special attention to placement in career ladder jobs must be emphasized. Training and development for women must include many opportunities for decision making and leadership action. Special attention to decision points and skill in stating problems, seeking alternatives, and projecting outcomes must be emphasized to assure effective decisions. Translation of decision to action will need constant attention, and evaluation of action results against stated objectives must be frequent.

Salary scales must be reviewed and equalized so that everyone receives equal pay for equal work. The description of that equality must be examined carefully to eliminate unconscious bias. Recognition and acceptance of the interplay of factors within the individual, between others, and practices within the organization which are prejudiced in nature is everyone's business. Women need help, encouragement and support, if they are to maximize their contribution in the world of work. We cannot afford to under-utilize any resource, therefore we must act now.

NOTES

[1] *Monthly Labor Review* (April 1974), pp. 21-27; or Special Labor Force Report 164.

[2] Jon J. Durkin, "The Potential of Women," Johnson O'Connor Research Foundation, Bulletin #87, 1971.

[3] Maryjean Suelzle, "Women in Labor," *Transaction* 8, No. 1 (November-December, 1970), pp. 50-58.

SUGGESTED READING

1. Ginsberg, Eli and Alice Yohalem (ed.), *Corporate Lib.* Baltimore: Johns Hopkins University Press, 1973.
2. Gordon, Francine and Myra Strober (ed.), *Bringing Women Into Management.* New York: McGraw-Hill, 1975.
3. Jongeward, Dorothy and Dru Scott, *Affirmative Action for Women: A Practical Guide.* Menlo Park, California: Addison-Wesley Publishing Company, 1973.
4. Loring, Rosalind, and Theodore Wells, *Breakthrough: Women Into Management.* New York: Van Nostrand Reinhold Company, 1972.

DISCUSSION QUESTIONS

1. In what ways have you seen parents, friends, and teachers channel children into sex roles?

2. Do you agree that women are viewed as either sex objects or servants? Explain your answer.

3. What signs have you seen that women have negative images of their self-worth?

4. What examples have you seen of females who were not made to assume the consequences of their own decisions simply because they were female?

5. Do you know any families who educated their sons but not their daughters? How else do families discourage daughters from making long-range goals?

6. Do you agree that many women do not know how to lead effectively, use analytical ability, make decisions? Do many men have the same failings?

7. Do you agree that women are not achievement oriented? Explain your answer.

8. Have you seen examples of women not supporting one another or not pulling together as a team?

9. List all the women and all the men you know with job titles of "Assistant to" or "Administrative Assistant." Which list is longer?

10. What examples have you seen of situations in which women do not command respect?

11. What is the difference between a quota and a goal?

12. What companies have you seen publicize their goals, target dates, and evaluations? How have they accomplished this openness and commitment?

13. What actions could be taken to insure that women will get the same consideration for promotions as men?

Sharon Kirkman:
Mind Over Myth

John Minahan

Minahan: Is fear of legal action the primary reason why corporations are seeking the advice of your company?*

Kirkman: I think there are many reasons why they're seeking the advice of our company, but certainly legal action is a primary reason. The settlements have been substantial, and there's tremendous media exposure.

More and more women understand their legal rights and are being urged, by the media and women's groups, to use those rights, to demand them. If you look back at the legal settlements, in many cases it was one of the most unexpected women in the company who brought suit—the quiet woman who had worked there for sixteen years, and finally decided to demand her rights. In other words, it's not necessarily the more radical or outspoken women who will bring suit. So, there's a real concern on the part of corporations, and there should be. Settlements are getting larger and larger.

Minahan: If the law hadn't been passed, what would have been the probability of major corporations getting into this kind of examination and introspection in the near future?

Kirkman: I don't think there would have been any chance at all.

Minahan: From your professional experience with people in top and middle management, what are the biggest obstacles to the progress of qualified women in business?

Kirkman: The biggest obstacles are the men and women themselves, and what they're thinking. It's the conditioning we've received as to what con-

Author's Note: Sharon Kirkman started at IBM. She is now a principal in Boyle/ Kirkman Associates, a management consultant firm specializing in affirmative action programs for women.

stitutes being a man and what constitutes being a woman in our society. In general, history and tradition have dictated that men are providers and women are mothers. That's the root cause of the problem. Essentially, what we're trying to do is change centuries of tradition.

Minahan: Tradition that had always been inculcated in childhood; conditioning that usually started before we reached the age of reason.

Kirkman: And still goes on. And if we could understand that more, we men and women, and work on that particular point, it would make it so much easier. We don't give conditioning as much importance as we should. It's the reason we do almost everything.

Women have a tremendous problem in business, because we've been conditioned our entire lives that we're not supposed to be in business. But we *are* here. And we *want* to be here, which creates great conflicts. Men in business have been conditioned to believe that they are supposed to be leaders and managers, and women are supposed to be followers, and that men are supposed to take care of women. And now, men are being told that we don't want to be taken care of, we want to compete with you, be equal, and, in many cases, we want to be better, we want to manage you. And a man's conditioning doesn't really allow him to accept that.

Minahan: I take it for granted that significant psychological adjustments have to be made by men. What are the major psychological adjustments that have to be made by *women?*

Kirkman: The major thing that women have to do is to become terribly realistic about what their lives are going to hold for them.

Back again to what we're conditioned to believe—that we're going to grow up and find a man, fall in love, get married, and he's going to take care of us. We aren't conditioned to believe that anything is going to go *wrong* with that plan.

What we try to get women to do is realize that there's a strong possibility that they're going to be employed for a major part of their lives. If we can get women to think that way and plan that way, we've won half the battle. But what we as women tend to do is put all of our emphasis on the fact that we're going to be wives and mothers, and many of us never end up becoming wives and mothers. Consequently, we spend our whole lives seeking something that we never get, and we don't have a viable alternative. Hence, a lot of very unhappy people.

But if you add to the great American dream of love, marriage and family, the idea that we're also going to work for the rest of our lives, then you have a very different situation. And as soon as you can get women to understand that, the light bulb goes on. And they say, "Aha, *that's* what you're talking about. Okay, that's what we *want.*"

Minahan: Would you say that most women in middle management today are ready, willing and able to accept the rigorous demands of time and energy that are axiomatic disciplines in making it to top management?

Kirkman: Women have seen other women devote that kind of time and attention to their jobs, and still not succeed. Consequently, they don't have a lot of faith that if they work from eight to eight they'll get any further than if they come in at nine and leave at five. As soon as they get rewarded the same way that men have, other women will have proof that it works, and the motivation will be much stronger.

Minahan: Other than the chance for advancement, are the motivational factors for women the same as for men — money, status, power, satisfaction?

Kirkman: I think if you take all of the normal motivational factors, you could apply them equally to men and women. Again, because of conditioning, it's harder for women to express what motivates them, because they've never really thought about it. Men can express it a great deal more easily. But with most women, when you get down to it, down to what really motivates them, you come up with the same list as you would for men.

Minahan: In your observations, are most women executives as physically and emotionally capable of handling high-pressure jobs as men?

Kirkman: The majority of women are as physically capable — or even perhaps more physically capable — to handle the pressures. Physically, I don't think there's any problem at all.

Emotionally, women are terribly strong, but we've been conditioned to express our emotions differently. A man at work who gets angry may curse, shout, slam a door or a file, to release his anger. A woman has been conditioned that those things are not feminine — but that it's acceptable to *cry.* And now we're saying, "No, it's not acceptable." So now what're they going to do? How do they express their anger? Well, most successful businesswomen that I know have picked up the man's way of expressing themselves, and given up crying. They adopt the man's way of dealing with the situation, and, when they do, a lot of men find it offensive.

Minahan: How do you answer people who claim that the menstrual cycle can be a significant problem for a woman executive?

Kirkman: I think that's the world's greatest myth, that somehow or other, every month, because we have a certain bodily function, it reflects what's going on in our minds and emotions. You're almost talked into it as a child. It's the "curse," it has names that are foreboding and bad and that go back to medieval times.

Minahan: And it's instilled in men's minds at a fairly early age.

Kirkman: Of course. It's instilled in everybody's mind, and then women grow up to think they're going to be grumpy, uncomfortable, have pain. Some women have legitimate medical problems and *are* physically uncomfortable. But the majority of women don't have any medical problem at all—it's a psychological one. And it's a tremendous device to be used on men, negatively. If I'm a clerical worker, and you bring some big project over to me, all I have to say is, "I don't feel very well today." Or, I may just take a day off every month.

As I said, some women have genuine medical problems, and they ought to have them corrected, but for the majority of women, it's an absolute myth. Medically, different things happen to you, yes. Your body does change; but does it affect my decision-making ability or my ability to handle my job? No.

Minahan: I understand that when you were conducting an "awareness" session for women employees in a major corporation, one woman said: "We have seen the enemy, and it is us." What prompted that reaction?

Kirkman: A lot of women tend to think that the reason they don't have a responsible job in the organization is because "they wouldn't let me"—*they* meaning the corporation, the men who have the power in corporations. Women think that "they have kept me down, and that's why I haven't succeeded." Well, to a major extent, that's been true in the past, and is still true today.

But it's also true that the majority of women today don't have a positive self-image, and have a tremendous lack of self-confidence in many business situations.

Why? Take the analogy of sports. Boys are involved on a football team. They work well together, because they *learn* how to work together. Sometimes somebody's better than they are, and sometimes they are better. They learn how to win and how to lose; how to say, "We lost today, but next time we'll win." You have different leaders, and you learn how to take tremendous criticism from the coach. And while he's giving it, you're thinking. You're taking it, you're listening, but you're thinking: "I'll show him; I'll show him next game. I won't make the same mistakes again." And this whole process conditions men so well for business, because these are precisely the things that happen in business.

Most women don't go through any conditioning that teaches them these things. So, when they go into business, they don't know how to work as well with other people, how to follow instructions, how to take really difficult criticism and then think: "Next time, I'm going to win." They didn't have that competitive instinct drilled into them. In many cases, they don't know how to win *or* lose.

Minahan: As a result, do you find defensive behavior to be the norm?

Kirkman: This is a very big problem women have, defensive behavior. There's a saying, "Ask a woman where she's going, and she'll tell you where she's been." In the sessions we have for women, we can point it out very easily. We go through some exercises, and women will explain and explain, and defend and defend. It's part of our conditioning. If I don't have a good self-perception and a lot of self-confidence, when you ask me a direct question, my answer is going to reflect those things. I'm going to couch it as much as possible, without coming out with a straight answer.

It's easy to teach women not to do this, once you point it out to them. Most women are unaware that they're doing it at all. But when you point it out to them, it becomes crystal clear when they've done it, why, and how to avoid it in the future.

For example, if you tell a woman, "That's a really pretty dress," she'll tell you where she bought it, what she paid for it, and say it's really old; she'll defend herself against the compliment. And once she begins to realize that she does this over and over, and that it's viewed by men at work as not positive, not a position of strength, then she can begin to avoid that kind of defensive behavior.

The men in corporations who are the most successful, if you really listen to them, never speak in a defensive way. They make decisions constantly. Or they say, "In my opinion." If you say, "I don't know if you'll go along with this, but, in my opinion — ," it sounds a great deal different.

Minahan: I saw you in a fascinating situation, on a television program, when you were in a room full of top executives, getting them to verbalize their problems with women in business. Is this a standard procedure?

Kirkman: Yes, because it's a mistake to assume you know what the problems are in any given group. And so you ask them: "What's the problem?" And we've been very successful in creatng a climate in which people feel quite comfortable in defining problems. Because we don't say, "You are wrong, bad guys." We say: "What's the problem?" And once we get the problem out, it's: "How do we solve it?"

And an effective way is to get into relatively small groups and ask one simple question, and let them answer it. The question is: "What are all the reasons that you believe account for the fact that women are predominately employed in the United States in clerical positions, as opposed to being in professional, managerial, or, for that matter, production positions?"

Then you break them into small groups, and they'll come back with everything they really believe about women. And you'll come up with a list of twenty-five or thirty reasons — every myth and stereotype that you've ever heard. And they believe them. That's a very important point — the majority of management people *believe* those myths and stereotypes. They believe that women don't want more than a clerical job, they believe all women are going to cry, can't stand stress, will have a problem with their period, are weak physically and can't handle endurance. And it's never one woman, it's *all* women. *All* women are going to cry, get married, get pregnant, leave the job.

One of our primary responsibilities is to identify exactly what the myths and stereotypes are in each individual case, explore why they are believed, and find solutions. Not just to satisfy the law, but to throw some long-needed light on the logical fact that women in business represent a tremendous talent pool — a resource that corporations need today, more than ever, and will find invaluable tomorrow.

DISCUSSION QUESTIONS

1. Do you believe that women would have had any chance at all without the laws that have been passed? Explain your answer.

2. What examples have you seen of women who do not have a realistic view of what life really holds for them?

3. Do you agree that women will be willing to put in the extra time and effort that management demands as soon as they receive the rewards? Explain your answer.

4. What examples have you seen where money, power, and status motivate men and women equally?

5. How have you seen men and women express anger at work?

6. What examples have you seen of defensive behavior in women? Do you see men as less defensive? Explain.

7. Do you believe learning to play team sports is an advantage for a future management position? Explain.

The Potential
of Women

[*The following dialogue occurred in the House of Representatives on September 8, 1971. The speaker is the Hon. Patsy T. Mink of Hawaii.**

Mrs. Mink: Mr. Speaker, my attention has recently been directed to a study on "The Potential of Women" by the Johnson O'Connor Research Foundation Human Engineering Laboratory. The study was written by Jon J. Durkin. It found that in 13 measures of ability between men and women, there was no discernible sex difference, while in eight aptitudes differing levels of ability were observed between men and women.

In the eight areas of differing ability, women were superior in six. The two in which men excelled were grip — a measure of physical energy — and structural visualization — as measured by the assembly of three-dimensional puzzles.

As women were superior in all measurable areas of skill except those attributable to biceps size and the ability to assemble puzzles, the report wondered about the predominance of men in various occupations as opposed to women. The report said:

> In most occupations, if positions were based solely on aptitudes, men
> and women would be found in approximately equal numbers.

I agree and see no reason why there should be more men in Congress than women, for example. There is no reason why a woman should not aspire to any position, including President of the United States.

The article follows:]

THE POTENTIAL OF WOMEN

Jon J. Durkin

Since its inception in 1922, the Human Engineering Laboratory/ Johnson O'Connor Research Foundation, Incorporated, has seen four men go through its program of aptitude assessment for every one woman. Per-

Jon J. Durkin, "The Potential of Women," Human Engineering Laboratory/Johnson O'Connor Research Foundation, Incorporated; *Congressional Record*, Vol. 117, Part 23, 92d Congress, 1st Session, Sept. 8, 1971, pp. 31088-89.

haps this made some sense thirty to fourty years ago, since far fewer women then may have contemplated full time, non-domestic careers. In the past decade this lopsided ratio of 4/1 has altered slightly so that the actual ratio now is more like 3.5 men to each woman. However, beginning with the Second World War (when women inundated the entire labor market) enormous changes have taken place regarding the occupational importance and aspirations of women. In 1970, forty-four per cent (44%) of all adult women were employed outside the home. In other words, the ratio of men to women in work is nearly 2/1. According to the Department of Labor this trend will definitely continue through the foreseeable future.

The job of the Human Engineering Laboratory/Johnson O'Connor Research Foundation, Incorporated, is the discovery and accurate measurement of inherent aptitudes and the measurement and teaching of acquired knowledge. When we look for differences in level of measured ability between men and women we find the following facts.

I. THOSE APTITUDES WHICH SHOW NO DISCERNIBLE SEX DIFFERENCES

1. Analytical Reasoning.
2. Eyedness.
3. Foresight.
4. Inductive Reasoning.
5. Memory for Design.
6. Number Memory.
7. Objective Personality.
8. Subjective Personality.
9. Pitch Discrimination.
10. Rhythm Memory.
11. Timbre Discrimination.
12. Tonal Memory.
13. Tweezer Dexterity.

II. THOSE APTITUDES WHICH DO SHOW A SEX DIFFERENCE

1. Finger Dexterity — used in all manner of activities involving deft digital manipulations (handling, demonstrating, assembling). At the 50th percentile, 17 year old men fill 77 holes in a pegboard, 17 year old women complete 82. Women excel in Finger Dexterity.

2. Graphoria—Originally termed accounting aptitude, this work-sample measures clerical speed and efficiency (accounting, auditing, statistics, actuarial work). A 17 year old boy at the 50th percentile takes 7.20 minutes to complete this worksample, a 17 year old girl completes it in 6.48 minutes. Women excel in Graphoria.

3. Ideaphoria—a measure of rate of flow of ideas used in activities involving persuasion and verbal fluency (sales, teaching, writing, advertising). At the 50th percentile, a 17 year old boy writes 267 words in 10 minutes, whereas a female peer writes 290. Women excel in Ideaphoria.

4. Observation—This worksample measures one's ability to perceive small changes, alterations, in physical details and is used in activities involving close visual inspection (insurance adjustment, police work, factory inspection). At the 50th percentile a 17 year old male amasses 85 points, a female gets 88. Women excel in Observation.

5. Silograms—measures the ability to easily form associations between known and unknown words. A measure of a memory most useful in acquisition of languages and professional terminology (chemistry, medicine, law). At the 50th percentile, a 17 year old boy remembers 27 words out of 80, a girl remembers 35. Women excel in Silograms.

6. Abstract Visualization—the theoretical complement of Structural Visualization, this aptitude is not measured directly but is inferred from the absence of Structure. Found in banking, management, politics, writing and sundry non-technical professions. 75% of women possess abstract visualization, whereas only 50% of men do.

7. Grip—a measure of physical energy, useful in those activities requiring large amounts of muscular exertion (construction worker, athlete, weight lifter). At the 50th percentile, a 17 year old woman exerts 90 kilograms pressure, a 17 year old boy exerts 144. Men excel in grip.

8. Structural Visualization—measured by worksamples involving rapid assembly of three dimensional puzzles, this aptitude seems central to the technical/scientific professions (engineering, architecture, surgery, mechanics, building). At the 50th percentile a 17 year old boy completes the worksamples in 1.75 minutes, a 17 year old girl in 2.75 minutes. Men excel in Structural Visualization.

We can find no discernible difference between men and women in acquired knowledge as measured by tests of English Vocabulary.

CONCLUSIONS

Out of the 22 aptitude and knowledge areas measured above, there is no sex difference in 14; women excel in 6; men excel in 2. We could speculate endlessly as to the reasons for these similarities and variances but that would obscure the point of this article. The point to be made is a simple one. There is no field which can, with absolute assurance, claim to be the exclusive domain of either sex. Men will predominate to some degree in those fields requiring Grip and Structural Visualization; women in those which call upon Graphoria, Dexterity, Ideaphoria, Observation, Silograms, and Abstract Visualization. In other fields there ought to be no favoritism. Neither a girl nor a boy ought to peremptorily dismiss from consideration any endeavor solely because it has been the preserve of the opposite sex.

People come to us primarily to gain information about themselves which they can use in developing a full, satisfying, and successful life. It has been the general observation of the staff that most women seem timid in their search for a lifestyle. Rather than aspiring to law, they aim for law clerk, architectural assistant rather than architect; private secretary rather than corporation president. In a word, subordinate positions.

We can find no substantiation for this timidity in measured ability. Many women claim, since they expect to marry and raise children, that they need not be so serious in making a vocational choice as does a man. This, we feel, is a short-sighted viewpoint, and one which can prove to be ultimately quite detrimental to the individual woman who chooses it. When children are grown and no longer a maternal responsibility many women find themselves experiencing increasing ennui and frustration with the diminished role as keeper of an empty house. This is not a pleasant prospect to anticipate or experience. It can lead to marital and emotional difficulties, degrading everyone, benefiting no one.

We urge that women take their lives as seriously as any human being ought to, and prepare for a vocation, a life's work, which will continually challenge all their abilities and knowledge; a vocation which will be harmonious with self-development and continual personal growth. We say "be a doctor instead of a nurse if such is your aptitude and desire." We say "grow and enjoy life as an independent individual not simply as a satellite dependent upon a larger planet." Get the experience, education, and fortitude necessary for a large life. Do not allow your freedom of choice to be diminished by well-meant, but meretricious advice.

The present period is monumentally critical to the future of all mankind and we feel that it is the responsibility of each person to do what they can to ensure the continued positive growth of the human race. It seems reasonable to assume that women, through full and unfettered realization of their potential could do much to further this end.

Our society, perhaps the most heavily industrialized one in history, places a premium on the expert use of structural visualization. This aptitude, the gift for three-dimensional thinking, underlies successful performance in the physical sciences, medicine, all forms of real engineering, architecture, city planning, building, mechanics, etc. Fewer women than men possess this aptitude. The exact figures are one woman in four, one man in two. However, none of the above mentioned professions are 25% female in population. This is a case of cultural bias. Parents treat boys and girls differently from birth. It's a rare parent who will give their daughter an erector set or carpentry tool which are delightful presents for a youngster who is high in structure as ¼ of girls are. At best, a high structure girl may exercise her aptitude through dressmaking, jigsaw puzzle assembly, or unauthorized use of her brother's toys. It seems to be a case of the few being made to suffer for the characteristics of the many.

Another example can be seen in the field of management. The aptitudes which seem to underlie successful management are: Objective Personality, Abstract Visualization, and high English Vocabulary. Equal numbers of men and women possess objective personality and high vocabulary. More women have abstract visualization than men. The ratios are three women in four, one man in two. Theoretically at least, there ought to be more women in management than men. However, in reality, this is definitely not the case. Even the most cursory perusal of most companies will reveal few, if any, women in higher management positions.

In most occupations, if positions were based solely on aptitudes, men and women would be found in approximately equal numbers. This is not how things actually are. Women are encouraged, both overtly and covertly, to seek lesser positions for a variety of reasons, many of which, when examined closely are found to be based on biased and spurious information. In other societies, this type of bias is not so obviously operative. One is reminded that the first woman astronaut, who orbited the earth several years ago, was not an American. The prime ministers of India, Israel and Ceylon are not men.* These are facts. The Johnson O'Connor Research Foundation respects facts whatever they may be. Since in the course of virtually fifty years of research it has found no facts which substantiate the great discrepancy between women's potential and their actual accomplishment it feels bound to present these facts to the world. If it leads to a greater development of ability on the part of all people, then our job will be done.

*Author's note: This article was written in 1971.

The Myth
and the Reality

Women's Bureau
U.S. Department of Labor
Employment Standards Administration

THE MYTH

A woman's place is in the home.

Women aren't seriously attached to the labor force; they work only for extra pocket money.

THE REALITY

Homemaking in itself is no longer a full-time job for most people. Goods and services formerly produced in the home are now commercially available; laborsaving devices have lightened or eliminated much work around the home.

Today more than half of all women between 18 and 64 years of age are in the labor force, where they are making a substantial contribution to the Nation's economy. Studies show that 9 out of 10 girls will work outside the home at some time in their lives.

Of the nearly 34 million women in the labor force in March 1973, nearly half were working because of pressing economic need. They were either single, widowed, divorced, or separated or had husbands whose incomes were less than $3,000 a year. Another 4.7 million had husbands with incomes between $3,000 and $7,000.[1]

Women's Bureau, U.S. Dept. of Labor, Employment Standards Administration, "The Myth and the Reality." (Washington, D.C.: U.S. Government Printing Office, 1974).

Women are out ill more than male workers; they cost the company more.

A recent Public Health Service study shows little difference in the absentee rate due to illness or injury: 5.6 days a year for women compared with 5.2 for men.

Women don't work as long or as regularly as their male coworkers; their training is costly – and largely, wasted.

A declining number of women leave work for marriage and children. But even among those who do leave, a majority return when their children are in school. Even with a break in employment, the average woman worker has a worklife expectancy of 25 years as compared with 43 years for the average male worker. The single woman averages 45 years in the labor force.

Studies on labor turnover indicate that net differences for men and women are generally small. In manufacturing industries the 1968 rates of accessions per 100 employees were 4.4 for men and 5.3 for women; the respective separation rates were 4.4 and 5.2.

Married women take jobs away from men; in fact, they ought to quit those jobs they now hold.

There were 19.8 million married women (husbands present) in the labor force in March 1973; the number of unemployed men was 2.5 million. If all the married women stayed at home and unemployed men were placed in their jobs, there would be 17.3 million unfilled jobs.

Moreover, most unemployed men do not have the education or the skill to qualify for many of the jobs held by women, such as secretaries, teachers, and nurses.

Women should stick to "Women's jobs" and shouldn't compete for "men's jobs."

Job requirements, with extremely rare exceptions, are unrelated to sex. Tradition rather than job content has led to labeling certain jobs as women's and others as men's. In measuring 22 inherent aptitudes and knowledge areas, a research laboratory found that there is no sex difference in 14, women excel in 6, and men excel in 2.

Women don't want responsibility on the job; they don't want promotions or job changes which add to their load.

Relatively few women have been offered positions of responsibility. But when given these opportunities, women, like men, do cope with job responsibilities in addition to personal or family responsibilities. In 1973, 4.7 million women held professional and technical jobs, another 1.6 million worked as nonfarm managers and administrators. Many others held supervisory jobs at all levels in offices and factories.

The employment of mothers leads to juvenile delinquency.

Studies show that many factors must be considered when seeking the causes of juvenile delinquency. Whether or not a mother is employed does not appear to be a determining factor.

These studies indicate that it is the quality of a mother's care rather than the time consumed in such care which is of major significance.

Men don't like to work for women supervisors.

Most men who complain about women supervisors have never worked for a woman.

In one study where at least three-fourths of both the male and female respondents (all executives) had worked with women managers, their evaluation of women in management was favorable. On the other hand, the study showed a traditional/cultural bias among those who reacted unfavorably to women as managers.

In another survey in which 41 percent of the reporting firms indicated that they hired women executives, none rated their performance as unsatisfactory; 50 percent rated them adequate; 42 percent rated them the same as their predecessors; and 8 percent rated them better than their predecessors.

NOTES

[1] The Bureau of Labor Statistics estimate for a low standard of living for an urban family of four was $7,386 in autumn 1972. This estimate is for a family consisting of an unemployed husband aged 38, a wife not employed outside the home, an 8-year-old girl, and a 13-year-old boy.

Women in Work Force Post Better Records for Stability in Jobs

Mike Tharp

The personnel-placement order is simple enough: A new assembly-line inspector is needed; someone who is reliable, works at a steady pace and isn't apt to quit in the middle of a production push; someone who will also be willing to shoulder some managerial responsibility when the pressure is on.

In the old days, the solution would have been simple enough, too: Hire a man. But today, the answer is increasingly the opposite: Hire a woman. As Betty Friedan, the feminist leader puts it, "The cliche of women's absenteeism and turnover isn't valid anymore."

Male chauvinists may accuse Betty Friedan of having an ax to grind, but the fact is that more and more companies are finding that the traditional characterization of a working woman as a flighty factor in the nation's work force is invalid today. Quit rates, turnover and absenteeism, among women are dropping—not only in comparison with levels in prior years but also, in some cases, when measured against the levels for male employes. (Turnover refers to movement of workers in and out of employment; quits are terminations of employment initiated by employes for any reason except retirement, transfer or armed-forces service.)

A FEW STATISTICS

Although the Department of Labor hasn't broken out quit rates by sex since 1968, the bookkeeping of individual companies indicates that women are staying on the job longer. At American Telephone & Telegraph Co., for example, female turnover rates in the first quarter of this year fell to 11.5% from 19.6% in the first quarter of 1971. Male turnover for the period also dropped, but at a slower rate, to 5.1% from 7% three years ago. At General Motors Corp., female quit rates, though still higher than male, decreased to 4.7% in 1973 from 5.3% in 1972, while men's quits rose to 2.3% from 1.9% during the period.

Polaroid Corp. says its turnover rate is highest on lower-level jobs, and that "men in those slots now show exactly the same turnover rates as women." And at Aetna Life and Casualty, a unit of Connecticut General Insurance Corp., the turnover rate for women in technical, managerial and professional jobs was 8.3% in 1973, well under the 11% for men in those positions.

The underlying reasons for these changes, observers say, are manifold. Labor officials heavily attribute the drop in women's turnover to economic factors. Double-digit inflation and rising unemployment, they say, tend to make workers of both sexes reluctant to leave a job, either to look for another or to quit the labor force entirely. As the cost of living has soared this year, the quit rate in manufacturing, usually a bellwether index for the state of economy as a whole, slipped to 2 workers per hundred in September from 2.7 at the end of 1973.

If economic conditions worsen and layoffs increase in the automobile and other industries, the rate of voluntary quits can be expected to shrink even further for both sexes.

But much of the improvement in the stability of women on the job antedates the present economic woes, and many companies agree that a change in the corporate attitude toward women is an equally important factor. Indeed, many concerns now are echoing a belief long advanced by women: that unreliability and job-hopping among workers are related more to job satisfaction, salary, occupational level and age than to sex. And as companies, whether under pressure or on their own, are upgrading their treatment of women, the women are responding positively. Says Donald L. Liebers, director of human resources and development at American Telephone & Telegraph Co.: "Women have long been a stabilizing force here, but that's increasing now with their additional opportunities." Adds Paul Armknecht, a Department of Labor economist: "Women are no longer under pressure to leave the labor force. Thus they're more permanently attached than in the past."

ENHANCED FRINGE BENEFITS

One way in which companies have improved their treatment of women is by enhancing benefits, particularly in the area of maternity leaves. For example, in December 1971, Noreen Haffner took a leave of absence from her job at Southern New England Telephone Co., an AT&T unit, to have her first child. Existing corporate policy required a female employe to leave work at the end of her seventh month of pregnancy, and she wasn't paid for the time off. However, pressured by female employes and the possibility of equal-employment lawsuits, the company subsequently liberalized its policy.

Last year, Mrs. Haffner left the company on a Friday to have her second child, which was born on the following Wednesday. Four weeks later, she was back at work. Although she again didn't receive disability pay, the 29-year-old data-systems manager says she was "much more satisfied with the corporate policy the second time. I don't think it hurt me, my baby or my job."

(A Labor Department survey shows that the availability of maternity leave with full reemployment rights rose 14% in the past five years; maternity leave with pay increased 12% from 1969. These figures are based on a national probability household sample of 1,500 workers. They are open to some dispute since they reflect not only an actual rise in availability of maternity rights but also an increased awareness among women as to what their rights are. Nevertheless, "child-bearing is the same as a broken leg now," says Susan Ells of Polaroid's equal-employment office.)

The corporate change of attitude toward women has in large part been caused by pressure from the women themselves. The simple fact is that women, no longer willing to take a back seat to their male counterparts, have been able to exert growing legal pressure on the nation's companies. (Women constituted 39% of the U.S. work force in 1973.) True, some companies maintain they are acting altruistically; but the fact remains that that failure to act could lead to massive lawsuits from disgruntled female employes.

GREATER SATISFACTION

In any case, the new upward mobility accorded women in many corporations is apparently being reflected in greater career satisfaction. What's more, as pay differences between males and females performing the same jobs has lessened, the effect has been to make "women in those jobs more career-oriented," as a Dow Chemical Co. personnel director puts it.

Women's morale, and hence their inclination to stay put, has also been advanced by a number of firms through equal treatment regarding on-the-job training, transfer plans and well-publicized posting of job openings. Women in unions have spearheaded many of these changes. (According to Labor Department statistics, women's membership in labor unions increased to 4.5 million in 1972 from 4.3 million in 1970.)

Societal factors have also come into play in women's stability in the work force. Shirley Johnson, professor of economics at Vassar College, says that because of the nation's growing divorce rate, many women find themselves as heads of households and therefore "won't be in and out of the labor force as much." At the same time, pregnancy rates are dropping; and Elizabeth Koontz, formerly of the women's bureau in the Department of Labor, notes that those working mothers who do have small children now are more readily able to find child-care facilities.

Ironically, along with the various positive reasons behind women's increasing job stability is a major negative: Some women say they are staying put not because they're happy but because of discrimination. A chemist with RCA Corp. contends that she hasn't been eager to look for another job because "few companies are willing to hire a female chemist—it's traditionally a male position." Furthermore, despite their upward advances into the executive ranks, many women say they aren't being funneled into the pipeline for so-called corporate headhunters. "Executive search firms are very sexist," says Gloria Gerry, manager of the equal-employment program at Aetna Insurance Co. "They reflect the sexism of their clients."

However, Millie McCoy, a vice president of Handy Associates Inc., a New York search firm, disagrees. "Most of our clients have gone out of their way to find minorities, women or other 'protected classes,'" she says. "And once they've hired them in supervisory positions, the old stereotypes disappear."

Certainly, although the extent is a matter of dispute, times are changing. And as stereotypes are being shattered, the effects aren't being lost on the women themselves.

Two examples:

—Merle Daniel, a special correspondent at United Services Automobile Association, a San Antonio-based insurer, has taken three insurance courses, and the company paid for the courses after she passed them. "The benefits have made this job more attractive to me," she says. "I've considered working other places, but I've remained here because it seems more advantageous to stay."

—Mildred May, a business office manager for a New England firm, left the company in 1947 to raise her two daughters. She returned in 1965 and has since held a succession of managerial-level jobs. "The first time around, what incentive did a woman have?" she asks. "She knew she was going to be a secretary or stenographer and couldn't be anything else. Now, the sky's the limit."

DISCUSSION QUESTIONS

The last three articles by Durkin, Women's Bureau, and Tharp contain research findings that debunk the myths and stereotypes about working women. As you review them, answer the following:

1. Which findings surprised you the most?
2. Which findings surprised you the least?
3. Which findings do you think will be the most helpful to women in gaining equal opportunity?

"Fifteen years ago, median annual earnings for men working fulltime were 65% more than for women. Today, the typical male worker is making 75% more than the average woman.

"According to the Wall Street Journal, *the average female college graduate earned less last year than the average male high school dropout. The Department of Labor reports that last year the median income of working women was 57% of the median wage of men, a decrease from nearly 64% in 1955.*

"Although the educational levels of men and women are similar, men are earning a higher dollar return on each year of additional education. The average woman's return on her education is only 55% of the average man's return."[1]

"Limited career opportunities for women heads of families result in limited earnings for these same women, which, in turn, result in limited educational opportunities and limited job opportunities for their children."[2]

[1] Address by Secretary of Commerce Elliot L. Richardson, prepared for delivery before the Twentieth National Assembly of the LINKS, Inc., Washington Plaza Hotel, Seattle, Washington, July 16, 1976, p. 4.
[2] *Ibid.*, p. 7.

II

Implementing
Equal Opportunity
for Women

Once we accept the principle of equal opportunity, implementation becomes the vital area of consideration. Some very "nitty-gritty" down-to-earth approaches are necessary. The articles in this section present methods that have been tried successfully.

Familiarizing yourself with these implementation methods should give you a great deal of empathy for all those involved, employees and managers alike. You will also appreciate the fact that affirmative action is no small job. Implementing affirmative action takes budget commitment, trained staff, data collection, statistical analysis, careful record keeping, periodic evaluation, and constant follow-up. In other words, it is just plain hard work. Sometimes there are touches of glamour — travel, meeting new people, speaking before groups. However, these are small considerations for the work involved. The real payoff will be the improvement in the quality of life for women and their families and the improvement in the productivity of organizations basing employee selection and promotion solely on qualifications.

Real Equal Opportunity
for Women Executives

Bette Ann Stead

April 2, 1972 is now history. But an event occurring on that date carries implications for business and industry that will probably be felt for years to come. On that date Revised Order 4, issued under Executive Order 11246, went into effect. Within 120 days from the commencement of a federal contract, each prime contractor or subcontractor with fifty or more employees and a contract of $50,000 or more was required to develop a written affirmative action compliance program setting forth goals and time tables for the employment and promotion of *women.*

This law seems to cover most companies; even if a company does not deal directly with the federal government, it probably deals with companies that do. So a question has arisen: "How does a company go about giving its women employees equal opportunities?"

A COMPANY-WIDE SYSTEMS APPROACH

If a company does not have a manpower plan, the preparation of one should become a high priority item. Such a plan is based on a complete assessment of the whole situation and will turn up some interesting considerations — including a manpower shortage:

> By the mid-70's industry will be hit by a million man shortage in the 35-45 age bracket according to the U.S. Bureau of the Census estimates. There will be a famine of the middle management gap, and it will come at a time when industry is hungry for talent.[1]

The well-run company realizes that planning is necessary for continued success. A manpower plan that identifies positions that will be open during the next five years provides the company with an effective

Bette Ann Stead, "Real Equal Opportunity for Women Executives," *Business Horizons*, (August 1974), pp. 87 – 92.

tool for implementing the "developmental management" concept. This concept encourages employees to identify their levels of aspiration with the company. For example, an employee could be asked to put in writing what she sees as her next two jobs with the company. A program is then tailored to help the employee prepare herself for her desired future. A company that maintains an open mind toward equal opportunity for women will find a number of examples of "what is good for women is good for the company" and vice-versa.

The developmental management concept has another implication. It can be documented that men who rise successfully in companies have had male mentors. Because so few women are able to rise to executive positions, women rarely have the opportunity to gain the necessary support of female mentors. Cultural biases may explain why few men have acted as mentors for women. A strong manpower plan that employs the developmental management concept would automatically give women the necessary mentors. Implementation and periodic review of a specific progress program for selected women employees would insure the needed help and emphasis.

COMMITMENT—THE FIRST STEP

Both the success of equal opportunity for women and the success of women in managerial positions depend upon a commitment from top management. The support of top managers can be gained usually by alerting them to the significance of equal opportunity for women and the necessity for their support.

Reality forces us to admit that some top managers still defend the attitude that "the first mistake we made was fifty years ago when we gave women the right to vote!" These managers must be presented with a clear statement of the law along with some examples of how expensive noncompliance can be. Two large utilities, both guilty of sex discrimination, have paid over a half million dollars; a manufacturing firm paid $901,000; and a university, $94,295. The total discrimination cost to business since 1964 has been over $42 million.

There are some managers who doubt that discrimination exists in their companies, but a review of their manpower plans would provide convicting data. Discrimination against women is insidious; it exists and continues, although for many executives it may be unintentional. A manpower plan would point out such areas as differences in salary for the same work, differences in numbers of men and women in levels of management, and differences in job placement according to educational background.

Top management can display its support by formally and informally rewarding those who make positive contributions toward equal opportunity for women. Top management can also maintain low-key visibility by attending a company showing of the film, *51%* (described below), participating in the game "Profair," or appearing at meetings of special programs for women.

USEFUL "EQUALIZING" TOOLS

An excellent movie has been made with the title *51%* which emphasizes the fact that women make up over 51 percent of the total population.[2] The film, which runs twenty-five minutes in color and is tastefully done in a businesslike manner, presents three short episodes depicting common work situations involving women.

The first episode shows a young couple considering an apartment. He is just out of the service and starting a new job; she has received excellent ratings in her present job and is sure of a raise so that they can afford the apartment. The scene shifts to her boss, who is discussing her with a colleague. He automatically assumes that, since her husband is home from the service, she will be quitting soon. He regrets losing her because of the load she has assumed. Both men and women who view this episode are struck by the hope in the face of the young woman, who is unaware that she has been automatically rejected professionally because of false assumptions.

The second episode depicts an attractive woman who has been with a company more than ten years. An honor graduate from both college and the company training program, she gets along well with everyone and has had experience in several areas of the company. Yet through the years, she has watched the men who joined the company when she did pass her by. Her father worries because she is not married yet and tells her she makes "good money for a woman." She responds that the right man has not come along and that her taxes, grocery bills, and rent have not been lowered because she is a woman.

She returns to her job and asks for a promotion. Her immediate boss, who knows how competent she is, is willing to promote her, but she is doomed to continue in her same capacity because she is a woman. Both men and women, particularly those with daughters, are moved by the predicament of this intelligent, competent, and hard-working human being who is not allowed to progress.

The third episode is probably the most difficult for men in the audience to accept because it depicts a woman winning a promotion over a man. She is obviously better qualified. This is the most important segment because it is an extremely fine example of implementation of the vital developmental management concept. The woman concerned was lucky enough to have had a male mentor who asked her to identify the next two company positions she desired. She explains, and most of us would agree, that such a task is not an easy one; however, it is vital to planning future individual development.

The final scene shows the woman facing the man over whom she was promoted and starting him on an individual development program so that he will be ready when the next job opens up. Both men and women who view this segment should be struck by the fairness of promoting a woman who is obviously better qualified than a man and the positive impact the developmental management concept can exert throughout business and industry.

Another tool that can be useful in emphasizing equal opportunities for women is a program called "Profair."[3] Although designed for use among company executives, "Profair" may be used successfully with a group of both executives and women who are being considered for promotions, since it is valuable in eliciting discussions on such issues as absenteeism and turnover among women.

"Profair" begins with a questionnaire that determines some attitudes towards working women. Personal data are presented on two employees, a man and a woman, who are being considered for the job. The participating executive is asked to choose one of them for the position. Then the participants are told that the computer made an error and that the employee that they had been told was a man is really a woman and vice versa. They are then given a chance to change their minds as to which employee should get the job. The program then states that the woman was chosen and asks each participant to list the reasons for promoting her, whether or not she was the first choice.

"Profair" then gives some objective information about the laws of discrimination. The participants are divided into groups of five, and each participant is given a role to play. Some of these roles support equal opportunity for women and others do not. Then the large group reassembles to discuss the reasons for any changes in attitudes toward supporting or opposing women. The initial questionnaire is repeated so that the group members can determine whether any attitude changes have occurred.

The inclusion of behavioral management science information can be useful in administering "Profair." For example, an explanation can be made of how people develop stereotypes, for example, most people have a stereotype for the concept "manager"—and that stereotype is a *man*. This explanation can help illustrate why women can also be guilty of discriminating against women.

IDENTIFYING CANDIDATES

Many firms have ways of identifying people who have high potential for executive training, and today many companies include women in their managerial training programs. Generally, programs which have proved successful in training men for managerial positions will prove useful for women too.

Prospective women participants should be interviewed to determine if they are interested in working toward a more responsible position. They should be told exactly what a managerial training program will include and what will be expected of them during and after the program. They should be allowed a reasonable amount of time to decide if they want to participate. Any women who decides not to participate should not be made to feel that she is attacking the principle of equal rights for women.

Some women may refuse for two reasons. First, if they have been in their jobs for many years or are close to retirement, they have probably been acculturated into their supportive positions for so long that it is too late for them to change. Second, they may realize or believe that they are not managerial material. These two statements can be easily applied to men also. For example, some men would also refuse managerial training if they had held the same low-level job for years or realized that they did not want managerial responsibility.

Equal opportunity does not mean that women are asking for the moon. Implementation of the developmental management concept (asking women to put in writing the next two company jobs they would like to occupy) has shown that many women make reasonable requests. Many jobs which are not considered as responsible as middle or top management positions are a step above — in both responsibility and salary — the traditional strictly supportive women's jobs. These jobs can be filled by loyal and competent women when openings arise.

Some managers cry, "We can't find qualified women!" But talented women are not hard to find. Why is a woman with a liberal arts degree not "qualified" when men with liberal arts degrees are found sprinkled throughout companies? Secretaries can be found with BBA degrees and teaching certificates. Why can a woman who is qualified to teach business subjects not be used as a full-fledged staff member in the training department? Why can women with journalism degrees not be used as full-fledged staff members in publications departments? Again, a look at the company manpower plan will identify women with a good education doing reliable work in jobs for which they are overqualified or temperamentally unsuited. Jobs that match their abilities and temperaments would release their talent.

Many companies are now using the task force approach to solve problems. The task force is an area where women can be given immediate experience and recognition at no extra salary expense. When a woman is placed on a task force, she should *not* be put in the stereotyped role of secretary.

WHAT TO INCLUDE

Many of the concepts found in management programs have traditionally been directed at men, but can be useful to women. A partial list would include:

- Maslow's hierarchy of needs
- Herzberg's motivators and dissatisfiers
- McGregor's theory X and theory Y
- Blake and Mouton's managerial grid
- Individual behavior concepts
- Group behavior concepts
- Group decision making as opposed to individual decision making
- Conflict resolution
- Complex organization modeling
- Management by objectives.

Women also need experience in decision making. Since most of their professional activities have been in supportive roles, they generally have no concept of the logical problem-solving process that leads to executive decision making. Each woman who is being groomed for a managerial position should have the following experiences:

1. She should define a real company problem. The problems could be stated as follows: What kind of travel control center should XYZ Company have for their personnel? How should the accounting department change the present method for distribution of cash receipts? How should XYZ Company secure and handle job applicants from external sources? Why should XYZ Company exercise control over their contractors' insurance requirements? The ability to define a problem can indicate whether the woman has managerial potential.

2. After the problem statement has been made, the individual should be required to find published readings related to this problem. Sometimes the search is not easy. When she finds an article, she may

have her first appreciation for a bibliography at the end of the article which will lead her to further related material. And she begins to see why her boss is continually taking home a briefcase stuffed full of reading material.

Most executives will read everything they can concerning current problems facing the company. This literature review will provide the individual with information on what progress has been made toward solving certain kinds of problems and may lead to ways in which a problem can be approached.

3. Her next step is to prepare a research design that will gather and treat company data in such a way as to reach conclusions and make recommendations about the problem. Data are usually collected in one of three ways: questionnaires, interviews, or company records.

For example, in the problem concerning a travel control center for personnel, company records for the last three years would show the increase in travel volume in terms of air fare spent, hotel reservations made, and cars rented. These records would show the increased volume and need for change. A survey of computer systems could provide information on which system would be most beneficial for the company's particular situation.

4. The individual is then taught to organize data into a meaningful form. She should learn that reading off lines of numbers or facts will make little impression, but if she organizes the facts into pie charts or bar graphs and puts the numbers into tables, the information becomes meaningful. In discussing her illustrations, she should be cautioned not to repeat all the data but simply to state high points, low points, and trends that are evident. She will also learn that employing simple techniques like color or stick figures can dramatize the presentation.

5. She should then draw conclusions from her related readings, questionnaires, interviews, and company records. These conclusions should be stated in the form of a list.

6. Her recommendations should be based on her conclusions. They also should be stated in the form of a list.

7. She should then be given the opportunity to make an oral presentation from her written report to her department members or middle management. Many men "on the way up" make frequent oral presentations. Her presentation should be limited to ten minutes followed by a question-and-answer session.

She should learn that proper research reporting includes a statement of the problem, an explanation of how the data were collected and treated, and the conclusions and recommendations. Her tables, charts, and graphs can be used during the presentation. By following these seven steps, she will have experienced a scientific decision-making process and, more than likely, will have actually done the company some good. Positive reinforcement should be given if she is deserving, and praise for her oral presentation should provide another opportunity to show support for equal opportunity for women.

This article has maintained that a number of methods that could help make "equal opportunity for women" a reality are now available to managers. In summary, these tools include:

- The specification of future job openings by studying present and future attrition rates reflected on company organization charts
- The implementation of a specific progress program for each woman employee
- The periodic review of each woman's job preparation and promotion schedule
- Continued visible support from top management
- The identification of each woman's specific aspirations with a company
- The matching of a woman's aspirations to a future job opening
- The re-interviewing of each woman college graduate for accelerated placement in an area that would better utilize her abilities
- The placement of a woman on each task force appointed to solve a specific company problem
- The inclusion of women in all in-house training programs

NOTES

[1] M.F. Feilke, "Women, Women, Everywhere, But Not a Manager in Sight," *Iron Age* (August 27, 1970), pp. 63 – 65.
[2] The film *51%* was produced by Robert Drucker & Co., Inc. 10718 Riverside Drive, North Hollywood, CA 91602.
[3] "Profair," Transnational Programs, Corp., 54 Mail St., Scottsville, N.Y. 14546.

DISCUSSION QUESTIONS:

1.   Write out the job descriptions of the next two positions you want.

2.   List the training, experience, and other qualifications needed for the two jobs above. Include a timetable.

3.   Show your plans to a possible mentor for review and advice. (Asking someone for advice is usually flattering.)

4.   Prepare a table that lists court cases involving sex discrimination. Include a column showing amounts of cash settlements.

5.   List some ways managers can show visible support for their affirmative action programs.

6.   "You make good money for a woman." List goods and services for which women pay less because they are women.

7.   Interview several men who have working wives, daughters, sisters, or mothers. What problems related to sex discrimination have they seen these women run up against?

8.   Interview several women who have taken some management training programs. How have these programs been useful? *Not* useful? If the group was predominantly male, how were the women treated?

9.   Interview any women you know who have college degrees and are working either as secretaries or in dead-end clerical positions. What advice do they have for other women college graduates? Are they still hoping for promotions or transfers into "career-ladder" jobs?

10.   Define three company problems you see as needing work. State these as questions.

11.   Follow the seven steps on one of your problems. Submit steps one, two, and three to your boss for review before continuing.

Patrons, Rabbis, Mentors—
Whatever You Call Them,
Women Need Them, Too

Jacqueline Thompson

Paula Brown, 34, is already a legend at American Telephone & Telegraph. She's probably broken through more anti-female job barriers faster than any woman in the company's history. Even before the giant public service company signed the 1973 consent decree pledging to reform its hiring and promotion policies for women, Brown had pushed and shoved her way into such traditionally male preserves as the plant department—a unit that maintains a huge electromechanical switching machine for long distance calls—where she supervised 300 men.

The man who helped her get that job was one of two whom she refers to as her "sponsors," men who helped guide and promote her career. Paula maintains her case is not unusual. Behind every successful woman at AT&T, there is a mentor. "You can't be naive politically and succeed in a company as large as this unless you happen to fall into the Affirmative Action numbers game. And that will only take you so far."

Brown describes her sponsors—others refer to them as "rabbis," "godfathers," "patrons," or "mentors"—as men "who were receptive to looking objectively at what I was accomplishing despite the fact I am female." How did she get their attention? "By astounding them with such productivity that they didn't know what to make of it. It violated everything they'd been taught to believe that a woman should be doing." Brown concedes her mentors bucked strong head winds to help her. Why did they bother? Because they, untypically, found Paula's talent and ambition stimulating.

"The difference between my sponsors and the majority of men in the corporate world was not that they could identify 'male' qualities in me which would make me successful in business, but that they could accept them," she says. "Most men feel threatened and think: 'My God! Aggres-

Jacqueline Thompson, "Patrons, Rabbis, Mentors—Whatever You Call Them, Women Need Them, Too," *MBA* (February 1976), pp. 26-27, 30, 35-36.

sion is one thing in a man, but I don't want to see it in a woman.' They immediately relate to their wives and think, 'I don't want my wife to be like that. I might have to compete with her.'"

Eventually Paula Brown's patrons left the company and she experienced an immediate loss of power. "I knew why it was happening." she says, "but I couldn't believe it. It was so subliminal. I had a new boss who seemed to want me to fail." Paula has continued to advance, but her halcyon days with sponsorship are over.

Men have been getting ahead via the buddy system for years while equally gifted women got nowhere, stumbling on the lower rungs of the corporate ladder. Now some politically astute young businesswomen are exploring the benefits — and perils — of the patronage system, as they attempt to make their way through the corporate hierarchy.

It is more difficult for women than men to negotiate this particular corporate byway. Because there are few women in upper management, and fewer still who are willing to assume the role of godmother, young women must for the most part rely on god*fathers*. But sexual tensions, different interests and hobbies, and even jealous wives conspire to keep male-female patronage relationships from developing. Meanwhile, ambitious young men are busy cultivating easy friendships with their superiors on the golf course, over drinks, or at sporting events.

Ironically, however, women need the psychological and tactical support of a mentor more than men. The average businesswoman has not been inculcated with the same determination to succeed as her male counterpart, so she can generally be diverted from her career objectives more easily. A mentor will encourage her to replace small, timid steps with bold strides. Secondly, in most companies a woman still has to contend with barriers to advancement. A patron will run interference for his protege, as he grooms her for progressively higher-level jobs.

The women interviewed for this article have reaped rewards from this type of relationship and successfully avoided its pitfalls. Each had a strategic ally who carried her banner and advanced her when the right opening came up. And does merit play a role in the career of a woman? Yes. Merit got them their sponsor, say these women, but their sponsor got them their promotions.

None of the women consciously sought a mentor. The relationships developed naturally after the parties had worked together for a while and gained each other's professional respect. In one unusual case, the patron took an intuitive liking to the woman without knowing very much about her work. In another, chance played a large role.

With one exception, the sponsors of the women interviewed were men. And there is a lot of similarity in their personalities. For the most part, they are highly secure in their jobs, ambitious, willing to take risks, relatively young, and see themselves as mavericks. They choose their proteges of either sex carefully and do not make a habit of helping women. Nor have any of them tried to take advantage of the relationship sexually.

John Smith (not his real name) has helped two women during a 25-year business career. As a marketing executive in a giant corporation back in the mid-1960s, he tried to convince a superior to give him permission to promote his secretary to assistant product manager. The superior refused so Smith unofficially fired her. He gave her time off for interviews. he explained the circumstances and praised her potential to prospective employers. She eventually found a better job elsewhere.

He is currently president of a medium-sized manufacturing company, where he upset the pecking order when he offered the resigning director of personnel's job to the man's secretary — because she'd been doing the nuts and bolts work in the department all along.

In both cases, Smith claims his reasons for lending a helping hand were pragmatic. "I am not interested in identifying talent merely for the sake of identifying talent. Notice that I wanted to promote competent people who would be reporting to me. I wanted to put them in positions where they could strengthen *my* career. Their gender had nothing to do with it. A star performance is hard to find, and it doesn't matter what shapes, sizes, colors, or sexes it comes in."

In any discussion of a sponsor-protege relationship between a male and a female, the question of sex is bound to come up. As noted, the women interviewed for this article have not allowed their business relationships to become more than that. And the men who played the role of mentor are equally adamant about keeping the two things separate.

The manufacturing vice president claims that mixing the two relationships is the "last thing I — or any other intelligent man — would do. You've got to be a fool not to have a strong sense of survival in business. There is no way I would risk being accused of advancing a woman's career in exchange for a toss in the hay — by the woman herself or anyone else, since office affairs never remain a secret for very long."

David King, a career counselor who specializes in training and placing women in sales jobs, concurs. "A woman creates a monster when she gets into a sexual-business relationship, which she can turn to her advantage only temporarily if at all. I know women who have gotten their first promotion because they slept with someone. But from then on, they found they were shunned. Potential sponsors were afraid of having their motives called into question. I know of no one who made it up the ladder rung by rung by sleeping with patrons. The best and strongest patron-neophyte relationships I know are with men who would be heartbroken if their proteges suspected them of ulterior sexual motives."

In fact, the typical sponsor-protege relationship gets started much more casually. Melissa Allenbach's promotion from a packaging development job to an assistant product manager at Chesebrough-Ponds resulted from work on a joint project with her would-be sponsor. After mentioning, during a lunch, that he was looking for an assistant, he left it to her to pick up the cue. When she finally applied to his boss for the job, she discovered that he'd already been pleading her cause from his end.

In the case of Jackie Chatmon of IBM, a sponsor-protege relationship was sparked when a senior manager observed her conducting a class for the company's community fund drive volunteers. He was so impressed that he offered to help her advance within the organization.

In many cases, such assistance is used sparingly. "I'm going through proper channels for a promotion," says Chatmon. "If it doesn't come fast enough, I'll get a message to him."

Anne Lawrence, who works at a major bank, hasn't the faintest idea why a certain senior vice president took a personal interest in her career. She's never worked or lunched with him although they exchange quips when they run into each other. "But if I need something, I've learned to get in touch with him," she says. "It's a pretty one-sided relationship: he gives and I take."

Anne's mentor had a good job waiting for her when she left the bank's credit training program. He has since steered her into a post normally reserved for men — a lending officer maintaining customer contact with a major Middle Eastern oil exporting country.

Barbara Massey came to Donaldson, Lufkin & Jenrette 11 years ago when the investment banking firm had 70 employees. In the intervening years, she got married, had a child, took a leave of absence, returned, and became head of administrative services.

"There I was — den mother to 650 people. I should have been ecstatically happy. But the closer I got to serving all the needs of all men, the less satisfying I found the whole thing. Why did I always have to be the cost center while they were the profit center?"

She confided in her boss, who made a deal with her: he'd lay the groundwork for her to move elsewhere within the firm if she'd guarantee a smooth transition with her replacement. After conferences with various department heads, arranged by her boss, Barbara accepted a job as a retail sales trainee. She suspects the result would have been far different without her boss as advance man.

"If I had approached the head of retail sales directly, he probably would have said, 'Gee, Barbara, I'm sure you would be a great salesperson some day, but I am hiring guys who are already producing over $500,000 in commissions per year and I just don't want to train a novice.'"

It is likely to be some time before women start assuming the role of mentor. Younger women who ally themselves with "the sisterhood" have not risen to influential posts as yet while older women who have are often subject to the "queen bee syndrome." A "queen bee" likes being the lone female in a male world. She is unmoved by feminist causes. After all, if she could progress without benefit of equal employment opportunity legislation, why can't they?

An exception is Paula Brown, one of whose proteges, Marsha Mock, has moved from AT&T to other companies. But after AT&T, she has had to rely on godfathers. She says that "women in top spots are not generally big women's supporters. That's a terrible thing to say, but it's been my experience."

In Barbara Massey's opinion, many women executives not only shrink from helping other women, but too often stand as negative role models for the average, upwardly mobile, young career woman. "Most of the women who have gained entry to the men's club that we call 'business' are unique," she points out. "They've got some special drive or quirk or neurosis that got them there. Furthermore, they have usually sacrificed their personal lives for their careers. I don't think the average American female can emulate them in terms of type."

Natalie Lang, a vice president in charge of developing and executing social policy at Booz, Allen & Hamilton, is part of a tiny vanguard of women at decision-making levels who are sensitive to this problem.

"I think the women who are in middle and upper management who *want* to be identifiable role models—you can't force anybody—ought to make sure that they don't look for mirror images of themselves—insisting that 'I went through the system and paid my dues and that's what it's going to take for you to get through it.' Today, it doesn't require the same tricks to get through the system. Times have changed. Besides, everybody brings different pluses and minuses to the process. A mentor has to be able to ask, 'How can I help you?' not 'This is how it worked for me. Do likewise.'"

What should a woman look for in a mentor? Security and flexibility, according to Lang. "A mentor has to be secure enough to help a woman who may turn out to have more talent than he or she does," says Lang. "And he or she should be able to adapt to change. If a mentor has these two key elements, gender is unimportant."

HOW TO FIND A MENTOR

Any superior in a position to influence your career within your company is a potential sponsor. However, according to the women we interviewed, a female's methods to locate one should be suited to the size of her organization.

In a large company, where superiors may not even know who you are, let alone what you can do, a patron is *de rigueur*. But be careful. An aggressive search for a mentor among male managers can easily be misconstrued and trigger a sexual rather than a professional response. In a smaller company, where colleagues are better acquainted with each other's capabilities, a patron may not be necessary. If sponsorship is required — to break through a discriminatory roadblock, for instance — the close proximity of management to subordinates works in your favor. Here, a woman can more actively solicit aid without fear of misinterpretation.

To find a mentor, those we spoke to proposed these rules:

• *Publicize Your Goals.* Whether your goal is to rise quickly within your department or learn a new skill in another corner of the company, let people know. The day has not yet arrived when people automatically assume a woman wants to move ahead. They are more likely to assume that a woman wants a secure, routine job and dismiss any extra effort on her part as normal, supportive female behavior. Women, especially, rarely get promotions they haven't asked for.

• *Seek High Visibility.* In a small company, a high profile is built into your job. In a large one, you must create it. Take on projects that will widen your circle of acquaintances and introduce you to important people both inside and outside the firm; a compliment from a client never hurt anyone's career.

"It's harder for a woman to toot her own horn, but essential," says Linda Howes, sales manager of a small international company. "If you keep quiet like a little mouse, they'll bury you. If you call attention to what you've accomplished and what you deserve, they"ll label you 'pushy.' Since there's no way to win, a woman might as well err in a forward direction."

• *Take Risks.* Maneuver yourself into a responsible position where you can save the day. Accept the challenge of starting a new department; clean up the mess left by a predecessor; experiment in a small, unstructured situation where people work as a team and jobs are not gender-typed.

• *Read the Signals Correctly.* A sponsor (who will probably be a man) does not turn up one day wearing a lapel button with your name printed on it. In fact, the potential mentor may not even realize he has attained that status. The only thing he may know for sure is that he likes your work and has told you so. (Don't discount the person who thinks you're great and spreads the word to everyone but you.)

"When a patron appears, it is usually obvious," claims David King. "He will say, 'I like what you are doing. Keep up the good work.'" King warns that a woman's actions at this point can make or break the relationship. "A woman who tries to cultivate a male patron creates a problem for herself. Every time a woman becomes too solicitous, she falls into the traditional female enchantress role. The guy will either get scared and disappear or zero in. The worst thing a woman can do is sleep with a prospective patron. The second worst thing she can do is encourage him and turn him down."

DISCUSSION QUESTIONS

1. What examples have you seen of males or females acting as mentors?

2. What qualities do you observe in mentors about their attitudes toward others?

3. Ask several people who have been lucky enough to have had mentors how they attracted their attention.

4. How do you think male mentors who help women differ from male mentors who help only other men?

5. Ask several people who have had mentors, what happened when they lost their mentor.

6. What examples do you know of "queen bees" — older women who feel they made it alone so others can too, or who want to be the only female in a powerful position?

7. Do you know people who think you should have a hard time because they did?

8. The article titled "How to Find a Mentor" lists four rules. For each of these rules list several specific things you could do to find a mentor.

9. Interview some "successful women" to learn how they and their organizations planned their upward mobility.

10. What examples have you seen of inappropriate sexual issues being raised that have hurt women's struggle for equal job opportunities and pay?

11. Many women who fight against equal opportunity are full-time homemakers. They feel their whole reason for being is threatened by equal opportunity. How could they be shown that equal opportunity is necessary to the economic survival of very many families?

New Work Patterns—
for Better Use
of Womanpower

Felice N. Schwartz

"If women's entry into the work force continues to accelerate, and if their sights are on administrative, managerial, technical, and professional levels—will there be enough jobs to go around?"

During the past 12 years, this is a question I have been asked repeatedly by men and women, by those who are entirely sympathetic to career-oriented women and those who are hostile. The question is asked more frequently in periods of economic recession, and the prospect now of a slackening in the rate of industrial growth has magnified its importance significantly.

It is urgent that we face this matter directly. Repressing it does not make it disappear; it only leaves it unanswered and perpetuates the anxiety and anger it provokes. If women want to work at responsible levels and men feel threatened by that desire, conflict is inevitable.

Most women, however, do not want to enter the work force at the expense of men. To do so would be to shift to themselves the burden of financial responsibility for the family, and they don't want to assume it entirely. On the other hand, it would be wrong to say that they want to work simply for self-enrichment. In fact, they are motivated (and probably in this order) by a desire to earn money, to feel useful, to be recognized in their own right, and to utilize their minds and education more fully—in short, to feel productive and self-respecting and to contribute to the support of their families.

To an emerging industrial society dependent on population growth, this desire of women would be alarming because women would be needed at home to give birth to and nurture children. But our society no longer requires—indeed we are threatened by—population growth. Thus,

Felice N. Schwartz, "New Work Patterns—for Better Use of Womanpower," *Management Review* (May 1974), pp. 5–12. Reprinted by permission of the publisher from MANAGEMENT REVIEW, May 1974, ©1974 by AMACOM, a division of American Management Associations.

women who want to are free to work or pursue careers throughout their lives with, at most, a few years devoted in part or entirely to the rearing of children. Many women today are highly motivated to choose the career-and-family path. Not to be overlooked or deprecated, of course, are women who opt to take significant time off when their children are young to devote themselves full time to family responsibilities; however, even these women often return to work. Increasingly, women enter or re-enter the labor force as their home and family responsibilities require less time or are shared with their husbands.

TAPPING A RICH RESOURCE

A growing number of women—particularly those who are college-educated—want to express the full range of their capacities and avoid the parasitism of dependence on fathers, husbands, or public welfare. Although this desire should be applauded, it won't be if men perceive it as competitive.

Today, when those born during the low population-growth years of the early forties are filling management-level jobs, there is a shortage of brainworkers. The picture may change, however, when the post-World War II "babies" come of age and competition for management positions increases. If the picture does change, the number of women entering management could exceed the number of jobs available and men could then be correct in perceiving women as competitive—unless the work to be done is subdivided.

Currently, there are a great many skilled women who prefer to devote part of their days to career and part to family. The process of subdivision can commence, logically and without resentment, with these women if they are given the opportunity to work and rise along the career ladder on less than full-time schedules. The concept of permanent part-time employment at administrative, managerial, technical, and professional levels is taken seriously by a significant percentage of the nation's college-educated women. It should therefore also be seriously considered by employers who want to absorb this valuable personnel resource profitably, and want also to establish patterns of employment that will best accommodate future needs.

By implementing varied work patterns, employers can open the doors of employment and advancement to a vast, rich resource: the many women whose skills and capabilities are vital to today's and tomorrow's work force. College-educated women with ongoing family responsibilities seeking less than full-time employment bring to their positions not only significant work skills but also a high degree of stability, efficiency, loyalty, and job commitment—all characteristics that reduce turnover and increase quality of performance.

Although women are the first beneficiaries of flexible work patterns such as part-time employment, men will follow in rapidly increasing numbers, because the life/work desires of men and women are converging. As more and more women want to move out of their homes at least part time, many men are becoming disenchanted with work for its own sake and are increasingly concerned with additional time intentionally allocated for participation in family, leisure, and public service activities.

Traditionally, women and children have depended on men's employment for support; so the specter of financial insecurity for men that lurks behind the question of whether there are enough jobs to go around is unsettling, to say the least. But it is valid only if we insist on a fixed and full-time work schedule for all who work. If we are willing to forego this rigidity, our capacity to provide employment for every man and woman who needs or wants it will be significantly expanded.

With part-time scheduling, both men and women will be able to pursue broader-gauged, less-pressured lives, sharing the burden of financial support for the family. They will also be sharing, then, other aspects of family life, such as time spent with children, so that fathers as well as mothers are in a better position to decide how much time and which time should be devoted to on-the-job responsibilities and to off-the-job areas of concern and interest.

EXAMINING PART-TIME WORK PATTERNS

When part-time schedules become widespread, the advantages for employers can be considerable:

• A larger recruitment pool will be available to the employer seeking part-time as well as full-time staff. This will enable the employer to be far more selective about the applicant's qualifications than when he or she was restricted to hiring only full-time personnel.

• Because of the shortage of part-time jobs, the turnover rate among those who work part time is usually substantially lower than that of full-time workers. The low turnover rate is reinforced by the stable life situation of the vast majority of those seeking part-time employment today—i.e., women with young children.

• Time off from work can decrease. Whereas full-time employees usually take time off from their work to attend to personal chores, part-timers take care of such matters during free daytime hours.

• Employment can be tailored to the time needed for the job duties rather than to fill the traditional five-day, 35- or 40-hour work week. Furthermore, jobs can be divided by levels of skill and pay so that the traditional work schedule is not filled with a skilled person doing less skilled work at a higher pay level.

There are several basic forms of part-time employment that are particularly well adapted to the needs and abilities of college-educated women who wish to take on less than full-time career responsibilities. Although these part-time work patterns were tested primarily with women, they also can be beneficial to men who seek less than full-time employment.

Each of these flexible forms — and variations on them will probably occur in the future — can yield for the employer greater productivity, reduced absenteeism, lower turnover, and decreased costs.

The split-location position.   A split-location job is one that may be done partly in an office and partly at home, depending on the particular communication and concentration demands. Creative work such as that performed by an editor, artist, or industrial designer is often adaptable to this flexible pattern.

The Sperry & Hutchinson Company in New York City employs Elizabeth Morrison Baker, a part-time senior systems analyst, in a split-location position. Formerly a full-time S&H employee, Ms. Baker helped design the corporation's merchandising system. When she changed to a part-time schedule she initially wrote a manual documenting that system, and later she designed a flow chart for the system to serve as a teaching aid for new S&H analysts. In her current post, she consults with other analysts but also works on independent research-oriented projects. She works a total of three days a week — Mondays and Thursdays from 9:30 a.m. to 5 p.m. at S&H headquarters in New York, and the same number of hours one day a week, usually Wednesday, at her home in Brookhaven, Long Island. She is paid on a per-diem basis.

Her switch from full-time to part-time employment at S&H came after her son was born in 1972, when she wanted to devote additional time to home responsibilities without sacrificing her career and the professional level she had attained. The present arrangement, according to her supervisor at S&H, has actually increased her value to the company. The key advantage, according to Ms. Baker, is that her split-location part-time position "keeps me in touch with a rapidly changing field."

The Straight Part-Time Position.   This position is one in which one or more individuals work less than a full-time, five-day week to perform a function that would otherwise be performed by one or more full-time persons.

The United States Department of Labor in New York City employs Patricia Wager McGuire, a senior compliance officer in labor relations, on a part-time schedule. She works 26 hours a week, from 10 a.m. to 5 p.m. Monday through Thursday, traveling for troubleshooting assignments when necessary. Her annual salary is prorated and she receives fringe benefits as well. She previously worked for the department on a full-time basis, switching to part-time after her first child was born.

Collaborative Research, Inc., in Waltham, Mass., employs Allison Taunton-Rigby, a senior research chemist, in a part-time position. Dr. Taunton-Rigby, who considers her position at the medical research laboratory half scientific and half administrative, works almost three-quarter time, for which she is paid an hourly rate based on the annual full-time salary. She lives near the laboratory, works parts of five days a week, and takes long lunch hours, which allows her to take care of her family responsibilities at home. Prior to her child's birth she worked full time; afterwards she worked part time on a lighter schedule; and eventually she expanded her part-time schedule to 30 hours a week.

The Consultant Position. A consultant position is one in which a particular type of expertise is needed on less than a full-time basis, so that a part-time professional may become a permanent part of a firm's labor force on a regular schedule.

Massachusetts Mutual Life Insurance Company in Springfield, Mass., employs Mary Pollard Breyer as a personnel consultant. Working on special projects, research, and action programs, she sets her own schedule and is paid by the hour. She averages 30 work hours per week, usually working in the Massachusetts Mutual office from 8 a.m. to 4:45 p.m. Monday through Thursday. She previously worked full time as a programmer and with trainees in data processing and personnel. She likes the independent aspect of her consulting job. Her supervisor recently said: "We've all gotten sort of locked into thinking of full time as the only way to get things done. But this has worked out ideally. Her part-time performance may be more efficient than most people's full-time efforts."

Paired/Shared Positions. A paired position is one in which two individuals divide one full-time job with equal responsibility for the total job. Each person works half-time and together they provide full-time coverage. Often, in the event that one of the team is absent, the other is able to cover both halves of the job in the interim. A shared position is one in which two individuals also divide one job between them, providing full-time coverage, but each is responsible for only half the work. Often, the job functions of one are distinctly different from those of the other within the overall job.

Carol Greenwald (Schwartz) is employed by the Federal Reserve Bank of Boston as assistant vice-president and economist in a paired position. The first woman to become an officer of that bank and the only part-time assistant vice-president in the entire Federal Reserve System, Ms. Greenwald has duties that range from analyzing business conditions and forecasting the economic outlook to handling research and publishing. Her paired arrangement is with Stephen McNees, a full-time economist who has worked with Ms. Greenwald for two years and covers for her when she is not at the bank. He answers inquiries for her, attends meetings in her place, and, according to Ms. Greenwald, "provides the continuity of communications as well as shares responsibilities." Ms. Greenwald averages 20 work hours a week and is paid 55 percent of the annual salary plus complete company benefits.

She suggested a long-range plan for part-time work at the bank even before her first child was born. Variations on her part-time schedule have ranged from working from 9 to 5 one day and from 9 to 1 three days to a schedule of five afternoons to accommodate child care arrangements.

COMMUNICATION AND FRINGE BENEFITS

Although better utilization of time—a benefit to employer and employee—can result from nontraditional work patterns, the benefits are not always immediately evident to employers.

In the past, for example, many executives were reluctant to hire part-time middle-management personnel because of a preconceived idea that everyone in the work force must work the same hours or a communications gap would arise among employees or between a company and its clients. However, officials of companies that have moved away from rigid work styles indicate that variations in employees' schedules result not only in increased involvement with and commitment to the job, but often in better internal and external communications as well.

This ease of communication has been demonstrated clearly in flexible working hours or flextime, a nontraditional full-time work pattern which currently affects more than one million men and women in European countries and which is rapidly gaining momentum in the U.S. Under this system, individual employees begin and end their work day at times of their choice, within certain limits, as long as they work the prescribed number of hours. It generally means that employees may arrive within a two-hour time span in the morning and leave any time within an end-of-day time span, but everyone is required to be on hand during whatever core or fixed hours are set by that company. Companies that use flextime report few communication problems despite the fact that employees do not all have the same schedule. In fact, communication often becomes more efficient when concentrated in the core period.

Another reason some employers are reluctant to hire people on a part-time basis is that they are afraid the cost of fringe benefits to part-time employees will result in extra expenses to the company.

This is a misconception. A benefits package can be constructed that is equitable to both the employer and the part-time employee and that essentially is based on a pro-rated share of the benefits available to full-time employees.

Pro-rating based on earnings is possible in areas of compensatory benefits—e.g., paid vacation, paid holidays, paid jury duty, and sick leave—and most supplementary benefits—e.g., long-term disability insurance, life insurance, pensions, and profit sharing. When pro-rating is not possible—as in the case of medical insurance, which is based not on individual earnings but on per capita costs—employers should be able to make other adjustments in the benefits package.

The important category in which pro-rating is not feasible for computing part-time personnel benefit costs is that of statutory benefits: social security, unemployment, state disability insurance, workmen's compensation.

The most significant of these is social security benefits. If, for instance, the salary of one full-time employee is $12,000 or the combined salary of two part-timers is $12,000, the social security cost to the company is identical. The cost doubles to the company when the combined salary reaches $24,000 compared with a single salary of $24,000. The cost does not increase when the salary goes beyond $24,000 for one full-timer or two part-timers.

Since a large portion of the work force is within the $12,000 to $24,000 salary range, in the case of part-timers it is realistic for employers to calculate greater costs in social security. This should be viewed, however, along with the many other fringe benefits that are fixed or can be pro-rated. For example, the degree to which the employer finds that the cost of statutory benefits for two part-timers exceeds the cost for one full-timer would be the degree to which optional benefits could be reduced by an equivalent amount in computing the remainder of the benefits package.

FOCUSING ON THE FUTURE

In summary, companies and organizations that learn to utilize college-educated women with ongoing family responsibilities effectively in part-time programs today will be better equipped to utilize the entire work force more effectively in the years ahead.

As men increasingly demand more time for active involvement with their families and as increasing numbers of women set serious career goals, innovative work patterns such as part-time positions and flexible work schedules will attract many members of the present and prospective labor force. These work concepts are proving beneficial not only to the executives who adopt them but also to the employees affected by them as they move up the career ladder, because new work concepts like these mitigate conflicts between an individual's professional and personal needs.

Judging by the current widespread interest in varied work scheduling patterns, the future undoubtedly will bring greater innovation in scheduling work hours of both full-time and part-time employees. Concern with clock and calendar will — hopefully — be replaced by concern with the needs and capacities of the individual in relation to the job to be done.

DISCUSSION QUESTIONS

1. What advantages do you see from part-time scheduling (a) for the employer, (b) for the employee, (c) for the family?

2. Interview several personnel officers or wage-and-hour employees to determine what a benefits package could be for part-time employees.

3. Would separate incomes for both husband and wife lead to mutual respect and better marriages? Would this depend on the individuals involved?

The Assessment Center:
Opportunities for Women

Douglas W. Bray

Personnel practices naturally, and of necessity, reflect current mores and assumptions about people, and, until recently, one set of assumptions that business has gone along with had it that the great majority of women would work for only the few years between leaving school and marrying, that they did not aspire to careers, that they should not be assigned to "unfeminine" jobs, and that, in fact, they lacked the ability to qualify for many types of positions. These beliefs, virtually unchallenged for years, have been expressed in employment policies that consider female applicants only for certain beginning jobs, in which those who are hired often find themselves at a dead end, with little chance to transfer into other job families and even less chance to work their way up into management. As a result, many organizations have a large number of female employees mostly in clerical and low-skilled jobs. Some may have advanced to the lowest level of supervision, but if so, they supervise other women in the same kind of work from which they themselves advanced. The few who have risen further are nearly always in staff assignments, rather than line management.

That situation is now changing, however, thanks to strong legal and social pressures for full equality of opportunity for employment and advancement. But effective change requires both motivation and method. Motivation to provide greater opportunity for women there is in abundance, not only in legislation and unrest among female employees, but in management's growing awareness of the tremendous hidden waste incurred in the failure to let women use their full potential. Method, however, is something else. Good intentions alone won't go far to correct imbalances and injustices that have been years in the making. Programs and techniques are needed.

Douglas W. Bray, "The Assessment Center: Opportunities for Women," *Personnel* (September-October 1971), pp. 30–34. Reprinted by permission of the publisher, ©1971 by American Management Association, Inc. All rights reserved.

Organizations characteristically have internal barriers that inhibit the free movement of employees from department to department or even from job family to job family, so even a white male who encounters no attitudinal resistance may not be utilized as well as he might be. These barriers include the inability to identify employees with unrealized potential, the reluctance of a department head to accept a transferee on somebody else's say-so or to part with a good employee, and candidates' lack of relevant experience to qualify for transfer. And if the white male employee has difficulty moving anywhere but straight up in the organization, it is all the more difficult for a woman. It is going to be very hard to convince managers who might take her on a transfer basis into a job usually thought of as "male" that she has the requisite ability. Even her own boss may be skeptical about advancing her, since the undemanding nature of many entry jobs for women does not allow a real demonstration of ability. What is needed in both instances is solid evidence that the woman candidate has the qualities called for by the proposed job.

A thorough evaluation of potential is needed not only as a persuader, but to determine that the candidate actually does have the abilities needed. A program of fuller utilization of women will proceed much more quickly if those who are transferred or advanced do well in their new assignments; too many poor choices would constitute a major setback. The answer may be the management assessment center, which has been demonstrated to be both an accurate method of evaluating potential and one that line managers are ready to accept. Introduced a little over a decade ago, this method is now being widely utilized in 15 large companies, including the Bell System, where it was designed, General Electric, IBM, and Sears, Roebuck and Company, as well as several government agencies.

HOW ASSESSMENT CENTERS WORK

The assessment center evaluates managerial ability and potential by putting the candidate in standardized performance situations where behavior can be observed and rated. These situations are especially designed to bring out dimensions important in supervisory management, such as leadership, flexibility, communications skills, planning and organizing, aptitude, decisiveness, and motivation. Although assessment centers use at least one well-known method, the interview, most of the candidate's time at the center is spent in special simulations. One of these, the in-basket, is used widely as a training as well as an evaluation device. It consists of a carefully planned sample of management problems presented to the assessee in the form of letters, reports, memos, records of incoming telephone messages, and the like. Both the management problems and the written material are tailored to the level of management for which the candidate is being considered. He works through the material, making decisions, scheduling meetings, writing memos and letters, as he would on the job, and is then interviewed to explore the reasons for his decisions, the depth of his perceptions, how he assigns values, and so forth.

A second type of simulation used in most assessment centers is the leaderless group discussion, with assigned roles. In this exercise the participants, usually six in number, are told that they are members of a task force, committee, or some other group, such as a school board. They are to assume that they are attending a meeting to make some sort of group decision—for example, the apportionment of a limited amount of money. Each participant, furthermore, is given a written briefing outlining the project that he is to push. The group then meets, with each participant trying to get a favorable hearing for his particular proposal while working with the others to reach a final decision.

Another group exercise is the short business game, in which the six participants are told that they are partners in a business enterprise. They may be asked to buy parts and put together simple articles that they sell back, in both cases at fluctuating prices. Such exercises are intended not to measure business acumen per se, but to reveal leadership, decisiveness, organizing ability, and comparably relevant qualities.

All exercises at the assessment center are observed by members of a trained staff, who pool their observations at a meeting in which each candidate is intensively reviewed. The candidate is rated on a number of management factors and a final judgment is then made about both the degree of management ability possessed and future developmental needs. A summary of these deliberations is sent to the appropriate level of management and face-to-face feedbacks to the individual participants are given within a week or two, often handled by the assessment staff members themselves.

WHAT ASSESSMENT CENTERS ARE DOING AND CAN DO

The assessment center has most often been used to evaluate candidates for promotion to management within their own departments, but more recently, one of the Bell System telephone companies has applied the technique to facilitate the interdepartmental movement of employees who have already reached managerial levels in their departments. This procedure has enabled first-line managers in departments where there was a surplus of employees with second-level potential to move to departments short of second-level managers—transfers that had been very difficult before because the departments with the shortages were not sure that the candidates proposed actually were capable of rapid advancement in a new department. (About half of the candidates processed were, in fact, *not* recommended for transfer by the assessment staff.)

To repeat, many organizations want to open up channels of advancement for the many women now on their payrolls in jobs of little scope or opportunity, but management hesitates because of doubts that it can accurately identify those with high potential, because of the usual barriers to movement across departments and job families, and because of a lack of confidence on the part of some candidates themselves that they have the ability to move into a new job and advance from there. The assessment center can make a major contribution to the solution of all these problems. First, over ten years' experience has demonstrated that its methods greatly increase the accuracy of selection. Second, line managers have become more willing to accept recommendations from an assessment center than from other evaluation methods. And third, personal feedback interviews with successful candidates about their performance in competition seem to encourage them to accept the risks of transfer and accelerated advancement.

This discussion of assessment centers so far has been concerned with women who have been employed by an organization for some time and have already advanced into lower-level management, or at least into higher-skilled nonmanagement jobs. Many other women, however, are constantly being hired into routine entry jobs. Not all, of course, have a high degree of promotability, but even those who are more capable are likely to go undiscovered for years or resign before their possibilities are appreciated. What is needed is some type of early identification program. Assessment centers offer promise here, too. Procedures would not have to be as extensive or refined as in the centers outlined here. Those centers are aimed at a judgment of immediate promotability, and important decisions are based on the results, but in the case of an *early* identification center, all that is sought is the identification of those with notably higher ability. Those spotted would, of course, be moved along faster than others, but actual advancement to management or to a higher-level specialist's job would depend on performance in the post-assessment period.

If it is not feasible to assess every new employee through a one-day assessment procedure, assessment can be limited to those noted as promising by the employment office, trainers, and first-line supervisors. Later once the program is under way, employees who want to volunteer might well be included.

Early identification need not, of course, be a women-only program; minority-group males, now being employed in greater numbers, should certainly be included. Women would reap great benefits, however, since they tend much more than men to be assigned to less demanding entry jobs, where their abilities cannot be observed so easily. A method that evaluates them objectively would be a powerful counterbalance.

No one argues that assessment of those already employed will solve all problems of giving women opportunities and rewards equal to those of men; equal opportunity at the employment office for women to be assigned to entry jobs on the same basis as men is fundamental. The assessment center can go a long way, though, toward opening up greater opportunities for the female employee and bringing about fuller utilization in the shortest possible time.

DISCUSSION QUESTIONS

1. List all the women you know (1) in supervisory jobs supervising other women (2) in staff positions (3) in line positions. Which list is shortest?

2. Do you know any examples of women who have been held back because their boss did not want to lose someone who took a load off his back?

3. What examples do you know of bright, well-qualified women assigned to less demanding entry-level jobs?

4. If you were a member of a trained staff who observed women candidates at an assessment center, what kinds of qualities and qualifications would you look for?

5. Talk with some company recruiters about innovative ways they use to recruit women.

6. Talk with some high school and college counselors to find out what efforts they have made to guide women into such areas as accounting and engineering.

7. Talk with several organizations to find out how they evaluate women recruits.

"More men are entering what have been traditionally female jobs, reports the U.S. Bureau of Labor Statistics. There was an increase in the number of male secretaries, from 17,000 in 1965 to 29,000 in 1975. According to the Bureau's statistics, the average weekly salary for a male secretary is $179; the average pay for a female secretary is $145 a week."

"Double Take," *Monitor* (January/February 1977), p. 5.

Accountability—
The Key To
Successful Affirmative
Action

R.B. Maddux

A review of any authoritative source of labor statistics quickly reveals the growing dependence of American business on women in the work force. A steady upward trend since the early 1940's was reflected in the 1970 census by a worker population that was forty percent female. Interestingly enough, less than four percent of these women held positions as managers or administrators.

Countless speeches have been delivered and innumerable articles written to point out this inequity, to offer reasons for its existence, and to suggest how it can be corrected. Most have been helpful and much has been done by business and other institutions to better prepare women for entry into management. Why, then, do the numbers of women in managerial roles continue to inch rather than leap upward? Why isn't the percentage of female administrators and managers becoming more quickly representative of their population in the labor force?

Perhaps one important answer lies with those who control the selection and placement process in American industry — the incumbent managers.

An increasing number of these managers have been sensitized to the career problems of female employees and many have recognized the legal ramifications of overt discrimination. Unfortunately, few have taken the deliberate steps to plan and carry out specific courses of action within their jurisdictions which will speed upward mobility and which will be ultimately required to comply with increasingly favorable corporate policies as well as federal regulations.

A change of this magnitude in the culture of American business and industry does not automatically happen because women want it, the

R. B. Maddux, "Accountability—The Key to Successful Affirmative Action," *Women in Management*, published by Simmons College Graduate Program in Management, July 1976, pp. 2–3.

government assures it, top management endorses it and employee relations personnel push it. The change occurs when the incumbent manager who controls positions and position hierarchies wants it to occur. It is doubtful that very many managers believe this issue will fade away, but there are many whose priorities indicate they think they may outlive the necessity of personally dealing with it. Unless these priorities change, the statistics reflecting the number of women in administrative and management positions will continue to inch, not leap, upward.

Personal accountability appears to be the ultimate answer. Managers are the most responsive and attentive to things for which they are directly answerable. When ignoring company policy or federal or state laws brings the same rewards as compliance, there is little incentive to undergo the trauma of changing the traditions of the past to meet the demands of today.

Accountability in today's complex business processes can be elusive, but almost any business has segments of organization which are of suitable size, which contain an adequate variety of positions and which have enough turnover to permit goal setting and establishment of individual accountability for affirmative action. Results can be measured and recognized through appropriate administration of the reward system.

Atlantic Richfield has had the continuing and growing support of its supervisors and managers in the area of Equal Opportunity Affairs, and recently implemented a system of direct affirmative action accountability in each division of the Corporation to achieve more consistent performance and a greater emphasis in long range planning.

Under the new program, the executive in charge of each of the Company's major divisions is responsible for setting affirmative action goals and will be held accountable for the achievement of those goals by the division. Performance against goals will be reviewed annually with the President and upwards of 20% of the executives' merit salary adjustment will be related to his affirmative action performance. In addition to performance against numerical goals, evaluation of performance on more subjective criteria will also be made. These criteria include:

LEADERSHIP

• Personal endorsement of the Company's EEO policy and the requirement that it be endorsed throughout the organizational structure.

• Dissemination of Equal Employee Opportunity Policy throughout the division.

• Personal, active and continuous participation in the development of the divisions' EEO programs and affirmative action plans with required periodic program review and evaluation.

• Established responsibility for implementation of EEO and affirmative action programs.

SUPPORT

• Personal good faith effort to achieve minority and female goals.
• Implementation of training and development activities.
• Personal example in the selection of direct subordinates.

UNDERSTANDING

• Demonstrated attitude of non-discrimination in all personnel actions.

• Demonstrated support of community programs intended to identify and develop qualified minority and female candidates.

• Updated policies, procedures and practices with any which might tend to be discriminatory eliminated or changed.

Ideally, it would be desirable to evaluate the performance of every manager or supervisor in a like manner, but in a large organization, this would be too complex to be practical. We do believe, however, that direct measurement of the performance of the division executive will influence the entire management structure in implementing the concepts of affirmative action in a manner appropriate for each division.

Programs emphasizing personal managerial accountability applied in any appropriate industrial setting should bring the responsibility of incumbent managers to "open the system" into much sharper focus and stimulate them to give this issue much more of their personal attention and a much higher priority. As this occurs, women who are willing to prepare themselves accordingly should find a more clearly defined track to follow and a higher level of achievement possible.

DISCUSSION QUESTIONS

1.   Do you know any examples where unqualified women were deliberately promoted to higher positions so that they would fail in order to prove "women can't make it."

2.   Can you think of any innovative ways to track and reward managers for specifically implementing equal opportunity?

3.   Talk with several organizations to find out how they change attitudes among male managers.

4.   See if you can get copies of the top management policy statement on affirmative action from several organizations and compare them. List the strengths of each one.

Preparing for the Future: Commitment and Action

Sandra Ekberg-Jordan

Many companies will have to initiate more vigorous affirmative action programs if larger numbers of women are to be brought into management soon and given the opportunity to experience the same sense of options about their careers that men have. If a business organization wishes to improve its compliance with EEO requirements and to be known as progressive, it should incorporate many of the following concepts into its affirmative action program. I would suggest the following steps:

1. Discussion of the company's written affirmative action policy with, and distribution of the policy among, as many employees as possible. Fears may exist among some men that they will be replaced by women; thus any step the organization takes to clarify its objectives and their implementation will help to create a more realistic and favorable atmosphere for acceptance of the affirmative action policy.

Employee meetings also serve to reinforce top management's belief in affirmative action and intention to correct any existing imbalances. Where programs exist only on paper and are not reassessed and reaffirmed at regular intervals—at least annually—little attention is likely to be paid to the programs.

2. Appointment of an affirmative action officer who reports to top management. In most organizations it makes sense for a woman to be appointed to this position, in part because such an appointment publicly affirms the company's belief in giving women good jobs. In addition, a woman is more likely to be sensitive to the problems experienced by other women in the organization and is thus more credible to them.

Sandra Ekberg-Jordan, "Preparing for the Future: Commitment and Action," *Atlanta Economic Review* (March–April 1976), pp. 47–49.

In those companies in which equality of opportunity is a genuine goal, the affirmative action officer should be assigned internal responsibilities — meeting with department managers, women employees, and advisory committees within the organization and top management to report on progress and problems and to recommend new action.

3. Recruitment and hiring of qualified women. This can be accomplished through on-campus recruiting programs and by using the services of executive search firms that specialize in finding women for all levels of management jobs.

If a company is honest about its efforts to hire women, it also will take a close look at its annual report and its recruiting materials. One thing that discourages potential women applicants is company literature that makes no reference to women. Many larger corporations have been revising their materials to include photographs of women in professional, technical, or managerial positions and references to managers as "she's" as well as "he's." As women develop greater awareness of the subtleties of employment discrimination, they will look more critically at a company's written materials.

4. Reassessment of career paths. No longer should any woman who expresses interest in a career be placed in a dead-end job, whether it be at a clerical or staff level. To assure all interested employees of career ladders, many firms may need to analyze existing positions and possibly reassign job responsibilities so that upward mobility will be possible from a larger number of positions. Salary scales for all positions should be equal for both men and women.

5. Career counseling for women employees. Women employed by the organization may never have had career counseling during their school years, and they may be unaware of the need to think ahead about career paths. Regular meetings led by personnel staff or outside consultants to talk about affirmative action plans and the company's career ladders can help currently employed women to learn what career options exist and to define long-range career goals. Such meetings also will assist corporate personnel staff members in learning which women may be interested in further responsibilities and which may prefer to remain at their current level.

6. Informal meetings for new women in management. Established woman managers employed by the company or by other companies in the area should be invited to meet with new managers. The experienced women will serve as role models for the newer managers and may be able to offer advice and to share experiences that will be helpful to the neophytes.

7. Encouragement of women to improve their knowledge. Information should be made available to women about credit courses that will prepare them for new levels of responsibility as well as conferences and professional meetings that will contribute to their personal development.

If women have not had an opportunity to complete undergraduate course work and if having degrees is important to their long-range career goals, they should be encouraged to look not only to traditional undergraduate programs, but also to those programs that offer adults credit for skills learned on the job or through workshops or other non-credit courses.

Those for whom graduate business course work is considered an advantage should be encouraged to investigate special MBA programs designed for working men and women. At Pace University two daytime master's level business programs have been established to encourage corporate employees to return to school. One is the Executive MBA Program, which is designed for those with at least eight years of business experience. Its classes meet alternate Fridays and Saturdays. The second is the Friday/Saturday Program within the Graduate Management Program for Women. The latter is open to those with undergraduate degrees and no specific business experience. Classes meet all or part of the day Friday and Saturday during the first year of study and are supplemented by special seminars, a communications workshop, and assertiveness training, features which are designed to help new managers become more effective on the job. During their second year of study, students continue their course work at night.

8. Development of an assessment technique to measure the progress made by women in different departments. If individual career programs have been developed for all women selected for management level positions, an affirmative action staff member will be able to sit down annually (or more frequently) with each department manager to learn how each individual woman under his or her supervision is doing, what additional training or experience she needs, how she can best obtain it, and when she will be ready for further responsibility.

To assure that women managers are being groomed for continued advancement, each department manager should be held responsible for the development of women within his department. If his own performance evaluation includes an assessment of how well women have been counseled and given the professional exposure they need, the department manager will be motivated to treat the women under him as seriously as he would the men.

9. Public posting of all open positions and access to personnel representatives with whom to discuss the openings. The installation of bulle-

tin boards in prominent locations for posting weekly listings of new openings can help to make women aware of what advancement possibilities exist.

10.   Establishment of a Women's Advisory Committee to recommend programs and policies to the affirmative action officer or to senior management. This committee might be composed of men and women representing different departments. Permitting women to select some of their own representatives will be helpful in getting legitimate feedback as to the women employees' true feelings.

11.   Sponsorship of sensitivity workshops for men and women at managerial levels to explore their attitudes and develop an awareness of how they feel about women in management. Their purpose would be to dispel stereotyped attitudes and to change discriminatory behavior. Such workshops might be led by consultants specializing in affirmative action or by trained staff members.

12.   Development of a sponsorship procedure for women managers. In many professions and businesses, an older man will assume sponsorship of a younger man, introduce him to colleagues, and generally acquaint him with the informal customs and rituals of the field. Similarly, corporations need to encourage middle and senior male managers to act as sponsors of women.

13.   Establishment of flexible hours and part-time positions where possible, which will allow women, as well as male employees, with young children to work different schedules from those of regular employees. The government has been attempting to develop increased numbers of part-time positions, particularly as a means of allowing educated women to balance family responsibilities with the use of their skills and experience.[1]

14.   Reevaluation of policies regarding maternity leaves, making it possible for new mothers to return after a specified period without loss of credit toward vacations, retirement, or other benefits. In addition to maternity leave, companies need to consider paternity leaves, as many young couples are interested in sharing the parenting process.

15.   Review of relocation policies. Concern over the need for relocation is expressed by employers and by potential and actual women managers. Although some single and some married women may view relocation as an exciting prospect, others may consider it unpleasant or impossible. Some single women object to transfers as they feel it is more difficult for them to build a social life in a new community than it is for a family, which, through the children's school and the community associations developed by the wife, can readily acquire new friends.

For married professional couples who do not wish to live apart, a relocation decision may rest on economic considerations, with the highest wage earner having the most say in any decision. A few married couples—with or without children—prefer to pursue their individual careers in whatever directions they may take them and to commute weekends so as to spend time together.[2] Although the latter concept has not been widely adopted, it may become more popular—at least among childless career couples—in the future.

Two-career families may well become more commonplace in the future; thus assessment by a company of its relocation policies is important. Is it really necessary for someone to relocate in order to gain the experience thought necessary for career development? Or will some other kind of experience, not requiring relocation, do as well? The need for reviewing relocation policies should not be based on a desire only to accommodate women. Undoubtedly, as both husbands and wives work and share more equally in their financial contributions to the family, men, too, will begin asserting their preference not to move.

16.   Funding of day-care centers. Thus far, our society has not accepted the position that good child care is a government responsibility. Existing child care centers are available to only a few, and the care of children has remained largely a personal family responsibility. Supporters of women's rights are seeking alternate solutions, for private arrangements are costly and government tax allowances for private child care deductions are limited to certain income levels. In the future, companies interested in attracting women with young children may offer day-care services for their employees. In an area where several companies are clustered, a center might be jointly built and operated. Parents with young children could leave their offspring during working hours and visit with them at lunch.

CONCLUSION

Women are becoming more optimistic about what the future holds for them. This is especially true for younger women, many of whom are excited about job opportunities. According to a 1974 Roper poll, more than half of the women surveyed indicated that they plan to combine careers with marriage and children.[3] Thus, the female job applicants with whom corporate recruiters and personnel managers talk in 1976 and the decade ahead will expect many more opportunities for advancement than did women employees of 5 or 10 years ago.

Women also are becoming more knowledgeable about their legal rights, and are being urged through the media and by women's groups to ask for their legal due. Women are bringing suits against companies, the effects of which can be financially costly and damaging to the organizations' reputation. John Kenneth Galbraith has argued that legal pressure is needed to break the male monopoly on jobs and has recommended that major corporations be given a ten-year period in which "to bring the representation of women at various salary levels into general accord with their representation in the work force as a whole.[4] Galbraith's view is not universally shared. Others have argued that giving companies a set number of years in which to bring themselves into compliance provides the companies with convenient excuses for not bringing about real change in the interim.[5]

Whether corporations are given a ten-year grace period or less, all business organizations face the need to develop the policies and programs that will make it possible for women to experience true equality on the job within the near future. It's up to each business to contribute to societal change through a commitment by senior management to an affirmative action program that guarantees elimination of sexist policies and practices. The time to make that commitment is today.

NOTES

[1] U.S. Civil Service Commission, "The Federal Women's Program — A Point of View" (Washington, D.C.: U.S. Government Printing Office, 1972).

[2] Francine E. Gordon and Myra Strober, *Bringing Women into Management* (New York: McGraw-Hill, 1975), pp. 139–47.

[3] "The Virginia Slims American Women's Opinion Poll," Vol. III (The Roper Organization, 1974), p. 1.

[4] John Kenneth Galbraith, *Economics and the Public Purpose* (Boston: Houghton Mifflin Company, 1973), p. 258.

[5] "Female Employment Opportunities: Some Recent Findings" (Philadelphia: Hay Associates, June 1974), p. 9.

DISCUSSION QUESTIONS

1. Interview some female affirmative action officers. How long have they held their positions? What do they feel will be their next step in the organization? Has their present position created any future barriers in the organization for them?

2. Interview some "head hunters" (executive search firms) as to their experiences in recruiting women. What advice do they have for women? For prospective employers?

3. What cues can women identify in organizations that point toward awareness and implementation of affirmative action?

4. Interview several companies to find out how they arrange career-path planning for employees.

5. Interview several women who have achieved some success in their organizations. Do they consciously try to do anything to act as role models for other women?

6. What educational opportunities exist in your area that would help a woman get a traditional or nontraditional job or progress professionally?

7. Moving is a significantly unsettling experience. Talk with some two-career families about how they intend to address the subject of "moving" if the situation arises.

8. What actions can be taken to insure that women will not discriminate against other women?

9. Ask for copies of any company affirmative action literature available to you. Check it against the suggestions in this article for both completeness and new ideas.

Guidelines for Interviewing and Hiring Women Candidates

The following guidelines were compiled by the Women's Association of the Harvard University Graduate School of Business Administration. They are based on Equal Employment Opportunity Commission guidelines and/or court rulings on specific cases.

A. WORKING CONDITIONS

In general, all working conditions, such as requirements for travel or long working hours, should be described to any candidate, but it is entirely for the candidate to decide whether she or he is willing and able to meet those conditions and how those conditions can be met.

B. IT IS ILLEGAL TO FAIL TO HIRE BECAUSE:

1.   A company's customers would not want to deal with a woman, or because a woman's field work is thought to lack credibility.

2.   Company co-workers might object.

3.   Of the employer's preference about the hiring of women (i.e., the company's president does not want women).

4.   The position involves travel and/or travel with members of the opposite sex.

5.   Of unusual working hours or lack of restroom facilities.

C. QUESTIONS, STATEMENTS, OR ACTIONS CONSIDERED TO BE DISCRIMINATORY

1.   Unintentional discrimination is considered as unlawful as intentional discrimination.

"Guidelines for Interviewing and Hiring Women Candidates," *Journal of College Placement* (April–May 1973), p. 55.

2. Any question asked of a female applicant not asked of men seeking a similar job is evidence of discrimination, such as questions about children, marital status, marital plans, plans to have children, and child care arrangements.

3. Any family history or personal background asked for by an interviewer must be asked of both male and female applicants. In addition, a company must be able to prove that questions asked in an interview are specifically job related.

4. Evidence of discrimination includes any statement by an interviewer exhibiting hiring preferences for either married or unmarried women.

5. It is unlawful for an interviewer to begin discussing a stereotyped female job with a female applicant, especially if the applicant is applying for another job.

6. It is evidence of discrimination if unfilled positions which are more commensurate with a female applicant's ability are not discussed with the applicant.

7. Any job benefits or conditions which pertain only to heads of households or principal wage earners are discriminatory.

8. Evidence of discrimination includes any statement or implication by any supervisor of belief in any female stereotypes, such as: women are not aggressive enough, women are too emotional, women should not travel alone or stay overnight in other cities, or women never stick with a job.

9. It is considered evidence of a general pattern of discrimination if an interviewer brings and distributes brochures and company information in which employees are consistently referred to only as "he."

10. If is considered evidence of discrimination for an interviewer to refer to an adult female applicant as a "girl" or to refer to adult female employees of the company as "girls."

D. EQUAL PAY

1. As of June 23, 1972, the Education Amendments of 1972 extend the Equal Pay Act of 1963 to cover executive, administrative, and professional employees.

2. It is illegal to offer a female applicant a lower salary than her predecessor, or than was advertised, or than was offered to another applicant with an equivalent background.

DISCUSSION QUESTIONS

1. Talk with several personnel directors to determine how they are training their managers to be aware of pitfalls in interviewing women.

2. Talk with a college placement director to determine how s/he insures that students will not be asked inappropriate questions during interviews.

3. Talk with some women graduating seniors to determine if they are being asked inappropriate questions during job interviews. If so, what are the questions and how are they dealing with them?

III

Getting Along
with
the Corporate Woman

What are women like to work with? They're just like men: there are good ones and bad ones! With all the emphasis on sex in our society, we sometimes forget that women—just like men—are human beings. They have the same kinds of hopes and dreams for themselves and their families that men do. Perhaps they are more alike than they are different. Until now, most men and women have viewed woman's role as related to an "accident of birth"—the fact that a woman was born a woman, and, therefore, could only be interested in what society defines as "woman's work." Perhaps one of the most positive contributions of the women's movement will be to give all women and men a broader view of women that encompasses their role as human beings.

Because the women's movement is a major social movement that will affect all our lives eventually, it is appropriate for us to read and discuss various perceptions of the differences in relationships with the corporate woman. In the final analysis, we may find that what it takes to get along with the corporate woman is the same as what it takes to get along with the corporate man. Then we can turn our attention to what it takes to get along with the corporate human being.

The Struggle
for Status:
accepting the aggressive
female executive

Dee Estelle Alpert

"Do your executives feel uncomfortable working with your first woman manager?" I asked a potential corporate client for my management consulting services. "Oh, no," he replied, whereupon his female assistant walked in, shouted "I quit," hurled a copy of *Male Chauvinist Pig* onto his desk, and barged out, slamming the door. Continuing, as though without interruption, he said, "The girls say I treat them quite well." Thus ended another meeting with an Affirmative Action officer unable to comprehend the rationale behind EEO seminars for managers.

During my conversation with him, this man exhibited distress over whether or not to light the five cigarettes he had driven me to smoke; insisted upon helping me off with my coat (dropping my scarf in his effort to grease the social wheels); and showed me his marvelous collection of exotic plants, which his (ex-)assistant had watered so well. He treated the "girls" well, but they quit in droves nevertheless, leaving him entirely perplexed.

Explaining to confused male managers why "girl" is now a forbidden word could easily become a lifetime preoccupation. "But my wife *loves* being called a girl," is the standard argument; "it makes her feel younger" — to which I cannot help but reply, "Dammit, I'm not your wife."

But the argument is revealing, for, regardless of her real job, a woman in business will commonly be treated as either a) wife, b) mother, or c) lover, or, better yet, as someone having the ability to become any one of the three on a moment's notice. In fact, if she's not a), b), or c), and she works, there is no clear-cut way of defining exactly what she is. (The term "businesswoman" has too many ambiguous implications.)

At the root of the problem is a basic double standard. Men are permitted two separate roles to play in our society. At work they are, optimally, Toughman, tearing through their days, justifying means with ends,

Dee Estelle Alpert, "The Struggle for Status," *MBA* (February 1976), pp. 25-28.

and bottom-lining throughout. At home, however, they become fathers, husbands, lovers. We have an entirely different set of expectations for men at home and at work, with respect both to the work they do and to the behavior they are supposed to exhibit while doing that work. Men are handy at home; male managers are not expected to be handy at the workplace — they don't fix the plumbing or paint walls. At home, men may take out the garbage; at the office, someone else handles the refuse.

Woman's work, in contrast, is commonly transferred from home to the office and added on to the job function for which she was hired. In effect, we transfer women's roles from home to the office while permitting men the luxury of leaving one set of expectations and activities at their front door, not to be reassumed until they return again at night.

The *New York Times* illustrated this phenomenon in an article about male secretaries. A new male employee was told that his duties would include watering the office's plants — a carryover from his female predecessor. "What do you think I am," he replied, "a gardener?" A similar kind of shock awaits a new female manager when informed that, on top of all her other duties, she must also bring in coffee for the men. She hasn't been hired for her cooking or serving ability, and excelling in food service won't accelerate her corporate career, but she'd better learn how to do it smoothly or face some awkward situations. In the absence of a role we could call "worker (woman)," female employees are treated as "women workers."

A West Coast bank, which is now the target of a class discrimination suit, made it a practice to serve in-house luncheons to all its employees at reduced cost. It reduced the cost by making all female employees both cook and serve the food. Incredibly, all women workers, including bank officers, had to participate in the mass mothering, while the lowliest male had not a single dish to wash. It has not been determined whether Equal Employment Opportunity Commission charges cause indigestion.

The image of women workers as primarily mothers, wives, and lovers helps create a great deal of confusion over why women work at all. It is widely accepted that women get married, have children, and keep homes because they want to — for the pleasure of it. If women carry out many of the same tasks at the office, must it not be then that they are also working at jobs for the pleasure of it? The answer, according to the Department of Labor's Women's Bureau, is a resounding no. Since well before the 1970s, seven out of ten American women have worked because they are single, divorced, widowed, separated, or have other head-of-household status, or because their husbands do not earn enough to keep the family above the poverty level. Seven out of ten women work because they need the money — which explains in part the dramatic rise in sex discrimination charges on file as unemployment has risen. (However, 11 years after the tough federal nondiscrimination laws were passed, full-time working women earn only 55 percent of what full-time working men do, and the level of education of both groups is equal.)

Yet the prevalent assumption seems to be that women just don't need — or work for — the money. A male regional director of one federal civil rights agency asked a job applicant not long ago: "What's a single female like you with no dependents doing asking for a salary this high?" (She was interviewing for a professional position requiring significant education and experience.) Similarly, sitting on a television panel, I was recently asked what to do if a male factory owner decided to give a promotion to a male rather than to a superior female employee because the male had a family to support. I replied, "Help the owner decide whether he's running a business or a charitable trust."

When an aggressive female manager takes the initiative by asking for a raise, transfer, or promotion, strange things can happen. "Why, I hadn't thought of you in that light" is one common reaction. Women are not automatically included in the career progressions developed for males, and demanding access can subject the demander to all the indignities of an outraged ego — or worse. One woman with whom I am presently working was doing an assistant manager's job at a clerical pay rate. When she demanded an upgrade and increase, she was given a token raise (for her good attitude) and no promotion. She refused the raise — and was fired the next day ("poor attitude"). It's not hard to see why. Imagine, if you will, a wife demanding a promotion from her husband. What can she be promoted to? Wife is a dead-end job.

Assumptions about why women work also dictate where women are placed within a company. While men handle operations, industrial sales, and other line functions, women traditionally are placed in staff or service-oriented jobs. In a new version of an old cliche, business says: Those who can (male), do it in line jobs; those who cannot (female), help on staff. Let us not forget that one of the primary jobs of the housewife is to make the household machine function so that men can do their work more easily and efficiently; they are expected to act as support for the efforts of their children and husbands in the "real world."

Corporate personnel recruitment groups are put in a curious bind here. The same hiring standards are frequently used for both male and female applicants in management-level slots; business education must be good and the individuals should be aggressive self-starters as well. But, while aggressiveness is usually necessary for sales or operation positions, it is decidedly not appropriate for a staff job with small dollars, little responsibility, and spaced-out promotions. The same qualities that make a woman attractive as a potential employee may well make her profoundly miserable in a staff job. If she's really "good," those characteristics will most likely propel her into a different job in another company. It's been my experience that motivated women will not rest content when underutilized on the job.

Companies often claim that they have difficulty finding women within their own ranks who will go after — or accept — upgrading. Close examination reveals that the firm has, often as not, lost those very women who should have been groomed for advancement; they became disenchanted and left. The women who remained in more traditionally female jobs were not willing to risk losing the job security they had obtained, nor willing to experiment with the slightly unorthodox behavior called for in nontraditional jobs.

Hiring women who are capable of becoming fine executives with training and experience, and losing them to other companies (or to personal demoralization), leads firms into precarious waters. These will often be the first to file discrimination charges, and usually have the strongest documentation for their cases. As good leaders, they are quite capable of organizing and recruiting other less energetic women into women's caucuses or other groups aimed at ending the discrimination they feel they have suffered — regardless of the cost to the employer. It is probably wiser not to hire strong female candidates at all if they're not going to be effectively utilized.

One New York bank is famous for hiring and training the best female candidates available in the United States for its lending programs. But it loses most of them after the second job assignment — usually staff researcher or a line position in community lending or, that old standby, estates and trusts — and therefore cheaply supplies other New York banks and many corporations with a large number of capable executives ready to start line assignments at hire. (Women in the legal and financial communities, incidentally, were originally placed in the estates and trusts sections because they were thought to be "good" with widows and children.) While this bank's training programs are properly rated as the Harvard in the field, long-term cost effectiveness relative to females trained is strictly bush league.

The mother-wife-lover aura has other consequences for the unwilling bearers of these role identifications. First of all, the woman is seen as a temptress, with all the attached implications. Consider these phenomena: If a business problem arises because of sexual relations between a male and a female employee of the same company, the woman will get the ax 99 percent of the time. (In the other 1 percent, she's the boss's daughter.) If a female employee complains of sexual advances made by a male employee, she is the one moved or terminated. Many companies terminate women who have had illegitimate children, but males never suffer such discipline. (Of course, it is easier to tell if a woman has been promiscuous; but how many employers ever inquire about male sexual behavior?) Parallels can be drawn between the attitude taken toward female workers and the common reaction to rape victims: She asked for it; she had it coming. Blaming the victim for that which befalls her is as pervasive in corporate life as it is in private life.

An informal survey I took in late 1974 of women in administrative and managerial jobs showed that over half of them, regardless of age, appearance, or marital status, had had passes made at them by at least one coworker or supervisor that year. Most said that the passes were quite perfunctory, and that there was no retaliation following. But one friend of mine was fired after such an incident. Her newly divorced supervisor called her into his private office after lunch and a few drinks too many, calmly took off his shoes, shirt, and trousers, and said, "Let's get down to business, honey." She said, "Yessir," took his pants and shirt out to the receptionist's desk, and hung them on a coat hanger. The managerial initiative, for which she was trained, went unrewarded.

Personal appearance presents a delicate problem to female job applicants above the clerical or secretarial level. Some companies think a woman, to be successful in sales, must be terrific-looking. Others regard good looks as a disadvantage, distracting customers from the product. (Attractive women are occasionally not hired because it is felt that a man will snap them up soon and take them away from their job.) In either case, they are perceiving the female applicant as a potential lover, and judging how that aspect of her will affect her performance as a worker. Indeed, male corporate buyers often decide whether or not to see a female salesperson on the basis of her appearance — and the potential follow-through. It's a no-win situation, and women who sell industrial products are full of stories about sly hints, aghast remembrances of passes past, and so on.

Older women frequently have a difficult time getting jobs, because they do not fit easily into the roles of wife, mother, or lover. They are seen as biologically unemployed — past their prime for their "real" functions. Yet it is seldom recognized that these women, having passed the unsettling problems of child care, divorce, alimony, and so on, represent a truly unique labor group — people who can work for 15 or 20 years more, with less chance for long-term interruptions or distractions.

The wife-mother-lover role confusion is the basis for a number of excuses used to bar women from corporate advancement. One of these "disqualifiers" might be called "the curse of cursing." It's common to have been taught by one's mother not to use profane language in public. In business, significant numbers of women have been excluded from first-line supervisory jobs because of the rough language of the men on the line, or because the men would feel uncomfortable watching their words all the time. Women are rarely consulted about their preferences or sensitivities in this regard — the decision is made for them by someone who "knows" how they'd react. As often as not, however, the shock is on the other side. A woman manager using a profanity can shut down a production line or an accounting department for hours as the guys recover from their surprise.

Another disqualifier is based on the "helpless woman" model. Because of presumed inabilities, women aren't assigned to certain kinds of jobs, certain shifts, and so on. Travel causes particular problems. A lone woman traveling in strange cities is presumed to be a target for all kinds of sharpies. If she's taken on a trip with the boys, there's the "problem" of whether or not to escort her in the evening. One is almost led to believe that hotel rooms rented to females are devoid of television sets and reading lights, that movies bar out-of-town women, and that women can't handle passes in strange towns that they've been handling at home for years. One executive told me that he couldn't travel with his assistant because she was too young to be his wife and she didn't look enough like him to be his daughter. It was the old "what will everybody in Kennedy Airport think I'm doing with her" routine. When a woman is married, she will almost never be offered the chance to travel; it is assumed that her husband won't let her, the kids need her at home, or some such thing—although the assumption may not be justified.

The female manager in a position of authority can cause the stickiest problems of all. Men have difficulty working for her because: 1) they're adults now and don't have to take orders from mommy; 2) they're married and get enough nagging at home; or 3) they're more concerned with making it with her than doing things for her. It should be pointed out that women are frequently as unwilling to take orders from a female manager as men are. Why not? Since they are all expected to play the same wife-mother-lover role, why should one woman have authority over another? In addition, a female manager who has at least partially broken out of the role represents a threat to other women, since she is living proof that choices are possible.

Women who have made it as managers and executives have done so, most often, after a significant period of adjustment on the part of those around them; after proving their competence a little bit more than should be necessary; and after having set up effective personal relationships, which define them to their co-workers as individuals rather than as members of a sexual group. The solution: more of them.

DISCUSSION QUESTIONS

1. What kinds of "woman's work" (watering plants, cooking for males, etc.) have you seen in organizations?

2. Can you identify males in your organization with higher salaries and fewer dependents than females with lower salaries and more dependents? What should be the basis for hiring and promoting individuals — their professional qualifications or the number of their dependents?

3. List the women you know in line positions and in staff positions. Informally discuss with one or two from each group (a) the advantages of being in line or staff, and (b) the strategies to get moved from staff to line. Are staff positions generally considered a part of the organization's profit-making center? What implications would this have on the prestige of line positions as compared with staff?

4. Many attractive, successful career women don't run into the problem of males making passes. What is their secret?

5. A stable, pleasant woman with good grades and a brand new BBA degree applies for a job. She is over 40. Will the affirmative action laws help her become employed in organizations you know? Would the age discrimination laws be of any use to her or a comparable male applicant?

6. List reasons why women may not want a female boss. Could personal prestige or family attitudes be a basis for same-sex discrimination?

7. What actions could be taken to insure that travel requirements are not considered in a negative light when considering women for a job?

8. Is "socializing" with other employees and bosses vital to career advancement? Give reasons for or against. Why is "socializing" difficult for many women?

Humanizing the World of Work

Sharon B. Lord

"We are an equal opportunity employer," states the ad; and the employer would like to believe that statement is true. "We don't discriminate; we just never find any qualified women," says the personnel manager sincerely. "I would be willing to hire a woman, but I'm afraid of the problems it would create in our office," explains the concerned president of a small company.

Affirmative action. Equal employment opportunity. Changing sex roles definitions. Women's rights. These are only a few of the reasons for the growing concern surrounding employment policies and practices in American business and industry. And the concern is justified, for the goal of equal opportunities in employment is a long way from being achieved.

Critics of governmental affirmative action efforts argue that weak governmental enforcement and lack of employer commitment have contributed to a program which has not significantly altered the status of women in the world of work, but has instead, created unrealistic job expectations for women through the highlighting of a handful of token women in key positions. Employers respond defensively, either with exaggerated reports of progress or overly-simplified arguments as to why no progress has been made. In reality, the situation is complex and the problems to be confronted and understood are multi-faceted.

In order to explicate the social and psychological aspects of the challenge of integrating women fully into all levels of employment in American business and industry, four topics will be examined: the nature of the changing roles of women in society; the subtle, unintentional modes of discrimination in the work world; special "problems" of women in a male-dominated work force; and ways of "humanizing" the world of work.

Sharon B. Lord, "Humanizing the World of Work," *Survey of Business*, (May-June 1975), pp. 8 – 11.

THE CHANGING ROLE OF WOMEN
IN AMERICAN SOCIETY

It is no longer necessary to establish evidence that the traditional role of woman is being questioned and broadened in society. One has only to look to legislation, the evening news, popular magazines, professional journals or television shows in order to see that woman's role and lifestyle is changing.

An examination of earlier or more primitive societies, i.e. societies lacking in sophisticated technology, reveals that their members spent most of their energies simply struggling for survival. Because it was difficult to fulfill basic needs such as food and shelter, and because they had no methods of birth control, distinct role differentiation usually resulted. In many cases, the females in the society produced, nursed, cared for and reared children for the major part of their lives, especially since their life span was very short, while the male worked toward hunting, fighting, or contributing to other basic work tasks necessary for that society's survival.

In contrast, in complex, "advanced" societies like our own, technology has freed human energy to pursue what some psychologists would label *higher order* needs, such as the need for self-fulfillment, the need to know, the need to think and to create beauty. And if human energies are freed to seek knowledge, then the technology advances further. In this society, technology has provided efficient ways of producing food, shelter and clothing without requiring that everyone in the society be involved in the same few basic tasks. Also, technological change has provided women a means for determining if and when they will have children; safe, sufficient substitutes exist for the breast feeding of children if the mother so chooses. Finally, the roles and jobs available in the world of work in a complex, advanced society are very diverse.

Although any student of sociology would predict that if technology changes, social changes will naturally occur in a society, a reality of life is, and always has been, that social changes—i.e., changes in attitudes, beliefs, values and role expectations—occur much more slowly and lag far behind technological changes. Today we are experiencing the changes in sex-role expectations that are a predictable outgrowth of a society dramatically altered by its technology.

We have advanced to a point that we formally educate the majority of the population, both male and female; educators like to believe that students are prepared to think, to create, to problem-solve. And yet, when two human beings decide to marry, to commit themselves to sharing a lifetime together (or at least a portion of a lifetime), it is still assumed that the possession of a female-type body automatically qualifies its owner for domestic type tasks.

It is argued today by psychologists such as Sandra and Daryl Bem that it is just as unreasonable and insane for society to consign a part of its population on the basis of sex as it is to consign the individual with a black skin to the role of janitor or domestic help.[1] It should be emphasized that it is not the quality of the role of housekeeper or homemaker questioned here, but the fact that in spite of their unique identities, unique abilities, unique interests, the majority of American women end up in the same role. If women do choose to work outside the home, it is usually expected that they will assume supportive, passive, low-paying positions.

While the assignment of tasks and roles to individuals on the basis of secondary sex characteristics rather than skill, interest, and educational background (i.e., sex-role stereotyping) has been a common, acceptable practice in our nation, it is no longer socially or legally acceptable.

SUBTLE, UNINTENTIONAL MODES OF DISCRIMINATION

Many discriminatory practices in the world of work are often unintentional, sexist behaviors which are related to sex-role stereotypes; however, these behaviors usually operate effectively and consistently to the detriment of women. Frequently the occurrences are related to the supportive, second-class citizenship roles in which women are customarily placed.

Since language is a symbol-system which represents and reflects the concepts which we "carry around in our heads," an examination of office language reveals the male/female — superior/subordinate class system in operation.

For example, a newly-hired, 55-year-old female administrative assistant, with 33 years of experience in the field, arrives for her first day of work and is addressed as "Susie" by the 29-year-old, "wet-behind-the-ears" male administrator with whom she works. He, of course, expects to be called "Mr. X," and would consider it insubordination if she called him Dale and inappropriate if she asked to be called Ms. Y in their personal and professional interactions. What is the rationale behind the practice?

Perhaps it is the same rationale which dictates the common practice of referring to working women, such as secretaries, as the "girls in the office," while a reference to working men as the "boys in the office" would be considered an insult. The far-fetched left-field type reasoning which tries to twist this practice into a compliment to women is as ludicrous as trying to argue that mature, black men should find it a compliment to be addressed as "hey, boy." The phrase, "girls in the office" or "let my girls take care of that" relegates women to an infantile, powerless, second-class status and is as demeaning as the racist phrases, "yard boy" or "house boy."

One might argue that the language discrimination is related to *rank* within the office rather than sex; however, this argument breaks down when one is presented the evidence that even when a woman is promoted upward through the ranks she is more often than not addressed by her first name by superiors, peers and subordinates alike. The class system within the office setting is definitely one in which sex and rank interact.

Forms of address reflect status in society; one can't really consider herself equal when she is "Susie" among a group of "Mr.'s." The difficulty of a woman being treated as an equal, in those rare cases when she is promoted up through the system, should be obvious.

An even more subtle barrier is posed for the professional woman who encounters the resentment of female subordinates who are so thoroughly entrenched in sex-role stereotypes that they willingly accept their assigned second-class citizenship *so long as it is imposed by men.* However, when confronted with the reality of a female "boss," the second-class citizenship becomes glaringly obvious, and the resentment and hostility toward the exploitative system is displaced to a less threatening object — the female "boss."

An unaware female administrator may find herself the unsuspecting object of sabotage and resentment to such a degree that her job performance can be drastically affected. If she does not understand the common psychological principle in operation, that of individuals choosing to aggress against objects which pose the least threat (and members of the subordinate class, i.e., the female sex, would be viewed as less threatening in a class system), she may find herself assuming total responsibility and guilt for an unhappy situation which she did not create.

Another set of behaviors or practices which place women at a disadvantage have been fondly labeled by aware women as "the boys in the back room" practices. Frequently occurring and often unintentionally discriminatory, "boys in the back room" practices are an outgrowth of the informal, fraternal-type interactions which occur among male co-workers at poker games or in men's social or civic groups

Since business conversation is not limited to the confines of the office, much important information can be shared through the "boys in the back room" network. Job openings, previously unavailable data related to business considerations — there is no end to the business-related content shared in informal settings. And if the setting precludes the presence of half of the human species, then that half of the human species is more likely than not to be excluded from the considerations at hand.

Individuals are often fired and hired through the use of "the boys in the back room" network, imposing one more form of discrimination on "the girls on the outside."

SPECIAL "PROBLEMS" OF WOMEN IN
A MALE-DOMINATED WORK FORCE

Situations are defined as problems in relation to the population which is doing the defining. For example, in an efficiency-oriented work setting where the primary emphasis is on maximizing output at the expense of worker satisfaction, a person-oriented employee might be labeled a problem; on the other hand, in a setting where worker satisfaction is valued on an equal basis with production, a person-oriented employee might be viewed as an asset.

Individuals who anticipate that the employment of women will create problems are often guilty, either of perpetuating myths about working women or of labeling an anticipated situation a problem because of their narrow perspectives. As a result, many of the hypotheses held by employers fearful of hiring women go untested and unvalidated, yet are used as arguments against hiring women.

The labor department has provided data which explode a number of the most common myths about working women; yet these myths are currently employed to justify denying employment to multitudes of women. One common argument against hiring women is that female workers are ill more than male workers and, therefore, cost the company more; however, a recent Public Health Service study shows little difference in the absentee rate due to illness or injury.

The reader is encouraged to review the government pamphlet, *The Myth and the Reality*, which provides data which *negate* arguments such as "women aren't serious workers, and their training is wasted" or "married women take jobs away from men, and shouldn't be in the labor force."[2] Employers must move beyond making hiring decisions on the basis of such myths.

However, there *are* some special problems related to being female in a male-dominated work force, and one of the major problem areas is tied directly to sex-role stereotyped expectations. If women choose to be direct, assertive and efficient in their approaches to work, they are often labeled "unfeminine" or aggressive by coworkers who believe that femininity is synonymous with "sweet, passive, indirect, and manipulative." The traits of rationality, calmness, sensitivity and assertiveness traditionally have been viewed as positive and desirable in a male employee; their presence in a woman often cause her to be labeled "undesirable" in one way or another, depending on who is doing the labeling.

Moreover, there is the additional problem that is always associated with classes of people who have historically been placed in a second-class citizenship position: persons in the dominant class find it difficult to accept being supervised or managed by them. Even though a worker may never have experienced a female supervisor or even a female peer, he or she may report that they "would never want to work for a woman." This places even the most competent women at a disadvantage when being considered for a management position. How can interviewer evaluations be objective or fair when historical built-in bias exists?

Finally, the age-old fear exists that a female co-worker might be a distraction to the male workers in the office. This form of reasoning is a classic example of an oppressed class being punished for the "hang-ups" or problems of the dominant class. If a male has so objectified women that an attractive female is viewed as a sex object regardless of the setting, that is a *male* problem, not a female problem. He should seek counseling or be removed from his job. A woman should no longer suffer from or be subjected to the assumption that her femaleness makes her fair game for every male in the office.

It is amusing to see the male reactions when a female worker points out that she either works with or anticipates working with handsome men, and she doesn't feel it will be a problem. It seems that men never turn the situation around and try to see it from the female point of view.

In the case of a female worker who is distracted by her handsome male co-workers, this indeed would be a *female* problem, which *she* should have to confront. However, there is no justification for preventing attractive women or men from being employed on the basis of the anticipated or real "hang-ups" of their fellow or sister co-workers. This occurrence would probably cease immediately if a male employer could ever experience being informed, "We'd love to hire you; you're the best man for the job. However, we can't, because the females in the office would find you too attractive."

WAYS OF HUMANIZING THE WORLD OF WORK

Before the problems associated with sex-role stereotyping and sex discrimination in the world of work will ever be eliminated, they will have to be understood and taken seriously by employers and employees. Just as Americans have begun to recognize and attempt to deal with the racism that is at the base of every institution in our nation, they must now begin to recognize and deal with the sexism and sex-role stereotypes which are also at the base of American institutions.

Management training programs must incorporate a serious, intensive treatment of problems related to sexism and sex-role stereotyping. Competent consultants on the issue should be employed with the same commitment and seriousness with which we employ lawyers or other type professionals to advise and educate business persons.

Women employees must be educated to understand and deal effectively and assertively with the subtle dynamics of sex-role stereotyping and its interaction with the world of work. The employer who recognizes the need for human relations training in the area of sexism as it relates to male-female relations, female-female relations, and male-male relations will ultimately reap the benefits of a more integrated, balanced work force.

The problem, being multifaceted, must be attacked on every level with every available technique. If you're still at the point where you think it's a woman's problem, you still have a long way to go.

NOTES

[1] Sandra and Daryl Bem, "Teaching the Woman to Know Her Place: The Power of a Non-Conscious Ideology" in Michele H. Garskof, *Roles Women Play* (Belmont, California: Cole Publishing Co., 1973).

[2] U.S. Department of Labor, Employment Standards Administration, Women's Bureau Bulletin, "The Myth and the Reality" (Washington, D.C.: Government Printing Office, May 1974). (*Au. note: Included in this anthology.*)

DISCUSSION QUESTIONS:

1.   Do you know women who ended up with family responsibilities and limited job opportunities due to lack of education?

2.   Do you know any women who have excellent minds, good judgment, and plenty of drive, and who might have had a job other than housework had they not been born with a female body? We know a baby's sex is determined both by chance and by the father. Should women be relegated to a life based on the chance happening of their sex?

3.   It is now more socially acceptable for women to work in "nontraditional" areas. Would they ever have received this opportunity without the backing of the law?

4.   Can you think of work groups that include a woman who is called by her first name, while she addresses the males as "Mr."?

5.   Can you think of informal male gatherings — lunches, poker games, etc. — that exclude women in your organization and include shop talk that later affects the job?

6.   There are definite occasions when aggressive behavior is called for. This behavior is admired in men and negatively labeled "unfeminine" in women. If aggressive behavior is appropriate for the situation, should it be negatively labeled for either sex?

7.   Emphasis on sexual connotations has permeated our advertising, language, and entertainment media. Is this emphasis on sex in our society detrimental to women sincerely trying to do a good job.?

A Businessman's Guide
to Women's Liberation

Gene Marine

For most of us reasonably grown-up and well-adjusted males, today's dedicated feminists fall into two categories: wearily objectionable and downright obnoxious. And that was true even before we got bored with the subject.

But—there they are. Some of us may go on insisting that women's liberation is a fad like hot pants or televised ghost stories and that if we just stare resolutely at the wall it will go away. But it isn't and it won't.

Not only that, but all across the land, in corporate offices and banks, in the world of brokers and investment counselors, there are going to be more and more women. They are going to be found in more and more responsible positions. And we men are going to have to work, more and more, with women as peers and even as superiors. Of course doctors and lawyers and bakers and telephone linemen are going to face the same thing, but that doesn't change it for us. We shall simply have to learn the rules.

Learning the rules, however, needn't be all that grim. The image of feminists as raucous and belligerent is largely a newspaper creation with a little help from some TV sitcoms. Newspapers may employ women, but they are essentially male places. There is no need for the rest of us to be slaves to the fears of the middle-aged ink-stained wretches of America's city rooms, no matter how adroit they are with headlines.

It helps no one's understanding when a (female) reporter for *Women's Wear Daily*, doing a story on a prominent feminist, describes typical "feminist heavies" as "buxom women with biceps and bullhorn voices."

A *San Francisco Chronicle* interview with Miss California involved a reporter asking, "Is there anything Women's Lib advocates that you

Gene Marine, "A Businessman's Guide to Women's Liberation," *MBA* (February 1974), pp. 27–31.

firmly disagree with?" "Yes," she replied, "I like to wear bras." Nothing in the story indicated that this was a stupid or an uninformed answer — but it was. At about the same time the top social reporter in Washington, D.C., Betty Beale of the *Star*, described a luncheon given by Perle Mesta in support of the Equal Rights Amendment. "None of these ladies is for Women's Lib," wrote Beale, " 'I want to keep my bra,' said Perle."

Even the journalistic habit of capitalizing — "Women's Liberation" or "Women's Lib" — is a stereotype. There is no organization called Women's Liberation, with a set of bylaws and a position, like the American Civil Liberties Union or the John Birch Society.

Over the past several years I have met a lot of feminists. Some I like. Some I don't and never will. As a group, however, I find them more intelligent and therefore better company than a lot of other women, and I find them pleasant people with fine senses of humor and a remarkable amount of patience. They are no more difficult to be around than anyone else who may be trying, in an uncertain and often unprincipled world, to assert the importance of a principle.

The fact is, of course, that women — even women who are feminists — are no more alike than violinists, or than red-haired men. To classify "feminists" in such a way would to be to do to them exactly what they say that we have always done to women as a whole: to stereotype an infinite variety into one or two narrow molds, and thus to believe a lot of simplistic nonsense.

So the first rule is: relax. Defensiveness toward the subject of women's liberation tells much more about you and your insecurities than it does about the movement or any member of it.

Beyond the first rule, there are not many that can be applied by rote, and most of them are already well-known. Most of us have learned by now not to refer to the "girls" in the office, some of whom may be old enough to be our mothers. We don't call the fellow at one desk "Harold" (his name) while we call the woman doing the same job at the next desk "Sweetie." Such obvious masculinisms are, of course, as degrading to an entire class of human beings as it would be to call Harold, if he happened to be black, "Boy."

What we may not so quickly recognize is that changing such small patterns actually helps to change the ways in which we see the world. Picture a white male who has called black males "Boy" all his life, confronted with a working situation in which he now forces himself to say "Mr. Smith." He will, in spite of himself, begin to see the black man differently. The same thing works with women. We begin to see them more accurately as people — and that applies even when the women aren't "peers" in the on-the-job sense.

All those newspaper stereotypes about feminists have some of us still worrying about things like lighting women's cigarettes or opening doors. The only sensible "rule" for such situations is: don't worry about it. If you and I, both male, are leaving a building together and I reach the door first, of course I'll open it for you; I may even make a little extra effort to get there first, as a simple act of courtesy. Beyond that there is a point at which struggling to reach the door first would look silly. In general, courtesy is not a put-down, unless by your manner you make it into one.

Worse than any question of opening doors or lighting cigarettes, for some of us, is the question of language. I am, I guess, what my mother calls "foul-mouthed" in my conversations in male company, and even in a business conversation with a man I've never met before, I fall easily into the use of whatever words may now be running through my head. Narrowly speaking, to treat a woman as "an equal" must mean that I would talk the same way to her or in her presence; if I don't, I'm cheating on my convictions.

The first thing to say on that subject is that, in fact, a lot of women in the movement demand this same freedom of language as a prerogative. One of the things that they resent is the idea that because they are women, they are not permitted, culturally, to say whatever word might occur to them, while we males are. And as might be expected whenever a sizable group of people is devoted to a cause, there are some who push the prerogative on purpose, to make the point even when it isn't all that "natural."

That much seems reasonable to me, and in real life I am, in fact, quite comfortable around women who say "fuck" as thoughtlessly and carelessly as I do. I simply don't hear it any more as "a women saying that word."

But of course that doesn't answer the problem. Perhaps the biggest question is: How much of our concern about language is about what the woman feels, and how much is actually about our own hangups? And the answer to that, of course, is again to learn to see the woman, not as a woman, but as a person.

Yet there is also, in the question of language, a hidden and deeper question — the fear that a lot of us feel, that the admission of women to a position of genuine equality means only that they demand and we surrender. On the contrary, we are quite justified — if we do it sincerely, and don't use it as an excuse to cling to unwarranted privileges — in saying, "You are welcome to this world and welcome to share it, but as it happens this world, as of right now, works in this way, and if you want to share it you must share the parts you don't like as well as the parts you do."

Or, in other words, when men include a woman in their plans for a social, shop-talking lunch, and one of them uses one of Those Words, there's nothing wrong with looking her straight in the eye and saying (and once should be enough), "That's how we talk, and making an effort to talk differently would get in the way of our talking freely." The chances are that one of her biggest frustrations, throughout her career, has been exclusion not from formal notice but from the informalities of peer-group socializing; and if she has enough sense to be your peer in the first place, a few so-called "dirty words" will be a cheap price for her to pay.

I know of a case in which there are four young executives who are on substantially the same level in their company; three are men, one is a woman. At times they are called upon to consult as a group. Since their jobs are similar and equal, it is also natural for them to socialize somewhat outside of work assignments.

Frequently all four have business lunch. Rarely, however, is the woman included when the others go to lunch simply because it's lunch-time, or when there's time for a belt or two after work. And when she is present, one of the men told me, the three men do not act the same. In principle, my conversant wants the distinction to go away. In practice, he is simply not "comfortable" in the same relaxed sense.

Probably the first thing to remember is that she isn't comfortable in that same easy-going sense either. None of us is accustomed to the truly equal presence of members of the opposite gender. Quite simply, it has to be worked at, and learned.

The first step is to watch yourself in that small moment of discrimi-nation when it's lunchtime and you're hungry and you reach for the intercom or walk across the hall to say, "Let's go to lunch." If you'd like to break the pattern but don't know how, try a gimmick: When you get out to lunch ask her some professional questions about herself — whatever is appropriate to your work, from "How did you get interested in mutual funds?" to "What kind of ambitions do you have in this business?" (but avoid the form: "What's a nice girl like you doing in a place like this?").

If your working relationship is pretty good, you may be surprised to find that you can even go further, if you have any sense of tact at all. Or you can simply say, "I'd like to break this stupid pattern into which we are all shaped by our culture, but I don't know how."

Open and honest statements of this kind, especially when they have to do with our own uncertainties, come hard to males in this culture. All of our training is to appear self-sufficient, confident, breezily certain of our-selves (Glen Ford doesn't ride into a strange town saying to himself "Gee I do hope these folks like me"). But my surprising experience over the last few years, since exposure to the women's movement, is that people — female and male — blink through a few moments of surprise, and then respond almost immediately to the offered vulnerability. It may be, and I think it is, the best and in the long run the easiest way past all the stereotypes of "male" and "female," all the hangups that are in the way of a real equality among human beings.

Ironically, a possibly more difficult problem arises in dealing not with feminists but anti-feminists. If a woman is now in a position of authority or responsibility in an male-dominated field, the chances are that she got there by herself, not through any changes brought about by six or seven years of "women liberation." And if she got there by herself, she may argue — even with some contempt — that "if I did it, another woman can do it." A recent article in *Psychology Today* refers to this as "the Queen Bee syndrome."

She may go further and argue that discrimination does not in fact exist (as though Margaret Chase Smith proved that women can be elected to the Senate as easily as men). So believing, she sees women's liberation as an orgainized attempt to put women into positions that they do not deserve on their own — as she deserves hers.

At her worst the Queen Bee will not only let you open doors for her and light her cigarettes but will expect it, and then she will politely cut your throat a half-hour later. At her best she will be as easy and friendly to work with as any other colleague, except that she may be faintly annoyed if you really treat her exactly as though she were male — in the language you use in her presence, for instance.

With women who accept at least the basic idea of feminism, the drill is a little more complex. The latest Gallup poll on attitudes toward feminism reveals that more than half of American women now find something in common with what they see as the goals of the women's movement, but that doesn't make them all "feminists" — yet. There are certainly hundreds of thousands of women, however, to whom the term can be applied, and there are a few ideas on which most of them would agree. One of those few basic ideas is this: a lot of what is wrong with my life is not my fault, but results from what this society does to me solely because I am female.

(In passing, that explains why so many feminists do not like psychiatry, which is essentially a system for treating individual maladjustment for making the individual "fit" the society instead of examining the society to see whether it might, by its very structure, be harmful to individuals. This is not, of course, a question to be dealt with in a sentence or two, but the distinction is one that is essential to understand.)

We may have read Millett or Greer or both (most feminists do not consider either to be among their most important writers), but our understanding still will not approach that of movement women, who have encountered in their activities and reading a much deeper and more sophisticated kind of social analysis than most of us even know exists. Besides, they have been women all their lives, and we have not; they know what has happened to them, and we can only guess through a haze of our own preconceptions.

I was myself exposed early to the women's liberation movement, both professionally (as an editor) and personally (as a husband), and by 1970 I thought I knew enough about it to see how other men might be confused by this difference in vocabulary and background. Since I make my living, in a sense, by packaging and retailing information, I somewhat arrogantly thought of writing a book, by a man and for men, about the women's movement—partly to bridge this "vocabulary gap" and partly to describe the differences between the stereotypes of "women's liberation" and the complex reality of the movement. Upon writing it, I discovered that a full 60 percent of the book (*A Male Guide to Women's Liberation*) was needed to describe what happens to women in our society—and what happens to men.

I had to examine our schools, and children's books, and the stereotypes that most of us learn as children, to show how we are shaped into a preconceived picture of "men" and "women" that has nothing to do with our individual potential—nothing, indeed, to do with anything real other than simple prejudice. I examined cultural concepts about what it means to be "male" or "female," and found that (for men as well as for women) they startlingly limit our individual development. And I found that most of what most of us believe to be true about "men" and "women" is nonsense.

Since you have an MBA, you may have had the experience of being looked down upon by at least some fellow students because you choose to concern yourself with marketing and risk capital and entrepreneurship instead of an exegesis of Shakespeare, or the nature of authority in the modern state, or the universal significance of kinship patterns among the Nyakyusa. If, despite all that, you have gone on to do what you really want to do, then you have some vague idea of the personal importance of fulfilling what you know to be your own potential, despite noticeable cultural pressure to the contrary.

Imagine, if you can, that kind of pressure coming not only from a few people in a college or university who didn't share your goals, but from virtually all of society from the time you were six months old. Then, perhaps, you can begin to get a glimmer of how a woman might feel if she is determined not to let the stereotypical reactions of others limit her personal choices. When there are whole substructures of our culture based on those stereotypes, all of them standing in her way, and when she has the strength dispite all of that to insist on doing what she wants to do, then certainly she earns our admiration and our respect.

The trick, then, is to realize that in a sense she is assaulting a privilege that Western culture has made ours by birth, but that she is not assaulting us as individuals. In a given case, a woman may confuse that distinction (the same may happen with blacks who want a piece of what whites "normally" have in this culture), but her confusion need not be ours.

If there is a rule, it is to remember that we men, too, are trained from childhood for the roles we have. We learn subtleties, not only of business life but of social contact among colleagues, that we aren't even aware of. In face we have learned many of them by the time we reach high school. A woman (also somewhat like many blacks in this respect) is starting in our world much later and from scratch. And in our defensiveness we are likely to see any small deviation as "proof" that she "doesn't know how it's done."

We are likely to feel, we men, that if we have to face the idea of equality with women, our manhood is somehow involved. And this has additional meaning in the business world. There is an enormous amount of evidence showing a definite identity, in our male minds, between the ability to make money and the ability to make it in bed. Don't try to make rational sense out of it; it doesn't make rational sense. But we do somehow have a connection, somewhere in our psyches, between job performance and potency. A challenge from a women as an equal on the job is to most of us, albeit perhaps unconsciously, a sexual threat.

Writer Elizabeth Janeway has pointed out that most men do not object to the equality of women if it means, "A women may be as good as I am." In other words, men don't mind if equality seems to involve only an upward movement for women. But says Mrs. Janeway, many men — perhaps most men — do not, at least unconsciously, put it that way. To us, equality tends to mean, "I am no better than a women," and implies not an upward movement for women but a downward movement for men. Because we are, indeed, trained from childhood to think of women as at least a little bit inferior, we fight that unconscious definition of equality and thus tend to fight equality itself. If you add sexual overtones to those statements (and think of how we are trained as children to block any idea of "femininity" in ourselves), you begin to get a handle on why "women's liberation" sets up an immediate, irrational feeling of defensive hostility in so many males.

Not long ago, on a cross-bay bus from San Francisco toward Berkeley, I sat alongside an attractive, thirtyish woman who was obviously a "straight" female employee in some city office — the restrained and careful makeup, the dress, the nylon pantyhose, the neatly chosen accessories, even the manner were all testimony. She had even brought home, it seemed, some work from the office; at any rate she was reading with considerable absorption a sheaf of papers. A congenital nosiness being the primary characteristic of any reporter, I read for a while over her shoulder.

What she was reading was an analysis of the status of women employed by the Bechtel Corp., one of San Francisco's (and the world's) largest construction firms — and very interested she was, too. Obviously, there was a caucus, cell, call it what you will, at Bechtel, organizing itself to make demands—as female employees within the past few years have forced hiring and promotions changes, and changes in treatment, at such varied places as *Newsweek*, AT&T.

What does a male colleague do when such demands arise?

Obviously, if you are yourself in a position of authority, you have an obligation, whatever your personal predilections, to listen as openmindedly as possible and even, perhaps, to bend over a little backward to correct any felt injustice. But suppose it is touch-and-go, the boss inclines toward intransigence, your own convictions lean toward the justice of the women's cause. Is there anything you can, or should, do? Or are your better out of it, watching from the sidelines?

I happen to think (conditioned, perhaps, by 1930s Humphrey Bogart movies) that a man ought to stand up for what he thinks is right, even if it costs him an otherwise satisfying and remunerative job. I am also old enough to know that that's an easy statement for an unbeholden free-lance writer to make.

My advice would be: Ask the women. Assume that they are intelligent and understanding; you'll probably be right. If they do need help from the male employees, they will need it, not from one isolated man, but from at least a sizable minority of the males, who are willing to get together in support of their demands. You might be asked to sound out the other males, to see whether there is a sizable body of support for the demands of the women that can be made known without individual jeopardy; but almost certainly you will not be asked to stick your lone and unprotected neck out all by itself. Contrary to another of those masculinist stereotypes, movement women do not want their advances to come at the expense of men; they want them to come as a matter of merit, with a basis of equality.

But remember, too, that you need not wait for the women to organize before you change your own behavior. You can make the coffee, and you can look around for other ways to apply the same principle. If nothing else, the effect on *you* will, I can almost promise, be as important as the effect on everyone else.

All my life, it seems, I've heard both men and women say that they would prefer working for men—and I've heard some men say that they would refuse to work for a woman. Asked why, they all have reasons, and all of the reasons are couched in generalizations like, "A woman always ... or "A woman would be ..." Women who are good at what they do are of course aware of this, and many of them resent it mightily—partly because the generalizations that they hear do not in fact apply to them as individuals, and partly because they know that they're not receiving promotions that would on merit be theirs. The "next boss up," almost certainly a man, either believes the same chimerical stereotypes himself, or prefers keeping the subordinate males "happy" at the woman's expense.

It all reminds me of a close friend who was for many years personnel manager of the San Francisco branch of a nationwide retail chain. During his last years on the job he worked long and hard to overcome years of racial discrimination, not only hiring blacks and Orientals but seeing to it that, insofar as he had anything to do with it, opportunities for advancement and promotion are fully open to them. Yet I can remember, a few years before, his telling me that while he personally was a vehement opponent of racial discrimination, he couldn't hire black salespeople. Whites wouldn't buy from them.

Now, in his own bailiwick, people black and white and yellow not only work together, but advance into supervisory positions pretty much on merit — and people who once swore that they wouldn't and couldn't work alongside blacks now work under them. As before, some people don't like their supervisors — but that, too, seems to be a matter of merit. In the simplest terms: Don't knock it until you've tried it.

Obviously, there is no easy way to undo years of acculturization. But to begin that process at least in your work, remember that you do not usually think of yourself as working with men. You work with other people, who are infinitely varied. Women are people, too, and what's more they are people first and women second.

Behave as though equality is the way things ought to be — meaning equality upward for her, not downward for you. Try, whether you really believe it or not, to rid your speech and your actions of the stereotyped patterns of artificial sex roles. The odds are that your view of people at work and elsewhere will change, and you may discover that there are twice as many interesting people in the world as you thought.

And finally, if women are people, so are you. You're not a male gnu, and you don't have to paw the veldt in your best virile manner when a female appears. That's a way of not accepting the challenge, and the pleasure, of getting to know and to work with another complete and interesting human being.

DISCUSSION QUESTIONS

1.   Women make up 51 percent of the population. They now comprise more than 40 percent of the work force and that figure is growing. One out of four families is headed by a woman. Seven out of ten women work because of economic need. How long do you think the women's movement will last?

2.   Since women and men are human beings, can't they extend courtesy to each other based on the appropriateness of the situation rather than on the sex of the people involved? If you are going out a door, do you let it slam in the face of the human being following you? If a human being carrying a large package is nearing a door, do you help? If a human being is physically less able to open a door than you, do you help?

3.   Can't four-letter words be just as offensive to men as to women? Are they really necessary to any human being for successful communication?

4.   Do you know any "Queen Bees"? Why do you consider them "Queen Bees"? How can a woman avoid being a "Queen Bee"?

5.   Have you experienced incidents that illustrate that some men perceive equality for women as a step downward for men?

6.   Have you had experiences illustrating that women are most reasonable in their job aspirations and want their career paths based on merit?

A Handy Guide
to Everyday Dealings
With Women

Priscilla S. Meyer

It was a mortifying experience for everyone concerned.

As a top New York insurance executive recalls it, his company stood to lose the account of a sizable corporate customer unless certain sticky problems could be hashed out. Preparing for a long grueling session in the customer's office, he handed a nearby woman several dollars and told her to run out and bring back coffee for everyone. She refused, icily informing him that she was the company's general counsel. It was all downhill after that, and the insurer was not surprised that he lost the account.

He shakes his head now and comments, "I should have known better. One of our own attorneys is a woman."

Pure male chauvinism? Hardly. Like many businessmen he suffered from lack of awareness of a potential pitfall that's becoming more and more common as an increasing number of women move into responsible business positions. In fact, veteran businesswomen trained in a male business world sometimes make similar slips in their dealings with other businesswomen.

We're not talking here about the bigger issues of equal pay for women or equal job opportunities, but the sticky smaller problems that at first glance may seem petty. They aren't, at least to women trying to perform effectively on an equal basis in the business world.

Put yourself, for example, in the place of a financial reporter for this publication who recently met five high-level executives at the Marco Polo Club in the Waldorf Astoria Hotel for lunch. They had arrived early and been served drinks when she arrived — setting off fireworks. Women weren't allowed in the Marco Polo at lunch, attendants said. So the entire group, drinks and all, had to troop downstairs to the public Bull and Bear Restaurant.

Embarrassing? Perhaps nearly as much for her as for the president of the company who had set up the lunch.

Most women in business have collected a plethora of such mini-horror stories. Some businessmen, on the other hand, are struggling with such issues as whether or not to light a businesswoman's cigarette, apparently in dread fear of being branded a "male chauvinist pig."

In an effort to bring a little order to this confusion, more than 20 businesswomen — ranging from securities analysis to the president of an advertising agency — were asked for pointers to steer well-meaning executives away from the most common pitfalls. Here they are.

1. Don't assume a woman contacted in business or over a business phone is a receptionist or secretary — even if she answers a man's telephone. She may be his boss.

2. Avoid calling women "sweetie," "honey," or "dear," unless you're comfortable calling male business executives "buddy-boy," "pal" or "chum." If you do that, you probably aren't reading this anyway.

3. As for lighting cigarettes, opening doors or helping with coats, (or even telling off-color stories and using swear words, for that matter) do whatever comes most naturally. None of the women cared one way or the other, as long as men don't make a big production of it. But women see red when a man accompanies a light with a comment such as "I hope you aren't one of those women's libbers." If she opposed such things, she would have met your light with a simple refusal.

In fact, while a number of women executives keep up with the women's liberation movement, few are chip-on-the-shoulder militants. The entire topic of women's liberation is best left out of day-to-day business dealings, relegated off-limits with politics and religion. Businesswomen also don't appreciate a case-by-case description of every female clerk your company has promoted to executive assistant. They'd much rather get to the business at hand.

4. Avoid private clubs when you're setting, up a luncheon or gathering that will include women, unless you're absolutely certain women have equal access to club facilities, as they now do at Manhattan's Lawyers Club which has recently moved to total male-female integration.

This can be tricky. For example, while New York's Union League Club will assure you on the phone that women guests are now permitted, club personnel frequently forget to mention that women are relegated to a separate "ladies" entrance and elevator. To make matters worse, when a woman tries to leave by the League's second floor "ladies" elevator, which adjoins the kitchen, she runs into more difficulties. It doesn't appear to have a button. (Actually it's usually hidden behind movable paneling.)

Many clubs have separate "ladies" dining rooms for groups that include women, which is annoying enough. The Bankers Club in New York, which has its "ladies" dining room on the 38th floor, has its only women's bathroom on the 40th.

If a problem does develop, such as a group ouster from a private club, a woman appreciates a man's following her lead. If she tries to ignore the slight, brush the incident aside. But if she's clearly annoyed, back her up when possible. And a particularly thoughtful gesture is a letter of complaint to the management or individual involved, with a carbon to the businesswoman.

5. As for who pays the lunch tab, leave the decision to the business situation. Don't battle for the bill when lunching with an advertising executive who's trying to sell you a new campaign just because she's a woman. Her company expects her to pay. And don't make an issue of how uncomfortable this makes you. It shouldn't.

6. In addressing a letter to a woman, Ms. is acceptable to most businesswomen, unless they've indicated otherwise in their own correspondence. Some people do feel that Ms. pronounced miz, has an uncomfortable hayseed sound when spoken. None of the married women polled object to orally being called Miss, or Mrs. if you're certain they're married. But all objected to men making a big issue of it.

One advertising executive has a vivid mental picture of a marketing vice president who met her at the door with an enormous leer, slurping, "What shall we call you dear, Miss or Mizzzzzzz?"

7. Avoid sending out formal invitations to a businessman "and wife." It's as easy to engrave them with "and spouse" or even "and friend or guest," particularly if some of the invited guests are women.

8. When meeting with an executive group that includes one woman, don't automatically assign her the task of note-taking, assuming she takes shorthand.

9. Equally annoying to woman executives are men who lapse into patronizing explanations. Assume a businesswoman is intelligent and knows her job unless she demonstrates otherwise. The company probably wouldn't have made her their treasurer if she didn't know long division.

10. Avoid calling your secretary "my girl," or asking other executives — particularly in memos — to "have your gals" do something or other. If your company's secretaries and clerks are all women, and executives are all men, they probably shouldn't be. And anyway, the inference of ownership is demeaning. And if there are women executives and male clerks such comments are a slap.

These pointers won't be much use to businessmen who are truly opposed to women in business, or who operate from deep prejudice. But far more common is simple blindness to the entry of women into the real business world.

The St. Paul Companies, an insurance complex based in Minnesota, devoted almost all of its 1971 annual shareholder report to a proud recital of the progress of women in the company.

But temporary blindness resulted in the paradoxical inclusion of two final pages showing photos of the company's top executives — all men.

Awareness can help.

DISCUSSION QUESTIONS

1. Do you know any humorous-sad or just plain sad stories of professional women (a) being mistaken for clerical employees? (b) not being allowed in eating/meeting places or being asked to use another entrance based on their sex? (c) having to search for a women's restroom in such places? (d) having to get men off the subject of women's liberation and on to the subject of business?

2. Does "Miz" sound any worse than "Mizruz" or "Missuz"?

3. Can "Ms." be a convenient courtesy title just as "Mr." is? Does a woman's marital status indicated by "Mrs." have any relevance in a business situation?

"Queen Victoria summed up the prejudice against her sex in a letter to the Princess Royal. Her husband, Prince Albert, she said, shared with all 'clever men' the tendency to despise 'our poor degraded sex.'"

"Some Uses of Biography," *The Royal Bank of Canada Monthly Letter* (August 1973), p. 3.

'Women Executives Are Different'

Pearl Meyer

If the plaints of corporate personnel officers are to be believed, the female executive is industry's most wanted person. Bestirred by the pressure of women's groups, the guidelines of the Equal Employment Opportunity Commission and the new realities of the marketplace, just about every large company nowadays is beating the bushes for capable women managers. Unfortunately, their record so far points to one inescapable fact: When it comes to wooing — and winning — women executives, business must be doing something wrong.

How else can one explain the fact that of the 40 million American women who work — fully 40% of the U.S. labor force — the number who hold managerial positions is still only a meager 5% — virtually the same as five years ago? As for the room ostensibly at the top, forget it. Woman may be invincible, as Helen Reddy sings. But in the executive suite, she remains largely invisible. The ratio of male to female corporate chief executives stands at a blatantly sexist 600-to-1.

Part of this abysmal showing can be blamed on the continued blindness of corporate recruiters. Despite industry's highly vocal insistence that it is unable to locate talented women managers, the fact is that there are many of them out there. But due to years of unequal opportunity, they have held supportive staff or subordinate roles rather than highly visible executive positions. Knock on any company's door and you will find high-caliber female buyers but not merchandise managers, analysts but not research directors, tellers but not treasurers, assistants to presidents but not vice presidents — all positions of low visibility.

Corporate shortsightedness, however, is only part of the problem. The fact that seems to have escaped even those companies genuinely eager to acquire distaff executives is that women managers are different than men, not merely in the way they look but in what they want in the

Pearl Meyer, "Women Executives Are Different," *Dun's Review* (January 1975), pp. 47–48.

way of salary and beneifts. With few exceptions, companies treat the female executive, in effect, as one of the boys. They offer her compensation and pension packages originally designed to attract middle-aged male managers. While similar, these offers are generally less than those dangled before male executives. And then companies wonder why their recruitment programs are not more successful.

And that is too bad. Bad for women, certainly. But worse for industry. For a curious paradox now confronts us. Numerically, U.S. business is currently staffed with the smallest management generation in modern history; executives between the ages of 35 and 45 are Depression babies, born when the nation's birthrate fell to its lowest point before now. On the other hand, recessionary business conditions have made companies less tolerant of poor executive performance; managers who do not shape up are being shipped out. These new realities of executive recruitment — urgent need, rising standards and short supply — are working directly counter to each other in the managerial marketplace.

FACING THE FACTS

There is no getting around the fact that within the next five years, the number of women in managerial positions — now about one for every twenty males — will triple. The women's movement is clamoring for it and, more importantly, the EEOC is putting sharp teeth into regulations aimed at achieving it.

So far, the EEOC has filed some 250 employment discrimination suits against both corporations and unions. But none has more landmark significance than the recent Patterson *vs.* The American Tobacco Co. In that decision, a federal district court required the company to appoint a woman or a "minority individual" to the next position to become vacant at the supervisory level at one of its facilities. The shocker in the case is that, unlike previous rulings, in which a company was given a number of years to comply, American was ordered to name a minority member to the *very next* management post to become available or be subject to substantial penalty. What's more, the company was directed to continue to fill supervisory jobs with "females and blacks" until the percentage of those minorities approximate that in the company's local area, which happens to be Richmond, Virginia.

The point is, of course, that in the next few years companies will be hiring many more women executives — whether by choice, need or government ukase. They are already having trouble hiring the caliber of male executives they want; getting the best women executives will be even tougher. And to do it, they are going to have to reshape their male-oriented compensation policies. A top-notch woman cannot be enticed with a compensation package designed for men; her needs are different.

When it comes to salary, for example, companies may have to offer her more. In any functional area where there is a shortage of talent, the price is historically higher. That was true for the aeronautical engineers of the mid-Fifties and the counsels and controllers of the late Sixties. Today it is true of women managers. Besides that, since she has earned a traditionally lower salary than men in her years of struggle for equality, the woman executive does not have a capital accumulation equal to her male counterpart. To catch up, she is likely to want more salary and other capital vehicles than the company is offering male executives with comparable experience.

She also has different pension needs because she figures to live longer than her male co-workers. In fact, courts are starting to require the use of "unisex" mortality tables by insurance companies. Considering the unbalanced proportion of male and female executives in business, it constitutes a danger signal to companies that their pension programs may be too lightly funded.

Chances are good that the typical single career woman does not require the life insurance coverage (generally equal to at least one year's salary) that most companies extend to their head-of-household male executives. In the case of married women executives, however, companies will have to modernize their male-oriented policies regarding insurance. Most such coverage today is written on the life of the executive, usually male, with his spouse as beneficiary. It now behooves companies to allow for policies that are written on the life of a woman executive's husband, with herself as beneficiary.

THE "LESS-MOBILE" EXECUTIVE

Especially when it comes to enticing women to give up their present jobs for better opportunities elsewhere, corporations will have to rethink their policies. Relocation expenses are one consideration. Many companies will pick up all or most of the tab for moving a male manager and his family, and even pay the differential in the mortgage rate on his new house. But what of the single woman who lives in an apartment? Chances are she needs to live in a high-rent area that has good security and other services. She may have to pay a location fee as well as a large rent differential in order to make the move. Will her new company make up the difference in her new rent as it does for a man's mortgage?

Or consider the special medical benefits so important to women. It took a recent court decision to compel one company to grant temporary disability benefits to all women employees on maternity leave. In its ruling, the court noted that such benefits are just because companies were extending them to male executives for vasectomy operations and hair transplants. Yet there are many legal battles to come, and few companies include maternity leave in the compensation packages offered to women executives.

Even extending the standard status-enriching perquisites of office to incoming women executives suddenly looms as a major problem in corporate protocol. Imagine, for example, the woman executive who lists her husband as the "take-me-along" spouse at company meetings and conventions. And what about the key to the executive washroom? Women will want not only the key but separate — but equal — facilities.

Then, too, there is the sticky question of membership at the local private country or city club, where social contacts and facilities may be essential for the successful performance of a woman's job. Most are private organizations with male-only memberships. If a woman executive is married, her company would have to purchase a membership for her husband in order to provide her access to the club as a "spouse" or family member.

Yet women executives believe they have earned the right to demand all these benefits. The one thing they do not want is to be considered second-class corporate citizens. Nothing goads a woman more — or discourages others from following her into a company — than the realization that she is management's token female executive. One of the most important considerations women weigh before joining a company is to what extent it is already staffed with "role models"; that is, the number of women at various levels of the organization.

Unfortunately, companies frequently make the mistake of hiring a token female at the board level and filling the balance of their quota with women at the entry level. But many a woman executive is deterred from joining a company that practices token equality. One of the nation's major banks, for example, has a woman running its largest retail branch. But she is its "showcase" female manager; the bank does not have another woman vice president in a line supervisory role. The female executive of a huge department store chain is regarded highly enough to sit on the boards of several companies — but not her own.

To overcome that kind of traditional thinking, management will have to establish new horizontal, rather than traditionally vertical, avenues of job movement. Women — and other qualified minorities — will have to be given additional exposure in new jobs and duties at the same level in order to provide the seasoning necessary for upward advancement. Companies will also have to "lace" women throughout every level of the corporation — especially in middle management — to inspire employees at the entry level.

From considerable practical experience, I have observed that the companies most successful in recruiting people they deem essential are those who approach the problem flexibly and respond to the demands of the marketplace. They have learned to reject narrowly defined criteria in job specifications. And in their pursuit of women, they have stopped talking about the best man for the job and insist instead on the best person for the job.

DISCUSSION QUESTIONS:

1. Is it fair to recruit a highly qualified woman at an unusually high salary?

2. Do you know of any innovative examples of pay and benefit packages that companies are using to attract women?

3. Do you know of any innovative examples of job movement patterns that companies are using to give women the experience they need?

4. How are local, state, and national employment statistics useful to an employer?

5. What examples do you know of women "tokens"?

6. If women "tokens" prove themselves to be capable, dedicated professionals so that they move from the status of "tokens" to the status of respected, needed employees, how are other women helped?

What's It Like
for Women Executives?

Lee Smith

THEY'VE CERTAINLY COME A LONG WAY—
BUT MALE CHAUVINISM IS NOT DEAD YET

It was the kind of thing that happens often. Rita O'Brien, a manager of administration at giant AT&T, was invited to a luncheon business meeting at New York's University Club. On the morning of the conference, the executive who set up the meeting (not from AT&T) called Ms. O'Brien. "He said he was terribly sorry," she reports, "but he had just learned that the club did not admit women. But he added that it was no problem. The men would just go ahead and have lunch and then send me the necessary data. I was stunned."

The slur to Ms. O'Brien is hardly one that a man in her position would ever have to face. Nor are a number of other pressures that women executives are running up against as they become increasingly visible in what has long been a man's world. Like any manager, a woman executive spends a large part of her time giving and taking orders in an endless exchange with superiors, peers and subordinates. But for her, that demanding job is complicated by the fact that most men are not used to working with women in managerial positions, which they may show in all kinds of seemingly innocuous — but insulting — ways.

As women become increasingly accepted at management levels, the pressures may ease. But for the time being at least, women executives are still rare enough that they must, in effect, carry out their duties on what amounts to a public stage and in front of an audience that is likely to catch any slip. Indeed, in talking to a number of women executives, it is clear that practically all of them at some time have to deal with men who try to make them look stupid.

Lee Smith, "What's It Like for Women Executives?" *Dun's Review* (December 1975), pp. 58–61.

One is Carole Cushing, who operates a Los Angeles management consulting firm with her husband. At the age of 36, Mrs. Cushing has had a dozen years of consulting experience. Nevertheless, she says, "Sometimes during an interview at a client company, someone will give me some kind of 'baffle-gab' to see how I'll react, so he can then decide if I know what I'm talking about. They rarely put my husband to that kind of test."

Particularly vivid in Mrs. Cushing's memory is her experience earlier this year as a participant in the advanced management course at Harvard Business School, where she was one of two women among 158 men. "In the discussion groups I was always asked to go first," she recalls. "Finally, one of the men explained why. They suspected that I was a real dumb-dumb, and they wanted to see me fall flat on my face. It's excruciating," Mrs. Cushing goes on. "On the one hand, a woman has to be good. On the other, if she is good, she becomes a threat to men. So she has to be both thick-skinned for herself and sensitive to a man's feelings. It's a terrible vise."

These days, of course, the resentment of some men towards women managers is exacerbated by the shrunken job market. As some male executives see it, the influx of a large number of women into their ranks could not have come at a worse time. And even some women admit that men have reason to be concerned. "A knockout woman will move aside a mediocre man," states President Madeline H. McWhinney of the First Women's Bank of New York. "A man who in an earlier day might have moved ahead will be left behind, and he really has it rough. But no change comes easily," adds Ms. McWhinney, an economist and former assistant vice president of the Federal Reserve Bank of New York.

At First National City Bank, Vice President Marilyn E. LaMarche seems to have set out to demonstrate that a woman can work not only harder, but unceasingly. Ms. LaMarche, head of the business development department in the investment management group, arrives at her ninth-floor office at 8:15 a.m. and begins a fast-paced day that usually ends around 10:30 p.m., sometimes with a business dinner.

As Ms. LaMarche sees it, her sex has not presented any problem in most aspects of her job. "I have superb relationships with the clients," she says. Nor does she have any difficulty in dealing with the seven people who report to her, nor with her secretary. (It is sometimes argued that a woman executive and a woman secretary cannot work together harmoniously — that they will always be rivals. But one woman maintains that one reason a man can get along well with his secretary is that he can flirt with her and so breaks the tension between superior and subordinate. A woman executive cannot do that.)

But while Ms. LaMarche believes that women get the same opportunity as men at Citibank, she also comments on the aggressiveness of some male peers who in their eagerness to get ahead seem tempted to take advantage of a woman competitor. "There are guys who come in here and say 'I want this, I want that,'" she notes. "And then I have to say, 'Hey, wait a minute. You can't talk to me like that.' I've got to make them understand that they're not talking to their wives.

"I would say there are two kinds of men who might try to take advantage of a woman," she continues. "The first is aggressive, an overachiever. The second type is just the opposite, the guy with a very weak ego who sees all women as threatening. But I think there is a third type, with whom I can get along just fine. He is the guy who enjoys his job, enjoys each day, is ambitious but not fanatical."

A DELICATE PROBLEM

Dealing with male subordinates can be especially delicate. One very attractive woman executive recalls that for a while the men who worked for her were constantly missing her instructions because they were distracted by her appearance. "If a man spends his time looking at my legs," she says with resignation, "it may be very pleasant and flattering in some ways, but I know there is no hope of talking business."

Not every woman has that particular problem, but certainly most men have some difficulty accepting a woman as boss. "If you ask a basically healthy male if he minds working for a woman," says Dr. Frank Hartman, a consulting psychiatrist to two large corporations, "his first reaction is likely to be 'No, as long as she is competent.' His second reaction will be, 'Hell, yes, it bothers me,' because he probably has a traditional view of male and female roles. But his third reaction is likely to be, 'Let's see how it works out.'"

Perceptive women executives are attuned to such thought processes. "I wouldn't think of hiring a man without asking him how he felt about working for a woman—working *with* a woman really," says Betty Cott, a senior vice president at public relations firm Ruder & Finn.

Similarly, perceptive women realize that they create at least a mild stir when they are sent as emissaries to companies or organizations that are not accustomed to seeing women in high places. Ms. Cott, for example, has been advising Exxon Corp. on its Bicentennial program. "Each time I walk into a meeting at Exxon," she says, "I sense that it's a new experience for them. I don't think it's been an obstruction in this case, but there are times I've had to ask a client, 'Look, are you holding back on me because I'm a woman?'"

When G. G. Michelson, senior vice president in charge of labor, personnel and consumer relations for Macy's, started as a labor negotiator for the huge department store some years ago, union representatives were somewhat surprised to see a woman across the bargaining table. Ms. Michelson believes she has carried off her assignment successfully not by trying to match unionists in stereotypical hard-knuckles negotiating but by relying on her knowledge of law and human nature. "I do not pretend to be an expert in steam fitting," explains Ms. Michelson. "But I listen and have a certain sensitivity, and I think you bring people together better that way."

Interestingly, it is sometimes other women who have difficulty recognizing a woman executive as an authoritative figure. June Thursh, catalog creative planning manager for J. C. Penney Co., remarks that the young woman who delivers the mail always addresses her by her first name. "At the same time," Ms. Thursh continues, "she always uses 'Mister' in talking to the junior executive across the corridor even though I am clearly senior to him."

Ms. Thursh insists the familiar form of address does not bother her, but some women executives are annoyed by similar slights. One recalls being the only woman in a meeting when a secretary walked in and handed her a note. It was a message for one of the men in the room. "The secretary assumed that as a woman, I must have been there to take the minutes and handle messages," says the executive. "I told her later that she should not make such assumptions."

As a number of women executives see it, their uneasy position stems largely from a twofold isolation within the corporate world. First, they feel excluded from the male executive's social world—bound together by old school ties, commuter lines to the suburbs and club memberships. Practically every woman executive has some tale of social humiliation to tell. Madeline McWhinney, for one, can recall the indignity of having to ascend to a meeting in an exclusive men's club in a freight elevator because the doorman refused to admit her through the main entrance.

Mingling with male executives socially can also be a problem. "Wives get very nervous when you are around and don't have a husband," maintains Janet Norman, an executive who helped design a computerized cash register for Singer Co. "And yet seeing top executives socially can be very important. In an executive environment, men invite one another to their homes and clubs. A senior executive will help promote a junior executive that way."

The importance of membership in the male tribal society, notes Carole Cushing, was impressed upon her not long ago when the vice president for finance at one of her client companies explained how he had hired a male assistant. "He told me that before the interview had gone very far, the candidate mentioned that he used to play ice hockey," she says. "The vice president said that was all he needed to know; the candidate must be a 'team player.' He therefore got the job. That one fact immediately set up a framework of understanding."

LEARNING THE TRADITIONS

Just as women may be isolated from executive society, they also feel the absence of more experienced women who can initiate them into the traditions and even the mannerisms of the corporate world. "One of the things you need for success in business is to be at ease," says Pearl Meyer, executive vice president of management consulting firm Handy Associates. "You may know the accounting rules, but you also have to know the communications, the humanity of business. You have to know, for example, at what level you walk into a board meeting and address the chairman by his first name. Men learn those things by watching one another close at hand. Women don't have those same opportunities."

On the other hand, gaining acceptance into the executive "club" can also be a burden. One woman recalls that soon after she started her job, some of her male colleagues invited her to join them for dinner at their favorite restaurant. It was an end-of-the-week celebration so stable in its rituals that without bothering to inquire, the waiter unerringly distributed each executive's drink without being asked. He then asked the newcomer what she would like to drink. "I don't drink," she replied.

The senior executive at the table was slightly embarrassed, she reports. "To be one of the boys," he protested, "you have to have a drink."

"Well," the woman executive said, "I just looked at him, smiled pleasantly and said, 'I don't want to be one of the boys.'"

To be sure, some of the earlier awkwardness that arose when men and women met as equals seems to be disappearing. Few men, for example, are embarrassed anymore when a woman reaches for the check at a restaurant. "The higher up you get, the less difference it makes who picks up the check, because no one is going to question your expense account anyhow," says Pearl Meyer. "I do what is comfortable. If I were to take the chairman of U. S. Steel to lunch, I would pick up the check but I wouldn't hold the door for him. That would make him feel uncomfortable, and as a result I would feel uncomfortable too."

More than that, the hostility of men on the job seems likely to ease as younger executives increasingly take over. For women executives generally agree that the problem is largely a generational one. "I don't sense any discrimination coming from younger men," comments Cathy Wengert, who is business manager for the industrial relations division of TRW's systems group, "but I do among certain men of my age, in their fifties. There are still cliques of men on my level who don't even think of me when they put together an agenda for a meeting."

In fact, there is a danger in exaggerating the difficulties of women in the corporate world. Many women, for example, dismiss the importance of the female "role model." Argues Dorothy Gregg, vice president for communications at Celanese Corp.: "I'm not sure that some of our role models shouldn't be men. And for that matter women can be role models for men as well."

And it is also true that many experienced businesswomen have successfully adopted the customs of the men around them. Like men in the public relations business, Betty Cott is inclined to be open and informal, addressing people by their first names immediately. Madeline McWhinney, on the other hand, is much more reserved, maintaining a degree of formality considered decorous for bankers of both sexes. And why not; these, after all, are the traditional styles of the industry they work in.

Some younger women executives are even exhilarated by the lack of guidelines for women in management. "I like the idea of being a pioneer," says AT&T's Rita O'Brien. "If few women have ever run a meeting at AT&T before, that means that I can be part of setting the precedent, of deciding how women do things here."

As for the University Club, it has revised its rules to admit women to private dining rooms. However, women are still not admitted to the club as full members. And that, as many women executives see it, is about where matters stand everywhere.

DISCUSSION QUESTIONS

1.   Have you ever been in a business situation with a large group of members of the opposite sex? What did they do to make you feel uncomfortable or comfortable?

2.   Do you know any specific cases where a woman has been promoted when a man was being considered for the same promotion? Do you know why the woman got the promotion?

3.   Have you met any secretaries with women bosses? What do they say about working for/with a woman?

4.   Do you know any aggressive men who try to take advantage of woman competitors to get ahead? How do they take advantage?

5.   Have you seen women executives being slighted by others in terms of address or other treatment?

6.   Do you think women need women role models? How can women be role models for men? Are there any differences between successful male and successful female role models?

7.   Do men who discriminate fall into any age category?

Women in Management: How Is It Working Out?

Marion M. Wood

Women managers have the same problems as men managers: pressures of responsibility, problems with subordinates, accountability to top management. But the woman manager also has some unique problems because she holds a position that has long been considered a "man's job." Where women are moving into the ranks of management, however, all the signs indicate that the problems are less than the women managers and their male counterparts expected. Even though many men — and women — continue their passive resistance to resocialization of the traditional male hierarchy, the consensus of nearly 100 male and female managers surveyed was that women managers are proving their competence and winning increasing acceptance. Some executives in key positions in the companies participating in the author's study are going out of their way to encourage qualified women to train themselves and to compete for higher level jobs. These supporters firmly believe that once the labor-force projection of increasing numbers of highly trained women becomes a reality, corporate management will be competing for their services. And this will be because of their potential for contributing to the organization, not simply because of the organization's need to meet affirmative action goals.

WOMAN'S IMPACT ON THE CORPORATE CLIMATE

In late 1972, labor-force projections indicated the U.S. economy could look forward "to a substantial supply of well educated women" toward the end of the decade. Now, three years later, it would appear that little progress has been made by women in the higher echelons of the labor force. Follow-

Marion M. Wood, "Women in Management: How Is It Working Out?" *S.A.M. Advanced Management Journal* (Winter 1976), pp. 22–30. Reprinted by permission of the publisher, Copyright © 1976 by S.A.M., a division of American Management Associations.

ing the industry's three-year concentration on affirmative action programs in response to "Revised Order Four" [Executive Order 11246, Revised Order Four (1972) made it imperative for federal contractors to establish affirmative action programs that ensure equal employment opportunities for women in all ranks], statistics show that women still represent less than one percent of the officials, managers, and professionals in the nation's major corporations.

These statistics, however, obscure the gains being made by women in individual organizations. To clarify these gains, a study of 14 Los Angeles companies where women have joined the managerial ranks was conducted by the author to determine how these women's new roles were affecting the quality of life at work. Much of the data was collected through personal interviews and observation, but a mailed questionnaire supplemented the informal method.

Even with this opportunity to speak anonymously, males and females expressed essentially the same opinions in writing as they did in the face-to-face discussions. In general, the men and women managers surveyed varied very little with respect to their answers to the questions asked. When asked to identify personal and organizational adjustments that had been made in fitting women into the male hierarchy, neither the male nor the female managers indicated that significant adjustments in either area had been necessary. Over half said they had not observed any noticeable effects on the overall operation. More women than men reported organizational changes, but none indicated that they had been traumatic.

All the participants in the survey seemed to be in general agreement on basic impressions of women's initial impact on the organization. On the plus side, the novelty of women in management apparently has been easier to adapt to than some of the managers surveyed had anticipated. Tension is subsiding, initial feelings of threat are easing, and status-role conflicts are slowly being resolved. The major problems, the persons queried said, are *not* in adjusting man-woman roles and relationships but rather in (1) finding or motivating qualified women within the organization to seek advancement and (2) gaining more general resocialization throughout the company. (Many in corporate management must still be convinced that promoting women is economically feasible.)

FINDING AND MOTIVATING QUALIFIED WOMEN

Discussing the present scarcity of highly qualified women, both the men and women managers who have the responsibility of training, developing, and finding women for management positions admitted concern with the morality of pushing women — in fact, any persons — into something they don't want. When affirmative action was first required for giving equal opportunities to racial minorities, programs were developed to identify potential talent and motivate persons to set goals and seek them aggressively. Now training directors are trying to modify these programs for the recruitment and the training of women.

Of course, there is more than just an ethical question involved in implementing these programs. Until jobs can be guaranteed for every man and woman whom employers train for promotion, companies must accept the fact that they may be preparing their employees for other employers. And managers who are dedicated to helping women grow despite this risk face the additional fear of encouraging some women who may turn out to be not as qualified as they were thought to be at first. "All we need is one of these women managers to fail," said one man surveyed, "and it will confirm in some men's minds that women simply cannot handle the job at all. Sure, many men whom we push turn out to be disappointments," he admitted, "but these we're used to dealing with."

The woman who fails to meet the company's expectation of her sets the hopes for women way back — in that organization at least, if not on a far wider basis. Profit objectives have a higher priority especially today than do affirmative action goals; and the higher the employee in the company, the greater investment he or she is. A company must be convinced that promoting women into management positions is economically justifiable, and one bad example can easily tip the scales against further efforts by the company in that direction.

Knowing this adds to the pressure on a woman manager. So does the fact that even with everything else going for her, without the approval of her male counterparts, the gatekeepers, she will not be accepted in management. Consequently, in addition to proving her ability as a manager, a woman manager must sell a new image; she must help her male counterparts see the *self*-benefits in perceiving woman "as she is now rather than how she always has been."

It takes a very strong and sensitive woman to put this across effectively, but even this kind of woman may be unable to meet the challenge if she is the only woman manager in the organization. One woman in a group of men is easily overpowered and will fall back into her traditional subordinate role if she is not prepared, alert, and determined. In a position of "damned if I do and damned if I don't," she runs the risk of alienation if she comes on too strong and of suppression if she comes on too weak.

This dilemma is frightening some qualified women from seeking management positions. Aware of the difficulties involved, they are reluctant to move into conflict, a fact that may explain at least in part the seeming paradox of women who have been fighting for opportunity being reluctant to use the doors that are now open to them. Many are doing very well in traditional roles in their organizations and question the logic of changing to something that apparently offers more frustration than security.

It is not altogether that women do not want to advance. It is just that until recently few thought about making careers in business; neither industry nor business schools encouraged them. But now the schools are busy trying to make up the time lag caused by industry's long antipathy.

RESOCIALIZATION IN THE COMPANY

In this social revolution, is it true that women have all to gain and men all to lose? According to some reports, this is a common perception. The study conducted by the author, however, did not reveal such thinking among most of the male managers surveyed. To some, women's ability to perform management functions is simply "a reinforcement of what I knew they could do, once given the chance." To others, it is "a pleasant surprise," "the end of another barrier," or "something that is long overdue."

Most of the men who made these comments have never held strong prejudicies, though they did acknowledge that fitting women into their existing hierarchical scheme had taken some soul-searching. Adjusting to peer relationships with women who had been formerly subordinates or, more traumatic, accepting a female boss, had called for radical changes in self-concept and perception of society. The men had trained themselves to compete, particularly in terms of power, but nothing had prepared them for competing with women. As Michael Korda, author of *Male Chauvinism! How it Works*, wrote, "Behind their dogmatism and small guiles lies the fear that woman may in fact be a formidable competitor once she has made her choice."

The male managers surveyed did not cite significant examples of operational changes in their organization as a result of women's expanding role in management. They spoke candidly of efforts "to minimize or eliminate sex-role bias and misconceptions," and they specified obvious needs for change: special training for newly promoted female supervisors and managers, reevaluation of policies regarding salaries and hours, and new policies for business travel. There are problems with wives, one male manager admitted, "when men travel with attractive women in management." Other than this, the general feeling expressed was that women are making a significant contribution in their organizations.

HOW COMPETENT ARE FEMALE MANAGERS?

When asked to evaluate female managers' competence at decision making, their handling of emotions, and their reponse to criticism (three areas in which women are frequently stereotyped as being inferior to males), both male and female managers rated women high. Women evaluated themselves higher than men rated them as decision makers and in their ability to control their emotions. However, only two men graded women as less than moderately effective in decision making, and none considered them "not well in control" of emotions. The consensus among the men was that men in management tend to display their emotions more frequently than do women. Women, they explained, are trying so hard to break old stereotypes and create a new image that they keep their emotions well under control. In comparison, men will "blast off" at any provocation.

Only in the area of response to criticism did the men and women surveyed vary significantly in their evaluation of women managers. One fourth of the male managers sampled graded women as "somewhat subjective," and two men reported bad experiences that led them to evaluate women managers as "very subjective."

In general, however, the respondents felt that the sex of the manager does not affect ability or stability. In fact, most of the male and female managers queried were reluctant to assign unique characteristics to women managers. When crediting an asset to them, the man or woman was careful to qualify that the characteristic was not necessarily peculiar to women. Assuming, wrote one female manager, that women have met the same qualifications as required of men, unique characteristics of either are related to *individual personality*. Calling generalizations about women both "stereotyping and sexist thinking," the group sampled refused to make distinctions.

Nevertheless, in discussing the female managers' contributions to the organization, the male managers did point out that women have brought fresh new insights and new points of view to management and to the total organization. "Women are not steeped in traditional management," one male manager said. "They bring fresh ways of problem solving to meetings, and they bring a new value system to corporate policy making."

BETTER BALANCE IN THE ORGANIZATION

Many of the male managers sampled indicated that women have brought a long-needed balance to the organization. In particular, stressed several, women are providing a better balance in marketing management. Their understanding of the female psyche has been valuable in marketing all products, not just those that are female-oriented. The general feeling expressed was that women are making a significant contribution in their handling of customers, particularly women customers, both in the office and out in the field.

Women tend to be people-minded, opined both the men and women surveyed. They are generally more aware of the human factor in business relationships and more sensitive and concerned about the personal feelings of their peers. This sensitivity was described as good for management. Women as a group, the male managers said, bring a degree of sensitivity (not to be interpreted as weakness or softness) to the management style that allows a broader perspective in determining course of action and decision making. One man's comment spoke right to the point: "Generally there is too much 'machismo' and misconceived need to be hard in business organizations; the stereotypical male sex role model needs some softening."

Women also have a good effect on the environment, according to the male managers surveyed. "They remain calm," said one, "when we're at the explosion point, and this helps to keep our discussions more objective, less emotional. Women managers tend to be more rational and more able to cope with the pressures of short turnaround, crisis situations." All of this adds up to a more pleasant place to work, the majority of the male respondents said. "For one thing," one claimed, "women have put a damper on the cutthroat competition found in my organization." "It's calmer around here," another noted.

Most of the men confided that they have had to clean up their language and jokes. At least temporarily! Apparently the male managers made this decision arbitrarily, not because the women complained. In fact, the women managers surveyed felt the issue is only a minor one, like opening doors and offering chairs. They want to concentrate on more important problems than these symbols inherited from another era. Still, the male managers felt that having women in management had made them "more thoughtful about employees," as one manager expressed it, and more respectful of females at all levels.

ROLE-STATUS PROBLEMS

Adjustment problems reported most frequently by the female managers were the role-status conflicts they experience when learning how to relate as a superior to secretaries and as a peer to male managers who have known them as secretaries. Both secretaries and male peers tend to regard the new woman manager in her former status. "I have to walk a delicate line to gain acceptance and respect," one woman confessed.

There were some women who said that they had had no personal problems adjusting to a peer relationship with men. They explained that they had always worked with men, they liked working with men, and they had been lucky to work with "good men." Only recently, because of all the discussion about the status of women, had some of these "old-timers" even become conscious of male chauvinism. Nor had any of the women with recent promotions into low-level management positions ever experienced male chauvinism. At the same time, these newcomers confessed that they had to frequently remind themselves to "stop assuming male colleagues are superior," to "be more assertive with ideas and opinions," and to "ask fewer questions." With each passing week and with helpful feedback from many of the men, they report they are feeling less tense about their role in the corporate hierarchy.

Overall, the women surveyed have found men not as difficult to work with as they had expected. For the most part, the women believe that their male counterparts are accepting them and expecting them to be advanced. One sure sign, one female manager said, is that "I haven't been asked to pour coffee or take notes at a meeting in two years."

WORKING TOGETHER—
ITS PROBLEMS AND PROMISES

With rare exception, the male managers were optimistic that women can handle effectively the managerial positions they are assuming. They feel that the small problems women are experiencing right now are due primarily to lack of experience, a situation they will overcome in time. Emotional problems, several specified, cannot be helped. They will disappear, one male manager said, "with increased exposure." A number of the men reported having to help women get over their initial insecurity, gain confidence, and assume an active and not a passive role. But they spoke of these problems as temporary ones, not as issues of grave concern.

The two most critical faults of women managers, according to the men, are their demanding nature at times and their unwillingness to "reach out and help other females." "Women tend to be less flexible and to demand more from their subordinates—especially if their charges are also female," one male manager commented.

The female managers were less critical than the men with their comments. There was an occasional slur, such as "having to overlook men's running off at the mouth when they don't know an answer," and mentions of men's "emotionalism" and "over-reacting" at meetings, but, other than these observations, the women were not bitter or negative in their written or spoken comments. Just as the men evidenced understanding of women's need for more experience and time to adjust to their new role, women seemed to understand the conflicts that men are experiencing in working out new relationships with their female counterparts. The women managers said that they are ready to help face and overcome all the hangups and prejudices that exist, but they said that they do not feel it is altogether their responsibility. It should be a corporate venture, they pointed out.

It will be many more years, possibly decades, before women will be found more commonly in management. This is not because they are not doing a good job. They are. Nor is it totally because men are holding out. Many are, but women executives have the support of many others. This study has indicated that when asked for candid opinions, men have more commendations than complaints to make about women in management. When male management support will become sufficiently articulate and widespread to provide the freedom of choice that women are seeking is still subject to conjecture. But what appears to be clear is that whenever qualified women do make their way to higher positions in management, the worst of the struggle is over. Once there, men and women agree that the tensions, feelings of threat, and apprehensions rapidly disappear. Men seem to be surviving the changes. And they readily admit that, so far, there are more changes for the better than for the worse. That should be good news for women.

DISCUSSION QUESTIONS

1. Revised Order Four, compelling federal contractors to provide equal opportunities for women, went into effect in 1972. What significant effects have you seen in the years since?

2. Do organizations have to make any adjustments to admit women to management positions in a male hierarchy?

3. Do you perceive that women have difficulty in taking part in all-male discussions? in organizational conflicts?

4. Do men have any more difficulty in adjusting to peer relationships with former female subordinates than with former male subordinates?

5. Why should wives *not* be worried about their husbands making business trips with women managers?

6. What kinds of socialization processes have caused women to be considered more emotional than men? less competitive?

7. Will women's value systems help alleviate some of the past problems of bribery, industrial espionage, and other unethical behavior in business?

8. Women are perceived as noncompetitive. Perhaps they reflect their ambitions differently than men. Either way, can women's presence help alleviate cutthroat organizational climates?

IV

Identifying
Language Barriers
and Remedies

Utterances, marks on paper—our language seems simple. Yet what do these utterances and marks represent? Our feelings? Our dreams? Our reactions? The way we reason?

Our language both aids and limits our ability to reason. For years statements like "woman's place," "she makes good money for a woman," and "woman's work" have gone unquestioned. Today we realize that language has been one of the most inhibiting factors in women's progress toward equal opportunity.

Some people regret saying things in anger because they realize that once angry words have been said they can never really be taken back. Discriminatory language is the same. Once it is heard around a job, women cannot feel the same toward those who have said it. The situation may become unproductive or qualified women may quit to look for a fairer deal.

Formalized discriminatory language is illegal; informal language that includes only males is insidious. Job titles that have traditional male or female connotations are limiting. This section helps us analyze the discriminatory nature of language; it indicates the necessity of changing our language so that both males and females are included on an equal basis.

Including females does not mean that language must become awkward. The effort it takes to include females and at the same time have the language remain effective and smooth is not too much to ask. Good writers know that effective writing is hard work "any way you cut it!" The rewards will come in a better quality of life for all of us.

The Semantics
of Sex Discrimination

Bette Ann Stead

The field of general semantics is credited to Alfred Korzybski as a result of his 1933 publication *Science and Sanity: An Introduction to Non-Aristotelian Systems and General Semantics*. Korzybski gave us a new system of thinking which appears to be applicable to any subject. Since we reason with symbols, we find ourselves inseparable from our language in terms of our ability to progress. This dependence on language plays both a strong and subtle role in influencing human behavior. Numerous authors have applied Korzybski's work to various concepts. This article applies the principles of general semantics as described by William V. Haney. These principles may be used to explain some of the problems associated with barriers to equal opportunity for women.[1]

OBSERVATION OR RISKY INFERENCE?

Problems occur when people fail to realize they have made inferences and proceed to act on the inferences as if acting on factual observations. These people seem to easily confuse inferences and observations and end up taking uncalculated risks. For example, opponents of the Equal Rights Amendment (ERA) say that passage of the ERA will make women eligible for the draft. The inference is that the ERA will be directly responsible for women being drafted. However, the fact is that Congress already has the power to draft women.[2]

Raising the draft and other issues to fight passage of the ERA may bring about uncalculated risks that can damage (if the ERA is stopped) other significant areas of life—for example, credit privileges. Some women are working against ERA passage while they are being comfortably supported by husbands. Some of these women may find themselves responsible for their families in future years. Among all families, about one out of eight is headed by a woman.[3] Without men to back them and without their own credit ratings these women may face the frustration of desperately needing to borrow money with nowhere to turn. Without legislative protection, they will look long and hard for recourse.

BYPASSING

Sometimes a person correctly hears a word from a sender; however, the receiver gives that word a meaning different from the sender's. Persons may not realize that they are using different words to express the same idea. Both instances result in misunderstandings that lead to unfortunate situations. These situations occur because one may feel that words only have one meaning. To avoid "bypassing," one must (1) realize that meaning occurs only in people, (2) ask questions and paraphrase, (3) make oneself constantly open and approachable, and (4) consider context as an intrinsic part of understanding.

"Bypassing" may be deliberate. If the motives of the sender are appropriate, deliberate bypassing may be ethically used to dramatically illustrate certain situations. Bypassing was most appropriately used by Benson Rosen and Thomas H. Jerdee to effectively illustrate sex discrimination. Fifteen hundred *Harvard Business Review* readers responded to a survey by recommending the proper managerial actions in eleven incidents. The incidents were identical on the two forms used in the survey, except the sexes of the key roles were reversed. The researchers used different words (male name vs. female name) to identify the same key role in each incident. The study found that there is greater concern for the organizational careers of men than there is for the careers of women and that there is a significant degree of skepticism toward a woman's ability to balance work and family demands.[4]

ALLNESS

Allness is the attitude of a person who thinks he or she can know, say, or write all there is about a subject—an impossible feat. People continually abstract to derive information about what happens to them. Semantic problems occur when one evaluates a group on the unconscious assumption that his or her experience with one or a few group members holds for all members of that group.

Many of the myths concerning women are based on male opinions about the "few" women with whom the men have associated—"few" in terms of generalizing the opinions to the total population. These myths are being refuted by research. When one realizes that the myths are based on the observation of a few women, one can think of a few men who also fit the myths. Equally inappropriate would be to generalize the myths to all men. Examples of myths which illustrate the dangers of all-ness include: (1) women do not want responsibility, promotions or job changes that add to the work load; (2) the employment of mothers leads to the juvenile delinquency of their children; and (3) men do not like to work for female supervisors.[5]

INDISCRIMINATION

Sometimes we overemphasize similarities and neglect differences. These overemphasized similarities become strong stereotypes that discourage further analysis. When a group has been given a stereotyped image, a person assigned to that group finds that any individual distinctions, which may set him or her apart from the group, are overlooked.

Working women are stereotyped as secretaries. Frequently, professional women must patiently explain that they are not secretaries to office visitors and telephone operators. Even more serious though is the problem of women with valuable professional qualifications who continue to be kept in secretarial positions. A sad example is one woman who has a college degree in art and yet has had to spend two years doing clerical work in a graphic arts studio. Her only alternative is to change jobs. But how often must she change jobs before she is granted a position that is appropriate to her professional preparation?[6]

Many companies employ female college graduates who work long years as secretaries, gaining insights into the operations. These companies are slow to realize that these women, simply by their presence in secretarial roles, highlight both the firm's obvious discrimination and underutilization of talent.

POLARIZATION

Polarization happens when situations that involve several alternatives are considered to be only either-or events. Polarization has been at the root of many tragedies throughout history. One tragedy has been the loss of human resources by discouraging extremely bright women from entering the science professions. In December 1973, among almost

207,500 science and engineering Ph.D.'s in the U.S. labor force, only 7.9 percent were women. In January 1974, women constituted 6.7 percent of the full-time mathematicians at twenty leading universities.[7]

Our society polarizes women into two categories — feminine, and unfeminine. Feminine women receive obvious positive rewards from society; unfeminine women receive obvious negative rewards. Research has shown that women who switch study majors away from a scientific field rarely do so because of academic difficulty. Success in academic competition is associated with unfeminine characteristics and therefore leads to social rejection.[8]

THE FROZEN EVALUATION

When people ignore the fact that others are continually changing, the problem of "frozen evaluation" occurs. Unless evaluations are up-to-date, people do not function effectively. The work force has changed significantly due to the entry of more women. In 1920, women comprised 20 percent of the work force; in 1973, the percentage had risen to 39 percent. "More than four out of ten married women 25 to 34 years of age were working in March 1973, as compared with less than three out of ten in 1963 and about two out of ten in 1948." The number of working mothers with children under 18 has increased about ninefold since 1940; working mothers now number 13 million, a 3.7 million increase in the last decade. Women have made great strides in gaining education, too. Although they were only 9.1 percent of M.D. graduates in 1973, women were 20 percent of the fall 1974 entering class. Yet a "frozen evaluation" in terms of remuneration and professional opportunities seems to have occurred. Even though women constitute a significantly greater part of the work force, their salaries remain about 60 percent of male salaries — the same ratio that existed twenty years ago.[9]

GUIDE BY MAPS NOT TERRITORIES

We must use words (maps) to represent what we are talking about (territories). Danger occurs when the map does a poor job of representing the territory and when we do not realize we are dealing with maps and not territories.

For centuries our language (map) has been male-oriented. Two sad and deleterious effects have resulted. *First,* a subliminal psychological message has come through that females (half the territory) are inferior. *Second,* scholars using male-oriented language that omits all female references foster misleading or unproven assumptions of fact conveying the impression of female irrelevance. If women make up half the population (territory), how can half the population (territory) be so irrelevant as not to deserve mention? The old English rule that says use a male pronoun when both genders are referred to at the same time is finally being challenged. So far the efforts are awkward. People snicker at "Dear Person" and make jokes about "person-hole cover." But Nancy Russo and Serena Stier say that tolerance of some awkwardness in efforts to develop creative alternatives is a small cost, considering the potential benefits that nonsexist language may accrue.[10]

WORDS EVOKE FEELINGS

Sometimes we react to words as if we were reacting to what the word referred to. Trouble comes when we are unaware of this confusion. When our evaluation of a person is influenced by a negative label that is applied to that person, the label may evoke negative feelings in the evaluator.

The label "liberated women" has come to have a whole range of meanings. It may mean someone who wants equal opportunity for jobs and salary or someone who enjoys a professional career as opposed to remaining at home or someone who burns her bra or someone who writes books using lots of four-letter words. Because of the glaring publicity given to some aspects of the women's movement, the label "liberated women" has come to have a negative connotation to some people. Therefore, many women cringe at the thought of being labeled a "liberated woman" because of the negative connotation evoked by those headlines relating to some aspects of the women's movement.

The sincere, dedicated, hard-working woman is just like the sincere, dedicated, hard-working man—not very newsworthy. If these women were more newsworthy, perhaps the drive toward equal opportunity would have developed earlier.

BLINDERING

The way we go about solving problems is greatly influenced by our perceptions of those problems. Our perceptual filter, a product of our past experiences, can explain the way we try to solve problems. Because no one's filter ever includes all there is to perceive about a situation, we suffer from a limited view that may be termed "blindering." When we are unaware of our "blinders," they limit our problem-solving ability.

Opponents of the ERA claim that ratification would result in loss of child support payments. Many perceive child support as a solid foundation for children of divorced parents. Yet the sad truth is that one year after divorce only 38 percent of ex-husbands are in full compliance with court-ordered child support payments. After five years, the figure drops to 19 percent.[11] Far from being a solid foundation, child support is a tenuous situation for today's children. The ERA would not wipe out that conscientious 19 percent. If only those ERA opponents would remove their "blinders," realize today's sad child support situation and devote their efforts toward finding ways to correct it!

UNDELAYED REACTIONS

Reflex responses involve no thinking, are uncontrollable, direct, and immediate. Voluntary responses involve thinking, are delayed and controllable. Reflexlike responses are "potentially" voluntary, but through habit, panic, conditioning, or surprise resemble reflexes.

A key goal should be to develop the habit of "delay-while-evaluating" before acting. This delay, however brief, increases chances for self-control and situation analysis. Therefore, one has a greater chance to avoid the previously-mentioned pitfalls.

Because of the pitifully slow progress toward equal opportunity for women, frustrations continue to mount. Most women work for the same reason—economic need—as men and fear loss of jobs if they take action. Many women wonder, as the years go by, if they will see any concrete evidence to replace the lip service paid to equal opportunity.

Women are said to lack a sense of humor when men joke about equal opportunity. After years of frustration, it is difficult to keep from verbally lashing out (a reflexlike response) at male detractors. In conclusion, women should be encouraged to use the "delayed reaction" technique to give themselves more time to analyze their situations and respond appropriately.

The field of general semantics shows us that language continually affects behavior in a number of ways. Language—the symbols that we use from day to day—appears to be a significant factor in hindering efforts to get equal opportunity for working women. A closer look at our language is needed to understand some of the root causes of discrimination. More serious efforts at eliminating male-oriented language could go a long way toward enhancing a valuable natural resource—half of our population.

NOTES

[1] Alfred Korzybski, *Science and Sanity: An Introduction to Non-Aristotelian Systems and General Semantics* (Lancaster, Pa.: Science Press Printing Co., 1933).

William V. Haney, *Communication and Organizational Behavior* (Homewood, Ill.: Richard D. Irwin, Inc., 1973).

[2] League of Women Voters, *The ERA — What It Means to Men and Women,* Pub. No. 272 (Washington, D.C.: League of Women Voters), p. 3.

[3] U.S. Department of Labor, Women's Bureau, *Twenty Facts on Women Workers* (Washington, D.C.: Government Printing Office, June 1974), p. 1.

[4] Benson Rosen and Thomas H. Jerdee, "Sex Stereotyping in the Executive Suite," *Harvard Business Review* (March–April 1974), pp. 45–58.

[5] Rhobia Taylor, *The Myth and the Reality* (Dallas, Texas: U.S. Department of Labor, Women's Bureau, March 1974), p. 3.

[6] Margaret Price, "Rallying for Rights: Preamble to Equal Opportunity," *Today's Secretary* (October 1974), p. 11.

[7] Betty M. Vetter and Eleanor L. Babco, *Professional Women and Minorities* (Washington, D.C.: Scientific Manpower Commission).

[8] Deedee Pendleton, "Women in Science: Reshaping the Stereotypes," *Science News* (March 15, 1975), p. 181.

[9] U.S. Department of Labor, Women's Bureau, *Women Workers Today,* revised (Washington, D.C.: Government Printing Office, 1974), pp. 1–4; U.S. Department of Labor, Women's Bureau, *Twenty Facts on Women Workers;* U.S. Department of Labor, Women's Bureau, *The Earnings Gap* (Washington, D.C.: Government Printing Office, March 1975), p. 2; Vetter and Babco, *Professional Women and Minorities.*

[10] Nancy Russo and Serena Stier, "A Rose Is a Rose Is a Rose … Is a Four-Letter Word," *APA Monitor* (February 1975), p. 15.

[11] K. Eckhard, "Deviance, Visibility, and Legal Action: The Duty to Support," *Social Problems* (Spring 1968), pp. 470–74.

DISCUSSION QUESTIONS

1. How does language reflect our thinking and influence our behavior?

2. What examples do you know of deserving women being denied credit for their ability?

3. What unfounded emotional arguments have you heard about the Equal Rights Amendment? How do you know that they're "unfounded"?

4. What myths or stereotypes about women have you noted in our language?

5. What examples do you know of bright young women who have changed their college majors because of social pressures?

6. Define "liberated woman" in 25 words or less. Compare your definition with others. Can you divide the definitions into areas of perception?

7. What jokes do you know about equal opportunity for women that both sexes would enjoy? Why do you think it is said that women who are interested in equal opportunity have no humor? Can a cavalier attitude about your means of making a living be funny? Explain.

"'Only 25% of young women between 14 and 25 would choose the role of housewife, while 34% would choose a professional or executive career,' an Institute of Life Insurance survey says."

"Career First Choice in Poll of Young Women," *Houston Chronicle*, November 21, 1976, Sec. 1, P. 10.

A Woman
Is Not a Girl
and Other Lessons
in Corporate Speech

Patricia Hogan

If you listen carefully to businessmen's conversations, you can learn much about their attitudes toward women.

SCENE ONE: A planning meeting. Ten men are seated around a large, circular conference table. One of the men leading the meeting has forgotten to bring a crucial document. Discovering this, he says, "I'll have my girl bring it right over." Five minutes later, a woman who appears to be in her early forties knocks on the door, excuses herself for the interruption, and hands the man the document.

SCENE TWO: Mr. Z calls Sally Jones, one of the firm's account executives, into his office to congratulate her on landing an account the company has been pursuing for years.

"Sally, you did a first-rate job on the Mercer account," he says. "You really surprised everyone. Don't get me wrong—it's not that we didn't think you could do the job. It's just ... well, how did you manage to get old Mercer to sign? Never mind, we won't go into that," he says with a wink.

Later, Mr. Z sees Ms. Jones in the executive dining room, approaches her table, and again congratulates her. "Bet you guys don't know what a terrific little saleswoman we have here," he says to the men lunching with Ms. Jones.

By day's end, Mr. Z has commended Ms. Jones five times on her achievement.

SCENE THREE: Six men and a lone woman attend a luncheon. The table conversation turns to capital gains, product diversification, and a new Management Information System (MIS) that will facilitate financial reporting for the large multinational corporation for which they work.

Patricia Hogan, "A Woman Is Not a Girl and Other Lessons in Corporate Speech," *Business and Society Review* (Summer 1975). Copyright © 1975, Warren, Gorham, and Lamont, Inc., 210 South Street, Boston, Mass. 02111.

Halfway through lunch, one of the men leans over and whispers to the woman, "Are we boring you?"

SCENE FOUR: A group of executives meet to discuss a merger. During the course of the discussion, one of the male vice-presidents says, "This is going to be a bitch to pull off." He immediately turns to the two women present and apologizes for the five-letter word.

SCENE FIVE: A male manager has recently transferred to head a new department. On the third day in his new assignment, he emerges from his office and asks a female standing near the Xerox machine to make four copies of a report and to get him a cup of coffee. The woman introduces herself; she is one of the production managers who report to him.

As women advance in the business world, men are often confronted with situations like those above — situations which call for new forms of behavior and a new awareness of and effort to overcome the sexism inherent in daily conversations.

The men in these five situations have violated certain basic communications rules. In the first instance, the man has referred to a mature female as a girl. The term *girl* implies a certain dependency associated with children. The word is as denigrating when applied to a woman as the word *boy* is when applied to a man. Secondly, the businessman identified the woman by her sex and not by her function (in this case, secretary) as would have been appropriate in this situation. Thirdly, the man's use of the word *my* indicates that he thinks of the secretary as personal property rather than as an employee of the company.

In the second example, Mr. Z's repeated and overblown praise belies any conviction that women are competent. His comments demonstrate his astonishment at Ms. Jones's achievement. In addition, he tries to attribute her success to feminine wiles or to sexual favors granted to "old Mercer." Mr. Z also patronizes Ms. Jones by describing her as a "terrific *little* saleswoman."

In the third case, the man's question is based on the assumption that women are not interested in business matters. If he did not accept the stereotype of woman as primarily concerned with domestic and certain other interests, he would not ask the question. The very phrasing of the question ("Are we boring you?") reveals that he views the men as controlling the conversation and the woman as a passive participant. She is seen as a listener and not as an equal partner in the luncheon discussion.

In the fourth instance, the vice-president apologizes not because he thinks he has offended an individual, but because he has been conditioned to believe that certain forms of language are not used in the presence of women. In this particular case, the man apologized despite the fact that one of the women had called the president of the company being acquired a "fucking madman" during the course of the meeting, thus clearly indicating that she took no exception to such language.

The manager in the fifth illustration obviously assigns women to certain roles within the business world. He finds it natural to assume that a woman standing near a Xerox machine is either a secretary or a clerk, and his remarks flow from that assumption.

WORDS OFTEN EXCLUDE WOMEN

Businessmen do no better when it comes to the written word, as an examination of internal memoranda and other documents will show. Indeed, business has created and uses an extensive terminology that excludes women. Some of its more familiar phrases include manpower planning, man-hours, workman's compensation, the right man for the job, etc.

It can, of course, be argued that these terms are meant generically and therefore include women. However, the effect is frequently the opposite. To most executives, *manpower planning* means plotting the future careers of the key men in the organization or matching key men with key positions. Invariably, the generic evokes a masculine image, especially when used in a business environment, which has long been a male preserve.

Most business terminology can be easily changed without resorting to awkward or strained language. For example, manpower planning becomes *staff resources planning.* Workman's compensation becomes *worker's compensation.* Right man for the job becomes *right person* for the job.

Many companies already have issued guidelines to help executives achieve nonsexist writing. (The McGraw-Hill "Guidelines for Equal Treatment of the Sexes" is perhaps the most notable and comprehensive of these. Although aimed at authors of textbooks, the McGraw-Hill guidelines are valuable for everyone.)

De-sexing the spoken and written language, however, requires more than the invention and utilization of nonsexist words and phrases. Behavior modification and attitudinal change are required. And because language is the externalization of our thought processes, it is our thinking about women that must change. Women must no longer be perceived as inherently bound to play limited roles in society. Sexist stereotypes, such as the indecisive female executive, must be discarded.

Businesswomen must be seen as the equals—for better or for worse—of businessmen: competent, aggressive, ambitious, decisive individuals. They must be viewed as people serious about their careers. As effective managers. Only when we think of females in this way will we be able to approach communicating with them in the proper manner.

Compared with the spoken word, de-sexing the written word should prove easy, because people tend to think more carefully about what they commit to print. We take the time to revise and refine our words.

Conversations are more spontaneous, therefore more apt to show people's biases. Also, people sometimes play power games on the conversational field. Conversations can be used either consciously or subconsciously to "put a woman in her place" — to make her submissive. They can be used, as in the Mr. Z-Ms. Jones example, to make a woman doubt her own abilities. They can be used to draw inordinate attention to a woman (causing embarrassment or making an already uncomfortable situation more uncomfortable), as in the case of the apologetic male vice-president who feels compelled to excuse himself for his language. The message he has sent via his apology is that women are a special breed of people who must be protected from vulgar language. (The corollary being, of course, that they must be protected from the harsh realities of the business world and therefore denied the same opportunity for advancement as men have.) He has also called attention to the fact that, as he perceives it, two women are now intruding on the meeting being held by the male executives.

One of the chief mistakes made in everyday conversations is to regard people as the representatives of a group rather than as individuals. The apologetic vice-president in example number four did not consider the people to whom he spoke *as individuals*. If he had, he might have apologized to a man present who found the language being used offensive. If the manager in the fifth example thought in terms of an individual rather than a class of people, he would have taken the time to find out the woman's position before asking her to make copies of his report and fetch coffee.

Nonsexist speaking habits can be acquired only be redirecting thinking patterns, discarding all the old assumptions and learning to interact on a one-to-one basis.

DISCUSSION QUESTIONS

1. What examples could you add to the five scenes given in this article?

2. What examples have you seen of written documents with discriminatory language?

3. What examples have you seen of written documents that try to include women in their language?

4. What language examples have you seen that "put women in their place"?

"He" and "She":
Changing Language
to Fit a Changing World

Carole Schulte Johnson
Inga Kromann Kelly

A recent Washington, D.C., social news column featured a woman appointed to a high level government position. The columnist did not overlook the opportunity to point out that "She ... doesn't go in for that chairperson-instead-of-chairman nonsense."

But is it nonsense? Is the question of language usage simply one of individual preference, or are there implications, beyond mere preference, which ought to be taken seriously by educators? How do children react to certain aspects of traditional language? What are implications of current research findings? Are we aware of what is happening in the "real world" with respect to language changes?

As a framework for considering this matter, we propose an analogy. Suppose as a medical doctor you have the choice of prescribing Drug A or Drug B for a given ailment. Both drugs have the same probability of curing or relieving the ailment, but Drug A has the possibility of causing negative side effects for some people, while Drug B does not. As a doctor, which drug are you going to prescribe? Recognizing that life is seldom so clear-cut, we suggest that Drug A is analogous to traditional language. It does have the possibility of causing or contributing negative side effects for certain groups of people, while language of the Drug B type eliminates this possibility. Using the language analogy, Drug A would be labeled *exclusionary* language; Drug B *inclusionary* language.

Exclusionary language functions in two ways. First, its traditional usage excludes females in effect if not by intent, because words such as "chairman" and "newsman," allegedly gender-generic, tend to be interpreted as being gender-specific. Second, the reversal of traditional usage

Carole Schulte Johnson and Inga Kromann Kelly, "'He' and 'She': Changing Language to Fit a Changing World," *Educational Leadership* (May 1975), pp. 527 – 30. Reprinted with permission of the Association for Supervision and Curriculum Development and the authors. Copyright © 1975 by the Association for Supervision and Curriculum Development.

excludes males in effect as well as by intent when gender-specific terms such as "chairwoman" and "saleswoman" are used. Inclusionary language is that which does not exclude, either by intent or in effect, on the basis of sex.

"MAILMEN" ARE NOT "LADIES"

Young children react literally to language. We recently observed a three-year-old attempt to retrieve a bottle from a cabinet. The small space required that the bottle be tipped sideways first. "Use your head," cajoled her father, observing the dilemma. The youngster promptly stuck her head inside the cabinet and proceeded to push at the bottle. Use her head? She did as she was told!

This kind of literal language interpretation (coupled with firsthand observation) reinforces children's perceptions that certain occupations must be held by males. Listen to preschoolers argue that "policemen," "firemen," or "mailmen" are men, *not* "ladies," and reflect on the negative side effects of inaccurate concept shaping for both boys and girls. Traditional language constantly shapes and reinforces the concept that boys are "supposed" to be in certain occupations, while girls are not. At best, traditional language fails to contradict the exclusionary concept (regardless of how it is formed initially) while it does serve to reinforce it.

Children have no difficulty learning inclusionary language. The three-year-old son of one of the authors knows that people who fight fires are "firefighters." He uses the term because adults have provided him with this language model. "Firefighter" not only retains the important concept (and actually enhances the imagery), but the term encourages recognition that the occupation is open to all who have the ability and the desire to pursue it.

But, we are told, inclusionary language sounds so "funny." How awkward is it to say "salesperson" for "salesman" or "saleswoman"? "Salesperson" has been in common use for some time. A nine-year-old matter-of-factly explained to a faculty member that his father was the new department "chairperson." The youngster had no difficulty with the term; what our ears become attuned to is what sounds "right." Political figures, sensitive to their constituencies, use "his and her," and "person" nouns with gold-tongued ease. They recognize the impact of language.

Moreover, exclusionary language is inefficient. Young children learn that "man" means male, not only because they interpret literally, but because that is the sole meaning of the word as it is used at their level. Later, however, children must somehow unlearn this concept, or they must modify it to encompass the masculine used as the generic. This does not seem to be an insurmountable task, until we observe that there is no clear way to determine when "man" is generic, and when it is not. For example, does the club constitution which states that all "men" with certain qualifications are eligible for membership mean that the club is inclusive ("mankind"?) or sex exclusive?

At this point, let us offer a second analogy. To avoid some of the problems and hazards of living, we practice prevention by employing measures such as those which protect us against fires, disease, and accidents. Prevention usually requires the avoidance of certain actions as well as the inclusion of other actions or measures expected to have a wholesome effect. Thus, to remove the possibility of negative side effects of language, we need to avoid exclusionary language while consciously using inclusionary language.

RESEARCH IMPLICATIONS

Concern about the exclusionary nature of English is evidenced by the writing of people such as linguists Key (4) and Lakoff (6), social scientists Bosmajian (2) and Kidd (5), and educators Tiedt (8) and Burr, Dunn, and Farquhar (3). They write on the subject of language bias and include the generic use of "man" and the masculine pronouns in their analyses.

Three studies are of particular interest because subjects were asked to respond to different wasy of using language. College students in Kidd's research responded to 18 statements in which the masculine pronoun and "man" were used traditionally. They were to identify each pronoun antecedent according to several characteristics, including sex. For the first nine statements, the identification was open ended, so that the sex of the referent could be identified as male, female, either, or both:

The potentialities of *man* are infinitely varied and exciting.

Social status _____ Financial position _____
Sex _____ Race _____

The second nine statements were in a forced-choice format:

A painter may or may not acknowledge the laws of perspective. *He* accepts such limitation if they further the kinds of reality he is trying to achieve.

a. female-male
b. successful-unsuccessful
c. white-black
d. rich-poor

Kidd found that the subjects did not respond inclusively to the generic pronoun either in the free-choice or the forced-choice situation. In the free-choice, males were selected 407 times and females 53 times. Kidd concluded that the masculine pronoun as the generic is not generally interpreted as representing a neutral antecedent; it is, in fact, considered male. She suggests that since the intended purpose is not accomplished, its continued use seems unwarranted.

Schneider and Hacker (7) asked college students for newspaper and magazine pictures to illustrate a proposed sociology textbook. Two forms of chapter titles were used. Both forms contained eight common titles which were neutral in gender; for example, Culture, Ecology. In addition, one form used five "man"-associated labels such as "urban man" and "political man" while the other form contained comparable inclusionary titles such as "urban life" and "political behavior." Schneider and Hacker found that 64 percent of students receiving "man" titles submitted pictures containing only males, compared with 50 percent of those receiving the inclusionary titles. The authors concluded that a significantly large number of students did not interpret "man" generically.

Bem and Bem (1) asked high school seniors to rate twelve job advertisements on an interested-uninterested scale. Eight ads identical on all three forms contained inclusionary language. The language of four telephone ads varied. Operator and service representative positions were considered traditionally female, while "frameman" and "lineman" were considered traditionally male. The company's traditional exclusionary language was used in Form I. Form II employed inclusionary language while sex-reversed exclusionary language was used in Form III, for example, telephone operator was referred to as "he," while "frameman" became "framewoman." The following results were obtained when subjects were asked to indicate interest in the traditional opposite-sex jobs:

Language-Type	Women	Men
Traditional exclusionary	5%	30%
Inclusionary	25%	75%
Sex-reversed exclusionary	45%	65%

Because the only difference in these ads was the language used, the conclusion that for some people, both male and female, language has a strong effect seems inescapable.

EMERGING TRENDS

Sensitivity to the use of inclusionary language in the "real" world is growing. Leading publishers such as Scott, Foresman and Company and McGraw-Hill Book Company have issued guidelines for improving the image of women in books. Included in the guidelines are alternatives for exclusionary language, such as humanity, human race, human beings, or people for "mankind," as well as examples of alternatives to generic use of masculine pronouns. Iris M. Tiedt (8), editor of *Elementary English*, has provided guidelines for inclusionary language for those submitting manuscripts.

In the state of Washington, the Higher Education Personnel Board revised its job classifications to eliminate "man" terms. Thus, "appliance serviceman" is "appliance mechanic," "seedman" is "seedworker," "offset pressman" is "offset press operator." Similarly, the U.S. Department of Labor has changed its dictionary of occupational titles so that "person" replaces "man." Its Office of Workmen's Compensation Programs has been officially changed to the Office of Worker's Compensation Programs.

Thus, inclusionary language is already part of the "real world" of everyday speech, classroom interaction, and public addresses. Moreover, it is appearing with increasing frequency in textbooks, newspapers, and magazines. If we, as educators, view our role as that of facilitating individual development to the fullest, should we not also adopt the inclusionary language model? The trend is here. What is our choice — to help or to hinder? We predict that when our present preschoolers are adults, inclusionary language will be the norm and everyone will marvel at the fuss over language usage 'way back in the '70's!

NOTES

[1] S. L. Bem and D. J. Bem, "Does Sex-Biased Job Advertising 'Aid and Abet' Sex Discrimination?" *Journal of Applied Social Psychology* 3 (1973), pp. 6 – 18.

[2] M. A. Bosmajian, "The Language of Sexism," *ETC: A Review of General Semantics* 29 (1972), pp. 305 – 12.

[3] E. Burr, S. Dunn, and N. Farquhar, "Women and the Language of Inequality," *Social Education* 36 (1972), pp. 841 – 45.

[4] M. R. Key, "Linguistic Behavior of Male and Female," *Linguistics* 88 (1972) pp. 15 – 31.

[5] V. Kidd, "A Study of the Images Produced Through the Use of the Male Pronoun as the Generic," *Moments in Contemporary Rhetoric and Communication* 1 (1971), pp. 25 – 29.

[6] R. Lakoff, "Language and Woman's Place," *Language in Society* 2 (1972), pp. 45 – 80.

[7] J. Schneider and S. Hacker, "Sex Role Imagery and Use of the Generic 'Man' in Introductory Texts: A Case in the Sociology of Sociology," *American Sociologist* 8 (1973), pp. 12 – 18.

[8] I. M. Tiedt, "Sexism in Language, an Editor's Plague," *Elementary English* 50 (1973), pp. 1073 – 74.

DISCUSSION QUESTIONS

1.   For a week keep a diary of every example of exclusionary language you hear on the radio or television or read in the paper. Make an alternate list of the same examples using inclusionary language. Send some of your alternatives to the station manager or newspaper editor involved. Describe the responses you get.

2.   List five clothing styles that looked "funny" to you three to five years ago but now seem appropriate. Now list any inclusionary language that you are becoming comfortable with.

3.   Can you come up with a better term than "*man*power planning"?

Addendum to Style Guide for Authors

Academy of Management Review

GUIDELINES FOR EQUAL TREATMENT OF SEXES

1. *The Roles of Men and Women.* Men and women should be treated as people, and not primarily as members of opposite sexes. Their shared humanity and common attributes should be stressed — not their gender difference. Neither sex should be stereotyped or arbitrarily assigned to a leading or secondary role. Job stereotypes, life styles, and career options should be equally treated for males and females. *Equal proportions* of *illustrations* should be used.

2. *Portrayals: Human Terms.* Members of both sexes should be represented as whole human beings with *human* strengths and weaknesses, not masculine or feminine ones. Women and girls should be shown as having the same abilities, interests, and ambitions as men and boys. Characteristics that have been traditionally praised in males, such as boldness, initiative, and assertiveness, should also be praised in females. Characteristics that have been praised in females, such as gentleness, compassion, and sensitivity, should also be praised in males.

In describing men and women, they should be treated with the same respect, dignity, and seriousness. Neither should be trivialized or stereotyped, either in text or in illustrations. The following are illustrative of incorrect and correct usage.

... the *Academy of Management is dedicated to the proposition that each human being has a dignity and worth that is his or her own, and not related to race, color, religion, sex, or national origin. Recently the McGraw-Hill Book Company issued a series of guidelines for its authors regarding equal treatment of sexes. The Review has adapted these guidelines for use by potential authors ...*

"Addendum to Style Guide for Authors," *Academy of Management Review* (July 1976), pp.150 – 52.

Incorrect	*Correct*
the girls or the ladies (when adult females are meant)	*the women*
girl, as in: I'll have my *girl* check that.	I'll have my *secretary* (or my *assistant*) check that. (Or use the person's name.)
lady used as a modifier, as in *lady* lawyer.	Try to avoid gender modifiers altogether. When you *must* modify, use *woman* or *female*, as in: a *course on women lawyers*, or *the airline's first female pilot*.
female gender word forms such as *authoress, poetess*	*author, poet*
female-gender or diminutive word forms, such as *suffragette, usherette, aviatrix*	*suffragist, usher, aviator* (or pilot)
co-ed	*student*

Women should be treated as the rule, not as the exception. Generic terms, such as manager and supervisor, should be assumed to include both men and women, and modified titles such as "woman manager" or "female supervisor" should not be used. Work should never be stereotyped as "woman's work" or a "man-sized job".

Women should be spoken of as participants in the action, not as possessions of men. Terms such as *pioneer, manager,* and *engineer* should not be used as though they applied only to adult males.

Women should be recognized for their own achievements. Intelligent, daring, and innovative women, both in history and fiction, should be provided as role-models for girls.

3. *Language Considerations.* In references to humanity at large, language should operate to include women and girls. Terms that tend to exclude females should not be used.

The word *man* has long been used not only to denote a person of male gender, but also generically to denote humanity at large. To many people today, however, the word *man* has become so closely associated with the first meaning (a male human being) that they consider it no longer broad enough to be applied to any person or to human beings as a whole. therefore, alternative expressions should be used. Here are some possible substitutions for *man*-words.

Incorrect	*Correct*
mankind	*humanity, human beings, human race, people*
primitive man	*primitive people or peoples, primitive human beings, primitive men and women*
man's achievements	*human achievements*
If a *man* drove 50 miles at 60 mph ...	If a *person* (or *driver*) drove 50 miles at 60 mph ...
The best *man* for the job	The best *person* (or *candidate*) for the job
man-made	*artificial; synthetic, manufactured; constructed; of human origin*
manpower	*human power; human energy; workers; work-force*

The English language lacks a generic singular pronoun signifying *he* or *she*, and therefore has grammatically sanctioned the use of masculine pronouns in expressions such as *"one ... he," "anyone ... he,"* and *"each* child opens *his* book." The pronouns *he, him,* and *his* in reference to a hypothetical person or humanity in general should be avoided. The following alternatives should be used:

(a) *Reword* to eliminate unnecessary gender pronouns. ("An average manager drinks his coffee black," can be reworded "An average manager drinks black coffee.")

(b) *Recast* into the plural. ("Most managers drink their coffee black.")

(c) *Replace* the masculine pronoun with *one, you, he* or *she, her* or *his*, as appropriate. (Use *he or she* and its variations sparingly to avoid clumsy prose.)

(d) *Alternate* male and female expressions and examples. (e.g. "I've often heard supervisors say, "she's not the right person for the job," or "He lacks the qualifications for success."

Occupational terms ending in *man* should be replaced by terms that can include members of either sex unless they refer to a particular person who is in fact male. The following are some illustrations:

Incorrect	*Correct*
businessman	*business executive, business manager*
insurance man	*insurance agent*
statesman	*leader, public servant*
salesman	*sales representative, salesperson*
foreman	*supervisor*

4. *Parallel Treatment.* The language used to designate and describe females and males should treat the sexes equally. Parallel language should be used for women and men. (e.g. "The men and women *or* the ladies and gentlemen" should be used instead of" the men and the ladies.")

Women should be identified by their own *names* (e.g. Barbara Walters). They should not be referred to in terms of their roles as wife, mother, sister, or daughter unless it is in these roles that they are significant in context. A woman should be referred to by name in the same way that a man is. Both should be called by their full names, by first or last name only, or by title. (e.g. Bobby Riggs and Billie Jean King instead of Bobby Riggs and Billie Jean).

Insofar as possible, job titles should be nonsexist. Different titles should not be used for the same job when it is held by both males and females.

Incorrect	*Correct*
steward or stewardess	*flight attendant*
policeman and policewoman	*police officer*

Different pronouns should not be linked with certain work or occupations on the assumption that the worker is always (or usually) female or male. Instead either pluralize or use *he or she* and *she or he.* (e.g. "Consumers or shoppers ... they," instead of "Consumer or shopper ... she.")

Males should not always be first in order of mention. Instead, alternate the order, sometimes using: *women and men, gentlemen and ladies, she or he, her or his.*

DISCUSSION QUESTIONS

1.   What examples have you seen recently of sexist language being used in popular and professional publications?

2.   What examples have you seen of sexist language being used recently in advertising?

3.   What examples have you seen of publications making efforts to rid themselves of sexist language?

52 Job Titles
Revised to Eliminate
Sex-Stereotyping

Women's Bureau
U.S. Department of Labor
Employment Standards Administration

Changes in 52 sex-stereotyped job titles have been adopted in the U.S. Census Bureau's Occupational Classification System. They will help eliminate the concept of so-called "men's jobs" and "women's jobs," Carmen R. Maymi, Director of the U.S. Department of Labor's Women's Bureau, said today.

Ms. Maymi called the new job titles "a welcome step" toward eliminating sex discrimination in employment.

The changes were recommended by Women's Bureau and Manpower Administration representatives of the Labor Department and other members of the Federal Interagency Committee on Occupation Classification.

The suffix "men" has been dropped from most of the occupational titles, and replaced by "worker" or "operator."

"It is not realistic to expect that women will apply for job openings advertised for foremen, salesmen, or credit men. Nor will men apply for job vacancies calling for laundresses, maids or airline stewardesses," Ms. Maymi said.

The title for the major group, craftsmen and kindred workers, has been changed to craft and kindred workers.

Excerpt from United States Department of Labor Press Release of November 9, 1973, *Statistical Reporter* (October 1973).

Occupation By Major Group

Census Code	Former Title	Revised Title
	Professional, Technical and Kindred Workers	
086	Clergymen	Clergy
192	Public relations men and publicity writers	Public relations specialists and publicity writers
	Managers and Administrators, Except Farm	
210	Credit men	Credit and collection managers
	Sales Workers	
260	Advertising agents and salesmen	Advertising agents and sales workers
266	Newsboys	Newspaper carriers and vendors
271	Stock and bond salesmen	Stock and bond sales agents
280	Salesmen and salesclerks, n.e.c.	Sales workers and sales clerks, n.e.c.
284	Salesmen, retail trade	Sales workers, except clerks, retail trade
285	Salesmen of services and construction	Sales workers, services and construction
	Clerical and Kindred Workers	
333	Messengers and office boys	Messengers and office helpers
	Craft and Kindred Workers	
423	Printing trades apprentices, except pressmen	Printing trade apprentices, except printing press
424	Cranemen, derrickmen, and hoistmen	Crane, derrick, and hoist operators
433	Electric power linemen and cablemen	Electric power line and cable installers and repairers
441	Foremen, n.e.c.	Blue-collar worker supervisors, n.e.c.
442	Forgemen and hammermen	Forge and hammer operators
472	Automobile body repairmen	Automotive body repairers
475	Data processing machine repairmen	Data processing machine repairers
492	Miscellaneous mechanics and repairmen	Miscellaneous mechanics and repairers
495	Not specified mechanics and repairmen	Not specified mechanics and repairers
516	Piano and organ tuners and repairmen	Piano and organ tuners and repairers
530	Pressmen and plate printers, printing	Printing press operators
531	Pressman apprentices	Printing press apprentices
542	Shoe repairmen	Shoe repairers
550	Structural metal craftsmen	Structural metal workers
552	Telephone installers and repairmen	Telephone installers and repairers
554	Telephone linemen and splicers	Telephone line installers and repairers
575	Craftsmen and kindred workers, n.e.c.	Craft and kindred workers, n.e.c.
586	Craftsmen and kindred workers—allocated	Craft and kindred workers—allocated
	Operatives Except Transport	
603	Blasters and powdermen	Blasters
605	Chainmen, rodmen, and axemen; surveying	Surveyor helpers
613	Dressmakers and seamstresses, except factory	Dressmakers, except factory
622	Furnacemen, smeltermen, and pourers	Furnace tenders, smelters, and pourers, metal
666	Stationary firemen	Furnace tenders and stokers, except metal
	Transport Equipment Operators	
701	Boatmen and canalmen	Boat Operators
704	Conductors and motormen, urban rail transit	Conductors and operators, urban rail transit
705	Deliverymen and routemen	Delivery and route workers
710	Motormen; mine, factory, logging camp, etc.	Rail vehicle operators, n.e.c.
712	Railroad brakemen	Railroad brake operators and couplers
713	Railroad switchmen	Railroad switch operators
	Laborers, Except Farm	
752	Fishermen and oystermen	Fishers, hunters, and trappers
760	Longshoremen and stevedores	Longshore workers and stevedores
761	Lumbermen, raftsmen, and woodchoppers	Timber cutting and logging workers
770	Warehousemen, n.e.c.	Warehouse laborers, n.e.c.
	Service Workers, Except Private Household	
901	Chambermaids and maids, except private household	Lodging quarters cleaners, except private household
902	Cleaners and charwomen	Building interior cleaners, n.e.c.
911	Busboys	Waiters' assistants
931	Airline stewardesses	Flight attendants
961	Firemen, fire protection	Fire fighters
962	Guards and watchmen	Guards
964	Policemen and detectives	Police and detectives
	Private Household Workers	
983	Laundresses, private household	Launderers, private household
984	Maids and servants, private household	Private household cleaners and servants

(Robert Raynsford, Statistical Policy Division, Office of Management and Budget.)

V

Understanding
Organizational Constraints

"Organization behavior" has emerged as one of the most researched and respected fields of study in departments of management in colleges of business administration around the country today. It is an area that some managers overlook as appropriate for formal study and research. But as time passes, more and more managers will have exposure to this field.

The informal work system within the formal organization is probably the most powerful force in either boosting or slowing production. Some managers refuse to recognize the informal work system because they feel threatened by it. But refusing to recognize it will not make it go away. The informal work system will always be there in some form. The good manager is able to get the informal work system to work for organization goals instead of against them.

Because of the power that comes from both the formal and the informal organization, it is useful to look at the organizational constraints that have hindered equal opportunity for women.

Differential Recruitment and Control: The Sex Structuring of Organizations

Joan Acker
Donald R. Van Houten

Organizational theory and research has neglected analyses of sex differences in organizational behavior. When sex differences have been noted, they have been explained in terms of differences in biology, socialization, attitudes, and role commitment. On the basis of a reexamination of the Hawthorne studies and Crozier's work on two French bureaucracies, this paper suggests that sex differences may also be due to more structural factors such as differential recruitment and sex-linked control mechanisms. On that basis, the paper suggests a reinterpretation of the findings from those studies. The sex structuring of organizations needs to be taken into account along with organizational factors to arrive at fuller explanations of organizational phenomena.

Sex differences in organizational behavior have been recorded in the research literature since systematic research in organizations began (for example Blauner, 1964; Roethlisberger and Dickson, 1939), and the sex segregation of the occupational world is being increasingly recognized as a significant aspect of social structure (Gross, 1968; Epstein, 1970; Oppenheimer, 1970). The relationship between these two phenomena has been suggested (Epstein, 1970; Etzioni, 1969; Marrett, 1972), but has been studied primarily within the professions, with other occupations largely ignored. Whyte's (1949) study is a notable exception. Sex differences in organizational behavior, when they have been commented on at all, have been variously interpreted, but rarely related to sex segregation and differential sex power in organizations.

We suggest, along with Caplow (1954: 230–247), that there is sex structuring in organizations, which consists of differentiation of female and male jobs, a hierarchical ordering of those jobs so that males are higher than females and are not expected to take orders from females. As a result males generally have more power in organizations than females; we call this the sex power differential. Furthermore, this sex structuring of organizations may be as important as social psychological factors in understanding sex differences in organizational behavior and may provide alternative or additional explanations for some well known generalizations in the organizational literature.

THE MALE BIAS IN ORGANIZATIONAL RESEARCH

Organizational theory and research has been heavily weighted toward the study of male society. Studies of top level managerial and professional workers usually focus on men, since men are usually in positions of power and leadership. In industrial sociology and organizational research which focuses on the lower participants of organizations, the samples studied are often entirely male (for instance, Tudor, 1972; Goldthorpe *et al*, 1968); but even when women workers are included, the research has largely ignored or dismissed sex power differentials.[1]

Most organizational analysts attribute sex differences largely to differential patterns in socialization and adult roles outside the organization, such as women's family roles not shared by men (Blauner, 1964; Furstenberg, 1968). One cannot rule out the importance of such differences in trying to explain the sex structuring of organizations, but what is disturbing is the neglect of other processes that sociologists have commonly associated with problems of social organization: patterns of selective recruitment and social control mechanisms other than socialization. Specifically what has not been sufficiently examined are (1) differential recruitment of women into organizational roles demanding passivity and compliance, and (2) unique mechanisms employed in organizations to control women. We suggest that these factors are at least as important in explaining sex differences as socialization, role, or biological differences. The necessary data are not available to prove this assertion, but we are going to examine the possible interaction of sex and organizational factors in two well-known studies in the field for questionable or incomplete interpretations resulting from failure to consider adequately the sex dimensions of organizational processes.

The studies to be analyzed are one of the earliest, (1) the Hawthorne studies, and a more recent example, (2) Crozier's study of two French bureaucracies. These particular studies were chosen because they are classics that have had considerable impact upon the field of complex organizations.

THE HAWTHORNE STUDIES

Textbooks still mention the Hawthorne studies and people still talk about the "Hawthorne effect," which refers to the positive reaction of research subjects resulting from their being selected out and treated as special and interesting in the course of a research project. Another finding of the Hawthorne studies, and one which led to many other studies of organizations, was that workers responded to friendly supervision and increased autonomy in the work situation with the development of group solidarity. In one small group in the factory, output increased. In another group, output was restricted. Commentators on the original research have not noted that the group with increased output was all female, and the group with restricted output was all male. Landsberger (1958) in his lengthy defense of the Hawthorne studies did point out that many of the workers were unmarried women of immigrant background, but did not explore the implications of this fact. In order to explore the implications of that observation, we examined the original reports of the research (Roethlisberger and Dickson, 1939; Whitehead, 1938) to determine how the experimental treatment differed with the female group and the male group, and whether there was some relationship between the differential treatment and the effects of the sex power differential. The following discussion deals with only two of the studies, the First Relay Assembly Test Room and the Bank Wiring Room—the studies most extensively referred to and criticized in the literature.

The women in the Relay Assembly Test Room (five assemblers and one layout operator) were individually subjected to a great deal of contact with male supervisors and administrators (Whitehead, 1938: 109, 112–114), and there may have been some implicit pressure in these individual contacts. For example, the women subjects were individually and informally selected for the research[2] They were then interviewed (Whitehead, 1938: 26, 103–104; Roethlisberger and Dickson, 1939: 32) by the plant superintendent to make sure that they really wanted to participate. Four of them were either 19 or 20; the two others were slightly older. All except one were living at home with their parents in first-generation Polish, Italian, Norwegian, and Czechoslovakian families (Roethlisberger and Dickson, 1939: 23; Whitehead, 1938: 16–17). These young, unmarried women from traditional families were brought in by the bosses and asked if they wanted to participate; it is not surprising that they all agreed.[3]

The point is not simply that these female workers probably had been socialized to obey males in positions of authority but that the sex power hierarchy in the home and in the factory were congruent; and when there is such a congruence sex power differentials outside the organization act as a power multiplier, enhancing the authority of male superiors in the work place. When there are no alternative experiences with different distributions of male and female influence and power, there is little experiential basis for questioning the legitimacy of the existing status hierarchy. Thus, at a social psychological level, we would expect greater acceptance of a given system of authority relationships if there is consistency in these relationships across the main institutional areas in which men and women interact.

There may also have been a power multiplier effect in the economically disadvantaged position of the women. We suggest that an economically dependent position in one domain reinforces powerlessness in other areas of life. At least four of these young women lived at home and gave their wages to their parents, who then gave them a small allowance (Roethlisberger and Dickson, 1939: 44). Economically their position was similar to that of children; but, at the same time, their families probably desperately needed their added income. The family situation, then, did not provide a secure economic base from which they could challenge the authority of the male supervisors upon whom they were dependent for their jobs. Furthermore, the work place probably did not provide a base from which they could question parental-paternal authority; their wages were probably too low for them to establish independent lives, even if culturally and psychologically this presented itself as a possiblity.

In spite of the effects of socialization and the power multiplier, some of the women in the Relay Assembly Test Room were not compliant or cooperative. In response to this, both researchers and management made strenuous efforts at control. Some elements of direct coercion are implied in the published reports of the research (Whitehead, 1938: 111–112). Carey (1967) documents this well. For example, the operatives were told to "work like you feel," "don't make a race out of it," (Whitehead, 1938: 26); "The group were assured that the test was not being set up to determine the maximum output ..." (Roethlisberger and Dickson, 1939: 33). However, as soon as the experimental period began, if they did not work hard, or if they slowed down, they were reprimanded and told to work faster. Two of the women objected, and kept saying, "We thought you wanted us to work as we feel," (Roethlisberger and Dickson, 1939: 53). In addition, they talked and laughed a lot on the job. They were frequently admonished about this (Whitehead, 1938: 116; Roethlisberger and Dickson, 1939: 53–55), and the chief offender "was told of her offenses" (Roethlisberger and Dickson, 1939: 55) by the test room authorities and later by the superintendent.

These two women also objected to being examined by a doctor every six weeks (Whitehead, 1938: 109, 114). The experimentors wanted to control for the effects of physiological changes on productivity, one of which was the periodic effect of menstruation. Their objections were, of course, very disruptive to the experiment, since data collection required the physical examination. This was another reason that the two women

who objected were viewed as destructive to the experiment and ring-
leaders of recalcitrant behavior. After about eight months the two
troublemakers were removed from the experiment and replaced by two
other women (Whitehead, 1938: 116 – 119).

The events following the replacement of the uncooperative women
seem to indicate manipulation by the researchers of the leadership structure of the group through the granting of special economic rewards. One
of the women replacements was providing for her whole family; her sister
had died, her father was temporarily unemployed, and she was desperate
for work. Soon after she entered the test room, her mother also died
(Roethlisberger and Dickson, 1939: 62, 171 – 172; Whitehead, 1938: 120 –
122), and she was given a special loan by management because of her
financial difficulties. She was also an ambitious woman who saw in the
assignment to the Test Room an opportunity for advancement (Whitehead, 1938: 120, 123, 158). She worked very diligently and was furious with
the other women if they did not do so also. At the same time that the two
new operators were brought into the experiment, "the daily hours of
work were shortened by half an hour but it was decided to *pay the operators the day rate for the half hour of working time lost"* (Carey, 1967: 309,
his emphasis; Whitehead, 1938: 121). A little later, further reductions in
work time were made, and again the women were paid for the time not
worked. The woman who had been given the loan became a leader of the
group, and group productivity increased. The interpretation by the researchers was that a very strong leader emerged from the group process.
Rather, what seems to have happened is that management inadvertently
found a strong leader, put her into the test room, and reinforced her leadership potential with special rewards not only to her, but to the entire
group.

There are also hints in the published reports of paternalistic attitudes and manipulation. The paternalistic attitudes of researchers and
managers is best documented by the repeated use of the term "girls"
throughout the texts of both Roethlisberger and Dickson (1939) and
Whitehead (1938) and throughout the excerpts from the research logs
published in both books. Examples of paternalistic manipulation are also
frequent. Participation by the workers in decisions about the research
was encouraged, while the real power was always retained by the male
researchers and supervisors. Although the women were asked for suggestions and comments throughout the experiment (Landsberger, 1958: 9),
some comments were incorporated in the research procedures, but some
of the more strenuous objections, such as the opposition to the physical
examinations, were not. Even on relatively minor issues, the unanimous
opinion of the subjects was not followed if the researchers did not agree.
Also, in a situation of great power differentials, efforts by those with
power to maintain a friendly atmosphere or to get comments or sugges-

tions can be seductively coopting. For example, the male observer stationed in the room had as one of his tasks to "create and maintain a friendly atmosphere in the test room" (Roethlisberger and Dickson, 1947: 22). To reduce objections to the physical examinations, the women were treated to a party with ice cream and cake after each physical (Whitehead, 1938: 109, 114). These parties were attended by the male doctors, researchers, and supervisors. Finally, on repeated occasions during the study, the "girls" were called into the superintendent's office to discuss changes in the study (for instance, Whitehead, 1938: 112). It is possible that such special and unusual contacts with high status and authoritative figures may not only have been coercive, but may also have had a particular reward value.

In summary, it appears that the cumulative effect of coercion, paternalistic treatment, and special rewards resulted in a rise in productivity.

In contrast to the female group, the members of the male group in the Bank Wiring Room (Roethlisberger and Dickson, 1939: chapt. 17), the group which restricted its production, were not selected and interviewed individually; only the group as a whole was under pressure to participate in the research (Roethlisberger and Dickson, 1939: 397, 398). That is, a preexisting work group was designated as a research group and "nothing was to be said or done in selecting the group to be studied, in explaining the study to them, or in removing them from the department which might alter their status in any way" (Roethlisberger and Dickson, 1939: 388). In addition, methods of observation which might make the workers apprehensive were avoided and "the observer was stationed with the group in the role of a disinterested spectator" (Roethlisberger and Dickson, 1939: 388). Types of worker activity which were viewed as disruptive to the experiment in the Relay Assembly Test Room were seen as only data to be observed in the Bank Wiring Room. No one was replaced during the course of the research, and no one was reprimanded even though there was slowing down, laughing, and talking.

Group norms relating to productivity did develop in both work groups, but they developed in relationship to the external environment of each group and the external demands in regard to increasing production were different for the two groups.[4] Furthermore, the immediate external environment was controlled by males in both experiments. But male control constitutes a different kind of external environment for a female group than for a male group because the effect of the sex-based hierarchy of the larger society is added to the structuring of control in the organization. For the women's group, the relationship was between powerful males and weak females; that is, the females, being weak, had to please the supervisors if they wished to stay in the test room, so they adopted the norm of increased production. Their attempts at developing some self-protection resulted in reprimands and eventually exclusion; compliance led to special rewards.

Since the research treatment was very different for the males and for the females, there still remains the question of whether the group of males would have responded similarly to the same combination of rewards and punishments. Of course, we do not know. However, having refined their hypotheses and their methodology, the investigators chose a group of males as subjects for further investigation. It is obvious that the researchers were not aware of the possible effects of the sex of their subjects on the outcome of the Relay Assembly Test Room experiment. They also seem to have taken no notice of the possible effects of variation in research procedures and the interaction of those variations with the sex of the subjects.

It is clear from our reexamination of the Hawthorne Studies, that the experimenters' treatment of the men in the Bank Wiring Room was very different from their treatment of the women in the Relay Assembly Test Room. The women were carefully recruited and closely supervised, and in numerous subtle ways were told that their productivity should rise. This is an amplification of Carey's analysis which has already pointed to the coercive elements in the research procedures in the Relay Assembly Test Room. The men, on the other hand, were recruited as a group and were allowed considerable autonomy in developing their own production norms. We argue that these differences in experimental treatment account to a considerable extent for the increase in productivity of the women's group and the restricted productivity of the men's group. Furthermore, we contend that the differences in treatment are at least partially attributable to the sex differences of the two groups. This reexamination of the Hawthorne researches suggests organizational processes related to sex based power differentials which may be found in other organizational settings.

CROZIER'S STUDIES

In 1964, Michel Crozier reported on his studies in the preceding decade of two French bureaucracies, which employed a large number of women: the Clerical Agency employed 4500 persons, most of them women;[5] and the Industrial Monopoly had women in two-thirds of its production jobs. At only one point (which we will identify later) does Crozier comment at all extensively about these facts of organizational life, and there he essentially argues that those facts are relatively insignificant. His neglect of the sex of employees is important in itself, but it gains in importance when one notes that there is considerable occupational segregation by sex within the organizations. We will discuss that occupational recruitment by sex, but also draw attention to portions of Crozier's data that refer to differential socialization histories as well as differential control patterns of women.

In the Clerical Agency located in Paris, although the majority of nonsupervisory employees were women,[6] most of the supervisors were men, most of the supervisors' bosses were men, and most of the union representatives were men. Women held jobs as strawbosses but these were not supervisor's jobs. Of the few men in nonsupervisory positions, all worked in auxiliary services, mail rooms, printing shops and maintenance work. Quotations suggest that this occupational and status segregation by sex was important and contributed to antagonism; for example, one woman commented: "Supervisors have no skill in human relations. They do not know how to deal with women" (Crozier, 1964: 42). Another woman complained about union representation: "But we are defended by men who do not understand the situation of women workers very well and are not able to talk the language of the average girl" (Crozier, 1964: 42). Crozier largely ignored the possible female-male basis of conflict and argued that the antagonisms were a function of a bureaucratic system that began with centralization and impersonality and developed a vicious circle which was dysfunctional for organizational effectiveness. He did not point out that sex differences may exacerbate the effects of the bureaucratic system and account for a substantial portion of the antagonisms.

The backgrounds of many of these women resembled those of the women in the Hawthorne studies. Most of them were "daughters of farmers, rural shopkeepers and craftsmen" (Crozier, 1964: 16). Crozier contrasted these women with rural backgrounds with the few with more urban backgrounds: "Parisian girls with the required schooling now very rarely accept the salaries and terms of employment of the lower grades of the civil service. Only girls who come from underdeveloped areas with few employment opportunities will accept them" (Crozier, 1964: 16–17). It isn't clear what Crozier means by the "terms of employment," though they might include the traditionally submissive role of women. Some support can be found for that in Crozier's discussion of the male supervisors who have been with the Agency for some time and who came from the same rural backgrounds as the women: "Twenty and thirty years ago, the southwest was sending its boys to Civil Service jobs in Paris. Now when its girls seem independent and are looking for employment, they in turn are going; *but the old network of relationships has not, in fact, changed very much*" (Crozier, 1964: 17, emphasis added). Crozier ends a section with that sentence and it isn't at all clear what he is referring to by the "old network of relationships." We suggest that he may be referring to traditional authority relationships between men and women that are more characteristic of rural families. The Clerical Agency then, exhibits a high degree of occupational and status segregation by sex, which appears overladen with traditional power relations between the sexes.

Besides recruitment and socialization differences by sex, there was some evidence of coercive control patterns. Crozier described a harsh discipline imposed by managers of the agency:

> It is sufficient to hold in check a woman employee whose feelings are easily manipulated by threats of public humiliation, such as official reprimands and insertions of criticism in the personal files. No kind of absenteeism is tolerated; mistakes are traced to the girls administratively responsible for them, and written excuses are demanded from each of them (1964: 20).

There were some male nonsupervisory personnel and these control patterns may have been used on them as well, but there was no mention of that, and Crozier referred specifically to women employees. Some of the controls were reminiscent of the treatment of children. For example, one woman commented about one of the managers: "I never saw him and I like it better that way, since one sees him only to get a scolding" (Crozier, 1964: 44). Whether or not the control tactics seem more appropriate to children or adults, they are still clearly harsh and the question remains whether male employees would have long endured them. Again, the impression is of a male group constituting the external, governing group for a female one and the controls being sex-based.

The bureaucratic system Crozier described certainly contributed to the antagonism and frustration characteristic of the Clerical Agency, but much of the conflict pattern may have been based on the oppression of women. The sex differences would at least seem to have amplified the effects of the bureaucratic system, or vice versa. And both patterns may have been a function of the French culture. Crozier suggests that the bureaucratic pattern is a reflection of that culture. We suggest that the sex power revealed in the organization may also be a part of the French culture, although certainly not restricted to it.

In the study of the Industrial Monopoly, Crozier argued that uncertainty in organizations cannot be eliminated, yet the achievement of organizational goals requires some degree of certainty; consequently, those individuals and groups who control important uncertainties have a basis for power in the organization. Principally because the Industrial Monopoly faced no competition from other organizations, the major uncertainty for it was at the production level. But production was highly routinized, and had few uncertainties. The principal uncertainty was around machine breakdown, and that uncertainty was the basis of considerable power for the men who maintained the machines. We suggest, however, that sex differences amplified their organizationally derived power.

The major disruption of the production work was machine stoppage. Production workers were "held personally responsible for all stoppages of less than one hour and a half and must compensate for the loss of production; if the stoppage is longer, they will be displaced or may be sent around to do menial jobs if there is no possibility of bumping less senior workers" (Crozier 1964: 109). Only maintenance personnel were allowed to cope with machine stoppage. The maintenance personnel were all men and the production workers were almost all women. Crozier (1964: 97) stated:

> Production workers, mostly women, behave as if they were dependent on the maintenance men and resentful of it. The sex difference, of course, is probably an important element in shaping the situation. But this influence should not be exaggerated. No comments were ever made about it, and there is a complete lack of differentiation between men servants and women product receivers.

This is the only point at which Crozier acknowledged that sex differences shape the work situation, but he was quick to deemphasize that factor. The fact that no comments were made about the sex differences is not altogether surprising. His second justification may be more convincing. If sex differences were operative in the general work situation, one would expect differences in resentments of women and men in the more auxiliary production roles, the men servants and the women product receivers. But, there were no differences in expressed complaints between men and women in these auxiliary roles, and both men and women in these roles made more complaints than the women machine operators. The problem is to explain the differences in open resentment in two groups of women. The women product receivers may have been a deviant group, who selected themselves out of work positions which had for them, excessive constraints against complaints. The product receiver job acted as a sort of safety valve for those women who could not tolerate the degree of dependence demanded in the machine operator's work. If a machine operator found her work intolerable, she could transfer to the product receiver job and many did, even though the pay was somewhat less. Women who remained as machine operators might be expected to be more compliant and submissive. Thus there seem to have been organizational mechanisms for accommodating contradictions between the demands of work positions and the personality orientations of particular workers.

The monopoly the maintenance men had over machine repairs was defended up the organizational hierarchy. For example, a new foreman did not accept a maintenance man's judgment that a particular machine breakdown was serious. He attempted to fix the machine himself, and found that the breakdown was not serious and was due to poor maintenance. Furious. he complained to three different superordinates, including the director of the organization, and received no satisfaction other than some sympathetic murmurs (Crozier, 1964: 127). That case testifies to the power of the maintenance men within that organization, but it is not altogether clear whether that power is solely based on the organizational uncertainties that they controlled, or partly on the fact that women were in the dependent role and controlled by men.

In his discussion of power and uncertainty, Crozier (1964: 156) noted: "Each group fights to preserve and enlarge the area upon which it has some discretion." One might add that they also struggle to manage the impressions other have of how large that area is; that is, groups struggle to control the objective bases of their power, but also others' perception of that area of uncertainty and therefore others' perception of their power. The maintenance men's ability to manage others perception of their power may have been enhanced by the presence of women rather than men as machine operators. As long as women are mechanically less competent than men or at least most persons believe they are less competent, the maintenance men have fewer problems managing others' perception of their power. Crozier (1964: 77) himself said that women are significantly more hostile to mechanization. In addition, quotations from the maintenance men showed that they believed women were not mechanically inclined or competent. "Workers do not care about technical problems. Workers do not understand anything beyond the narrow requirements of their own job" (Crozier, 1964: 97). The accuracy of these judgments is really irrelevant, for they need only to be believed to have important consequences. As long as the machine operators were felt to be too incompetent to understand let alone to repair machine breakdowns, maintenance men could maintain their position of power. Any complaints the women might have raised about maintenance men's judgment and performance would be discredited by male superiors. Male machine operators might challenge the seriousness of machine breakdowns, as the new foreman did, making the foreman's complaints credible. The degree of dependence may not, then, be due just to the character of the technology.

The dependency also tended to be personal. One maintenance man was responsible for the machines of three to six women machine operators; that is, women machine operators had continually to deal with the same maintenance man, who came to talk of "their machine operators." Also, maintenance men were allowed to intervene regularly in the work of "their machine operators," apparently because they thought their operators "rather careless" (Crozier, 1964: 97). And although they realized that the machine operators did not usually take their advice, about half of them continued to give their advice quite often (Crozier, 1964: 97). The picture one gets is of each woman machine operator being subjected to fairly close control by a single maintenance man.

We would agree with Crozier that machine breakdown was a critical uncertainty for the Industrial Monopoly, but the degree and character of dependence experienced by the machine operators seems to have been shaped significantly by sex differences. If the machine operators had been men, the dependency might have remained but might have been weakened considerably. Crozier is essentially correct, then, in stating that technology creates a dependency relation. However, the severity of the relation in this case was aggravated by the differential recruitment of women as machine operators. It may even be that the technology created a relationship of such dependency that only women could be recruited to such jobs and controlled in them.

The bureaucratic vicious circle, the influence of French culture, and the relations between objective organizational uncertainty and power remain as important variables in Crozier's analysis; but if our suggestions carry weight, Crozier's analysis is only a partial one. He neglected the impact of sex differences in socialization, occupational recruitment, and organizational control patterns.

CONCLUSION

Our reexamination of the Hawthorne studies and Crozier's work seems to support our contention that organizational structures and processes are influenced by sex. Specifically sex differences in organizational participation are related to (1) differential recruitment of women into jobs requiring dependence and passivity, (2) selective recruitment of particularly compliant women into these jobs, and (3) control mechanisms used in organizations for women, which reinforce control mechanisms to which they are subjected in other areas of the society.

These suggestions lead to specific research questions. For example, from the differential recruitment of women into jobs requiring dependence, one may expect that technologies, as well as occupations, are sex segregated, highly routinized technologies employing disproportionately women, and less routinized technologies such as craft and continuous process ones, mostly men. A related question would be whether women are disproportionately recruited to highly routinized jobs where machines largely control the work, which might be a better explanation of the frequent assumption that women are more antagonistic to mechanization, than early socialization.

It is not possible to suggest all the dimensions on which control mechanisms might vary with sex. Control mechanisms for women may more often resemble those used with children, as indicated by both studies analyzed in this paper. Also, in these studies, adult women were frequently referred to as girls. The use of this word shaped the construction of reality for both the men and the women, and allowed for control. Also, organizational rewards offered women may be often products or services stereotypically thought to be preferred by women, while rewards offered men are not so sex-linked. For example, women may be frequently rewarded with such things as flowers, trinkets, and so forth.[7] Women may be subjected to more personalized control arrangements than men. Men may usually face impersonal rules and regulations that are fairly universalistic for men occupying similar positions, while women may more often be required to adjust to rules that are particular to their relationship with a male supervisor.

Converse to sex-differentiated controls are possibilities of sex-differentiated power strategies. The power strategies which are available to participants in organizations are certainly shaped by the nature of the structure. But, it may also be true that individuals are differentially socialized to the appropriateness of different power strategies, and/or are differentially penalized for using different power strategies. Those differences may fall along sex lines. For example, women may be frequently proscribed from forming coalitions as a power strategy. The proscription may be communicated through primary socialization, or severe penalties may be imposed upon women if they try that strategy as organizational members. Similarly, women may be constrained more from complaining particularly about specific male coworkers or supervisors, and again this constraint may be internalized in early socialization or may be differentially penalized in organizations.

If women do experience different controls than men, those controls may be particularly effective if they are consonant with controls women experience outside of organizations as indicated in our analysis. For example, we expect that women who come from fairly traditional families with patriarchial arrangements would experience as employees the power multiplier and probably respond with greater conformity than women from less traditional families. If power distributions in organizations multiply larger patterns of power by sex, perhaps organizations with more sex segregated occupations are more hierarchical.[8] Also, in sex segregated occupations involving both men and women, one might expect that the sex power differential would be greater between male groups controlling female groups, than male groups controlling male groups, or female ones with female subordinate groups, or any power arrangements involving integrated groups.

We tentatively suggest, also, that organizations with occupational segregation by sex and embedded in traditional society contexts may exhibit less intergroup conflict. March and Simon (1958: 121) suggest a number of factors that may contribute to intergroup conflict. These factors may be dampened in organizations where males control female occupational groups. One factor, the need for joint decision making, may be felt less with such arrangements because the stereotyping of sex roles in the larger society would tend to imprint clearly separated domains for decision making. Conflict between the maintenance men and the production workers is a case in point. Women production workers did not challenge the decisions of the maintenance men; if the production workers had been men, there might have been more conflict. Consonant sex power hierarchies would tend generally to clarify goals and perceptions of reality, two other factors March and Simon referred to as possible sources of intergroup conflict. However, these relationships could be expected only where occupational sex segregation and power differentials correspond to patterns in the larger society and which continue to be viewed as legitimate by both men and women. Occupational segregation by sex may increase intergroup conflict where women have begun to question such arrangements. The segregation by sex would facilitate the sharing of such questionings, and provide greater opportunities to organize within the group to combat the power arrangements.

It may be that sex power differentials have a more profound effect in some cases than the organizational variables. In any case, sex power differentials can at least be used together with organizational factors to develop a more thorough explanation of variation in organizational phenomena.

NOTES

[1] Mechanic (1962) in a very perceptive analysis of the sources of power of lower level participants in organizations, describes a number of mechanisms used for enhancing personal power. Some of these would seem to be used more often by women than men, although Mechanic does not point to this possible sex differentiation.

[2] It is not clear exactly how the women were selected. They seem to have had some part in the selection. The accounts of Roethlisberger and Dickson (1939) and that of Whitehead (1938) differ on this point.

[3] Carey (1967), in a critique of the Relay Assembly Test Room research, discussed in much greater detail many of the problems with the research, but did not take account of the sex hierarchy variable.

[4] Economic conditions were also different for the female and male groups. The Relay Assembly Test Room studies began in 1927 before the Depression and continued into 1932, the Bank Wiring Room experiment took place during the bottom of the Depression, 1932. This undoubtedly was a factor in the differences in group behaviors. Landsberger (1958) gave a detailed discussion of this problem.

[5] Crozier does not provide the exact proportion of men and women.

[6] Again, Crozier does not provide the specific figures.

[7] Elinor Langer gives some excellent examples of gifts received by women in the New York Telephone Company (1970: 16, 17).

[8] Marrett (1972) examines the evidence for and against the hypothesis that female predominance in organizations encourages centralization. She concludes that the question cannot be resolved with the data presently available.

REFERENCES

Blauner, Robert, *Alienation and Freedom.* Chicago: The University of Chicago Press, 1964.

Caplow, Theodore, *The Sociology of Work.* New York: McGraw-Hill, 1954.

Carey, Alex, "The Hawthorne Studies: a Radical Criticism," *American Sociological Review* 32 (1967), pp. 403–16.

Crozier, Michel, *The Bureaucratic Phenomenon.* Chicago: University of Chicago, 1964.

Epstein, Cynthia, *Woman's Place.* Berkeley: University of California Press, 1970.

Etzioni, Amitai, *The Semi-Professions and Their Organizations.* New York: The Free Press, 1969.

Furstenburg, Friedrich, "Structural Changes in the Working Class: A Situational Study of Workers in the Western German Chemical Industry," in John A. Jackson (ed.), *Social Stratification,* pp. 145–74. London: Cambridge University Press, 1968.

Goldthorpe, John, David Lockwood, Frank Bechhofer, and Jennifer Platt, *The Affluent Worker: Industrial Attitudes and Behavior.* London: Cambridge University Press, 1968.

Gross, Edward, "Plus ca Change …? The Sexual Structure of Occupations over Time," *Social Problems,* 16, pp. 198–208.

Landsberger, Henry A., *Hawthorne Revisited.* Ithaca, New York: Cornell University, 1958.

Langer, Elinor, "The Women of the Telephone Company," *The New York Review of Books* 14 (1970), pp. 14–22.

March, James G., and Herbert A. Simon, *Organizations.* New York: Wiley, 1958.

Marrett, Cora Bagley, "Centralization in Female Organizations: Reassessing the Evidence," *Social Problems* 19 (1972), pp. 348–57.

Mechanic, David, "Sources of Power and Lower Participants in Complex Organizations." *Administrative Science Quarterly* 7 (1962), pp. 349–64.

Oppenheimer, Valerie, *The Female Labor Force in the U.S.* Berkeley: Population Monograph Series, No. 5. University of California, 1970.

Roethlisberger, F. J., and William J. Dickson, *Management and the Worker.* Cambridge, Mass.: Harvard University, 1939.

Tudor, Bill, "A Specification of Relationships between Job Complexity and Powerlessness." *American Sociological Review* 37 (1972), pp. 596–604.

Whitehead, T. North, *The Industrial Worker,* Vol. 1, London: Oxford University, 1938.

Whyte, William Foote, "The Social Structure of the Restaurant." *American Journal of Sociology,* 54 (1949), pp. 302–10.

DISCUSSION QUESTIONS

1. Would the all-female group react today by increasing productivity as they did in the '30s? Explain your answer.

2. How are male and female work groups treated differently today?

3. Is there still occupational segregation by sex within organizations today? What are some examples?

4. Do you know of any work situations today where women are treated like children?

5. How do men hold power today by having been both allowed and encouraged to become mechanically and technically proficient?

6. What sex-linked rewards do women and men receive today? What kinds of rewards would be more valuable?

7. What organization controls do women experience today that are reinforced by their experiences outside the organization?

"The average male spends one-month per year attending in-service training on company time. Women's participation has been less than a day per year."

Janice A. Kay, "What Do I Want to Do Next?" in *Affirmative Action for Women,* eds. Dorothy Jongeward and Dru Scott (Reading, Mass.: Addison-Wesley Publishing Co., 1974), p. 256.

Women
and the Informal
Organization

Donald W. Zacharias

One way to describe the informal organization is to characterize it as the network of people who exchange information over coffee, lunch, or at informal social clusterings for the purpose of stating their beliefs and aspirations. It is the network over which trusted associates, regardless of their organizational status, say to each other what they would like to say to their superiors, and give each other lists of convincing reasons why the people around them are erring. Myths and survival strategies are shared freely by people on the network. The emphasis throughout this undiagrammed system is upon interpersonal relationships, oral communication, and the sharing of "soft," timely information. Anyone may demand and receive a job in an organization; no one can demand to be included, informed, or respected by the informal organization.

When employees enter a new organization, they quickly learn how to relate to the work norms, social attitudes, and informal leaders. Women, especially those entering professions and positions traditionally held by men, are likely to find the informal organization their greatest challenge. Before examining some of the special obstacles and possible ways of handling them, a brief discussion of some principles of organizational communication might be helpful. Jay M. Jackson (1969) reached three major conclusions in his study of communication patterns within organizations. First, he found that people who are pursuing their work goals feel more constrained to communicate with those who will help them achieve their aims, and less interested in communicating with those who will not assist or may even retard their accomplishment. Henry Mintzberg (1973) in his study of the manager's job reports a similar

Donald W. Zacharias, "Women and the Informal Organization," in Meg Gerrard, June Oliver, and Martha Williams (eds.), *Women in Management Proceedings of the Conference, Women and Men—Colleagues in Management?* Austin, Texas: Center for Social Work Research, The University of Texas at Austin (1976).

finding: That people want to speak to higher status rather than lower status persons. For women who are still in the process of breaking organizational barriers this principle is likely to be troublesome because, unfortunately, they usually find themselves in the positions with less status.

Second, Jackson found similar forces at work causing people to direct their communication toward anyone who can make them feel more secure and gratify their need for reinforcement and away from anyone who threatens them, or makes them feel anxious. If men in the work situation feel threatened by a woman in the organization, there is little reason to expect that she will be invited quickly into the informal organization.

Third, Jackson reported that members of an organization always communicate as if they were trying to improve their positions. People communicate to increase their status, belong to more prestigious groups, obtain power to influence decisions, and expand their authority. Though this is information that women in organizations should know, it is not likely to make their chances of becoming a part of the informal organization any easier. In brief, it is fair to say that communication flows best along status and friendship channels within the informal organization.

What can women do to improve their position within the informal organization, assuming that success is related to success in the formal organization? No one can provide ten easy steps to a successful career, but one list of informative guidelines appeared in the appendix to Robert Townsend's *Up the Organization* (1970). In his section "Guerrilla Guide for Working Women" he recommends that women make every decision in the light of this question: "How would I do this job if I owned the company?" Furthermore, he argues that all organizations are 50 percent waste — waste people, waste effort, waste space, and waste time. "When asked," he says, "strike a blow against nonsense — no matter how entrenched and popular it may be."

Townsend is probably too flippant to be helpful. The advice of Marion M. Woods (1975) is more useful. From her interview with nearly one hundred women in the Los Angeles area, holding positions ranging from management trainee to president of the company, she has identified ten characteristics that a woman needs to learn if she wants to succeed in management. They are: competence, education, realism, aggressiveness, self-confidence, career-mindedness, femininity, strategy, support of an influential male, and uniqueness. "A woman needs a set of goals and a plan," she reports, "and, according to most of the women interviewed, women would do well to use men as their model for these techniques." One of the strategies men use regularly is bargaining. Dr. Wood's observations on this issue are direct: "Traditionally, women have not been trained to bargain. Most have not learned that a salary offered is not a constant, but a starting point for discussion." She concludes that men will continue considering women "cheap help" as long as women continue to accept lower offers than they are worth.

Bargaining and negotiation are worth studying even if you do not plan a career in business. Chester L. Karrass (1970) reports the major findings from an experiment using one hundred and twenty professional negotiators, all men. First, he found that skilled negotiators were very successful when they had high aspirations. Second, he discovered that successful negotiators make high initial demands, avoid making first concessions, concede slowly, and avoid making as many large concessions as their opponents. This study, of course, was an experiment and has to be applied with some caution to real situations. Its greatest limitation is the lack of information about how women should perform in negotiating situations.

That is what some of the experts say about succeeding in the informal organization. To assist in the preparation of this report, I asked some of my former graduate students who are now employed in business and education for their observations on how to handle problems in the informal structure. Keep in mind that these are recommendations from women who are having successful careers.

> Convince your young colleagues that you are serious about a career and sell yourself as a professional.
>
> Convince your older colleagues that you are competent.
>
> Sort out the important issues from the trivial ones early in your new job. Be aggressive about important issues, not trivial ones.
>
> Your male colleagues also have a right to feel comfortable about the way you wish to be treated. Talk over different perceptions of behavior when they occur.
>
> If you are a manager, remember to spend time establishing the ground rules for the working relationship with your secretary. Don't use your male counterpart as a model.
>
> Respect the rights of all women, especially the rights of those who are married to your male colleagues.
>
> Look for ways to help women inside and outside your organization. Women are now employed as professional movers; request an all-woman crew the next time you move.
>
> If you are married, convince your employer that you are still mobile because your husband is committed to your career goals.
>
> Look for successful women in your organization and use them as potential models for your career.
>
> Use informal communication channels to establish trust and friendship with influential men in the organization.

These are observations by women in key positions. There may be disagreement on some of them. On one point, however, most observers agree: Women must have clearly defined career goals and use a specific strategy to achieve them. The informal organization is an appropriate place to test these goals and develop a strategy for being included, respected and promoted.

REFERENCES

Jackson, M. J., "The Organization and its Communications Problem," in Norman B. Sigband (ed.), *Communications for Management.* Glenview, Ill.: Scott, Foresman, 1969.

Karrass, C. L., *The Negotiating Game.* New York: Thomas Y. Crowell, 1970.

Mintzberg, H., *The Nature of Managerial Work.* New York: Harper and Row, 1973.

Townsend, R., *Up the Organization.* Greenwich, Conn.: Fawcett Publications, 1970.

Woods, M. M., "What Does it Take for a Woman to Make it in Management?" *Personnel Journal* 54 (1975), pp. 38 – 41.

DISCUSSION QUESTIONS

1. List examples you have seen of the "informal organization" at work, school, or in organizations you belong to.

2. Use the examples in your list from question 1 to show how women can be hindered by the existence of the "informal organization."

3. Should women change to fit the organization's expectations? If so, how?

Informal
Interaction Patterns
of Professional Women

Sandy Albrecht

The focus of this study is the professional woman and her participation in the informal interaction patterns within the organizational setting. The available literature on the professional woman suggests that women do not benefit from informal interaction to the same degree as do their male colleagues; men get together for luncheons, coffees, sports, informal conversations, and so forth, while the professional woman is often left out of such activities. White (1972) under the heading, "Are women in the club?", cites a study of the woman PhD and her exclusion from the informal interaction network:

> ... the problem which bothers the woman PhD, who is a full-time contributor to her profession, is that she is denied many of the informal signs of belonging and recognition. These women report that even on such daily activities as finding someone with whom she can chew over an idea, or on larger issues such as finding a partner with whom she can share a research interest, the woman PhD has a special and lower status. (p. 303)

Similar responses by professional women in the BBC (Fogarty, 1971) reflect this feeling of being excluded from the social network. The women interviewed expressed the difficulty that they had had in breaking into the formal communication areas, such as the all-male meetings, but felt that it was even more difficult to gain acceptance into the informal network.

The picture that evolves is one of exclusion of women from the informal interaction network of the organization. H. M. Hacker (1951) applied minority group sociology to the study of women, and refers to the fact

Sandy Albrecht, "Informal Interaction Patterns of Professional Women," in Meg Gerrard, June Oliver, and Martha Williams (eds), *Women in Management Proceedings of the Conference, Women and Men—Colleagues in Management?* Austin, Texas: Center for Social Work Research, The University of Texas at Austin (1976).

that men, as the dominant group within the work situation, may want to establish some "social distance" between themselves and the women in the professional setting. Tiger (1971) suggests that men have a natural proclivity to band together in groups. Whether or not this is the case, these descriptions suggest that men and women do not interact on an informal basis within the organizational setting.

The interesting finding, however, is that this exclusion of women is not attributable only to males excluding females, but also is a product of self-exclusion. Epstein (1970a) found that women lawyers avoided joining colleagues in informal situations; the more informal the situation, the more they accepted the "rightness" of their exclusion. An example comes from a woman lawyer:

> Sometimes when the natural thing to do would be to join an associate and a client at lunch if you were a man, you feel, well, maybe I'd better not. It might be awkward for them. They might want to talk about something and might feel constrained. (p. 976)

Similarly, Bernard (1964) in a study of laboratory bioscientists, found that women, who comprised 68 of the 673 bioscientists, were less often sought out for informal communication by their male colleagues, and also, women were less apt to seek out their colleagues for informal communications. The pattern that develops, then, is one of segregated informal interaction patterns; both men and women seem to accept as "given" this exclusive nature of interaction and act within this structure.

This suggests the existence of what Peter Blau (1960) referred to as "structural effects." In a study of a public assistance agency, he hypothesized that the values of the group impose constraints on the individual and his values. Blau suggests that an individual, regardless of his own disposition, is more apt to discriminate against minorities if his community holds authoritarian values than if they hold nonauthoritarian values. In his research, he found that members of a group that held pro-client values as a group were more service-oriented than members of groups which held other values, regardless of their individual values. What can be described as the social climate of the group then, influences the behavior of the individuals within that group.

In an organizational setting, the structural effects of informal interaction patterns impose external constraints on the individual members. Because it is taken for granted that men and women do not get together for informal communications, this orientation creates structural barriers to professional women, preventing them from participating fully in the organization. In a sense, these segregated informal interaction patterns become the basis of institutionalized sexism. Because of a social climate characterized by segregated interaction networks, women are denied access to the channels of communication that could aid their mobility within that organization.

Campbell and Alexander (1965) propose that there is an intermediary step between the structural effects of an organization and the individual's behavior; that of the influence of *significant others*. It is the contact that a person has with significant others that influences attitude formation. Campbell and Alexander do not minimize the importance of the structural characteristics of the setting, for they accept that these effects create the "givens" in the situation. The structural factors will determine who will be defined as a significant other.

In the case of the professional woman, the structural characteristics of the organizational setting will determine the exposure she has to significant others. If she is excluded from the informal interaction network, then she will be limited in her contact with significant others.

Significant others have typically been defined as those persons who influence attitude formation. They are often defined in an affective fashion, based on the theory of interpersonal influence; one person influences another's attitudes because the two have an affective relationship to one another. Friends, parents, spouses are all usually considered significant others. The more information a person can supply, either by word or example, the more significant he becomes in influencing attitudes. It is equally plausible that the more information a person has about the situation, the more directly he can influence one's "life chances." The better person A is able to define the situation for person B, the better equipped B will be to perform within the given situation. Thus, the more contact B has with these significant others, such as A, defined in a structural sense, the better his performance will be.

It is to this formulation of structural significant others that this study is based. Members of an organization are considered structural significant others to the extent that they can directly affect a person's mobility within that organization. A member can be considered structurally significant in two ways. One, in his ability to act as a *situational definer*. That is, a person is considered a situational definer to the extent that he can provide relevant information about the situation and how he should act, and also to the extent that he can provide a model of behavior. Thus, the more contact one has with this information and model, the better equipped he will be to perform within the organization.

The second way a member can act as a structural significant other is as a *resource allocator*. Certain members of an organization, because of their position on the power hierarchy, are in control of various resources that affect ego's mobility. For example, recruitment, promotions, recommendations, and knowledge of the field can be considered as resources. Those members who have the ability to distribute these resources become significant to other members. The more contact a member has with these resource allocators, the better his chances of receiving these resources, which will aid his mobility.

Access to these *structural significant others*, then, becomes crucial to a person's mobility within the organization. He needs contact with both situational definers and resource allocators in order to perform well within the organization. It becomes problematical for professional women, however, because much of the contact, especially within the professions (Epstein, 1970b), is carried out in the one area where women have been most excluded — the informal channels of communication. What Bernard (1964) coined the "stag effect" seems to be operating; i.e., women's exclusion from informal communication results in limited participation within the system. That is, the nature of informal interaction patterns imposes structural barriers to women's access to significant others, which in turn retards their mobility within the organization.

The value of interaction networks as a channel of communication has been well documented. Studies of industrial organizations point to the role informal interaction plays in the structure and maintenance of an organization. Roy (1952, 1954) found that workers could restrict production through informal interactions and that an informally organized group had more control over production than management did.

A study done by Dalton (1951) on the selection patterns for managers also points to the importance of being part of the informal interaction network as a basis for promotion. He found that promotion was largely determined by such criteria as "ethnicity, religion, participation in specific out-plant social activities, political affiliation, and membership in accepted secret societies." In this sense, these members are acting as resource allocators and access to these members is through informal interactions.

Within the professions, there is a quite extensive use of situational definers, known as the protégé system or sponsorship pattern. Becker and Strauss (1956) note the importance of this channel of communication: "Until a newcomer has been accepted, he will not be taught crucial trade secrets." Older members, in informal communications with new members, pass on valuable information about the organization and how the new member should act to maximize his position. This interaction provides a basis of acquisition of knowledge about the situation, and equally important, provides a model for imitation for the new member. In a study comparing philosophers and physiologists, Becker and Carper (1956) found that the better the sponsorship pattern, the better an identification a member had with his profession.

Informal interaction between the new and old members of the organization is a valuable means of passing on information, and in this sense, old members then are significant in the definitional sense. But members are also put in contact with others who act as resource allocators. Everyday informal interactions put individuals in contact with a vital amount of knowledge about the field that might otherwise be missed. Sir Alfred Egerton has often been quoted as saying, "Of the total information extant, only part is in the literature. Much of it is stored in the many brains of scientists and technologists." (Epstein, 1970b) Through informal communication, members share this knowledge. Pelz (1967) found that high performers among the scientists he studied interacted often with their colleagues, both in interaction between a number of colleagues and the sheer volume of interactions. By informal communication, members discuss and refine ideas, and formulate new contributions to their fields; these communications provide "resources" to the individual in his production of research, papers, reports, and scientific findings.

Because of this importance of informal interaction as a means of connecting a member with structural significant others, women's exclusion from this network would have important consequences. Women would be denied access to those members who directly affect mobility, by possessing both the information and the resources of that organization. There are structural effects of informal interaction patterns that determine who is a significant other, and therefore who directly affects mobility. Because the professional woman is often excluded or excludes herself from the male informal interaction network, she does not have access to those significant others that would aid her mobility within the organization.

REFERENCES

Becker, H., and D. Carper, "The Development of Identification with an Occupation," *American Journal of Sociology* 61 (1956), pp. 289–98.

Becker, H., and A. Strauss, "Careers, Personality and Adult Socialization," *American Journal of Sociology* 62 (1956), pp. 253–63.

Bernard, J., *Academic Women.* University Park, Pa.: Pennsylvania State University Press, 1964.

Blau, P. M., "Structural Effects," *American Sociological Review* 25 (1960), pp. 178–93.

Campbell, E., and C. N. Alexander, "Structural Effects and Interpersonal Relationships," *American Journal of Sociology* 71 (1965), pp. 284–89. Reprinted in P. Lazarsfel, A. Pasanella and M. Rosenberg (eds.), *Continuities in the Language of Social Research.* New York: The Free Press, 1972.

Dalton, M., "Informal Factors in Career Achievement," *American Journal of Sociology* 56 (1951), pp. 407–15.

Epstein, C. F., "Encountering the Male Establishment: Sex-Status Limits on Women's Careers in the Professions," *American Journal of Sociology* 75 (1970a), pp. 965–82.

Epstein, C. F., *Woman's Place: Options and Limits in Professional Careers.* Berkeley: University of California Press, 1970(b).

Fogarty, M., A. J., Allen, I. Allen, and P. Walters, *Women in Top Jobs: Four Studies in Achievement.* London: George Allen & Unwin, Ltd., 1971.

Hacker, H. M., "Women as a Minority Group," *Social Forces* 30 (1951), pp. 60–69.

Pelz, D. C., "Creative Tensions in the Research and Development Climate," *Science* 157 (1967) pp. 160–65.

Roy, D., "Quota Restrictions and Goldbricking in a Machine Shop. *American Journal of Sociology* 57 (1952), pp. 427–43.

Roy, D., "Efficiency and 'The Fix'; Informal Intergroup Relations in a Piecework Machine Shop," *American Journal of Sociology* 60 (1954) pp. 255–66.

Tiger, L., "The possible Biological Origins of Sexual Discrimination," in C. F. Epstein and W. Goode, *The Other Half.* Englewood Cliffs, N.J.: Prentice-Hall, 1971.

White, M., "Psychological and Social Barriers to Women in Science," in C. Safilios-Rothschild (ed.), *Toward a Sociology of Women.* Lexington, Mass.: Xerox College Publishing Co., 1972.

DISCUSSION QUESTIONS

1. What are some ways that you would like to be included in the "informal organization" activities?

2. Who have you chosen as "significant others"? Why?

3. What organization barriers have you found barring your access to someone who might have been a "significant other" for you?

4. How have you observed the "informal organization" controlling production?

Women and Success
in Organizations

Martha Williams

The literature on women and success reflects a curious incongruity. On the one hand, there is plenty of evidence to suggest that women are less successful than men by any career measure you wish to choose. Although women represent approximately 40 percent of the labor force, they occupy only about four percent of the high-level managerial/administrative positions in modern organizations. Even in the traditionally feminine professions, such as social work and education, women do not occupy key decision-making jobs in proportion to their numbers. Women at the top are rare. In schools, women teach and men plan, organize, direct, and control. In social agencies, women who manage are usually middle managers supervising direct service workers, while the men plan programs, prepare budgets, and represent the agency in interorganizational activities. Women lawyers are concentrated in specialties which bring less pay and less status (Epstein, 1970). The same is true for female doctors (Vetter, 1975). When compared to their male colleagues in universities, women are more often lecturers and assistant professors than tenured professors. Certainly women are less often deans, departmental chairpersons, or presidents of universities and colleges. Money, which represents perhaps our most concrete measure of career attainment, is also differentially distributed; many studies verify that women are not receiving the income of their male counterparts (e.g., Williams, Ho, and Fielder, 1974; Perruci, 1970; Poston, 1972).

Yet, there are numerous studies of successful career women (defined typically as those who have received the highest degree in their professions) which indicate that these women are especially competent in just

Martha Williams, "Women and Success in Organizations," in Meg Gerrard, June Oliver, and Martha Williams (eds), *Women in Management Proceedings of the Conference, Women and Men—Colleagues in Management?* (Austin, Texas: Center for Social Work Research, The University of Texas at Austin (1976).

about every way. They are described as committed, independent, dominant, active, adventurous, sensitive, secure, and self-confident (e.g., Constantini and Craik, 1972; Helson, 1972; Cartwright, 1972). In reading the literature, one is struck with the unusually exceptional qualities of these women, regardless of their particular professional discipline.

Several hypotheses for explaining the uniqueness of highly educated women have been summarized by Almquist and Angrist (1970). One is the *enrichment hypothesis*, which holds that women who are successful have experienced enriched environments that have led to higher levels of personal adjustment and professional training and to greater motivation to succeed. Cartwright (1972) showed that women in medicine scored quite high on the achievement via independence scale of the California Personality Inventory (CPI). Over two-thirds of their fathers had at least a college degree and two-fifths had some professional training. The women are characterized by effective social and intellectual functioning, self acceptance, dominance, independence, and an "active" orientation. They came from stable families and often were first or second born or only children. Almquist and Angrist (1971) found that high achievement in career women is related to enriched family and college influences involving work-role models among parents, relatives, and teachers. Constantini and Craik (1972) found female politicians to have families of higher social class and more education than did male politicians. In personality, the women were found to be high on the ACL measures of self-confidence, dominance, and achievement (yet they also evidenced some doubt and concern about their place in society, and their push toward achievement was constrained by a sense of caution and propriety).

Rossi (cited in Almquist and Angrist, 1970) offers the *deviance hypothesis* to explain high career achievement in women. She argues that such achievement is related to a pattern of development different from that of other women. Successful women are likely to have begun dating later and dated less; they are less likely to marry, have children, value family roles, or spend time visiting relatives. These women are less likely to value working with people, to want to help others, or to try to please their parents.

The literature reflects a third explanation, the *idiosyncratic career path* hypothesis. This hypothesis relates the success of women to idiosyncratic factors not likely to be the norm for most women; such factors include husbands who are especially sensitive to their aspirations, protected work situations, and accidents or crises such as war. Surprisingly, the career paths of women who are highly successful are also often characterized by occupational drift, and a lack of long-range planning and career development. Many even drop out of careers after they have achieved a certain level of success and after their children are older.

In the study of women politicians by Constantini and Craik (1972), Werner is cited as finding that between 1917 and 1964 only 70 women had served in the U.S. Congress. Over half of these were either appointed or elected to fill a vacancy, often one caused by the death of a husband. The women typically had been active longer than their male colleagues in party affairs, had devoted themselves more to the work-a-day organizational burden of the political party, and had worked at the grass roots and local levels. These findings seem to lend equal support to all three of the above hypotheses.

Traditional women, on the other hand, are reported in the literature to suffer from several things, including the anti-success syndrome (Smith and Smith, 1970), the feminine mystique (Friedan, 1963), fear of success (Horner, 1972), and fear of failure (Hoffman, 1974). The anti-success syndrome includes four components:

1. *Fear of failure and lack of self-confidence.* Women are more apprehensive about performance, anxious about achievement, and fearful of failing grades. They are more discouraged by failure and more likely to downgrade their abilities.

2. *Dependence and need for social approval.* Adults are more attentive and affectionate toward female children, which may cause females to be more influenced by social pressure. Females also show greater concern with financial security, a greater preference for safe jobs with modest incomes, and more willingness to sacrifice their own success for a partner.

3. *Lack of aggression and competition.* Men are more active and aggressive. Women equate a good grade or a good job with hostile defeat of another person. Men work better in competition than alone, while women work better alone than in competition. Men compete more vigorously against women than against other men.

4. *Lack of achievement motivation.* The most capable students who *do not* go to college are women.

RETREAT FROM AMBITION

Other-directedness as a barrier to women's success seems supported by such studies as that of Constantini and Craik (1972). They report that men are more motivated to enter politics for self-serving reasons, whereas women are more often motivated by public service. The authors summarize as follows: "The female party leader, like the wife, tends to specialize in expressive functions or those concerned with the internal affairs of the system, and the maintenance of integrative relations between members and a supportive role of selfless service," (p. 35). A retreat from strong ambition is made in order to serve others. Betty Friedan's (1963) "feminine mystique" has been well publicized in the popular literature. She argues that women have equated sexual attractiveness with intellectual flightiness and personal dependency. Many women fear negative social consequences resulting from success. These add up to a parade of "terribles," including fears that successful women are masculine, socially isolated, rigid, and usually divorced or deserted by men, who look for more attractive partners (presumably more attractive because they devote themselves totally to the male ego).

The inconsistencies become apparent. The women who are successful in their careers are quite exceptional and enter the world of work from a strong educational base and with positive personal and social qualities, yet appear to falter somewhere along the way past college. They do not very often climb the executive ladder. They do not become the presidents of companies, colleges, or the country. They are not senators, nor often principals. They are not usually deans, directors, nor commissioners. They are not board chairmen, preachers, or newscasters on ABC, NBC, or CBS. Can we explain this curious phenomenon by such concepts as fear of success, the feminine mystique, or the anti-success syndrome? It is possible that these play a role in differentiating traditional women from nontraditional women, but these concepts seem not to account for the lack of advancement of highly trained and educated women in the professions. It is more likely, or at least equally likely, that women who graduate with advanced degrees immediately find themselves confronted with an organization that greets them with something between muted hostility and benign neglect. In other words, the organization is an equal opportunity employer for only about 24 hours after hiring, if then. The career woman is faced with many hurdles to overcome, including:

- Double standards of performance;
- Mentorism;
- Sex-typing of jobs;
- Misperceptions of the competence of women;
- Ambiguous reward (reinforcement) schedules;
- Informal social cliques;
- Attitudinal prejudice;
- Lack of career development counseling that is geared to women's needs;
- Inappropriately assigned tasks, and task expectations not commensurate with abilities;
- Less opportunity for advanced or in-service training;

- Lack of role models for women; and,
- Little consideration for the special problems of job-family role conflicts that many women face.

Epstein (1970a and 1970b) develops in more detail how many of these factors operate to exclude women from top jobs. Most are well known and are within the personal experience of many professional women. Two factors in the list are perhaps in need of additional clarification: *mentorism* and *task assignments*.

MENTORISM

Informal training is required for access to top jobs. Formal training is not enough. In most organizations and in the professions, people are selected to assume leadership roles via a complex protégé system. Not only technical knowledge is required for top positions, but also secret know-how. Special knowledges and skills are largely learned from an old pro, who must be observable as he practices his art. In all the professions, competence is created by exposing the new professional to the tasks, giving him the chance to learn from others and to avoid the pitfalls by coaching and by feedback. The inner circle must decide that a person is worth coaching, and then he must be exposed on a day-to-day basis to the tasks and situations that develop his abilities. (Epstein, 1970a).

The old pro seeks out the younger colleague just as much as the younger colleague seeks out the old pro. The two develop a positive relationship, a dyadic leader-follower, unwritten contract which has been very clearly conceptualized by Graen and Cashman (1975) in the context of administrative leadership. Several possibilities inherent in this type of relationship may pose special problems for women. First, women may simply not be chosen by the inner circle for special grooming. Men may not as easily recognize potential in women because it is of a different variety, or women may not be as vocal in advertising their worth. Women may wait to be sought out by mentors rather than actively seeking them out. However, some women do attach themselves to mentors. Then several other kinds of difficulties may arise. For example, the relationship may be more difficult to preserve as a strictly platonic one (sexual attachments may get involved). Even when the relationship is strictly formal, there may be more of a tendency for role-task specialization to occur, modeled somewhat after other male-female relationships, i.e., women may choose to perform, or may accept more readily, the supportive and maintenance functions in the mentor relationship.

Such a relationship can be very fruitful for both until it is time for the woman to advance to other things. At this point, the mentor may feel betrayed, and the woman guilty for putting her own interests above those of the mentor who has done for her what so many others have not done — accepted her as his protégée. Thus, she may tend to remain loyal rather than strike out on her own or may come to realize that she has not gained enough experience in the types of instrumental tasks (as opposed to maintenance tasks) needed for independent action. The result is that only the "king bee" gets the royal jelly in many organizational hives.

TASK ASSIGNMENTS

Task assignments present a second area for further scrutiny. Cecil, Paul, and Olins (1973) studied the nature of the qualifications expected of female and male applicants being considered for the same administrative position. In general, they concluded that when a women was being considered, those making judgments envisioned the job differently in terms of the kinds of qualifications deemed necessary. Women were seen as needing qualifications falling into the categories of personality/appearance and skills/education, whereas men were seen to need motivation/ability and interpersonal-relations skills. The inference was that men would be performing persuasive functions and making decisions requiring motivation, aggressiveness, and the ability to withstand pressure. Women, on the other hand, were seen as needing pleasant voices, immaculate dress and appearance, the ability to express themselves well, and excellent computational skills. The implication is that the same administrative job would be subtly defined differently for men than for women.

These findings are similar to those of Rosen and Jerdee (1974) who studied discrimination in assessment of applicants for routine versus demanding jobs (those requiring aggressive interpersonal behavior and decisive managerial action). Their study showed that there is much more discrimination against women when the job is seen as demanding and challenging. This leads to the hypothesis that women are channeled toward the routine, less challenging positions in an organization, even though they advance upward. In the long run, this may deny them the kind of experience and training they need for high-level positions which are almost always demanding. In other words, they have not been given early "boot camp" training. Therefore, they may either lack the self-confidence to take on tough assignments, or they will not have had the chance to prove themselves to their compatriots. Perhaps, more importantly, they may not have had the chance to practice leadership skills in middle level jobs. Obviously, women can move up along the ranks to a certain point assuming the more routine maintenance functions: Then, when it comes to a choice between a man and woman for a top-level job, the decision is made in favor of the one who has had more experience in withstanding the pressures and excelling in the tasks requiring initiative and aggressiveness. This occurs even though the male and female applicants are equivalent in education and tenure, and perhaps even have similar personalities.

Task assignments may affect women in other ways, too. Women may be assigned more haphazardly to spots which prevent the development of expertise. They may be used to fill gaps or take on unclear assignments that the men can see are dead-end in career terms, yet important in that someone must do them. Task interdependence, task clarity, and task feedback are important to success. Epstein (1970a) suggests that when these exist, women are more likely to move up in professional life. *Task interdependence* means simply assuming roles which require and reward interdependent activity with other professional partners. Such situations would lead to more exchange of information between role partners and more mutual support. *Task clarity* involves well-defined tasks where norms governing interactions are clear and division of labor and authority are not ambiguous. In such situations, women may be less likely to assume the maintenance functions and men the task functions. Finally, opportunities for *task feedback* must be available to women. This is, of course, less possible when the task is ill-defined or is not a traditional one within the organization. Furthermore, women may be assigned less measurable tasks to perform. On the other hand, mentors may be more reticent to give feedback to women, especially negative feedback, perhaps assuming that they can't take it and will react emotionally. It is also entirely conceivable that women will perform certain tasks differently than men; for example, women may bargain or negotiate differently, and although they may utilize strategies which are no less logical or worthy, they may be criticized simply because their style is different, the intrinsic assumption being that different equals wrong.

In sum, the area of task assignments may account for a large measure of the difficulties women encounter in developing their talents after graduation and, therefore, in moving up the organization ladder. For example, women may more readily assume, or may be more encouraged to assume, the less visible, less persuasive, less stressful, more routine, more ambiguous, and inappropriately difficult (too easy or too hard) maintenance-oriented tasks. These tasks may require less interdependent activity, and less feedback about performance may result. These tasks may not require decision-making so much as the implementing of the decisions of others. The subtle socialization pressures of task differentiation may never be consciously understood by any of the parties involved, and may or may not be accompanied by salary discrimination or conscious prejudice. The result, however, may be that a woman may go so far in an organization but no farther. As she approaches the top levels, someone with the decision-making power will review her qualifications and render the verdict, "She is not ready for this kind of very difficult job." The woman herself will perhaps even concur—for after all, are there not others who have had the critical kinds of experiences she has not had? Are they not obviously more qualified? The answer, too often, is "yes." The organization's socialization structure has seen to that.

REFERENCES

Almquist, E., and S.S. Angrist, "Career Salience and Atypicality of Occupational Choice among College Women," *Journal of Marriage and the Family* 32, (1970), pp. 242 – 49.

Almquist, E.M., and S.S. Angrist, "Role Model Influences on College Women's Career Aspirations," *Merrill Palmer Quarterly* 17 (1971), pp. 263 – 79.

Cartwright, L. K., "Conscious Factors Entering Into Decisions of Women to Study Medicine," *Journal of Social Issues* 28, No. 2 (1972), pp. 201 – 15.

Cartwright, L. K., "The Personality and Family Background of a Sample of Women Medical Students at the University of California," *Medical Women's Association* (May 1972), pp. 260 – 66.

Cecil, E. A., R. J. Paul, and R. A. Olins, "Perceived Importance of Selected Variables used to Evaluate Male and Female Job Applicants," *Personnel Psychology* 26 (1973), pp. 397 – 404.

Constantini, E. and K. H. Craik, "Women as Politicians: The Social Background, Personality and Political Careers of Female Party Leaders," *Journal of Social Issues* 28, No. 2 (1972), pp. 217 – 36.

Epstein, C. F., "Encountering the Male Establishment: Sex-Status Limits on Women's Careers in the Professions," *American Journal of Sociology*, 75, No. 6 (1970a), pp. 965 – 82.

Epstein, C. F., *Woman's Place*. Berkeley: University of California Press, 1970 (b).

Friedan, B., *The Feminine Mystique*. New York: Norton, 1963.

Graen, G. and J. Cashman, "A Role-Making Model of Leadership in Formal Organizations: A Developmental Approach," in J. G. Hunt and L. L. Larson (eds.) *Leadership Frontiers*. Kent, Ohio: Kent State University Press, 1975.

Helson, R., "The Changing Image of the Career Woman," *Journal of Social Issues* 28, No. 2 (1972), pp. 33 – 46.

Hoffman, L. W., "Fear of Success in Males and Females: 1965 – 1971," *Journal of Consulting and Clinical Psychology* 42 (1974), pp. 353 – 58.

Horner, M. S., "Toward an Understanding of Achievement-Related Conflicts in Women," *Journal of Social Issues* 28 (1972), pp. 157 – 75.

Perrucci, C. C., "Minority Status and the Pursuit of Professional Careers: Women in Science and Engineering," *Social Forces* 49, No. 2 (1970), pp. 245 – 59.

Poston, D. L., "On the Cost of Being a Female Worker." Paper presented at the Annual Meeting of the Southwestern Social Science Association, San Antonio, Texas, March 31, 1972.

Rosen, B. and T. H. Jerdee, "Effects of Applicant's Sex and Difficulty of Job on Evaluations of Candidates for Managerial Positions," *Journal of Applied Psychology* 59, No. 4 (1974), pp. 511 – 12.

Smith, C. P. and C. H. Smith, "Why Don't Women Succeed?" *New Society* 16 (1970), pp. 577–79.

Vetter, B. M., "Women and Minority Scientists," *Science* 189, No. 4205 (1975), p. 301.

Williams, M., L. Ho, and L. Fielder, "Career Patterns: More Grist for Women's Liberation," *Social Work* 19, No. 4 (1974), pp. 463–66.

DISCUSSION QUESTIONS

1.   List the women you know who have strong, positive self-concepts. List the women you know who seem fearful of success. Which list is longer?

2.   How have women you know shown fear of success by retreating from achievements?

3.   How have women you know shown that they equated sexual attractiveness with flightiness and dependency?

4.   What examples do you know of women achieving the same results as men by using a different style of behavior?

5.   What kind of job assignments have you seen women get that do not enhance their professional growth and, therefore, hinder their progress on the organization ladder?

"A 1970 survey showed that 19% of women with college degrees and another 17% with some college training were working in clerical, semi-clerical and unskilled jobs."

Affirmative Action and Equal Employment, Volume 1, U.S. Equal Employment Opportunity Commission,, Washington, D.C. 20506, p. 51.

VI

Analyzing
Women's Leadership
Style and Motivation

Leadership—one of the most researched management concepts. What is it? What characterizes a successful leader? Who is capable of leadership?

The problem is that many of the findings of past research were gathered within a male context. Good research is being done today on females in leadership. But much of what is being written either ignores past research findings completely or is applied to females from a male context.

As you read this section, it is important to ask yourself if males and females may be more alike than they are different. Our culture emphasizes the physical differences. But isn't it possible that these physical differences are not as important as the fact that both men and women have intellect, spirit, hopes, dreams, disappointments, joys, *and* analytical ability, problem-solving ability, and leadership potential?

The
Female Leadership
Dilemma

J. Brad Chapman
Fred Luthans

The major reason for the lack of attention given to female leadership is the fact that women have traditionally been relegated to relatively non-leadership areas in clerical, operative, nursing, teaching, and social service areas. Today, of course, women are playing an increasingly important role in leadership positions in both the public and private sector. A sampling of reasons for this new thrust include:

- Increased incidence of women in the work force.

- Increased emphasis given EEOC/affirmative action programs specifically related to the employment of women.

- Improved education and training opportunities for women.

- Changed/changing cultural values concerning the role of women in society.

- Increased employment trends in the service-producing sector as opposed to the goods-producing sector.

- Dispelled myths about women in the work force.

- Increased activism on the part of female employees to attain job equality.

Any one or a combination of the factors mentioned above, plus many others, points to the need to know more about women as leaders.

J. Brad Chapman and Fred Luthans, "The Female Leadership Dilemma," *Public Personnel Management* (May – June 1975), pp. 173 – 79. Reprinted by permission of the International Personnel Management Association, 1313 East 60th Street, Chicago, Illinois 60637.

RESEARCH REVIEW

1. Female Leadership Styles

Both women and men are placed into sex role stereotypes which influence their personality and behavioral patterns. For example, at least in the past, it has been generally accepted in our society that women are considered passive, accommodative, and intuitive, while men are assumed to be aggressive, active, and authoritarian. Therefore, it follows that women leaders exhibit a style which is more human-relationship-oriented than their male counterparts. On the other hand, women may also exhibit a leadership style significantly more task-oriented than their male counterparts because their very survival in a leadership position may be one of "getting-the-job-done."

Research either verifying or discounting these expectations is just beginning to surface. The traditional sex role stereotypes, although not completely disappearing, are certainly being questioned, if not condemned, in current management literature. However, the fact remains that much of the empirical research that is being reported supports the opinion that there is a distinct difference not only in the leadership behavior of males and females, but also in the perceptions of a woman's potential in a leadership position.

In one comprehensive study of the relationship between sex role stereotypes and management characteristics, Virginia Schein found that successful middle managers are perceived to possess characteristics, attitudes, and temperaments more commonly ascribed to men than to women.[1] For example, successful managers were more similar to men than to women in emotional stability, aggressiveness, leadership ability, self-reliance, certainty, vigor, desiring responsibility, seriousness, objectivity, knowledge, and straight-forwardness. On the other hand, characteristics such as understanding, helpfulness, and intuitiveness were more commonly ascribed to women. In essence, this research indicates a relationship-oriented leadership style for women as opposed to a task-oriented or autocratic style. Other research tends to substantiate this conclusion. For example, Bond and Vinacke, in an experimental study of mixed-sex triads, indicated that males tended toward exploitive behavior, while the more successful females, in terms of task accomplishment, tended toward more accommodative behaviors.[2]

Research conducted by Denmarke and Diggory indicated, "It is clear that on the average men are more authoritarian than women with respect to the leader's exercise of authority and power in the matter of group goals and control of the behavior of individual members."[3] However, of the 19 items included in their questionnaire, women report and approve more authoritarian-leader behavior than men in only five of the items; there is no sex difference in five other items. In the remaining nine questions, men report and approve more authoritarian-leader behavior than women. The study did not conclude that women are not authoritarian. Instead, the study showed that men are *more* authoritarian than women.

Another study by Philip Sadler has direct implication on sex differentials in leadership style. Sadler's study revealed that, out of his sample of 319 women, only 15 percent indicated a preference for authoritarian ("tells" or task-oriented) leadership.[4] The implication from this study is that women tend to be relationship- or participative-oriented as opposed to task-oriented. Yet, Sadler's sample of 1,270 men shows only 8 percent of the men accepting an authoritarian approach to leadership. Thus, the conclusions are tentative at best.

To clarify the question of leadership style for females, the authors of this article recently conducted a study with Fred Fiedler's widely used Least-Preferred Coworker (LPC) instrument to measure leadership styles. Fiedler indicates that "a high LPC person derives his major satisfaction from successful interpersonal relationships, while the low LPC person derives his major satisfaction from task performance."[5]

Using practicing males and females in a civilian and military organization as subjects, it was discovered that: (1) there was no significant difference in male and female leadership styles, (2) there was no significant difference in male and female leadership styles in situations where the degree of task structure, position power, and leader-member relations was comparable, and (3) there were no significant correlations between leadership style and demographic variables for either males or females.

Thus, our study found that there may not be a difference in male and female leadership styles. However, there may be a difference in actual leadership behaviors.

2. Female Leadership Behaviors

The implications of sex-role stereotyping are not only important to leadership styles but also to actual leadership behaviors. How a leader behaves, how he or she is expected to behave, and what behavior is appropriate in a given situation may not be the same for men and women. For example, Megargee conducted a study on the influence of sex roles on leadership behaviors.[6] Using primarily a sex dominance characteristic, his research investigated how social sex role prescriptions influence the expression of leadership behaviors by high *Do* (dominance) men and women. In his first study, it was found that when high *Do* men and women were paired with group members of the same sex, 75 percent of the high *Do* men and 70 percent of the high *Do* women assumed the leadership role. When high *Do* men were paired with low *Do* women, 90 percent of the men assumed the leadership role. However, when high *Do* women were paired with low *Do* men, only 20 percent of the women assumed a leadership role. In other words, women may exhibit different leadership behaviors with other women than they do with men. The high dominance females, because of sex-role stereotyping, and self-image, did not exhibit behaviors when paired with low dominance men.

In another study of dissonance behaviors (psychological conflict behaviors resulting when an individual is faced with two or more closely valued alternatives to a decision), Steiner and Rogers found that: females made less use of rejection than did males, females were more inclined to tolerate conflict, and the effect of anxiety upon an individual's choice of dissonance-reducing responses depended upon the sex of the individual.[7] Similarly, Vinacke and Gullickson found that in competitive activities women tended to form coalitions in an accommodative manner while men were more exploitive and used coalitions to gain individual advantages.[8] The conclusions from these two studies would indicate that women do have different leadership behaviors than men and that these behaviors are accommodative in nature.

3. Self-Image and Belongingness Needs of Females

Besides the styles and behaviors of females, in an analysis of their leadership roles, there must be some understanding of what women think of themselves and their need to be part of and accepted by a group. In a comprehensive study of 1,300 persons, aged 15 – 64, Bennett and Cohen found that women, in evaluating themselves as compared to men, felt a greater social benevolence, social propriety, lack of self protection, personal satisfaction, controlled rage, and democratic feeling.[9] On the other hand, men normally felt a greater need for attainment and being uncompromising and ruthless. These self-profiles are further supported by other researchers. For example, Kohn and Fiedler found that women generally perceived significant persons in their environment more favorably than did the males in their study.[10] In other words, the individual's sex had a consistent effect upon his or her interpersonal perceptions.

Two studies by Exline provide further insight into the interpersonal or affiliation patterns of women leaders. In his first study, Exline found that women's messages were significantly more person-oriented than were men's. In women's, relative to men's groups, subjects whose coworkers were visible requested significantly more personal information than did those whose co-workers were not visible. The need for affiliation was significantly and *inversely* related to the degree of control over the other's behavior attempted in the first message written in the process of group problem-solving.[11] Exline concluded that there was no evidence that the need for affiliation *per se* affected the degree of personal, as opposed to task-oriented, communications. A follow-up study basically found that females interacted significantly more than their male counterparts.[12] In essence, this latter study replicated his earlier findings that need affiliation did not have a significant effect on the degree of interaction, although interaction was much greater for high and low need affiliation women than men.

THE FEMALE LEADERSHIP DILEMMA

The primary determinants of any person's (male or female) ability to influence group performance would consist of the leader him/herself, the group being led, and the situation.[13] But from a female leadership perspective, the interaction of these leadership variables poses a dilemma. For example, a female leader in an achievement-oriented situation may have a fear of failure; but, perhaps more importantly, she may also have a fear of success. Matina Horner defined this female fear of success as, "the fear that success in competitive achievement situations will lead to negative consequences, such as unpopularity and loss of femininity."[14] The consequence of such a fear would be to adopt more accommodative strategies in leadership situations. This accommodative approach taken by female leaders tends to be supported in the research literature.

Further compounding of the "failure/success dilemma" is the self-image women have regarding their lack of acceptance by male and female peers, superiors and subordinates. In other words, because of social role stereotypes and the resulting stereotypical behaviors on the part of women, there is little organizational or peer reinforcement for success in the traditionally male-dominated organization.

Primary work-group acceptance and reinforcement could overcome many of the obstacles confronting women managers and diminish the fear of success. Unfortunately, this work-group acceptance does not appear to exist. In a study by Bass, *et al*, it was found that many men regard working women as having different skills, different habits, and different motivations, which make them undesirable as workers.[15] Male managers in this study felt that: (1) men and women have defined societal roles which govern their interaction, most notably rules of etiquette and politeness between the two sexes in public; (2) men and women would prefer having male supervisors and would be uncomfortable with a woman supervisor; and (3) males perceived females in the work environment as having a lack of dependability.

Although most would agree that women are exhibiting less stereotypical behaviors now than in the past, male attitudes may still be a major
impediment to equal status. For example, Orth and Jacobs concluded that
the major obstacle to equal status for women in the work place included
fixed attitudes, confused career patterns, and outmoded notions.[16] All
these factors primarily represent the negative or indifferent attitude
males have for female leaders.

A large national survey (conducted by the Bureau of National
Affairs) regarding organizational reactions to equal employment
opportunity and affirmative action programs indicated that one of the
major problems encountered by the respondents was "difficulties in educating supervisors and middle managers, or in some cases the entire work
force, in the need for supporting EEO efforts."[17] This group acceptance
problem may be very difficult to overcome, especially in light of a study
by Bass, *et al.*, which found that "men who did not work with women had
more positive regard for women than the men who did."[18]

The third major determinant of leadership effectiveness is the situation. Today, most companies have adopted aggressive affirmative action
programs. Yet, despite meeting the letter of the law, it seems many
organizational climates do not support female leadership. A recent study
by Rosen and Jerdee found that: (1) managers expect male employees to
give top priority to their jobs when career demands and family obligations conflict; they expect female employees to sacrifice their careers to
family responsibilities; (2) if personal conduct threatens an employee's job,
managers make greater efforts to retain a valuable male employee than
the equally-qualified female and (3) in selection, promoting, and career-
development decisions, managers are biased in favor of males.[19]

The result of such attitudes as these is to create an organizational
environment where the female manager is made to feel inferior and inadequate in a leadership role. Qualified females occupying responsible leadership positions in an "acting" capacity until a suitable male replacement is
found to fill the position permanently is not uncommon. In other
instances, a woman subordinate is asked to train a male to assume the
position as her superior. In this latter case, the inconsistency of the organization to recognize female competencies on the one hand but not
follow through with commensurate leadership responsibilities on the
other, helps to reinforce the female dilemma of incompatible sex-role
stereotypes.

The leadership influence system — made up of the leader, the group,
and the situation — does not appear to be very favorable to women. The
female leader is caught in a dual conflict situation involving not only the
group and the organizational situation but also herself. If she adopts accommodative leadership behavior patterns, which may be more

congruent with her basic personality, she will be subjected to the common male criticism of being too intuitive, undependable, and passive. However, if she adopts an autocratic or task-oriented leadership behavior, there is the self-perception of losing her "femininity" and the resultant conflict between fear of success and fear of failure. Overcompensation in either direction may result in one or both of two consequences: (1) she will feel uncomfortable with her behaviors or (2) she will be the subject of considerable male suspect as to her ulterior motives. The end result in each consequence is to reduce her total leadership effectiveness in attaining organizational goals.

SOLUTIONS TO THE DILEMMA

What are the alternatives for a female caught in the current leadership dilemma? What responsibility do organizations have to mitigate the problems, both real and imagined, confronting their current and future women leaders? Unfortunately, the answers are not easy. Many organizations, in responding to the demands for equity by their women employees and the increased governmental action through the EEOC, have resorted to short-run, stop-gap measures which may actually be promulgating, rather than abating, the problem. Myopic solutions can result in increased female dissatisfaction and lower self-image and increased male prejudice. The solution is not just one of placing more females in responsible management positions. Instead, the longer-run solution to the female leadership dilemma involves new thinking and specific programs in the areas of recruitment, selection, placement, training, and organizational development.

1. Recruitment, Selection, and Placement.

Organizations should recruit, select and place female managers based on well-defined needs. The criteria for selection should be based on personal qualifications, and the placement should involve a match between these qualifications and the job requirements. Organizations should avoid the practice of hiring females and placing them in "fabricated" managerial positions to avoid subsequent governmental action. Such practices are self-defeating. Mere tokenism will result in male resentment and female disillusionment.

2. Training and Development

For female managers, emphasis should be given to the development of specific managerial skills designed to increase necessary technical, human, and conceptual abilities. Particular emphasis should be given to creating a learning climate which makes the female management trainees comfortable with the vocabulary and protocol. However, of equal importance in training the females is the development of training programs designed to make males more receptive to female peers, subordinates, and superiors. Training programs conducted with males and females interacting on an equal basis is one approach to reducing many of the stereotypes commonly ascribed by males to the woman leader. However, careful selection must be made so that the women and men in a mixed program are equally competent.

3. Organizational Development

Overall organization policies which discriminate against female employees in areas such as job design, appraisal, travel, promotion, transfer, lay-off, discipline, and benefits must be analyzed and redefined to live up to the spirit as well as the letter of the law on equal opportunity for females. In other words, the organization cannot expect the female manager to go through a complete change process without the organization indicating a willingness to change itself. A total OD effort to change the beliefs, attitudes, values, and structure of the organization to accommodate the female leader is necessary. Team building, job enrichment, sensitivity training, and organizational behavior modification techniques of OD can be used to accomplish the end of a more supportive and reinforcing organizational environment for female leadership.

CONCLUSION

As societal and legislative pressures increase to place more women in responsible leadership positions and women themselves become more vocal and active in demanding job equality, both public and private institutions must adopt more aggressive and realistic policies and programs designed to fully utilize the female leadership potential. Such policies and programs must be founded on sound, research-based information which clearly indicates what steps can be taken. Short-run, stop-gap measures designed merely to satisfy legislative requirements or stave off female antagonism will be self-defeating and actually reinforce prejudice and thus result in dysfunctional organizational consequences.

This article suggests that female leadership research shows there is probably no significant difference between male and female leadership styles but that there is a difference in leadership behaviors. Women tend to behave in a more accommodative manner when in a leadership role. In addition, research generally shows that neither males nor females themselves have a very high opinion of female leadership capabilities. Women are not generally accepted by the groups being led. The organizational situation as a whole tends to be nonsupportive of female leadership. However, it is important to note that in those situations where women have been traditionally accepted in managerial positions—such as in Air Force operations where WAF's are typically used—there appears to be no significant difference between the leadership styles or behaviors of men and women. However, when women are being recruited or when they are initially placed into organizations which have been traditionally male dominated, social-role stereotypes become an important determinant of leadership. The female faces the dilemma of being successful yet fearing success.

By viewing leadership as an influence system consisting of the leader, the group and the situation, the myopic view of looking only at individual leadership differences attributable to sex can be avoided. The ability of a leader to influence subordinate behaviors and thus be effective is certainly a function of individual traits; but, perhaps more importantly, it is also a function of the group and the organizational situation. If sex prejudices are reduced in the group and the organizational situation is supportive of female leadership, then long-run headway can be made to live up to the spirit as well as the letter of female equal opportunity in leadership positions in today's organizations.

NOTES

[1] Virginia Ellen Schein, "The Relationship Between Sex Role Stereotypes and Requisite Management Characteristics," *Journal of Applied Psychology* 57 (April 1973), p. 95.

[2] J. R. Bond and W. E. Vinacke, "Coalitions in Mixed-Sex Triads," *Sociometry* 24 (1961), pp. 61–65.

[3] Florence L. Denmarke and James C. Diggory, "Sex Differences in Attitudes Toward Leader's Display of Authoritarian Behavior," *Psychological Reports* 18 (Southern University Press, 1966), pp. 867–68.

[4] Philip J. Sadler, "Leadership Style, Confidence in Management and Job Satisfaction," *The Journal of Applied Behavioral Science* 6, No. 1 (1970), p. 10.

[5] Fred E. Fiedler, *A Theory of Leadership Effectiveness* (New York: McGraw-Hill Book Company, 1967), p. 45.

[6] Edwin I. Megargee, "Influence of Sex Roles on the Manifestation of Leadership," *Journal of Applied Psychology* 53, No. 2 (1969), p. 377.

[7] Ivan D. Steiner and Evan D. Rogers, "Alternative Responses to Dissonance," *Journal of Abnormal and Social Psychology* 66, No. 2 (1963), pp. 128–36.

[8] Edgar Vinacke and Gary R. Gullickson, "Age and Sex Differences in the Formation of Coalitions," *Child Development* 35 (1964), pp. 1217–31.

[9] Edward M. Bennett and Larry R. Cohen, "Men and Women: Personality Patterns and Contracts," *Genetics Psychology Monographs* 59 (1959), pp. 101–55.

[10] A. Robert Kohn and Fred E. Fiedler, "Age and Sex Differences in the Perception of Persons," *Sociometry* 24 (1961), pp. 157 – 63.

[11] Ralph V. Exline, "Effects of Need for Affiliation, Sex, and the Sight of Others upon Initial Communications in Problem-Solving Groups," *Journal of Personality* 30 (1962), p. 556.

[12] Ralph V. Exline, "Explorations in the Process of Person Perception: Visual Interaction in Relation to Competition, Sex, and Need for Affiliation," *Journal of Personality* 31 (1963), pp. 1 – 20.

[13] See: Fred Luthans, *Organizational Behavior* (New York: McGraw-Hill, 1973), p. 504.

[14] Matina Horner, "A Bright Woman is Caught in a Double Bind. In Achievement-Oriented Situations She Worries Not Only About Failure But Also About Success," *Psychology Today* (November 1969), p. 138.

[15] Bernard M. Bass, Judith Krusell, and Ralph A. Alexander, "Male Managers' Attitudes Toward Working Women," *American Behavioral Scientist* (November 1971), p. 233.

[16] Charles D. Orth, 3rd and Frederic Jacobs, "Woman in Management: Pattern for Change," *Harvard Business Review* (July/August, 1971).

[17] ASPA – BNA, "Equal Employment Opportunity and Affirmative Action Programs," *Bulletin to Management*, Survey Report No. 20 (December 1973), p. 8.

[18] Bass and Krusell, *op. cit.*, p. 233.

[19] Benson Rosen and Thomas H. Jerdee, "Sex Stereotyping in the Executive Suite," *Harvard Business Review* (March/April 1974), p. 47.

DISCUSSION QUESTIONS

1.   Think of a successful male and a successful female manager/ supervisor you know. List the behaviors that each exhibits. Do they really differ? If there are differences, how many can be attributed to the situations rather than the individuals?

2.   Do you know any *successful* women who fear success?

3.   Do you know of any examples where males are asked to train their own supervisors?

4.   Do you know of any examples where women leaders are not accepted just because they are women?

Women in Management:
Keys to Success
or Failure

Lois Ann Koff
Joseph H. Handlon

Despite the increase in Affirmative Action programs for women, the debate about placing women in managerial positions still continues. But that debate no longer centers on whether women *should* be managers; rather, it is now *which* women will succeed as managers.

It had been assumed that once the long-standing barriers against letting women become managers were removed, there would be a flood of applicants vying for the available positions. But the response in many organizations has been little more than a modest trickle. The reasons why women have either ignored or actively resisted such opportunities have been both a puzzle and a source of concern to many organizations now searching for women to promote.

Research has revealed a number of reasons why some women are so resistant to becoming managers or supervisors and why, once promoted, women in management succeed or fail. We firmly believe that if these reasons were better understood, steps could be taken to deal with the resistances and failures in ways that would be mutually beneficial. In addition, we further believe that there are appropriate positions for women at *all* levels of an organization, but that what is needed is a way of matching the qualified woman to the proper position. This is what we will discuss.

The information contained in this article is a brief synopsis of a six-year study into the factors causing success or failure of women in supervisory and management positions. A total of 1,775 women, ranging in age from 20 to 55 and employed in various business and industrial organizations throughout the United States, were interviewed by the senior author.

The patterned interview, case history method was chosen to furnish data not only on the *what*, but the *why* involved in all of the participants'

Lois Ann Koff and Joseph H. Handlon, "Women in Management: Keys to Success or Failure," *The Personnel Administrator* (April 1975), pp. 24–28.

239

thinking and actions. The subject of each case history was interviewed from four to eight hours, depending upon her age and business experience. Then her supervisor, peers and a sampling of her subordinates were interviewed by the senior author. The interviews were designed to reveal the woman's attitudes toward seeking out or accepting positions, response to various types of training programs, how she was selected for promotion, her managerial effectiveness, etc.

The resulting data show that women can be categorized by different degrees of motivational proneness for upward mobility within organizations.* (This categorization is determined by such factors as degree of self-confidence, evidence of desire to achieve, prior patterns of success, reasons for motivation, personal commitment to career development, maturity, etc.) This motivational proneness is, in turn, related to a probable degree of success in the role of manager or supervisor. Further, the study shows that the kinds of psychological resistances displayed by some women when encouraged to take on these new roles can also be categorized. As defined, these categories provide a means for understanding and applying the optimum utilization of the obvious talents of women. These conceptual tools can help answer many questions, including:

- Which women will be motivated to go beyond entry level supervision or management?
- Which women will be more successful in line positions as compared to staff responsibility?
- Which women will be able to become effective generalist managers?
- What type of training program will most benefit a particular category of women and why?
- What kind of work environment is most likely to work best with what type of woman?

The research proved that the women studied could be divided into two main types: those who are basically more motivationally upward-mobile prone (at present 30 percent) and those who are basically more

---

*I personally resist the use of labels when applied as identifiers of human beings because it strips people of their individuality. In many cases, these labels can be more harmful than helpful. The requirements of individuals are complex and simplistic labeling can overlook a wide range of personal needs and feelings.

But, at times, labeling can promote understanding, can focus attention on problems and get more immediate action. When it became apparent during my 4,000 hours of research that women fell into different patterns of motivational achievements, the clearest method of explanation was to describe these patterns as groups and assign them labels.

prone to stay put in their current positions (70 percent). (Eighteen percent of the women under age 30 who had graduated from college were more mobile prone than those under 30 who had not received a college degree.) Within normal limits, the degree of intelligence, marital status and number of children did not differ between the two groups. Within each of these two main groups, there are a number of important sub-groups, each with its own unique characteristics.

UPWARD-MOBILE PRONE GROUP

Women in this major category are positively motivated to take on more responsibility and to move up the organizational ladder. But the degree of motivation for promotion varies considerably for each of the three sub-groups within this category.

Pioneers

The most upward-mobile in their motivations, these women are the innovators and the initiators and comprise the top 10 percent of the up-ward-mobile prone group. They are self-propelled and seem almost addicted to challenging situations. Pioneers are not afraid to take risks and their strongly upward-mobile motivations are made possible, in part, by their own very positive sense of self-worth. They feel that they are superiorly endowed in natural and acquired talents and are very comfortable with this sense of self-worth.

Pioneers are high achievers. They expect to be successful and usually are. They often break new ground and serve as important role models for their less risk-taking sisters. If these opportunities are not forthcoming in any given situation, Pioneers will change employers, usually gravitating to large urban centers for greater career opportunities. These women know what the salary ranges are for their positions and demand top dollar.

Pioneers operate independently and autonomously. They pursue their individual goals despite lack of support or even during resistance from others. They are not easily discouraged and can keep going even during periods of considerable adversity. Indeed, the more difficult things are made for them, the harder they will strive.

Pioneers get their rewards from the achievements they gain and from the sense of accomplishment they feel at being given increased responsibility.

Climate Sensitives

These women share strong positive motivations for upward mobility and achievement with Pioneers (they are the middle 10 percent of the major category) but they are more sensitive to the psychological climate around them. Climate Sensitives tend to relate and rely on *positive company climate* to develop their self-confidence to the point where they will tackle middle and senior management positions. While these women do not need to be pampered, they respond best to approval or recognition of their efforts by top managers and executives than immediate superiors. This approval permits them to take many of the risks that Pioneers will take unquestioningly.

In contrast, Climate Sensitives tend to have a more singular view of goal achievement. While the Pioneer is always looking for new challenges, the Climate Sensitive, once her original goal is achieved (particularly when it is related to proving her worth) is quite content to do nothing further on her own to broaden her areas of expertise or develop new goals. Indeed, some members of this group who have proven themselves may even retire from the marketplace and be content to work part-time or become traditional housewives.

The majority of Climate Sensitives tend to stay with the same employer until an outside situation causes the termination of employment. After such a job-break, close to 60 percent of these women will seek employment within the same career speciality but change the field of business. To them this is risk-taking.

Substantial data show that Climate Sensitives are not without a healthy sense of their own worth, but they seem to need to have these positive self-perceptions validated on a regular basis by professionals they respect. Once such support is given, this group can be as upward-mobile and as successful as the more daring Pioneers. Salary demands for Climate Sensitives are moderate because opportunity for advancement is their prime consideration.

Support Seekers

This group, the bottom 10 percent of the major grouping, can be upward-mobile and achieve success in their managerial roles, but they need more "stroking" and "hand holding" than Climate Sensitives. The upward path for them needs to be cleared of external obstacles and personal resistances from others reduced to a minimum. They need to consistently receive a reassuring input of approval from employer and family.

Support Seekers become easily discouraged and readily lose confidence. During such times, much encouragement is required to remotivate them. They are security conscious and, as such, have trouble taking risks unless they feel the chances of failure are practically nil. Before taking risks, Support Seekers spend time checking all the possible things that might go wrong. Once they feel secure, and with skilled training, they can become innovative and as high achievers as their less self-doubting sisters.

Unlike Pioneers, Support Seekers are usually very faithful to a single organization. Given the kind of training, support and approval they most require, they willingly demonstrate their loyalty and dedication to the job in many ways. Salary requests and wage acceptances are below average for the jobs held for nearly 80 percent of this group. They are the least responsive of the upward-mobile prone group in accepting lateral transfers and in sacrificing personal time for career development. While Support Seekers need approval from many sources to build confidence, approval is most meaningful when it comes from those closest to them— immediate supervisors, subordinates and close family members.

STAY-PUT PRONE GROUP

Women in this category shun new challenges and avoid increased responsibilities for a variety of reasons. They are often seen by others as being passive, low risk takers and lacking ambition and energy. They are plagued by low self-esteem. They are motivated by security needs and by personal comfort and they express a decided lack of interest in assuming any sort of supervisory or managerial role. For them, upward mobility and achievement are fraught with certain "catastrophic expectations." The content of these fears form the basis for our categories and have implications for overcoming these women's resistance to advancement.

Fear of Conflict with Tradition

For the women in this group, especially for those over 30, being upward mobile in the work situation means taking on new roles that are in conflict with strong family and/or subculture traditions. These traditions are often widely accepted "rules" about appropriate sex roles. Typical of such "rules" are:

• Because her place is in the home, a truly successful husband ought to be able to support his wife without compelling her to work; but if she must work, then:

1. a wife should never earn more than her husband;
2. a wife should never have a higher status job than her husband;

3.   a wife should never be in a job that demands more skills, knowledge and experience than does her husband's job.

The underlying theme behind these "rules" is that women in the work situation should not pose a psychological threat to the important men in their lives.

Bear in mind that the psychological threat to the husband posed by the violation of these "rules" by the wife is often not verified by the concerned spouse. The wife simply *assumes* that what she is contemplating doing would be too threatening were it to happen and she is not willing to take this risk for fear of possible negative results.

For many present day women there is clearly a good deal of ambivalence about the traditional woman's role with its many implicit and explicit "rules." But for all its qualities of second class citizenship, the traditional role is, at least, one most women have been well taught and it has paid off for some of them. Learning a different role can be risky; it seems awkward if the woman is not used to it. The payoff is likely to be uncertain and, therefore, the new role is avoided.

The degree of social pressure upon women to maintain the traditional role can vary greatly from subgroup to subgroup. For example, a woman living a highly visible life in a small rural community may have more difficulty resisting pressures to remain a traditional woman than one working within the anonymity of a large city.

Can these women overcome their fear of conflict with traditions and move from the stay-put prone group to the upward-mobile group? With EEO, Affirmative Action and community mores giving women more approval, about 12 percent of the stay-puts will consider advancement to supervision. But will her spouse approve? Most women say their husbands wouldn't like them in supervision without ever really discussing the matter, something a woman being considered for an upward move should be encouraged to do.

Fear of Disloyalty to a Peer Group

These women see their work peers as comprising an important "family." This family is often the primary source of confidence, emotional support and personal security for the individual. To move upward, and thus out of the family, particularly when part of the family mythology is to take a dim view of all bosses, is tantamount to rejecting the family. The woman fears that she will be viewed by them as being disloyal and that the caring support and security that she relies upon will be withdrawn.

Moving upward in the organization is seen as being risky enough; but without the reliable support of this important peer family, such a move is seen as too dangerous and to be avoided. Implicitly, a bargain is struck: "I won't move out of the group and join the enemy if you will continue to love me."

Fear of Failure Group

Women in this group are reluctant to take a job with increased demands because of a fear of not being able to "hack it." They perceive that they do not have the intelligence, knowledge, skills, experience, personality (the list is endless) required to do the job. They dread failure and are not willing to risk it.

Often such women have very high self-imposed standards of work excellence. Any move to a position of added complexity and responsibility is a threat. They fear they will be unable to maintain the same high standards and reputation for superior achievement. It is probably this ability to maintain high standards that put them in the running for a promotion. But they will refuse such offers, saying, in effect, at least we know how to do a good job in the position we're in now.

Fear of a New Social Status Group

These women represent a special case of fear of failure. They resist moving up because it means entering a new social strata with which they are not sure they can cope. Their fears take many forms: "I'm ashamed of the way I talk—I don't use all those fancy words." "My manners aren't good enough." "I don't have the right clothes." And so on.

Promotion is seen as moving into a socio-economic class with which the woman feels she has had little or no experience. This is potentially threatening, the great fear being that "I'll make a fool of myself and everyone will make fun of me. Who wants a fool for a boss?"

OVERCOMPENSATORS

In addition to the group just described, there is another motivationally important group of women—the Overcompensators. They can be found in both the upward-mobile and in the stay-put prone groups.

Upward-Mobile Overcompensators

This group uses their job situation to make up for what they feel are deficiencies in other aspects of their lives. Sometimes they feel that something is missing in their image of themselves. Sometimes a crisis, such as a recent divorce or death, has robbed them of something they wanted very much and they are trying to make up for the unjustified loss. Sometimes it is an unfortunate family history so that the woman feels she has to prove to others the real worth of "my family" or "my people".

Upward mobile overcompensators are often not as successful as they might be in their managerial or supervisory roles. They seem to lack the flexibility required to be a truly successful manager and there are a number of ways in which this managerial rigidity manifests itself.

Because of their strong need to prove themselves to others by "showing them," plus a singular lack of interest in developing their subordinates, Upward Mobile Overcompensators are often reluctant to delegate appropriate responsibilities to others. This is particularly true when they need to be sure that the job is done satisfactorily and that they will be blamed if it is not. However, when they can be sure that they will not be blamed for what is done, Upward-Mobile Overcompensators will not hesitate to delegate — even swamping their subordinates with work to demonstrate their obvious incompetence in contrast to themselves.

Because they are overly sensitive to actual or implied criticism, since this makes them feel "one-down," they respond poorly to censure. In addition, because of their low degree of trust, Upward-Mobile Overcompensators respond to criticism, even when intended to be helpful, in a rigidly defensive manner rather than in an accepting and growth promoting fashion.

And since their concept of a successful boss is often an unrealistic stereotype, they emulate the model of the somewhat autocratic male. In this way, they believe that they can demonstrate how competent they are, thus making up for any self-doubts that they may have about their own ability.

Stay-Put Overcompensators

The desire to make up for some believed lack in other aspects of their lives does not become fulfilled within this group's work situation. These women do not feel it appropriate to use their jobs in this way. Instead, they are most likely to find other outlets in their lives — family activities, sports and hobbies, church or club work — as a means of making up for the lack of confidence and the deficiencies they feel. Of course, intense involvement and over-preoccupation with devising and implementing such nonwork overcompensation strategies can still play havoc with effective work motivation and will eventually result in less than optimal job performance.

If women are to be encouraged to assume an equal place with men among managerial ranks — including the very top echelons — then there are important implications to be drawn from the findings described here.

• Women's motivations to be moved or to resist being moved into managerial positions vary considerably, just as they do for men. Among the reasons why women resist becoming managers are:

1. Lack of motivational proneness — they are Stay-Putters.

2. Lack of company training programs or programs considered inadequate or too sophisticated by potential candidates. Fear of failure or ranking low in class. They are now doing great jobs, but fear loss of esteem if they don't do well in class.

3. On-the-job training programs under the supervision of harried, busy managers without time, motivation, patience or knowledge to train effectively.

4. Lack of self-confidence and fear of criticism.

5. Unsure of the support and relationship they will have with a new supervisor.

6. No women role models or mentors.

• The nature of these motivations must be understood by organizations if they are to be able to optimize the chances for success of women moving into managerial roles.

• The proper assessment of a potential candidate for promotion in terms of her upward-mobile motivations is needed as a crucial first step.

• The training and educational needs of potential women managers differ, depending upon individual motivations. We are becoming more sophisticated about setting up such differentiated programs. For example, we must:

1. Utilize the motivational proneness of women being employed by or recruited for a company.

2. Include positive techniques in training programs that will make them more meaningful to potential women managers.

3. Educate and train the managers who will be guiding and developing women so that they understand the needs of women and can counsel them for positive results.

4. Make available in-house, or through tuition, courses that will assist women in gaining the insight to deal with their fears.

5. Help women understand that good managers or supervisors can be either male or female and that leadership styles are really asexual.

• There is a place in the organization for women of whatever motivational pattern. A woman's worth to the organization should not be judged solely on what managerial potential she may have.

• All employees, both female and male, can realize their maximum potential in a work environment which is both perceptive and receptive. Organizational development is a needed adjunct to individual development.

DISCUSSION QUESTIONS

1.   This study of 1,775 women found that 30% were basically more motivationally upward-mobile prone. Would this percent have been higher, lower, or about the same in an all-male group? Why?

2.   Identify some *pioneers*. Let them read the description of *pioneer*. Ask them how they develop their courage.

3.   Interview one or more top managers. Let them read the descriptions of *pioneers, climate sensitives,* and *support seekers.* How many of each kind would they prefer to have work with them? Why?

4.   How do members of committees and/or families put social pressure on a woman to maintain her traditional role?

5.   Ask several working women what kind of training or supportive climate they would need to move up in their organization.

"A woman developed the explosive which made the Apollo moon landings possible. It was relied on to lift the landing module off the moon, enabling the astronauts to return to their spacecraft."

Jayne Baker Spain, "Women in Government and Affirmative Action," in *Affirmative Action for Women,* eds. Dorothy Jongeward and Dru Scott (Reading, Mass.: Addison-Wesley Publishing Co., 1974), p. 79.

Women in Management:
The Fallacy
of the Trait Approach

Linda Putnam

J. Stephen Heinen

Legal and social pressures to increase the number of women executives in the United States have resulted in the publication of a wide array of books and articles addressing the issue of sex stereotypes and effective management. Many of the authors provide women managers with advice on personal attributes necessary for successful female leadership. This advice, however, is predicated upon sex-linked stereotypes of effective and ineffective leadership. Reading the "advice to the female manager" columns is likely to lead to confusion and heightened anxiety for many women. In some cases, it may even be poor advice because of the problems connected with the model of leadership upon which it is based. The leadership model referred to is the *trait theory model.* The model originated with the study of the characteristics of the great male leaders. This theory assumes that a leader possesses some unique innate physical and personality traits that enable the person to assume a leadership position in any situation. Early approaches to the study of leadership searched for those personal characteristics which distinguished leaders from non-leaders. After many years of research the trait approach has failed to differentiate between effective and ineffective leaders. Now, many people seem to be reviving that theory for women managers even though it is unsupported for male managers. This appears to be occurring because gender is a trait which directs attention to other traits associated with leadership.

In this article the authors will illustrate how the trait theory has been applied to women managers, point out how continued adherence to this approach will slow down the development of effective women man-

Linda Putnam and J. Stephen Heinen, "Women in Management: The Fallacy of the Trait Approach," *MSU Business Topics* (Summer 1976), pp. 47–53. Reprinted by permission of the publisher, Division of Research, Graduate School of Business Administration, Michigan State University.

agers, and briefly, describe a more comprehensive model of leadership behavior.

THE TRAIT THEORY AND THE DOUBLE BIND

In our society the image of a successful leader is a person who is aggressive, forceful, competitive, achievement oriented, self-confident, and independent. These traits tend to be more often associated with men than with women. Women are generally depicted as emotional, passive, dependent, nurtural, intuitive, and submissive. Thus a woman manager often finds herself placed in a double bind. If she displays the culturally defined traits of a woman, she is rejected as an unacceptable manager. If she acts according to the male defined role of a leader, she is condemned as being unfeminine. Since the woman manager cannot simultaneously conform to society's expectations of both woman and manager, she is faced with a paradox. The either-or nature of these choices polarizes those who advise women managers and confuses the women with contradictory recommendations.

In publications for the woman executive, three commonly mentioned sets of personality traits are aggressiveness and dominance, self-confidence and self-esteem, and emotional control and sound judgment. A review of this literature illustrates that *(a) women face a double bind in the management role, (b) the advice they receive is often contradictory, and (c) the research on these traits does not support the belief that they are critical to effective leadership.* The first two points refer to the fact that these traits are considered culturally desirable for managers but culturally undesirable for women. Different authors contradict each other on what the woman should do about this problem. Overlooked in all these articles is the evidence on the trait theory itself, which is our third point. Little support can be found for each of these personality traits in distinguishing effective from ineffective managers.

AGGRESSIVENESS AND DOMINANCE VERSUS DEPENDENCY AND SUBMISSION

The words *aggressiveness* and *dominance* often appear interchangeably in the literature about women in management. Even though these terms may connote different aspects of the same concept, authors rarely differentiate between them. Some writers agree that aggressiveness is an essential quality for women managers, while others temper this conclusion by pointing to the negative effects of too much dominance or suggest that men are repelled by aggression, yet critical when women managers lack it.

As an advocate of the former position, R. Bremer contends that female executives should:

> be aggressive when called for, force yourself to be assertive. Subordinates rely on you to settle grievances, get them remuneration that they deserve, and take action on problems they are not in a position to solve. Fear of making a mistake may seriously impair your ability to function on the job. However, women should not become defensive about being a woman and overcompensate by being aggressively high-handed or heavy handed in dealing with them (men.)[1]

On the other hand, D. C. Basil's survey of 316 managers (102 female, 214 male) supports the belief that aggressiveness is a negative quality for female managers. He found:

> Negative attitudes on the part of men appear confined to women executives who show a tendency to demand equality, to try to be masculine, to insist on asserting ego, to be domineering and aggressive....
> Some of the attributes found necessary for success in management, such as aggressiveness, have been found by women in their social role to repel men.... If men cannot accept harshness and aggressiveness in women, can women perform a managerial function utilizing more womanly attributes and be accepted?[2]

Due to the paradoxical link between these two seemingly contradictory positions, it is not unusual to find both stances advocated within the same publication. When E. Lynch enumerates the attributes for successful female leadership, she urges women

> to be strong but not aggressive... (to) be self-assertive, (to) make the right decisions quickly and (to) handle subordinates with humor and firmness.[3]

Later she points out that fear of being too aggressive is one of the hangups female supervisors face in executing their managerial duties.

Discussions of aggressiveness or dominance as personality traits of female leaders suffer from ambiguous meanings aligned with these words. This is evident in the wide variety of terms and situations used to describe aggressiveness; these include

> *assertive, heavy handed* (Bremer); *demanding, asserting ego, domineering, harshness* (Basil); *firmness, strength* (Lynch); *self-initiative, drive, fortitude* (Woods); and *overreacting, forwardness* (Epstein).[4]

It is apparent from this semantic confusion that the term *aggressiveness* and *dominance* do not refer to a comparable set of leadership skills and behaviors. The definitions of these traits are not interchangeable.

The feminine traits of dependency and submissiveness are outgrowths of a lack of self-assertion. What our culture deems feminine are derivations of dependency. Men usually select aggression or detachment when faced with anxiety, whereas women traditionally are supposed to opt for dependency which, in turn, can lead to submissiveness, self-efface-ment, and fear of self-assertion.

As management peers, women and men work together for a common goal in non-traditional ways. Such peer relationships between male and female may seem strange and even threatening. For some male executives, a woman must meet their expectations of a dependent female or she threatens their masculinity. If she is not dependent on them, they may withhold information she needs or use her as a scapegoat.

As with recommendations about aggressiveness, advice on female submissiveness is often inconsistent. Some authors feel that dependency is a negative attribute for successful female leadership; others tend to qualify their rejection of this trait with reservations about when and how women should relinquish it.

One question left unanswered by many of these writers is whether these traits actually are important to one desirous of being an effective leader. Research does not support very strongly the truth of the assump-tion.[5] In the area of dominance, the relationship to leadership was gener-ally found to be low and dependent upon a range of situational factors. No evidence can be found to link aggressiveness to such management skills as tackling challenging assignments, setting achievable goals, planning, organizing, persuading, conciliating, and conveying enthusiasm. Thus the notion that successful managers are dominant or aggressive may depend on the situation she or he encounters. It seems futile to talk about degrees, too much or too little aggressiveness or dominance. Con-sequently, when authors admonish female executives to be more or less aggressive, they continue to nurture the double bind women face.

SELF-CONFIDENCE AND SELF-ESTEEM

Lack of confidence in her abilities to excel is another problem a woman in a management position faces. In a survey of the relationship of self-concept to sex role stereotypes, it was found that women have more nega-tive opinions of their self-worth than men do. This phenomenon seems linked to the high social desirability of masculine characteristics. In a follow-up study of female college students, G. K. Baruch found that daughters of career-oriented mothers score higher on self-esteem and on competence ratings than do other women.[7] Thus self-esteem seems inversely related to femininity, yet positively linked with feelings of com-petence. These separate findings seem to reinforce the notion that a woman must choose between being viewed as feminine or being viewed as professionally competent. However, most of the research has been with women who are college age and younger. Since there have been few studies of self-esteem of women beyond college age, it is difficult to determine whether there are clear differences between male and female managers.

Self-confidence is one characteristic which has shown a relatively consistent positive relationship with leadership in studies conducted from 1904 to 1970.[8] The findings suggest that leaders rate higher than followers in self-confidence and self-esteem. However, the development of self-confidence is highly dependent upon the way one is treated. In a job setting, workers need support and positive feedback to increase confidence in a particular job, and this reinforcement is contingent on effective performance. Therefore, whether one becomes self-confident depends upon what the situation is and how one has been rewarded for performance in similar situations.

EMOTIONAL CONTROL AND SOUND JUDGMENT

Emotional versus logical is a popular stereotype for contrasting sex differences in making decisions. In Basil's survey, almost three-fourths of the 214 male respondents (71 percent) and a significant percentage of the 102 female supervisors (49 percent) said that women are more emotional and less rational than men.[9]

Surveys of male managers consistently report that men believe that women are temperamentally unsuited for management, that they are too emotional and tense for work that requires objectivity, analytical skills, and careful reasoning.

Some writers who acknowledge the prevalence of this belief caution female executives to control their emotions, avoid being whimsical or disorganized in reasoning, and to remain cool and dignified in a crisis. This advice, of course, tends to foster the double bind facing a woman manager. If she is too emotional, she is an ineffective executive who behaves like a woman; yet if she is too cold and aloof, she becomes a parody of a man.

Again, the research findings do not support the contention that leaders are characterized consistently by a high degree of self-control or by a lack of emotional expression. Many studies show a slight positive link between these factors and leadership, but some also show no relationship at all or even a negative relationship.

Throughout the literature on personal factors for effective female leadership, writers disagree as to whether masculine or feminine traits should be emphasized; consequently, they present antithetical recommendations to prospective women managers:

The quality of a woman executive which gives her an upper hand on the management level is her feminine responsiveness. It is not only possible but preferable that a woman retain her feminine responsiveness without losing the power of assertion or even of command. Gentle assertiveness on the part of a woman is not only more becoming but, likewise, more effective....

The world of work is a man's world. Women must either play by the rules or suffer the consequences.[10]

PITFALLS OF THE FEMALE TRAIT APPROACH

Trait theories dominated leadership investigations conducted between World War I and World War II. However, they later fell into disfavor because of the inconclusiveness of the results. The trait approach to defining leadership centers on an individual's qualities such as initiative, dependability, extroversion, dominance, and intelligence. These qualities often are viewed as innate attributes of a potential leader. The various personal characteristics studied were not found to yield consistent differences, but were found to differentiate leaders from followers and effective from ineffective leaders under specific conditions. Vestiges of the trait approach still haunt many companies in their selection practices and performance appraisals.

The failure of the trait approach can be traced primarily to its limited perspective. It ignores the fact that the situation facing the leader in terms of the type of task and organization and the nature of the subordinates interact with the characteristics of the leader to determine effective and ineffective leadership. Secondary problems include the fact that traits operate in combinations rather than singly; also that the present conceptualization and measurement of specific traits are inadequate.

Given the inadequacies of the trait approach, one might paraphrase Kurt Lewin's question: "Are the differences between males and females on various traits differences that make a difference?" Following the trait approach in studying female management may have several inherent difficulties:

• *The trait approach to studying leadership is antiquated and it is not likely that we will learn much about female management by using it.* More than twenty-five years of extensive trait studies produced inconclusive results. Should we repeat this approach in our study of women managers?

• *The study of sex-trait differences is likely to increase rather than lessen the double bind women managers face.* The presence of counter-positions in advocating appropriate traits for female leaders seems ironical in that most authors agree that organizations should break away from sex-stereotyping of managerial roles. Yet, the very nature of dwelling on sex-linked traits seems to emphasize male versus female attributes. Our language also contributes to this problem. The words we use to describe sex roles, *masculine* and *feminine,* are defined by culturally prescribed traits; consequently, when we use the terms *male* or *female* we inadvertently refer to the personality factors that define these words. The inverse then follows. When we discuss these personality traits we connote references to sex. Furthermore, the terms *male* and *female* appear in dictionaries and on personality tests as antonyms, void of any mutually shared traits. Our language system then depicts men and women as opposites and defines male and female as a personality trait. Due to this language, then, discussions of personal attributes for effective female leadership project an implicit assumption that women should reject femininity. When authors recommend that women become more assertive, less emotional, and more logical, they imply that females must acquire these *masculine* traits. Yet, when writers suggest that female executives use their soft and gentle feminine style, they imply she should not exhibit any male-oriented traits. Opportunities for the self-fulfilling prophecy to take effect may increase with continued emphasis upon the differences in male-female traits.

* *Focusing on sex-linked traits also may result in inappropriate leadership behavior by the women in light of a particular situation.* S. L. Bem has found that both men and women holding rigid traditional sex-role concepts often do not behave adaptively when the situation demands change in relation to sex-role stereotypes.[11] Personality research has found that the socialization practices of males allow incorporation of the positive male and female linked behaviors much more so than do the socialization practices of women. Following the suggestions to develop a particular trait may make a woman less effective because the trait is inappropriate for the situation she is to face.

* *Emphasis on the trait approach could lead to the demise of many potentially competent female managers.* With the lack of female role models, women do not have the opportunities that men have to observe how different behavioral strategies work in different settings. Thus these women become significantly more dependent upon expert prescriptions for effective managerial behavior than do their male counterparts. This dependency may not only lead her to some behaviors inappropriate to the particular situation, but it may force her to develop behavior patterns that are contrary to her particular strengths.

SITUATION MODEL OF FEMALE
MANAGERIAL BEHAVIOR

Basically, the trait approach is not useful because it characterizes leadership in terms of personal characteristics. It ignores the nature of the task, the organizational context, and any characteristics of the followers. In addition, this approach neglects the important fact that leadership is not static, but dynamic. The accomplishment of the task involves a complex interplay of forces between the leader and the situational factors that she or he faces. Utilizing a trait approach tends to lead a person to the conclusion that differences between the sexes in organizations must be biologically based; utilizing a situational or interactive approach helps us recognize that some sex differences are situational or interpersonal effects rather than trait differences. For example, much recent research suggests that women are not lower than men in need for achievement but have redirected their achievement drives in more socially acceptable ways.[12] It is the author's contention that managers might focus more on providing conditions which will encourage women to express achievement drives, rather than to assume that women have low needs for achievement.

The situational approach focuses on what behaviors a manager needs to perform to be effective and attempts to determine what behavior patterns will work in a given environment. Based on the trait perspective, the female manager may be told to be aggressive or forceful with her people. In contrast, an advocate of the situational approach would examine the interaction between the situation and the people. If the woman is managing a group of people with little experience to accomplish a task which is ambiguous and for which the organization has offered few guidelines, she might provide direction to the group for the goals to be accomplished, and clarify what work paths should be followed. However, if she is managing a group of research specialists on a project similar to one they have done many times, she may allow them to set their own goals, and use some of their suggestions for modifying the work process. If this same manager is attending a budget review meeting she may argue assertively for her department's needs, present her viewpoints clearly and point out flaws in others' ideas. But in a meeting to discuss problems in her department, she may listen attentively, clarify feelings being expressed, and ensure that minority viewpoints are heard.

The situation model also assumes that, in a particular setting, managers with different characteristics may use different behavioral approaches to accomplish the same end. In working with the poor performer, a dominant and highly knowledgeable manager may attempt to teach the subordinate all the correct procedures. On the other hand, a supportive and considerate manager may use her interpersonal skills to help the individual identify the cause of the poor performance and reinforce the subordinate's efforts to improve his or her ability.

It is not the intention of the authors to state that there are no biological or cultural differences between male and female managers, but that those differences may or may not be relevant to their managerial capability. The contention here is that to focus on appropriate situational responses for leaders over time will make the question of the manager's gender relatively unimportant. Traits may be sex-linked, but behavior patterns are not necessarily so. However, during these times of social transition and upheaval, both men and women are being influenced in their behavior by past social conditioning and present expectations. Women managers who are inconsiderate of their subordinate's needs and feelings may have less satisfied subordinates than do their male counterparts because our social conditioning leads us to expect women to be more considerate than men. Therefore, it is important to look at how women and men respond to similar conditions and how different environments give rise to adaptive and non-adaptive behavioral strategies.

We would discourage advising a woman to develop a certain trait; rather, we would suggest adapting her behavior to the situation. Development of a universal set of traits will force her into a predetermined mold (traditionally male-defined) which may be ineffective for her and her situation. Moreover, following a situational model will increase the emphasis upon changing certain aspects of the environment rather than trying to change the person.

NOTES

[1] R. Bremer, "When the Supervisor Is a Woman," *Supervisory Management* (July 1973), p. 16.

[2] D. C. Basil, *Women in Management* (New York: Dunellen Publishing Company, 1972), pp. 96 and 108.

[3] E. Lynch, *The Executive Suite—Feminine Style* (New York: American Management Association, 1973), p. 27.

[4] See Bremer, "Supervisor Is a Woman"; Basil, *Women in Management;* Lynch, *Executive Suite;* also see M. Woods, "What Does It Take for a Woman to Make It in Management?" *Personnel Journal* (January 1975), pp. 38 – 40; C. Epstein, "Women's Place," in E. Ginsberg and A. Yohalem, eds., *Corporate Lib—Women's Challenge to Management* (Baltimore: Johns Hopkins University Press, 1973).

[5] For a comprehensive review of all the research on trait studies of leadership, see R. M. Stogdill, *Handbook of Leadership: Theory and Research* (New York: The Free Press, 1974).

[6] P. Rosencrantz, S. Vogel, H. Bee, I. Boverman, and D. Broverman, "Sex-Role Stereotypes and Self-Concepts in College Students," *Journal of Consulting and Clinical Psychology* (June 1968), pp. 287–95.

[7] G. K. Baruch, "Feminine Self-Esteem, Self Ratings of Competence and Maternal Career Commitment," *Journal of Counseling Psychology* (September 1973), pp. 487–88.

[8] Stogdill, *Handbook of Leadership.*

[9] Basil, *Women in Management.*

[10] L. C. Hackamach and A. B. Solid, "The Woman Executive," *Business Horizons* (April 1972), p. 102; J. Dunlap, *Personal and Professional Success for Women* (New Jersey: Prentice-Hall, 1972), p. 21.

[11] S. L. Bem, "Fluffy Women and Chesty Men," *Psychology Today* (September 1975), pp. 58–62.

[12] A. Stein and M. Bailey, "The Socialization of Achievement Orientation in Females," *Psychological Bulletin* (November 1973).

DISCUSSION QUESTIONS

1. List some ways that women might act in a leadership situation that could be branded "unfeminine."

2. Since no evidence has been found to link aggressiveness to management skills, are all the current "assertiveness-training" programs appropriate? Will assertiveness training prove to the another fad foisted on unsuspecting people?

3. List any emotional outbursts you have witnessed from women at work. Now list any emotional outbursts you have witnessed from men. Which list is longer?

4. Is it possible that males and females are really more alike than they are different—having the same kind of hopes for themselves and their families? Is it appropriate to define "male" and "female" as personality traits?

VII

Viewing
Past Accomplishments
and Future Strategies
for Progress

On their own, women have made surprisingly significant contributions to management—a field that has been closed to them. It is good to identify those women who have been prominent in upgrading women's quality of life. These women can act as role models for all of us.

So far we have examined the problems that women have faced and are facing in gaining equal opportunity. In the final analysis, women themselves must put forth the effort to claim their rightful place in the working world. This section includes some ideas and strategies that will help women climb career ladders.

Continuing education is a key to success today. With the world's knowledge doubling every three to five years, no one can stop studying and still hope to remain professionally successful for very long. Women must know not only what kinds of strategies to use but they must also upgrade and continue their professional development through education.

It is clearly *not* my intention to advocate that qualified women should begin in organizations as secretaries with the hope that they will be promoted into management positions. In fact, qualified women should *not* begin as secretaries since they become so stereotyped into that supportive role that it becomes virtually impossible for them to be considered for anything else. There are still job counselors today who advise women college graduates to take a secretarial position "just to get a foot in the door." This kind of counseling is not only unnecessary in this enlightened age of equal opportunity but it can also deal a blow to the future growth and development of the individual.

However, it *is* important to recognize that there are literally thousands of women today who either have some college education or an earned degree and who are working in dead-end clerical or secretarial positions. Many of these women have either aided in or actually made many important decisions and also have an excellent overview of the organization and how it functions. Therefore, they have earned the right for upward mobility; this right is yet to be fully acknowledged.

It is also important to recognize that the secretarial field could be a natural training ground for management; but only when managers consider it as such, and when male employees also participate fully in this role will it be safe for women to enter the secretarial field as a starting place toward upward mobility.

Women's Contributions to
Management Thought

Bette Ann Stead

The evolutionary process through which the field of management has come since the turn of the century can be briefly described in three eras: 1910 to late 1920s—scientific management (work-measurement approach); late 1920s to 1959—human relations (contented-cow approach); and 1960 to the present—behavioral management science (interdisciplinary approach using psychology, sociology, and anthropology). To each of these areas, women have made significant—but largely unrecognized—contributions. These contributions may be termed highly unusual since women traditionally have been barred from management careers.

Why have women been moved to contribute to an area in which neither they nor their contemporaries could find a future? We may see the answer in the nature of woman herself. Women have always been interested in the betterment of life for all people. Women have worked in fields devoted to improving the human condition, such as nursing, teaching, and social work. It follows as a natural progression that women would be interested in bettering the human condition in the vast area of the work environment. This article reviews some of the past and present contributions made by women to the field of management.

THE SCIENTIFIC MANAGEMENT ERA

The scientific management era began about 1910 and is credited to Frederick W. Taylor. Much of the thinking during this era was characterized by the notion that people work for only one reason—money. Much of the work was organized as piecework, and workers were paid by the number

Bette Ann Stead, "Women's Contributions to Management Thought," *Business Horizons* (February 1974), pp. 32-36. Copyright 1974 by the Foundation for the School of Business at Indiana University. Reprinted by permission.

of items they produced. Therefore, much of the research was aimed toward influencing workers to produce more pieces. The notion was that, since people worked only for money, they could be treated as machines and trained to produce more and more. No one contributed more to this era of management than Lillian Gilbreth (1878-1972).

Probably more is known of the personal life of Gilbreth than any of the other women discussed in this article. The Gilbreth family has been immortalized in books; *Cheaper by the Dozen, Bells on Their Toes,* and *Frank and Lillian Gilbreth: Partners for Life* all portray the events and characters that made up her life. In addition, Myrna Loy's touching portrayal of Gilbreth in the popular 1950 movie *Cheaper by the Dozen* is still run occasionally on television.

We know that Gilbreth felt the burden of discrimination in her life. Her Phi Beta Kappa key was delayed. She coauthored with her husband a significant work, *Primer of Scientific Management,* yet only her husband's name appears on the work. The publisher did not want a woman's name to appear as collaborator. Her thesis "The Psychology of Management" was refused by several publishers, who explained that they could not accept a book on such a subject by a woman author. Finally, in a series of articles appearing from May 1912 – May 1913, the magazine *Industrial Engineering* published it, and in 1914 a book publisher accepted it. However, in both instances her name appeared as L. M. Gilbreth, and no publicity could be given to the fact that the author was a woman.

Even in later years, after she had been honored with awards, honorary degrees, and memberships on prestigious committees, she was denied entrance to two clubs. The University Club in New York refused to let her in, even though her name was printed on a program as a participant in an event being held inside. The Engineering Club denied her entrance, although she was a member of an American Society of Mechanical Engineers committee which was meeting within. The committee members told her to eat alone at a nearby restaurant, and that they would meet with her later for a few moments. However, her record of continuing honors showed that she would not allow these slights to deter her work.

Frank Gilbreth died in 1924, and Lillian Gilbreth remained a major figure in management for more than forty years after his death. Together, they began the field of motion study, which combined the fields of management and mechanical engineering. But it was Lillian who quickly recognized that the key to managerial success is the individual and his feelings. Her thesis dealing with the psychology of management presents the underlying theme of all her work. As early as 1911, she was recognized for her work, which was absolutely different from that being followed by any other researcher in the scientific management field. She stressed that the emphasis in good management must be more on the man than on the work, and that effective teaching would enable the man to make better use of his abilities.

She never put quantitative results over the consideration of the quality of the worker's life while he was on the job. She genuinely believed in political democracy, and was convinced that its preservation depended on industrial democracy.

THE HUMAN RELATIONS ERA

A new management era dawned in the early twenties when the famous Hawthorne studies began. These studies brought with them a significant breakthrough in management thinking—people's feelings must be considered. We can look back at Gilbreth's work to see that she had been heralding this approach for a long time. Mary Parker Follett (1868–1933), another woman who had been calling for the consideration of the worker as a person, had made her mark in the field of management. Ironically, she died near the beginning of the era she had worked to bring about.

Follett's philosophy and approach came fifty years ahead of their time. She stressed that intelligent organization and the administration of government and industry should work toward an honest integration of all points of view, to the end that every individual's efforts are mobilized so that he counts both as a person and as an effective part of the group and of society. These ideas ring of today's management theme of encouraging the individual to meet his own needs as well as the needs of the organization.

As a noted political scientist, her work with the Boston Placement Bureau, Vocational Guidance Bureau, and Massachusetts Minimum Wage Board, as well as her books, brought her into contact with the thinking of many businessmen. She made the natural transition to social administration, then to industrial organization and administration.

Her thinking can be clearly seen in the current behavioral approach to management science. She applied her knowledge of psychology and sociology to industrial problems. Today colleges of business administration are removing the word "business" from their titles as they realize that the principles of administration can be applied to many areas of activity other than business. Follett saw too that the principles that are discovered in the social sciences are applicable in many areas. Her viewpoint that every human activity is merely a moment in a process can be seen in today's systems approach. Her notion of reciprocal reaction in solving differences through conference and cooperation is indeed a forerunner of today's conflict resolution techniques. Follett's approach involved having the parties evoke each other's latent ideas based upon the facts of the situation, come to see and understand each other's points of view, and integrate those viewpoints by uniting toward a common goal.

She was already searching for how business management might become a profession—a problem which still needs a solution. Among her writings are more than twenty-five papers presented here and in England about business organization and administration. Her wide acceptance by businessmen would be enviable today but may be considered a phenomenon of the time in which she lived and worked.

THE BEHAVIORAL SCIENCE ERA

The human relations era had brought about a rash of extrinsic solutions for improving employee morale and increasing production. The years between 1930 and 1959 introduced coffee breaks, plush carpets, fine office furniture and equipment, and piped-in music. All of these accoutrements were intended to treat the worker as a human being or make him into a "contented cow." But they only worked up to a point.

By 1960 the "affluent society" had become a reality for many people. Management discovered that not only had all the coffee breaks, plush carpets, and so on, not been completely effective, but labor problems were becoming more prominent. The era of behavioral management science began about 1960. During this era came the realization that our understanding of the worker had to be much broader than it was in the superficial human relations era. To get this deeper understanding, management turned to the disciplines of psychology, sociology, and anthropology, and considered these within the context of the work environment. This era is relatively new, but it was encouraged by Gilbreth through her work in psychology and by Follett through her efforts in sociology. Today women in increasing numbers are active in behavioral management science.

Truly a "superstar" in management today is Jane Mouton. Her research and writing with Robert R. Blake are known throughout both academia and industry. Blake and Mouton began as teachers, but now they are president and vice-president, respectively, of Scientific Methods, Inc., Austin, Texas. Their company is actively involved in management consulting all over the world. They have been prolific writers, and their work has appeared in scholarly journals, business journals, and books.

Their most well-known work is probably *The Managerial Grid*, a finely researched volume that presents an instrument for identifying leadership style. The authors show how a manager can simultaneously maximize two leadership styles—production- and people-oriented—thus achieving the benefits of both. By using the model in the book, a manager can study and change his own leadership style.

Beginning managers may have scientific, engineering, or business service skills and yet there may be a missing ingredient. That ingredient is the ability to create the environment in which people will willingly work toward company objectives. Blake and Mouton, along with some other coauthors, have researched and written several books about this topic, including *Corporate Excellence Through Grid Organization, The Grid for Sales Excellence,* and *Corporate Darwinism.* Another work, *Corporate Excellence Diagnosis,* describes a means of total corporation health assessment through a 72-window rubric.

The Blake-Mouton writing style is clear and readable. Behavioral management science is new compared to other recognized disciplines, but these two authors have successfully analyzed and synthesized the research that has been done, and they have presented it in a form that industry can easily apply. This feature of applicability is a major break-through—a bridge between academia's research and industry's needs.

Joan Woodward, a faculty member in industrial sociology at the Imperial College of Science and Technology, is a social scientist of the first rank. Her works, *Industrial Organization: Theory and Practice* (1965) and *Industrial Organization: Behavior and Control* (1970) are considered "musts" for every graduate student in business who is studying organizational behavior. She is outstanding in her ability to conceptualize and hypothesize, and to do research that is aimed at building a strong body of knowledge for organization theory.

Her first book was a study of 100 firms in South Essex. By relating the firms' organization characteristics to three simple categories of technology, she found that specific organizational patterns were associated with each category. In the past, technology had been ignored and the predominant view was that there is one best way to run any manufacturing business.

Her second book looks at medium to large batch production firms and firms with a component assembly production system. She points out that variations in structure and behavior found in these firms depend more on the nature of the control system than on the technology.

Her studies in the field are all made within the same conceptual framework; in this way she identifies common threads that can be related to theoretical considerations. She stresses that patient and detailed exploration of what actually happens inside industrial firms is a prerequisite to developing an organization theory comprehensive enough to provide managers with a reliable basis for their decisions and actions. She asks that managers use her work as an explanatory framework to compare their own firm with the firms she describes to understand how and why theirs are different.

Riva Poor is known as a leading advocate for the four-day, forty-hour work week. As author, lecturer, and management consultant, her first book *4 Days, 40 Hours* was a collection of thirteen articles and five appendixes that assembled the writings and research of fifteen authors. She also pursued the topic of decision making.

She majored in social sciences at Bennington College and in organizational development at the Sloan School of Management, MIT. She holds a master's degree in city planning from MIT. Edward C. Bursk, editor of *The Harvard Business Review*, is her partner in Bursk and Poor Publishing. She has owned and operated several small businesses, edited several business reports and newsletters, and started a successful minority business program.

The "Acknowledgements" section of Poor's book gives some insight into her personal life. She credits her parents with rearing her to be a businesswoman and her husband for being a true helpmeet. We know that cultural biases from the family environment have done much to discourage or thwart the educational and professional development of many women. We have all seen girls who were brought up to believe that having a husband and children should be their only goal in life. We have all seen husbands who, insecure in their own right, have stood in the way of their wives' chances for any sort of development.

Christel Kammerer is known for her concept "gleitende arbeitzeit" or "gliding time." She is a West German management consultant who was hired by Messerschmitt-Bolkow to work on problems of absenteeism and punctuality. In 1967, the gliding time system was launched, and since then about 3,500 West German firms have adopted it. Some people are biologically programmed to be "day" or "early" people and are eager to get started in the morning. "Night" people do their most productive work late in the day. Companies using gliding time keep their doors open from 7 a.m. to 7 p.m.; employees schedule themselves to fill a forty-hour week.

In one West German company, one-day absenteeism dropped 60 percent under gliding time, while production went up 5 percent and morale soared. In this country gliding time has been successfully used by the American Optometric Association since February 1973. Of their seventy employees, forty are now on gliding time and, according to J. Harold Bailey, executive director, they seem to like it. Bailey states that the amount of work performed has increased while the amount of overtime has dropped considerably.

Gliding time may prove to be a real breakthrough. Not only can it solve problems of absenteeism and morale, but there may be some possible interesting and useful spin-offs. For example, how much traffic congestion could be relieved in downtown and office park areas if all employees could come and go at different times?

April 2, 1972, brought a new era for women. On that date Revised Order 4, issued under Executive Order 11246, went into effect. Within 120 days from the commencement of a federal contract, each prime contractor or subcontractor with fifty or more employees and a contract of $50,000 or more must develop a written affirmative action compliance program setting forth goals and time tables for the employment and promotion of women. If women have made significant contributions in the past to a field that has been closed to them, we can only speculate on what contributions they will make in the future to a field that is beginning to open to them.

DISCUSSION QUESTIONS

1.   Interview women who have made improvements in your organization and/or community. Write short biographies of them. Get the subjects' permission to submit these biographies to your company president for memberships on task forces, or to your mayor or governor for memberships on boards or commissions. (Note: Since many executives say they don't know any qualified women, they would probably find your biographies useful.)

2.   Do you know of women who have received "professional putdowns" and yet have risen above these disappointments to achieve some measure of success?

3.   What examples have you seen of work measurement being used today?

4.   Do you know of families who have put up road blocks to the professional development of women relatives?

5.   Identify some women who have published in some area of business during the past ten years. Make an annotated bibliography of their writings. Write to each for a brief biographical sketch that can be added to your bibliography. Can you identify any common threads in their lives?

What Does it Take for a Woman to Make it in Management?

Marion M. Wood

Interviews with nearly 100 women in the Los Angeles area, holding positions ranging from management trainee to president of the company, revealed convictions, compromises and challenges which they believe define the common characteristics essential for success in a male-dominated world. Men working with, over or under these women responded with almost identical opinions, when asked the same questions.

Of the many traits identified, ten characteristics are defined here, regarding what a woman has to learn if she wants to succeed in management:

Competence	Career-Mindedness
Education	Femininity
Realism	Strategy
Aggressiveness	Support of an Influential Male
Self-Confidence	Uniqueness

PROFILE OF THE SUCCESSFUL WOMAN

The successful Los Angeles businesswoman is well-groomed, soft-spoken, slim and youthful; probably has a bachelor's degree if she is under 35, possibly a master's or a doctorate. With or without a degree, at any age, she began with her company at a low entry level. She is just as apt to be married as not married. If not married, she is just as apt to be divorced as single. Those who are married profess to be happily so and feel strongly that it is quite possible to do both jobs efficiently. Of the unmarried, there

Marion M. Wood, "What Does It Take for a Woman to Make it in Management?" *Personnel Journal* (January 1975), pp. 38-41, 60. Reprinted with permission: copyright *Personnel Journal* January 1975.

are just as many who consider singleness an asset as who claim marriage will be welcome and will not interfere with career plans.

The divorced working woman usually has children, and her motive for seeking more responsible work is probably financial rather than a need for independence (though she candidly concedes it is difficult to say which is the stronger motive). Finally, no matter what her marital status, the woman over 35 is likely to have specific, established goals. If she's over 35, she "never dreamed" she would become a career woman and manager. She knows from experience that progress has been slow, with advances accelerating during the past five years.

COMPETENCE AND EDUCATION

"We have to learn from men at the same time we are competing with them," pointed out a female department head in a food manufacturing firm. "In spite of the law, we can't assume right now that we're equal to men. We still must approach with tact and discretion. Men need to be assured we are intelligent; we aren't after their jobs; there's room for all of us."

Both men and women agree that women aspiring to promotion up the corporate ladder must be competent and well educated. "Get a good education so you won't have to depend on the lucky breaks," they advise young women. "Attend management development classes. Let management know you're really serious." Women who have been promoted "thanks to lucky breaks" are securing their progress by taking advantage of company-paid tuition programs to work toward degrees or for specialized training.

Although competence is probably equally weighted when it comes to assessing potentiality of men and women, at this stage of history requirements appear to be tougher for the woman. "She has to work twice as hard as a man to prove herself," is a typical male opinion.

REALISM

Women are well aware of this disparity. "Recent developments have made it easier for us, but it's a hard, cold fact ... you've got to be better than a man or you may not get it," said a female engineer in middle management. "We have to be sharper than the average man in order to progress."

Men in a position to effect the promotion of women concede that the above is true. What's more, they say, a woman has to prove herself longer. "Women frequently have to wait much longer for promotions than men do. And when they are given more responsibility, we tend to ask them to take longer apprenticeships than the young men have to."

Another male executive responsible for finding women candidates for management explained, "We look for women with unusually sound qualifications so that top management won't have immediate barriers for rationalization (in turning them down). Women need as many calling cards as they can get. I hate to say it, but it's true that some women in management are working twice as hard as the men, and getting half as much."

Women recognize, too, that change takes time. Neither federal law nor the threat of losing contracts can make men accept women as competitors. Change of attitudes in individual men (and women) must come about before women will make significant progress, and astute women accept this fact.

"Don't buck the system," advises a woman engineer. "Work through it as it exists, and improve it. First find out the situation." And a woman production head points out, "We're in a transitional period. We will be, for at least another five years, so it's pretty crucial how we handle ourselves and our opportunities."

AGGRESSIVENESS

Just as crucial to a woman's success is her aggressiveness and, in particular, her ability to disguise it as self-initiative. "Male managers," most women claim (and many men concede), "are afraid of women with drive, yet lack respect for those without it; they want (a woman) to show initiative but not be aggressive." By any name, however, the achieving woman is aggressive and competitive.

"It takes an aggressive woman to get ahead," said a male executive in charge of industrial relations. "A passive woman doesn't have a chance. She must have confidence in herself ... be willing to take a counterposition, but not go out of her way to create conflict."

How do men define aggressiveness? During interviews, they gave considerable thought to this and came up with such diverse perceptions of "female aggressiveness" as "not being afraid of responsibility" ... "seizing opportunities when she sees them" ... "operating in an anticipatory manner" ... "extraordinarily high drive; first-rate professionalism" ... "self-confident, self-assured, knowing that she is capable; aggressive only to goal extent" ... "having to want it and being ready for stiff competition" ... "willingness to compete with men; living up to the same requirements of the job and not asking for exceptions and privileges" ... "producing" ... "putting her own ego aside."

Curiously, when men are forced to give aggressiveness a personal definition, they tend to be more accepting of the characteristic in women. When women try to define it, they are self-conscious, in view of men's strong reaction, so they, too, grope for softer terms. "Aggressiveness is important, but you don't need to be like a man," summarized a young woman manager. "Upward aggressiveness is good; hostility is not good. You can't wait around for someone to tell you what to do. If you do, they'll give you something that's not very interesting."

Women who have male managers subordinate to them are more candid. They don't need to be overly concerned with modifying their definitions. "I'm playing an aggressively competitive role. I'm a winner — to win but not to beat the other guy," one said. "For the woman who is aggressive and ambitious, I'll work long and hard to help her," said another, who sees little to be gained in wasting time with semantics. "Qualities for success are exactly the same for women as for men."

This, of course, should hold true for self-confidence, yet women apparently must make an extra effort to show the world how they feel about themselves.

SELF-CONFIDENCE

Never let it show if your self-confidence weakens at times, say the winners. Don't let yourself be put on the defensive; that leads to defeat. "Women underestimate their ability," in the opinion of many women. Their determination has to be stronger than men's ... they have to work on self-confidence. "Convince yourself first and see yourself as the person you want to be. Once you have your own self-image established, you can sell it to someone else."

"Change must come from within the woman herself, as well as from within the business. We block our own progress by refusing to change our attitudes or by being insensitive to the need to change self-concepts," say women who have learned from experience. "Many (women) are fearful of male competition, fearful they won't make it. Women are going to have to change their own minds about their potential. You can't run around with a chip on your shoulder. You can't look at affronts as personal. There are going to be a lot of disillusioned women. A lot of disappointments. Because success is dependent upon attitude. You have to believe in yourself as a person."

CAREER-MINDEDNESS

A corollary to making men believe that women believe in themselves is for women to convince men they really want a career. This is not easy, they report. "Convincing yourself of your capability and making a commitment are not enough, you have to make the men believe you are serious about a career." Men frankly admit there are women in their organizations who would qualify for promotion into management, but they find it difficult to believe that women are sufficiently career-minded to be a good investment. And, in spite of an increasing rate of turnover in male management, men still believe that women, particularly young ones, are more apt to abandon a career. They need special convincing.

Unfortunately for the women who are truly career-minded, men's fears are continually supported by experience. Many more women than men turn down opportunities for advancement. And, as one personnel manager pointed out, another fact is that men are "more apt to accept appointments and transfers of any nature. This is often because they really don't have a choice. Women do (have a choice) and they give us a problem. They reject transfers and we have to accept their decisions."

Not many concrete suggestions for convincing management were proposed by the women interviewed for this study. One suggestion was: "It's more helpful for women to be taking courses in management — more helpful than for men. Men don't really believe you're going to stick with it, so the more you do, the more you convince them of your intentions." The most candid advice was given by a male in top management who said if he were a woman who was asked how long she planned to stay with an organization, he would say, "As long as you keep me challenged."

Married women, in particular, must know how to respond convincingly to management concerning questions about their careers and homes. Women with the most responsible and time-consuming jobs reported that all their housekeeping chores are delegated to paid help. Some even turn over all the meal planning and marketing. One of the most difficult questions to answer is what will happen in the event of a transfer — of either the husband or herself. Solutions are being found. Most organizations have eased nepotism rules and some managements are going out of their way to find an acceptable job for the husband in the same company or in the city where the wife will be transferred.

The advice of many successful women is to give work the highest priority. "A job must come first, if we women are going to actually achieve top jobs in business, industry and education; particularly if we move into the offices in a corporate division," one female executive emphasized. Finally, women who have made it say that once given the opportunity, a woman must be constantly alert to the need to keep management convinced she is permanent.

FEMININITY

The management role does not mean playing a male role. Both men and women stressed this, even though perceptions varied widely on the distinction. Attempts to define femininity seem to stumble most when dealing with traits like aggressiveness and competitiveness.

"Women who get ahead tend to be a little more feminine," explained one male personnel manager. "They are not overly aggressive, not hard nosed, and more friendly." Another said candidly, "Women who can manipulate and use their femininity are much better at management than are men. The issue is to do it well."

Some men resorted to emotional modifiers in describing femininity while others defined it more pragmatically. "Femininity is soft, pleasing, warm, ..." "It's empathy ... ability to listen ... showing enthusiasm, capability ... being equipped ... patient, tolerant, humble. ..." "Femininity is sensitivity ... it's toning it down and still looking intelligent."

As for the women, some simply dismissed the subject, contending that too much is made of defining the term and worrying about it when the fundamental thing is to get the job done.

A few feared that if they get aggressive and take risks, they lose their femininity. More prevalent, though, was the feeling that all this is "nonsense," that aggressiveness is not exclusively a male trait, nor is it incompatible with femininity. To be successful, a woman must be both.

Women were even more adamant about the notion than were men. "Control your personality," advised one woman manager. "Dress like a woman. Conduct yourself like a woman. Be gracious and intelligent. Don't try to imitate a man. (The male establishment) has been with us too long. We can't change the environment; just adapt to it."

STRATEGY

To put all this advice to the most effective use, the smart woman must work out a strategy, and the study yielded a number of ideas for going about this. A woman needs a set of goals and a plan and, according to most of the women interviewed, women would do well to use men as their model for these techniques. "We have to learn from men at the same time as competing with them," admitted a young, ambitious manager. "Until I reached the supervisory level, I was not competing with men. When I went up to manager, I was." And that, she said, was when she discovered how much could and had to be learned from men.

What does it take to compete successfully with men? "Patience. Sensitivity. Understanding of their motives." Women have to start changing the men's thinking ... but they must learn the strategy of "not making it look like a threat." Said one woman programmer, "You have to gain the confidence of the men with the soft sell, but I guess my way is kind of sneaky. I've seen girls who are pushy and are left by the wayside. I'm not going to compete with the guys."

A middle-aged woman management training director cautioned, "Don't climb for one particular position within an organization. This is one of men's problems. You may have to go from company to company, area to area, to meet your goals."

Paychecks represent another sensitive area for women. Men claim it's up to women to get more money ... and women who are getting more money confirm this over and over. Traditionally, women have not been trained to bargain. Most have not learned that a salary offered is not a constant, but a starting point for discussion. She has to know her value and strive to make the salary match it. To gain success and status, she must learn to negotiate more to her advantage. Men—even those who acknowledge that women underrate themselves—will continue considering women "cheap help" as long as women continue to accept lower offers than they are worth.

One of the few women in top management in the Los Angeles area admitted that for years she had followed the familiar pattern of gratefully accepting incremental raises in a salary that had started below scale. Then someone advised her, "If you want to play in a man's field, act like a man." Through sheer self-discipline and actual rehearsal of her demand statement, she obtained a substantial raise. She followed this strategy year after year, pushing her salary level up to where she believed it should be by getting proportionally larger annual increases than she would have received by remaining silent. And if the strategy doesn't work within one organization, this woman advised, then move around. At one point in her own progress when she responded to one of several job offers, she said quite frankly, "Let's talk salary. My purpose in transferring is to get a higher salary level." And she did.

SUPPORT OF AN INFLUENTIAL MALE

No matter what a successful woman's strategy, it is certain that she had a supportive male influence and, for most, usually at each level in her career.

Fathers are reported as having been sources of encouragement during the early career-decision period of the lives of many women. They have helped intelligent, ambitious daughters to "dare to set high goals" and encouraged them to major in math, engineering or in some field which seemed to be open only to men. And, the women recall, their fathers "pushed them to achieve in spite of the subtle, if not overt, social stigma associated with career-oriented women."

Husbands, too, are a primary factor in a woman's decision to push success in business. They must be supportive, the women insist, not only to make their careers possible, but also to make their marriages work. "My husband is 100% behind me. Marriage would have been impossible, otherwise." As to their careers, husbands have been "very proud of my achievement" … "understanding, helpful" … "happy because I'm happy."

Husbands do not always wield strong influence, but when they do not, usually some other man has played a supporting role in the women's career. The single woman, for example, has succeeded without a husband. "I'm single, so I don't have to worry about competing with my husband," said an attractive woman in her thirties. "I don't have that load on me and couldn't live that way. The only way I'd get married would be when I wouldn't put any demands on a husband, and I wouldn't want any on me." Some divorced women spoke similarly, claiming they had left their husbands because they "stood in their way."

Although the majority of the married women interviewed believed that they could succeed both with their marriage and their career, some expressed apprehension: "A woman is torn between family and career and it's difficult in certain situations to determine the priority." Frequently, when married women face a dual allegiance, "husbands only make it worse," some claim. But just as many women feel differently. A female engineer, for example, reported, "My husband is also an engineer. He doesn't mind my being one."

In addition to supportive husbands and fathers, women who are succeeding in management also give substantial credit to bosses or friends who have provided encouragement and assistance. "I've been fortunate enough to work for managers who saw me as a person—recognized that I could do more than I was doing, and encouraged my getting more training," said one young woman in a management training program. "I've had an excellent manager who recognizes my potential and tries to do everything he can," said another, the first woman in the organization to be sent to a special company training conference.

Frequently heard was the statement, "She started with a man who had a lot of faith in women." A male manager describing the success of a middle-aged woman in his company, added, "Behind every successful woman you can be sure there's a man who has helped her." And a male

Equal Employment Opportunity director emphasized, "For a woman to succeed, there must be a man in her life who believed it's the right thing to do."

The seemingly conflicting characteristics discussed so far find congruence in a final category of advice offered by men and women who participated in this study.

UNIQUENESS AS WOMEN

Women have unique talents and qualities that complement those which men possess. Tasks and responsibilities, therefore, should be designed to make best use of male and female qualities—both independently and interdependently. So stated the persons who were interviewed.

Many men feel that women use men as models primarily because of the lack of female models, in management, but most believe it is unfortunate. "Women should capitalize on their assets," the men emphasized. Older career women, some pointed out, stay more uniquely women than do the younger ones moving up in the organization.

Men also admit they are discovering that women communicate with women better than men can, and some male managers are trying to put this capability to good use with their clients, feeling that women who are diplomatic in using their femininity are much better at getting things done the way they want it. Men don't seem to resent this; rather, they confess admiration for a woman who is "firm, yet feminine."

A male engineer, whose immediate supervisor is a woman manager, said he had been working with women for many years and found them easier to work with than men. They don't have a lot of the hangups some men have. For example, men worry about office size, office-with-windows and other irrelevancies.

More than one of the men interviewed pointed out that "Woman's strength is *sensitivity*. That is what she will get ahead on." And others, when considering fields in which they believe women would excel, recalled stereotypes which may carry more truth than many women wish to admit. Women should do well, they claimed, in responsibilities requiring "more detail and patience."

These comments imply that men see differences, but see them as assets which they hope women will retain when they assume managerial positions. Some men, of course, say there really aren't any differences. Said one, "There's nothing particularly unique in the personality structure of women supervisors. They don't ask for special favors. They want to be treated like human beings. One individual (on our staff) is a lot less emotional than men in the same position. We have some creative women in marketing, personnel and labor relations, as well as in traditional areas like home economics and accounting jobs."

How women feel about their uniqueness is summarized by a woman in top management of a large Los Angeles firm. "The answer is going to come from individual women who are able to open doors because they are qualified. Women who do a job on a professional basis. Women who are low key, who sell themselves and their abilities first, and then their product. It is important that women develop the same bond that men feel for one another. They must also look and act professional and not try to emulate men. Women have a special something to offer in addition to a fine mind and ability — intuitiveness, sensitivity, understanding, fairness, enthusiasm, and a fresh new approach."

To succeed in management, then, it would appear a woman has to be all things to all people. Assuming she is competent, and providing she has the support of her husband and/or another influential male, she is cautioned to be realistic in her expectations, to exude self-confidence even when she doesn't have it at times, to develop strategies both for assuring management she is career-minded and for pushing her way ahead, and to act like a man but stay feminine.

In short, she must temper her aspirations with an understanding of the situation as it is, in order to achieve a successful career in management.

DISCUSSION QUESTIONS

1. In any office building, more men than women seem to be "professionally dressed." Is this because they are better paid and can afford more professional clothes or is there some other reason?

2. What plan do you have for making yourself more competent in your particular field?

3. What examples do you know of women who have had to wait longer than men for promotion or who have had to serve longer internships?

4. "You can't look at affronts as personal." How do you accomplish this?

5. Are today's male employees readily accepting transfers without question?

6. Think of some men you have admired professionally. What qualities do they have that we could all learn from?

7. Identify some people who are successful at negotiating good salaries and fringe benefits for themselves. Get a list of helpful hints from them.

8. What examples do you know of men who are supportive toward their wives' careers? How do they show their support?

9. What are some ways a woman can remain "feminine" and still be a successful manager?

Keys
to the Executive
Powder Room

Caroline Donnelly

At long last women are being admitted to executive suites and board rooms, and not just to serve coffee or take notes. Prodded by government equal rights agencies, companies are hiring female graduates for management training programs that once were for men only, and promoting into the executive ranks women who have put in ten years or more as secretaries.

Times have changed to such an extent that now men are seeking the protection of antidiscrimination laws. In 1973 a court ordered American Telephone & Telegraph to pay $38 million in compensation to women and minorities who had been victims of discrimination. In June of this year, a judge ruled that AT&T must now compensate a male employee who lost out to a less experienced female. As part of the 1973 court settlement, AT&T set up an affirmative action program to encourage the hiring and promotion of women; the less experienced woman in the 1976 case had been promoted as part of that program.

WHEN COMPETENCE IS NOT ENOUGH

Yet sex discrimination — the old-fashioned antifemale kind — is still a fact of life, even in big, sophisticated corporations. On average, women with college degrees are paid less than men who are high school dropouts, according to the Conference Board, a business research organization. Many women with high-sounding titles whom companies point to with pride are, in fact, relegated to such traditional backwaters of business as research and public relations. Others fill newly invented and somewhat peripheral jobs carrying out affirmative action programs; the jobs have titles like "director of minority affairs and women's concerns."

Women who have succeeded in business insist that there are techniques women can use to get ahead. To find out what they are, *Money* talked to management consultants, executive recruiters and, in particular, women executives. (Most of the women declined to be identified; one of them contended that publicity helps a man's career but hurts a woman's.) Some of the tactics they suggested are commonly used by men, but women seldom think to use them. Other tactics are especially suited to women. Everyone agreed that competence is essential to getting ahead, but that just doing a good job is not enough. In fact, according to Margaret Higginson and Thomas Quick in *The Ambitious Woman's Guide to a Successful Career* (1975), a woman who does a good job must deal with the tendency of employers to view her as merely "reliable—a trait identified with subordinates, not bosses. The dos and don'ts for aspiring women executives that emerged from *Money's* interviews:

Shake Off Ingrained Attitudes that Hold You Back

"There are many companies that are looking for women in top management positions," says Pam Flaherty, 32, a vice president of Citibank in New York. "But it is women's own self-image that must change. Fifty percent of the battle is within women themselves." Women's biggest handicap in business is passivity, according to Margaret Hennig of Simmons College, who helped set up the first graduate program in management for women there in 1974. Women, she says, often expect to fail and then behave in ways that make failure almost inevitable. Ms. Hennig and others make several more generalizations about personality traits that hold women back:

• Girls less frequently have the experience of highly competitive team sports, which help teach boys how to set goals, anticipate opponents and spread the blame in the event of failure.

• Unlike ambitious men, ambitious women tend not to buck for promotions or raises, but believe that if they work hard someone will notice and give them their due. Meanwhile, because many women don't express interest in moving up, men are confirmed in their suspicion that women aren't really committed to careers. "I've encouraged many women to try a career, but they usually disappoint me," admits Patricia M. Howe, a San Francisco-based partner in L. F. Rothschild & Co., a brokerage firm.

• Women's tendency to concentrate solely on the task at hand can blind them to the larger picture. "Whether or not we like it, women are very petty," says Sandra Brown, who publishes the Executive Woman newsletter. "A woman will spend three days negotiating a $300 contract."

Employment professionals and successful women agree that if women want to succeed, they must learn to take risks and to flout convention to some extent. One New York businesswoman, who doesn't want her name used because she feels her hard-won status would be undermined if associates learned she was once a stewardess, recalls the risk she took that led to her first promotion. She submitted to airline management an unsolicited 20-page report on low morale among flight attendants. "I was *so* presumptuous," she says now.

Take a Long View of Your Career

A study of 108 women executives by Ms. Hennig and a colleague found that while women may work all their adult lives, they tend not to regard themselves as career women until they pass 30. As a consequence, they are as much as ten years behind men in their career planning. Women should regard their jobs the way men do theirs, simply as way stations on an upward-bound career path. Grateful for what they've got, women tend to linger in dead-end jobs. They usually don't know the techniques of job switching. They are too often self-deprecating in job interviews and on résumés. "Instead of saying 'I was responsible for such and such,' they say, 'I participated,'" says Barbara Boyle Sullivan, a partner in Boyle/Kirkman Associates Inc., a firm that specializes in advising companies on meeting affirmative action requirements.

Pick Your Job Carefully

Women should go where they are a novelty rather than to industries that have been hospitable to them, like advertising and publishing. An attractive woman who has good judgment and knows the language of her field is highly visible in a sea of men. Lynn Salvage, a vice president of Bankers Trust Co. in New York, says of her clients: "They may see umpteen bankers, but they remember the one who is a woman."

Sandra Brown urges women to go into sales and other jobs where they can make a tangible contribution: "If your job can be measured in dollars and cents, it doesn't matter whether you're a woman or a three-toed horse. If it can't, you get into personalities and what people think of you." Women should get out of back-room jobs that give them little exposure to customers and other outsiders who might help them get ahead.

Shop Around for the Right Kind of Employer

Large firms are more likely to have affirmative action programs or standardized promotion schedules and pay scales that apply regardless of sex. On the other hand, small companies can be more flexible and may give an able woman a chance to prove herself, often in a variety of jobs. John Sibbald, a Chicago management consultant, counsels the ambitious woman "to position herself in a company that is going to feel the heat from regulatory agencies, and right now that is the banks and insurance companies." Barbara Sullivan goes a step further and encourages women to seek jobs with companies that have been sued by disgruntled female employees, because the embarrassed companies will probably be eager to treat women well.

Dress the Part

Women executives should dress expensively and conservatively, but not primly. Clothes are a caste mark, so a professional woman should note how secretaries in her company dress and make sure her wardrobe sets her apart. If secretaries are wearing denim miniskirts this year, she should lean to knee-length knits. Authors Margaret Higginson and Thomas Quick prescribe an attaché case, which they note "is not pretentious, and nothing looks worse than a well-dressed woman carrying a manila envelope or shopping bag."

Act the Part

A woman executive must assert herself in small ways. If she has a report to be delivered at a meeting she should present it herself, not leave it with the secretary outside the board-room door. Once inside the conference room, she should take a prominent chair. She must convince co-workers of her professionalism — put in long hours, make a point of her willingness to travel, announce her aspiration to the next job up. To counter the common impression that women don't handle situations of stress and conflict as well as men do, she should avoid displays of emotion. Explains Peggy Wyant, a brand promotion manager for Procter & Gamble in Cincinnati: "There are acceptable ways to act in a social setting that are not acceptable in business. If a woman went to see *Gone With the Wind*, it would be socially acceptable for her to cry, whereas it wouldn't be acceptable for her to cry if she were turned down by a client."

Pursue Friendships that Help Your Career

Cold blooded as it may seem, many job counselors say that women who have been promoted should disassociate themselves from their chums in the secretarial pool and other female subordinates who make comfortable companions. Instead, over lunch, after hours and around the water cooler, they should socialize with their predominantly male peers and supervisors.

Women executives have long bemoaned their exclusion from the old-boy network of businessmen who make decisions or offer advice to one another on the golf course or over lunch. Pearl Meyer, an executive vice president of Handy Associates, a New York management consulting firm, admits that she took up golf for business because it gives male associates "a handle — something to talk about." Mrs. Meyer believes that sports talk is an important business ritual and that the woman who can take part has an advantage. "They're not really talking about baseball," she says. "They're really saying, 'Hello. How are you? We have a lot in common.'"

More often than not, successful women can point to a single person — a mentor, usually a man — who was largely responsible for her success. Sometimes a mentor is an immediate supervisor with whom a woman has rapport and who brings her along as his own career advances. Many women miss this opportunity, however, because "women have a tendency to work for weak supervisors," says Pearl Meyer. But a mentor need not be a boss. An ideal mentor might be someone in another department in whom a woman can confide and who is influential enough to pull strings with her supervisor.

A woman needs a mentor early in her career to open her eyes to the possibility that she can reach the upper ranks on the organization chart. Suzanne dePasse, a vice president of Motown Records in Los Angeles, says that Berry Gordy, the firm's founder, became her mentor when she joined Motown as his assistant in 1969. Gordy not only trained her, she remembers, but "he armed me with independence and gave me confidence."

Use Your Femininity without Using Sex

Bedding down with the boss as a means for a woman to get ahead is a poor stratagem today, job counselors agree. Not that there isn't plenty of office sex: witness the shenanigans of Elizabeth Ray and associates. If anything, casual sex has become too commonplace to trade off for advancement, and most corporate versions of the casting couch have turned into antiques.

An occasional feminine wile, however, is something else again. One businesswoman remembers how, at 14, she wanted desperately to be a handler at the pony rides at a school fair. So she got up early and went down to where the teenage boys in charge were assigning girls to lead ponies around the ring. "There I was in my raggedy little car coat and I didn't get a pony," she recalls. But she had learned her lesson: "Next year I wore a dress, and I went up to one of those disgusting adolescents and said, 'Could I have a pony?'" She got one.

Often men don't see female colleagues as competitors, a fact that some women have turned to their advantage. Disarmed, men tend to talk too much, sometimes to the point of indiscretion. Women who suppress their femininity on the job may put off male associates. Barbara Sullivan of the Boyle/Kirkman consulting firm observes that charm isn't an exclusively feminine trait: some manufacturers hire handsome and personable young men to sell office equipment to secretaries. "Attractive people get ahead," she says. "If there's any discrimination, that's it."

Don't Take Legal Action Against an Unfair Employer Except as a Last Resort

The Equal Employment Opportunity Commission normally has to disclose the name of a complainant to an employer within ten days. The Department of Labor's Wage and Hour Division pledges confidentiality on complaints about pay and fringe benefits, but only up to a point. If the case goes to court the woman will be named as an alleged victim of discrimination. In any event her employer may have figured out long since who provoked the investigation. While reprisals are against the law, they can be subtle enough to make the law unenforceable, job counselors say. The woman might suddenly find she has a nitpicking boss, or conversely, nothing whatever to do. The risks are especially great for executive women, since they not only may incur the wrath of their employers but also could become branded as troublemakers throughout their industries.

Is there any ethical reason why women should not use any of the special tactics available to them? Few women executives think so. The odds against women in business have been so great for so long, says Sandra Brown, that "we ought to use everything we've got."

DISCUSSION QUESTIONS

1.   Do you know of any women with fancy titles but little responsibility or pay?

2.   Compare a Dun and Bradstreet *Million Dollar Directory* from five years ago with one today. What job titles have emerged at the corporate level that did not exist five years ago?

3.   What is there about a twenty-page report that could lead a person to a promotion?

4.   How would you dress and act the part of a woman executive in today's environment?

5.   What informal topics (like golf) can you discuss comfortably with men?

6.   If you were suddenly promoted, how would you break ties with your "old gang" at work?

Educating Women
for Administration

Bette Ann Stead

Colleges of business administration all over the country have begun to meet the special needs of women students from all segments of the university. Women who hope to progress — not only in business but also in professional careers relating to government, education, social work, journalism, engineering, and science — are looking toward the colleges of business administration. Topics courses can provide insights into the special problems women encounter in taking the first step on the administrative ladder. Some colleges are offering separate courses while others are devoting several weeks to women's needs within a social issues oriented course.

IDENTIFYING WOMEN'S SPECIAL NEEDS

The movement toward equality for women in terms of giving them the opportunity to support themselves and their families and achieve self-actualization has begun. However, the government does not have enough staff to review and evaluate all affirmative action plans. The headlines tell of massive back-pay settlements by a *few* companies, representing only a tiny margin of retribution for past injustices. In reality, most of the few organizations that have taken a stand for equality are simply paying lip service to it. Many will do nothing until federal pressure is applied. Situations still existing in 1975 demonstrate how little progress has been made.

The Department of Health, Education and Welfare (HEW) has an acute shortage of lawyers, and the lawyers HEW does have are hampered by inadequate training for work in the equal opportunity area. During the

Bette Ann Stead, "Educating Women for Administration," *Business Horizons* (April 1975), pp. 51–56. Copyright 1975 by the Foundation for the School of Business at Indiana University. Reprinted by permission.

House appropriations spring hearings, HEW revealed that the Office of Civil Rights had filled only one-quarter of its positions. The Higher Education Division has a shortage of personnel and cannot locate people who have higher education backgrounds and who can understand discrimination subtleties.

A startling statistic is that HEW has approved only fourteen affirmative action plans out of the 900 colleges and universities that have federal contracts. And so we see that full-time female professors earn $1,762 less than their male counterparts. Women's athletic department budgets also reflect disturbing differences. At the University of Minnesota, the women's athletic department budget was increased from $28,000 in 1974 to $87,000 in 1975. But the men's budget for 1975 will be $2,300,000. A quick analysis reveals that women receive 3.64 percent of the total athletic budget.[1]

After-dinner speakers, whose topics include "equal opportunity for women," frequently cite Leviticus 27:3–5, the passage that states that a man is worth 50 shekels of silver and that a woman is worth only 30 shekels (in other words, a woman is valued at 60 percent of a male's worth). The speaker will then apply the cigarette commercial slogan, "You've come a long way, baby!" to women's salaries today. But how far is "a long way"?

One out of eight families is headed by a woman. Even the strongest voices against equal opportunity for women admit that when a woman shoulders head-of-household responsibilities like a man she and her family deserve the same standard of living. But female heads of households average $134 per week while their male counterparts average $214.[2] No one should be surprised that $134 is 62.62 percent of $214. "You've come a long way, baby!" adds up to 2.62 percent since the day of the shekel. Progress is painfully slow.

The Equal Pay Act became effective June 11, 1964. But it was ten years before the Supreme Court handed down its first decision on June 3, 1974. The Court ruled that complete equalization of wage levels for *all* Corning Glass Works inspectors to the higher night-shift wage rate would achieve the law's purpose. Over a thousand women and 450 men working the day shift will share in the retroactive pay settlement. This Supreme Court ruling should end extensive litigation over various employer schemes and half measures to take corrective action.[3] With centuries of established cultural biases and little government pressure for change, it is no wonder that women still have difficulty in obtaining positions that are suitable for their education and background.

Because of the poor professional climate facing women and because there has never been a movement toward reducing women's food costs, rent, and other bills because they are women, women need as much preparation as possible to get an equal chance for success in the professional arena. The reality that is facing women today can be recognized and dealt with more effectively through a special topics course.

A WOMEN'S COURSE

Suggested Course Objectives

According to the course evaluation, the following objectives were met during a "Women in Administration" course taught in the 1974 spring semester at the University of Houston.

First, the course should prepare students to implement equal opportunity laws when they enter the working world. Equal opportunity laws add up to good personnel practices that enhance the working situation for all employees and employers. The law also provides the means for women to enter the administrative arena. It seems appropriate for students to learn to implement equal opportunity laws because they provide students with insights into ways women can be channeled into the administrative arena, and insights into far reaching social legislation that is now and will be impacting not only individuals but also profit and nonprofit organizations for years to come.

Second, the course should give students examples of role models (women) who are making positive contributions in administration. Role models have long been an effective tool for changing attitudes. Today some women can be found serving in administrative positions that are nontraditional roles. The students see and hear women talk about how they have gained administrative positions, solved problems of personal discrimination, and made positive contributions to their organizations. Their testimony gives evidence and hope of real equal opportunity. Bringing women from both profit and nonprofit sectors also seems to provide examples of all kinds of personalities that may be appropriate for different kinds of organizations.

Third, the course should present the problems that women in administration will face and suggest solutions. Problems can be described in the form of "minicases." They come from the newspapers, class members, and invited speakers. They range from sad to "hard-to-believe" to humorous. Women who are able to laugh at their situations say the humor helps to maintain their sanity. The minicases give students insights into the kinds of problems they may face and how others have dealt with these problems, a sense of shared feelings that builds empathy and group cohesion, and evidence that others have also faced problems of discrimination and dealt with them effectively.

Fourth, the course should review the current literature so that students will become aware of progress made toward putting women into administrative positions. There is a variety of good literature appearing in scholarly journals, business periodicals, trade journals, newspapers, and government publications. Given the dynamic nature of the environment, the students should be free to seek the latest developments and to find and use material that is of particular interest to them.

Fifth, the course should help prepare women students to successfully seek out administrative positions. There are few opportunities in college to tell students about the "nitty gritty" of résumés, job interviews, follow-ups, and the finding of opportunities for women to enter jobs that lead to administrative positions. Women who take this course will represent many different subject majors. They need preparation to effectively enter the business and professional world. Men with majors other than business have found their way into the administrative arena for many years. However, women have difficulty in locating jobs whether they have specific qualifications or general backgrounds. They need special help in avoiding traditional dead-end female clerical positions.

Sixth, the course should help prepare male students to aid in the development of both men and women for administrative positions. Men do take this course and make very positive contributions. They are certainly welcome. They can present the male point-of-view on issues. Their presence in the classroom lends itself to a more "real-world" atmosphere. Realistically, for the near future, more men than women will be in the position of actually implementing equal opportunity laws. Therefore, men do need to know the background and requirements of the laws.

Successful Class Activities

A number of different learning activities can be used in this course. Some of these are presented below.

Call in the Feds

Both the Equal Employment Opportunity Commission (EEOC) and the Women's Bureau of the U.S. Department of Labor are generous in providing speakers and handouts related to this topic. Field investigators and attorneys from EEOC make particularly interesting speakers as they have been on the front line in trying to settle cases both in and out of court. The handouts not only give statistical data about working women but also cover such topics as "Myths About Working Women" and "Why Women Work."

Show the Woman Administrator's Family Life

Is it possible for a woman to have both a successful administrative career and a successful family life? A panel of family members can give affirmative answers as well as poignant examples of close family cooperation.

Some examples of cooperation include a twelve-year-old boy who learns to make meat loaf as he takes his turn cooking supper; a newlywed who understands that he and his wife must attend many evening community functions related to her job; the son of a woman bank vice-president who is angered at the past and present discrimination he has seen his mother suffer; a nationally prominent female politician's husband who has to reassure his children when the press and unfounded rumors are causing difficult times; the Ph.D. husband of a woman entrepreneur who discovers that males of all ages can learn to share household responsibilities. The strong family unit can enhance the self-actualization of male or female. This kind of panel can provide not only food for thought but also insights into reality.

Discuss the Equal Rights Amendment (ERA)

Women attorneys and representatives from the League of Women Voters can provide oral and printed information that destroy the many myths of ERA. And there are many myths.

Present Successful Affirmative Action Plans

Companies only reluctantly send representatives to discuss their affirmative action plans in front of a class. A few companies have put women in charge of identifying and developing females for administrative positions. For the other panels mentioned students do very well in arranging for a variety of panel members. But in finding panel members for the topic of company affirmative action plans, the instructor will need to do some early groundwork.

Contact Sources for Finding Jobs

A most interesting panel can be drawn from company personnel officers, college placement directors, and professional personnel placement agencies that look for "executive" talent (headhunters). They can describe the current job outlook and also answer such nitty-gritty questions as, Specifically which companies and organizations are placing women in jobs with a real future?

The Class Makeup

The University of Houston class was offered at the senior level with no prerequisites. Graduate students were given credit for the course, and accounted for over half of the enrollment. Because of demand, a graduate course number has now been provided. The graduate and undergraduate students may meet together, but the major project assignments are geared to graduate or undergraduate levels.

Because of the diverse class makeup, some management theory was included — a description of the evolution of management thought; the communication process as applied to cases using Maslow's hierarchy of needs, McGregor's Theories X and Y, and Herzberg's motivators and dissatisfiers; and an introduction to leadership style. Women's contributions to management thought were also reviewed, and the stimulus-response bond was introduced as a concept to explain cultural reasons for why women discriminate against women. The course evaluations indicated that the management topics were well-received by the students. However, time constraints did not allow further emphasis. Students were counseled to take other business administration courses, and several are now doing so.

Three men completed the course. They had strong self-concepts and were among the most positive and successful contributors.

Course Requirements

The course grade is based on how well each student fulfills the three requirements. A discussion of the reading requirement, class participation, and the major project follows.

Reading Requirement

With so many diverse publications concerning the woman's movement toward job equality, using a single text does not seem appropriate. I recommend that each student prepare a twenty-five item (minimum) annotated bibliography. Each instructor can decide on the reading mix of books, journal articles, government publications, newspaper articles, and industry publications to be included. The annotated bibliography can contribute 25 percent of the course grade.

Class Participation Requirement

Participation is essential to the success of the course. There are many opportunities including arranging for panel members, reminding students of upcoming local and national events, keeping the class aware of pertinent news stories and other publications, and suggesting topics for discussion. A major factor in the success of the guest speakers was the wealth of relevant and incisive questions asked by the class. Class participation can count for 25 percent of the course grade.

Major Project Requirement

Students are given a choice of preparing a research paper, a game, or a case. The project can be worth 50 percent of the course grade. The students are asked to write proposals for their projects. The proposals are presented orally so the class can help with identifying related data sources. The instructor can also counsel each student individually.

If the research paper is chosen, the student may gather data from the community to support a hypothesis. The paper should (1) state the problem and the project's justification and limitations; (2) present data collected from questionnaires, interviews, organization records, or previously validated documents; (3) analyze the data through the use of figures; and (4) make conclusions and recommendations. Each student finally writes a synopsis including problem statement, methods, and findings. The synopsis and the supporting tables and figures are used for the final oral presentation.

This research method gives students opportunities to study administrative opportunities for women in such areas as the local police force and church business offices. Or a student may elect to study the magnitude of discontent among women in a local organization.

If a student chooses to develop a game, two alternatives are available—a role playing behavioral game or a board game. With either kind, the student may develop an enjoyable experiential learning method to teach job-related facts about the woman's movement. Therefore, each fact mentioned in any game should be traceable to a specific source. For the student's oral presentation, she or he teaches the class to play the game.

If a student develops a case, she or he writes a paper describing a real-life work experience in which discrimination plays a part. Then the student models the case by listing the human inputs involved (number of males and females, ages, values, skills, and educational levels); the technical inputs involved (machine and work skills); organization inputs—fringe benefits, hours, wages, and formal company policies; and social inputs involved—cliques, morale, and informal group leaders. Any item listed in the model should be mentioned somewhere in the case. The case may then be analyzed in terms of the literature, and conclusions and recommendations may be made. An oral class presentation is made. These presentations are valuable in allowing students to consider real-life discriminatory situations and to come to a reasonable solution through informal or formal company methods or through legal means (government intervention).

Student Evaluations

Student comments indicate that much "food for thought" was produced by the class activities and the student projects. Because the students represented many different majors, the limited amount of management theory was completely new to some and well-received. One male student, who had entered the class with traditional male-oriented ideas, stated that his own project demonstrating how female stereotypes are formed at early ages had erased many of his own stereotypes toward sex roles.

Two students did a feasibility study on the possibility of the University of Houston's Management Development Center presenting a workshop in cooperation with HEW and the Governor's Office on Equal Opportunity. The workshop would teach officials in other institutions of higher education how to write affirmative action plans. The results of the study were presented to government officials who liked the idea and agreed to do the workshop. The response to the workshop far exceeded the feasibility study's estimate, and a repeat program is being planned. Several students saw their projects become a part of the affirmative action data or plans for local organizations and companies.

It is to be hoped that this course will produce two results. It should help females deal effectively with discrimination that they are sure to face in years ahead, and it should prepare both male and female students to make specific contributions toward the development of women for administrative positions and the implementation of affirmative action programs.

NOTES

[1] Cathe Wolhowe, "Special Supplement on Education," *Women Law Reporter* (Sept. 15, 1974), p. 1.18; "Status of HEW Guideline," *Women Law Reporter* (Nov. 15, 1974), p. 1.78; "Congress: Women's Education Equity Act," *Women Law Reporter* (Sept. 15, 1974), p. 1.24; and Austin Wehrwein, "University of Minnesota Reacts," *Women Law Reporter* (Sept. 15, 1974), p. 1.21.

[2] "Trends in Earnings," *Women Law Reporter* (Nov. 15, 1974), p. 1.78; U.S. Office of Education, "Women in the World of Work" (Washington, D.C.: Government Printing Office, 1973), p. 1.

[3] Bessie Margolin, "The Impact of Corning," *Women Law Reporter* (Sept. 15, 1974), pp. 1.13 – 1.14.

DISCUSSION QUESTIONS

1. Call the community, junior, and senior colleges in your area to compile a list of women's studies courses being offered. Give copies of your compilation to local women's organizations.

2. Give some examples to show that equal opportunity laws are good personnel practices for all.

3. What topics would you like to see discussed in a "Women in Management" course?

"Plato believed women to be of equal intellectual ability with men, and he admitted a few women to his academy. Aristotle's view that the distinctive function of women required a different education from that for men reinforced age-old prejudice which held firm until well into the 19th century."

Franklin Parker, "Women's Education: Historical and International View," *Contemporary Education* XLIII, 4 (February 1972), p. 198.

The Consequences of
Equal Opportunity
for Women

Jane W. Torrey

Much is being written about the lack of equal opportunity for women in the American economy, about the obstacles to achieving it and about means of overcoming the resistance. However, very little is being said about what will happen to this man's world when equal opportunity happens. One reason nobody says much about it is that it has never been tried, at least not in any large organization, so there is no evidence. Nevertheless, we do know something about people and about organizations and the ways these influence one another, so it should be possible to make some educated guesses about what will happen when both of these have changed in all the ways necessary to make equal opportunity a reality.

MEN IN THEIR WORLD

What we know about people is that they are potentially many different things. They can be rational and emotional; they can be tough and tender; they can be ambitious and dependent. The cultural setting can enhance or suppress any of these tendencies and, thus, shape the kinds of personalities that develop. It can make women rational, tough and ambitious while it makes men emotional, tender and dependent. It also can do the opposite, or it can make men and women very similar temperamentally.[1]

People naturally think that whatever traits their culture produces are innate human nature, including the sex differences. Often, they interpret the structure of their society as being the effect rather than the cause of these traits. Thus it is argued that men are naturally better suited to going out of the home to earn a living because they are ambi-

Jane W. Torrey, "The Consequences of Equal Opportunity for Women," *Journal of Contemporary Business* (Winter 1976), pp. 13–27.

tious and rational while women belong at home because they are tender and emotional.

In the industrialized world, the culture assiduously cultivates in males the traits of dominance and ambition because these are required for success in public life, i.e., life outside the home, and it is the traditional task of males to manage that world. Organizations are formed rationally to maximize profit and productivity. Positions are defined by the purposes of the organization with the assumption that the people who fill positions will conform to the position's requirements either by selection or by adjustment. There is often very little room and no expectation for the performer to express himself through his work. Rationality is the dominant ethic of the world of professional management, and successful managers frequently are almost unable either to recognize or deal with the emotional relations among their colleagues.[2]

The ultimate satisfaction an organization offers its successful men is achievement, i.e., rising in the hierarchy. In the culture of public organizations, other people are either superiors, subordinates or competitors, and all interactions with them are determined mainly by relative status. If any other relations develop, such as friendship or resentment, they are regarded as irrelevant and potentially disturbing. In short, public life brings out and uses only a limited range of human potentialities and relationships among its almost exclusive male power structure.

At the same time, the existence of other traits and other needs is not denied totally. It is acceptable for men in business to have personal relationships and to find part of their fulfillment through nonbusiness interests, provided that this other side of their personalities is expressed outside the organization. At home or in their church it is all right for them to express their feelings. There, friendship or love is usually the connecting link among people, many of whom are women.

The lives and personalities of men, thus, are divided in time and space. At the place of work during business hours one set of motives, assumptions and personal relations exists while at other times and places, a man may be quite a different person and play many different roles. In addition to this division in time and space, there is another dimension that controls men's reactions, and that is the sex of the person they interact with. There are many women in the public world, most of whom are not part of the hierarchy of the organization, and men are often in contact with them. However, the business relationships discussed above do not apply to these women because they belong to a subordinate class from which movement upward in the hierarchy is barred. They have been described as a "productive parahierarchy"[3] whose work is essential, but who have little power and no voice in management. Because of this peripheral status, they are not, like other subordinates, potential competitors, so that interactions with them are not determined by the management ethic. Where women are involved, even in the public world, feelings are more legitimate. "Office wives" are thus similar to the home variety, not only in that they take care of the routine tasks that men feel are "beneath their own dignity," but also because they make possible some expression of the personal and emotional side of men's lives. Men can confide in their secretaries and get personal support from them much as they can from their wives.

The sexual division emphasizes the fact that the public world is a male phenomenon. Not only is it dominated by men, but also it serves men as an expression of their "macho" image. The culture of the public is a male one; clubs and meetings are more exclusive of females even than of blacks. Since femaleness is characteristic of the subordinate persons in this world, status depends upon not compromising the maleness of any activity. Men can assert their masculinity every time they give orders to a secretary because she is a woman and dominance is masculine. The economic exploitation of women in the public world parallels and resembles their exploitation in the world of playboy sex. The fact that men often use sexual relations as an expression of dominance makes it natural that they should associate their motivation to dominate in the public world with their sexuality. This aspect of their motivation is a very important factor in their resistance to equal opportunity for women. The coming of serious women competitors inevitably will require some serious adjustments in the personal attitudes of men in business. Some men feel their virility so threatened by any sign of competitiveness or lack of submission by a woman that they immediately feel she is "castrating" them. Men who have never had a female boss usually find it hard to accept the idea and often mention their anxiety about their sex in discussing it.

WOMEN'S WORK

The world of women is quite differently organized. At the office, as at home, women serve as support both in work and in personal relationships. Secretaries open mail and type letters; nurses distribute medicine and perform routine examinations; wives wash dishes and take care of children; programmers carry out plans set by other people; and teachers make the children literate. All this work is necessary and much of it requires high-level skills and abilities; however, most of it is either underpaid or not paid at all. In most cases, especially for women, this work does not lead to the higher levels occupied by men no matter how well it is done. Women in these positions usually are attached to men and derive what status they have from this relationship with their supervisor. The case of the wife is the extreme of this phenomenon, for her work is not paid at all, and her status in the world has almost no other basis than that of being this man's wife. In this world of women there is little competition because there is little differentiation of status among the kinds of work they do. As far as the work itself is concerned, no one knows which way is up, so each seeks her niche in terms of work satisfaction, personal relations or in terms of the status of the men they are attached to. Women's interrelations are also less limited than men's because the structure of their part of the organization is less hierarchical. Women are shaped by the culture to fit this destiny. Their own ambitions are not encouraged; independence is suppressed; and tender, submissive feelings are allowed certain expressions that are denied to men. (Of course, other emotions, such as anger, are permitted to men but denied to women.)

A well-programmed woman often finds great satisfaction in the support role, which is in some ways less personally confining and often less demanding than the public image required of men. However, the costs to women of whatever privileges they have are very great. One of the main costs is that female jobs often do not bring enough money to live on and rarely provide for anything like affluence. The fact that the work brings so little economic reward is probably the most important source of pressure for equal opportunity. The fact that it costs so little to have this work done may be the source of the greatest resistance to equal opportunity for women and of some of the biggest adjustments that will be required as equal opportunity becomes a reality.

Beside the cost to women in money, the kind of function their work usually serves in the world places another burden upon women, a subtler one, but one which still severely handicaps them in the public world. The support function, that of servicing another individual to free him for "higher-level" work, generally carries a rather diffuse job description.[4] In other words, there are few defined limits to this supportive work, so the boss may ask for almost any service, and the woman seldom has any clear right to refuse to perform it. "Women's work is never done" is the old adage that expresses this problem. Women are brought up to think of themselves as responsible for the work that other people won't do. Men think of their jobs as defined and limited. If it isn't in the job specifications, it just isn't their job. This is particularly true around the home. "Bringing home the bacon" is a husband's contribution. He may accept responsibility for certain other limited jobs, such as lawn care and car maintenance, but "women's work" is everything else. This is the reason why the work of keeping a house requires longer hours than the average industrial job. Furthermore, family women who are employed outside the home typically find that housework remains their all-but-exclusive responsibility. They are compelled essentially to "moonlight" for no extra pay in addition to whatever remunerative work they do. Women also commonly bear most of the burden of child care, including staying home when the children are sick in addition to whatever sick leave the mother requires for herself. The typical male worker at any level seldom has many such additional burdens. His employer can count on him to come to work refreshed after an evening of leisure; to be available for overtime or out-of-town travel; to provide business-related entertainment with the help of a live-in caterer; and to be able to pick up his family and move to another city without much regard to the convenience of the family. Thus, a male employee typically comes with all of his own personal maintenance provided free — his food service, laundry, housework and the care of his children — without having to do it in overtime. On the other hand, a woman has to do her own, and often other people's, maintenance work in addition to the hours she can give her employer. Men, in short, can be detached from their personal lives and used in their rational productive capacity as though they had no other responsibilities, whereas women usually cannot be treated as separate from their families. Their services must usually be shared with others to whom they feel obliged. As long as this situation exists, equal opportunity for women will be, at best, a limited possibility.

THE POSSIBLE DREAM

It follows that the equal opportunity whose repercussions are assessed here cannot be assumed even to exist without also assuming some rather fundamental other changes in the family as well as the public organization. However, lest this should seem to imply that equality is a long way off, let me cite several reasons why the economy and the family will be reprogrammed sooner than we think.

First, it is now clear that the world no longer needs to encourage child-bearing. The main justification for the housewife's career at home always has been to provide child care. Child care has also been one of the main factors in family-maintenance work. Not only will there be less child care to be done in the future because there are fewer children, but also social pressure on women to make a career of homemaking will have less justification. Most housework would be doing cooking and laundry for an adult man, who, after all, is equally capable of doing the work for himself. The national interest is now to discourage babies, and one of the most effective means to do that is to have wives employed outside the home.

Still, even one child requires a lot of extra maintenance work, and if women continue to bear most of that burden, they will continue to be disadvantaged in the world of work. One way to relieve women is the partial institutionalization of this work in the form of nurseries and daycare centers. Although there are very few such public facilities now for babies and preschool children, their advent is probably not far off. Congress already has passed a bill setting up a national system of daycare centers. The fact that the bill was vetoed once does not obscure the fact that the political backing for daycare is already strong. When daycare for children is done outside the home, it has to be paid for. This will have the effect of removing it from the class of work that normally is demanded automatically of women without compensation. It will be considered part of the gross national product for the first time which will help to relieve women of the feeling of obligation to perform it without counting it as "work." Even if do-it-yourself child care remains appealing to many, they will be able to think of it as voluntary. To the extent that men enter the profession of child care, it will lose its image of low-level, dull work that could be turned over to morons (and sometimes is). People with special abilities in this field will receive public recognition and higher pay, neither of which they do now.

The growing political power of women, which is related to the demand for public daycare, is another factor which is relatively new. This will move society faster than it has been going toward recognition of women's contributions to the economy. Women have in the past had very little political clout, and what they had was "in spite of" rather than "because of" the fact that they were women. Women in elected office recently have begun to be the representatives of women and to advocate women's interests. This will affect public policy in many areas, beginning with daycare and equal opportunity enforcement.

Another change already is developing which probably will help to reduce the disadvantage of women in public organizations, i.e., the trend in the psychology of management away from the strictly rational competitive hierarchy and toward more accommodation of the emotional and personal sides of life. A more "horizontal" organizational framework like that which operates among women[5] would allow men also to select their goals in terms of the kind of work they enjoy and the people they like to be with, rather than being always obliged to "aim higher" in a clearly defined hierarchical system. The ideas of job enrichment and participative leadership[6] are among the proposals for improving the quality of working life. Sensitivity training, flexible working hours[7] and reorganization of working groups to provide more responsibility and more individual satisfaction are techniques for humanizing the public organization. For the most part, these are discussed without reference to their implications for women, but they will move business organization nearer to the kind of cultural milieu in which women's personalities will be less alien than they are from the present system. Even changes in the value system of the business world seem to be coming when we find it seriously proposed that the purpose of business is to satisfy people and that profit is only a means to that end.[8]

Summary

To summarize, we have identified a number of psychological and organizational conditions which we can expect to change as equal opportunity is achieved. First is the fact that public life tends to encourage in men the rational, dominating and competitive aspects of their personalities and to suppress or exclude tender feelings, personal satisfaction and cooperative behavior. This not only alienates men from other aspects of themselves, but also puts women at a severe disadvantage in that they usually have not developed habits and motivations appropriate to the "dog-eat-dog" world. Second, by separating men from women in its status hierarchy, it leads men to regard their status in the world as a symbol of their sexuality. Thus any competition from women becomes, quite unnecessarily, a threat to their masculinity. Third, the separation of home from work gives men the excuse to treat the tremendous job of homemaking as purely women's work. This means that even when the man is no longer the exclusive breadwinner, the woman remains the exclusive homemaker, a fact which in itself would preclude equal opportunity for women even if the entire business world were knocking itself out to offer them an equal chance.

It follows from this third point that if we are to discuss the effects of equal opportunity, we already must assume a world in which women are as free as men or, rather, where men are no freer than women to give their full energies to the outside job. A description of a world of equal opportunity must include new provisions for accomplishing the job of personal maintenance which is necessary for every individual regardless of sex. Organizations often provide for medical care, recreation, daytime meals and other maintenance functions to keep their employees in working condition. We will have to imagine that they also will take into account other maintenance work and not, as they so frequently do now, assume that some women in the background will contribute that work for free.

THE BRAVE NEW SYSTEM: DOWN WITH THE DIFFERENCE

There will be two large categories of changes between the working world of the present and that of the future. First, in the future there will be a greater accommodation of family life. In other words, there will be recognition by the working organization of the personal maintenance work of house and family care and a less rigid separation of these two aspects of their employees' lives. No one will be able to be treated as though he had no personal life or children. Second, the business and industrial organization will be less of a male-oriented, male-image culture. This will come about both through the greater participation of women in the actual processes of management and decision-making and through greater emphasis upon personal and emotional sides of mens' personalities.

Family Life Goes to Work

In the absence of the personal maintenance services of housewives, every public institution will find that its personnel of both sexes have home responsibilities. Everyone will have to find an employer who can accept, and preferably ease, the performance of family tasks. One obvious way will be on-the-job child care. Instead of carting the children to separate daycare centers to spend the day without seeing either Mommy or Daddy, parents will prefer a daycare center at their place of work. Buildings already routinely provide toilets, lunch rooms and sometimes other facilities for personal needs. A nursery and a preschool will enable parents to be near their children for visits and emergencies, yet allow both parents and children to do their own thing without mutual interference, something which is rarely possible at home. Children will not feel they are being left behind, and parents will feel more confident about the care their children are receiving. Caregivers will be employed by the same institution, so that some parental participation and oversight will be appropriate and convenient. Another effect of having children nearby will be to reduce the employee's sense of alienation of work from personal life and the tendency of the employer to think of employees as impersonal machines.

Another provision for children probably will be part-time career jobs for young parents. If both parents work half-time, it will be possible to bring in a full-time income while, at the same time, caring for the children at home and getting the housework done. Of course such part-time work will have to be different from the usual part-time job today. Young people will not be attracted to peripheral low-pay, temporary jobs. They will want to have their salaries and experience prorated. Employers may find some advantages in this system. One experiment already has shown that two part-time social workers accomplished more than a single full-time one.[9]

Employment often will be a "package deal" for married people. Neither husband nor wife will be expected to accept a job unless the partner can get satisfactory work nearby. Neither husband nor wife ever will be automatically expected to go along with the other in a change of location. Many times employers will have to offer jobs to both in order to get either one. This is the opposite of the traditional "antinepotism," which usually operated to deny employment to wives. If such a switch seems revolutionary, it should be noted that such policies already exist for civil servants in France, where a spouse in the same service is given priority for jobs in the same location where the partner is located.[10]

The Classless Society in Public Organizations

One of the problems that equal opportunity may pose for many organizations is described by Tracy in a "Postscript to the Peter Principle."[11] According to the Peter Principle, each man in a hierarchical organization tends to get promoted on some kind of merit system until he reaches a level that is just above his capacity, his "level of incompetence." The result is that the organization tends to fall apart because of poor management. However, many businesses do not fall apart because there is a crew of lower-level workers, such as secretaries, who know how to run it. The reason these underlings are so capable in their jobs is that the Peter Principle does not operate with them, i.e., they are never promoted so they never reach their level of incompetence. Their organization is a horizontal one—one in which there is no upward movement, only sideways movement. Thus their only motivation is to find a place where their talents are used best. Tracy asserts that the dominant hierarchy in order to survive must create such a "productive parahierarchy." One of the reasons organizations have been able to keep such a crew is that women are a subordinate class throughout the world of work. They can be kept safely for very little money at low-lével, dead-end jobs, which they often do extremely well. Equal opportunity will mean that when a secretary has served a given manager long enough to know the ropes, she (or he) will be the logical successor to that manager. The job of secretary will have quite a different description. It will probably no longer resemble the old "office wife" who did anything and everything including going for coffee. A secretary will be more like an assistant, a trainee for more advanced work. She or he will have to command a salary on a par with other trainees, with the result that "secretarial" services will cost a good deal more. With a higher cost, there will be a closer scrutiny of the work, sorting out what really needs to be done from what doesn't. Possibly the luxury of expert typing for routine correspondence will be dispensed with as more people prepare their own mail for dispatch. Possibly fewer records will be kept and filed, and certainly more instant coffee will be prepared by the same people who want to drink it.

The problems of cost will affect the other productive parahierarchies, too. Researchers will cost more and be less experienced because, as they gain experience, they will become writers and be replaced by other beginners. It no longer will be possible to keep highly qualified women doing the work year after year at lower pay than neophyte male writers. University departments will no longer be able to keep a revolving crew of female lecturers to do the bulk of the teaching at low pay and be replaced after 2 or 3 years while less qualified young men are promoted into the tenured ranks.[12] Similarly, nurses, technicians and dental hygienists will expect to move up to higher-level and better paying jobs. Many, no doubt, will be doing the work as part of their preparation to become doctors, dentists or scientists. The only people doing work for low pay will be the newer inexperienced workers. In short, the "productive parahierarchy" will no longer exist.

It is an interesting question whether everyone then will be promoted to his or her level of incompetence. Tracy[13] proposes that the horizontal structure would be a better one for everyone. With no underprivileged class available to be kept at levels where they still can do a good job, pressures would exist to find another way to avoid moving everyone up out of the jobs they can do well. Some companies already have tried to eliminate some of the trappings of rank at the upper levels so that people will be less eager to move up merely for the sake of higher status. Walton[14] describes an attempt in one industrial organization to frame a system which would counter the tendency of alienation from work, which he says is inherent in the hierarchical system. Autonomous, self-managed work groups were given collective responsibility for accomplishing defined work. They handled not only production, but also maintenance, housekeeping and personnel work, such as hiring, within the scope of their work. Each job had both higher- and lower-level responsibilities. Pay increases resulted from an individual's mastering a greater variety of tasks within the group and later within the industry as a whole, but not from moving upward to a position over the heads of fellow workers. Any number could win in this game, so competition for the higher paid positions was eliminated. Production decisions often could be made by operators themselves, and status differentials between coworkers were reduced or eliminated. The system is one in which the feminine personality would be at less disadvantage than in a hierarchy. In addition, to the extent that it succeeded in eliminating status differentials, there would be less danger of female supervisors threatening anyone's masculinity.

This calls to mind another difference in the public world that can be predicted from the entry of women. With less stereotyping of males as high status and females as low status, there will be less of a tendency on the part of some men to equate success with masculinity. Sexuality will be more divorced from the motivation to achieve. The kind of competitiveness that is really a disguised form of sexual dominance will be less common since promotion no longer will have the same symbolic significance. Men who now think they would be "emasculated" by a female boss probably will find, as many have already, that with a woman boss, supervision ceases to seem like a sexual act, and carrying out someone's orders no longer feels like rape. Under these conditions, some men will be less motivated to rise to the top, and the top will no doubt be better off without them.

Many feminists have expressed the hope for a long time that the impact of the feminine personality itself will humanize whatever worlds women penetrate. Token or exceptional women have found more often that the male world changed them rather than vice versa, but it is reasonable to hope that as women become more numerous and their presence at higher levels more normal, they may be able to bring in a little of their traditional humanity. However, a firmer basis for the hope is the fact that management already is thinking of making greater allowance for feelings and individuality in the working group. It represents a recognition that men have these "feminine" tendencies, too, and already are seeking greater expression of them.

The Classless Society at Home

Since we have been arguing that the work of the homemaker is an essential service which should be recognized as a contribution to the economy, it is necessary to include it in this description of equal opportunity. First, it should be pointed out that equal opportunity depends upon the virtual elimination of the traditional career homemaker who does the service out of the goodness of her heart for no compensation other than her financial support. There are two ways in which this pattern is inconsistent with equal opportunity. First, it is not an equal opportunity for the homemaker herself. Without salary, worker compensation, paid vacations, job security and often without insurance protection, pension or any limits on working hours, her job as a job is the bottom of the scale. In prestige, her job has been rated as lower than that of her nearest industrial equivalent, the janitor. Although some wives of affluent and generous men share the good life of their husbands, their legal right to that share is tenuous. A man is required only under law to "support" his wife, but support is not defined and courts have held, for example, that a man cannot be required legally to provide heat for his wife in their Iowa farmhouse or to buy her a new winter coat when the old one is worn out. Much of the work is also stultifying and repetitious. It is seldom even considered as "work experience" in later employment.

A second reason why homemaking careers are inconsistent with equal opportunity is that the homemaker essentially provides for her husband all the personal maintenance services that women workers almost always have to provide for themselves. Women will never be able to compete with men in the public world as long as men can have cheap live-in household help simply by getting married. Of course, homemaking would not prevent equality if "househusbands" were as common as "housewives," but there is little reason to expect that they ever will be. Therefore, if one is to assume a world of equal opportunity, it has to be a world in which men share equally in their own and their children's maintenance work—where housework and child care are just as much the responsibility of husbands and fathers as they are of wives and mothers. Wives will be as likely as husbands to be employed outside the home, and, without discrimination in pay, they will be as likely as not to bring home more money. Women will not feel compelled to nag their husbands to get a promotion or a raise because they will be able to get these for themselves. In turn, this kind of home life will affect the motivation of workers. Men will no longer be likely to see supporting a family as a proof of virility or regard an earning wife as an intruder upon his breadwinning function.

Who Will Be the Winners?

An end to the dog-eat-dog competition of the hierarchical organization with its underdog parahierarchy of women will help both men and women, but it will help women more. Satisfying work demands a sense of identification with the goals of the work, a means of getting credit for good work and an opportunity to determine exactly how the job will be done, including which task comes first and how time will be apportioned to each segment of work. The female in the parahierarchy now holds the job with the least freedom of choice and the least opportunity for self-expression. She is under the thumb of her supervisor, she is at his beck and call to interrupt whatever she is doing and she has little chance to organize her own work. Men will lose something when they no longer have the privilege of unloading the dull work on someone else and when subordinates have to be paid a respectable wage. Women will gain when they no longer have to perform these services at low pay, but it is reasonable to hope that the accompanying changes in the quality of working life will, on balance, create a better life for everyone.

NOTES

[1] Margaret Mead, *Sex and Temperament in Three Primitive Societies* (New York: William Morrow & Company, 1935).

[2] Chris Argyris, *Interpersonal Competence and Organizational Effectiveness* (Homewood, Illinois: Irwin & Dorsey, 1962).

[3] Lane Tracy, "Postscript to the Peter Principle," *Harvard Business Review* 50 (July-August 1972), pp. 65–71.

[4] Jessie Bernard, *Women and the Public Interest* (Chicago: Aldine-Atherton, 1971), p. 26.

[5] Tracy, "Postscript to the Peter Principle."

[6] Richard E. Walton, "How to Counter Alienation at the Plant," *Harvard Business Review* 50 (November-December 1972), pp. 70–81.

[7] Alvar O. Elbing, Herman Gadon, and John R. M. Gordon, "Flexible Working Hours: It's About Time," *Harvard Business Review* 52 (January-February 1974), p. 18.

[8] John Adam, Jr., "Put Profit in its Place," *Harvard Business Review* 51 (March-April 1973), p. 150.

[9] Ruth B. Kundsin, *Women and Success, The Anatomy of Achievement* (New York: William Morrow & Company, 1974), p. 174.

[10] Bernard, *Women and the Public Interest*, p. 190.

[11] Tracy, "Postscript to the Peter Principle."

[12] Joan Abramson, *The Invisible Women: Discrimination in the Academic Profession* (San Francisco: Jossey-Bass, 1975).

[13] Tracy, "Postscript to the Peter Principle."

[14] Walton, "How to Counter Alienation at the Plant."

DISCUSSION QUESTIONS

1.   What tasks have you seen secretaries perform that male executives consider "beneath their own dignity"?

2.   Have you seen any men showing signs of threatened virility when women have come to work as their peers? What signs do you perceive?

3.   Have you seen an organization where secretarial status is connected to the boss's status? How?

4.   In large organizations, located in tall buildings, is status attached to working on certain floors?

5.   Torrey notes few defined limits to supportive work. Most secretaries, at the time of their employment, perceive that they are being hired for traditional secretarial duties. What unusual duties do you know that secretaries have been asked to do, which are not "secretarial"?

6.   List the women you know who are employed full-time and have full or most of the responsibility for homemaking. Now list the men. Which list is longer?

7.   Will it take men entering the secretarial field for (a) appropriate salaries to be paid for true secretarial work, (b) the field to be viewed as a training ground for management, (c) the "office wife" to disappear?

8.   Do you know any secretaries who have been promoted to management? Have they changed? How?

9.   Are there any parts of homemaking that could be considered "work experience" in later employment?

10.   We constantly hear that women must be *qualified* to move into management, and that it's hard to find *qualified* women. Can you think of any men who have been given promotions based on perceived potential—not on qualifications?

11.   List all the women college graduates you know in dead-end clerical positions. Now list all the men. Which list is longer?

12.   Do you know any women who have worked in the same job for a long time and have trained more than one of their own bosses?

Appendix A

Cases

Divide your class into groups of five. Let each group discuss the case and arrive at a consensus about the answers to the questions at the end of each case. Then let each group relate to the whole class the answers they have agreed on. Try to get the class to come to a final consensus about the answers.

AFFIRMATIVE ACTION EQUALS
GOOD PERSONNEL PRACTICES FOR ALL

Monday

Barbara decided to write a term paper entitled "Women in Business,"; she went to meet Dr. Emma Lang, who was teaching a "Women in Management" course. Dr. Lang gave Barbara some material for her term paper and, just as she was leaving, asked her when she would graduate. Barbara said she would finish in May, so Dr. Lang asked if she were job-interviewing yet. Barbara replied that she was, and that she thought her areas of concentration in finance and marketing would be good for the job market. Barbara then said she was discouraged because of what had happened to her in the university placement center three weeks earlier. She had interviewed with Giant Industries. The recruiter had told her that women didn't do as well as men in sales, and that it would take her ten years to accomplish what it would take a man six years to do at Giant Industries.

Dr. Lang couldn't believe her ears and had to stifle her anger. She knew that what had happened to Barbara was not only unkind but also illegal. All recruiters who came on the campus signed a statement that they were equal opportunity employers. She knew that some recruiters still made comments like those made to Barbara, and that students were afraid to report them. They didn't want to be branded "trouble makers" and jeopardize their chances for a job. Dr. Lang asked if she could report the incident. Barbara agreed, so Dr. Lang picked up the phone and, in a few minutes, related the incident to Tom Cole, the university placement director.

Barbara agreed to go to Tom's office immediately and give him the specific name of the recruiter and the time of the interview. Dr. Lang offered to go with Barbara, but she said she didn't mind going alone to relate her story to Tom Cole.

Thursday

Dr. Lang was at a downtown hotel attending a convention when she received a message asking her to meet with Barbara, another student, Tom Cole, and a representative from Giant Industries who was flying in from Denver. Tom had done some investigating and found that Barbara was not the only student hurt by the same recruiter. The meeting was set for Monday.

Monday

Dr. Lang arrived a few minutes early for the meeting, so she had time to talk with Tom Cole. Tom told her that when he reviewed the records and called all the students that the recruiter had interviewed that day, he found Paul Norris, a white male student, in serious trouble. Paul had worked his way through college supporting himself, his wife, and his two children. For the past four years he had been employed by Casey Distributors. Since he was nearing graduation, he decided to look at job opportunities, even though there was a chance that Casey might promote him upon graduation. He liked Casey but there was no harm in looking around. It happened that Giant Industries was negotiating a sale to Casey. The recruiter had called Paul's boss and told him that he had inter- viewed Paul but was not going to hire him. The recruiter apparently thought that would enhance the chances of the sale. Paul received a change in his work schedule and began hearing through his office grape- vine that his job would soon be phased out. It was still two months until graduation, and Paul had had hopes of receiving a promotion so he could stay with Casey. At any rate he needed that job to support his family and finish school. As Dr. Lang listened, she thought of the oft-heard statement "Equal opportunity and affirmative action are simply good personnel practices for all." Where you find no strong affirmative action plans, you may find many employees, regardless of sex or color, being given a raw deal.

Both a male and a female representative from Giant Industries arrived. Barbara and Paul retold their stories. Then Tom Cole took over. In a quiet, calm, deliberate manner, he placed the following requirements on Giant Industries: (1) the recruiter who had done the damage would be permanently banned from the university campus; (2) Tom was to receive copies of all future correspondence between Giant Industries and stu- dents; and (3) he was also to receive a copy of Giant Industries' own equal opportunity statement. Finally, he asked what Giant Industries intended to do about Barbara and Paul. The male Giant Industries' representative did all the talking. He apologized to both students and assured everyone that this was a highly unusual, isolated incident and that Giant Industries had a very strong affirmative action program. He then told Paul that if he lost his job with Casey Distributors, he would automatically have a job with Giant Industries. Dr. Lang then asked if Barbara could be reinter- viewed by someone else in another part of Giant Industries. The Giant Industries' representative hastily agreed; however, Barbara declined.

Dr. Lang kept tabs on the situation. The local head of Giant Indus- tries had lunch the next week with the president of Casey Distributors to explain what had happened to Paul and ask that his job be protected. However, Tom Cole thought that it might be best if Paul made a fresh start with another company. He began arranging some special interviews for him. Barbara was hired by a local company at a very fine starting salary.

QUESTIONS

1. How can Giant Industries prevent another "isolated incident"?

2. The recruiter had been in various positions with the company for fifteen years. What should Giant Industries do about his action?

3. How can Dr. Lang and Tom Cole communicate to students their interest in helping them?

THE *VERY* PRIVATE CLUB

Jane was entering the job market. She was well prepared for a professional position and had had several interesting interviews. The firm she was interviewing today seemed to have many challenging opportunities. Three people had talked with her and shown her around the offices. At noon, Tom and Curt invited her to lunch, she would spend the rest of the day meeting other firm members.

Tom and Curt told her they were taking her to the "Top-of-the Beanstalk"—the most prestigious private club in town with the best view and food. Jane was very favorably impressed, not only because she had detected no discriminatory treatment but also because this firm seemed really interested in her. The "Top-of-the Beanstalk" was well known, and Jane was happy to have the opportunity to see it and the beautiful view from forty stories up. Tom and Curt made several luncheon suggestions on the way over.

They entered the dining room and waited to be seated. Suddenly a man in an official looking blazer approached them. "I am sorry," he said, "but ladies are not allowed in the main dining room. I can seat you in another dining room we have." Tom and Curt looked astounded. The three of them followed "the official-looking blazer" into a small, side dining room with no windows. It was empty.

Tom and Curt apologized profusely. Jane had a knot in her stomach. She couldn't decide what to do. But she sat through the meal. At first she felt sorry for Tom and Curt but then she began to get angry. Why hadn't Tom and Curt left immediately? There were plenty of other places they could have eaten. She would gladly have forgone all the luxury for the dignity of being able to sit anywhere in the restaurant.

She tried not to show her feelings that afternoon, but she had a hard time keeping her mind on the rest of the interviews. She began to wonder how she could entertain clients in that empty dining room. She wondered how many lunches were held in the main dining room, with discussions of important information that she would need to know to do her job well. And she wondered if this were just the "tip of the iceberg" — if there were other discriminatory actions condoned by the firm.

About ten days later, she got an excellent offer from the firm, both in terms of job description and salary. She wondered if she should take it.

QUESTIONS

1. Should Jane have asked to leave the "Top-of-the-Beanstalk"?

2. What should Tom and Curt have done?

3. Should the firm take any action? appeal to the management? drop their membership?

4. Should Jane accept the job offer?

5. Under what circumstances would membership in the "Top-of-the-Beanstalk" be legal for this firm?

MS. PRESIDENT

Ruth was a single, attractive, middle-aged woman. She had been a member of a professional organization for sixteen years and was known as "an absolute work horse." She had served as secretary of the organization and then as treasurer. After doing an outstanding job in both offices, the members decided to combine the two offices and let her do both jobs. She also had done the major share of the work for several important committees. Whenever there was a fund-raising event or a service activity, Ruth could be counted on to be there giving 110% of her efforts to make the activity a success.

Over the years, Ruth had dated several of the members who were single or "between wives" but nothing serious had ever developed. She did not consider the professional organization as a "hunting ground" for a man. She enjoyed associating with people in the same kind of job and found both the speakers and the informal discussions at meetings about common problems to be very informative and useful.

Finally Ruth was nominated for vice-president, along with several males. The vice-presidency automatically led to the presidency. When the ballots were counted, Ruth had won a majority. She was both astounded and delighted. A reception was held before the next meeting to honor the new officers. Ruth was happy as she received many sincere congratulations; there was no mention about her getting the job because she was a woman.

But suddenly she realized something else. One man after another kept his arm around her during their conversation. She also became aware that much of the kidding was based on suggestive or double entendre comments. Everyone seemed to be joking and in good humor, but she found the whole reception rather unpleasant. She had wanted the vice-presidency for two reasons: (1) she had proved her dedication to the organization, and (2) she had the competence and experience to hold the office. She went home wondering if she would have to face a whole year of being "armed" and of hearing suggestive remarks. She felt that as the vice-president she deserved the same professional respect and treatment that others had received.

QUESTIONS

1.   Why were the male members behaving differently toward her than they did toward the male vice-presidents in the past?

2.   Could Ruth have done anything about their behavior during the reception?

3.   Can Ruth do anything over the next year that will retain the male members' goodwill and, at the same time, let them know that she wants more professional treatment?

THOUGHT YOU MIGHT BE INTERESTED

Janet met Elsa at the national convention of a professional organization to which they both belonged. The organization had a "Committee on the Status of Women in the Profession" which had done a lot to raise the visibility of women and increase their professional participation.

Janet and Elsa had coffee during the convention. It was an enjoyable conversation, discussing their activities and problems at work. Janet liked Elsa because of what she had accomplished professionally and because Elsa was a pleasant person to be with.

The women who attended the national meetings were intelligent and highly professional in their attitude toward their work. One ever-popular topic was about new methods of keeping current in their field. Janet found these women a refreshing change from many of the other women she knew. She liked her other women friends very much but found she could take just so much of hearing about family problems, soap operas, and clothes.

After coffee, Janet and Elsa returned to one of the meeting rooms to hear a speaker who was particularly interesting. As they were approaching the door to the meeting room, Elsa met a man she knew. Elsa introduced Janet and began a conversation with the man. As Elsa talked on and on Janet began to get uneasy, since it was time for the speaker to begin. She also felt that Elsa was asking the man some rather personal questions about a job interview he had had recently. Finally, Janet began to inch away. Elsa seemed to take the hint and said goodbye to the man.

As they were taking their seats in the meeting room, Elsa whispered to Janet, "He's a nice young man. Of course, I'm not interested, but I thought you might be." Janet was grateful that the speaker started just then and she didn't have to reply. She was upset by Elsa's remark for two reasons: (1) she did not come to these meetings on a "hunting trip" for men, and (2) she found the remark unprofessional for a woman of Elsa's professional status and, therefore, degrading to all women. Janet enjoyed dating but she had always resented people forcing situations on her. Elsa's remark also reminded her of the level of conversation of so many of the other women she knew. Perhaps the main reason that Elsa angered Janet was that the remark seemed to reinforce many of the male stereotypes about women.

Janet had difficulty concentrating on the speaker's remarks. She decided to try to get away from Elsa as quickly as possible after the speech.

QUESTIONS

1.   Why did Elsa behave as she did?
2.   Should Janet get away from her? talk with her about her professional attitude? try to forget the whole thing?

THE NEW CAR

Catherine was a teacher married to Charles, an engineer. She wanted to buy a new car and saved her money so she could pay the full price. When she had enough saved, she started her search for a new car. She went to a number of dealers until she finally found the car she really wanted. She asked Charles to go with her when she bought the car to see what he thought of her choice. Charles was always very supportive of her. He was proud of her and they had a good marriage. So Catherine did not ask Charles to look at the car to get his permission. She trusted and respected him, and asked him to go just as many family members consult each other when they are making decisions.

Charles looked at the car and agreed with her that it was a good choice and that she should get it if she wanted it. They sat down with Ralph, the sales representative. Catherine wrote out a check for the car. Ralph hesitantly took the check back to his manager and returned with it in his hand. He told Catherine that he could not accept the check and that she would have to write a check to her husband Charles who could then endorse it over to the dealer. Catherine and Charles looked at each other in astonishment. Since Catherine had spent so much time looking for the exact car she wanted, she decided to do as Ralph asked. She tore up the check, and wrote out one to Charles, who endorsed it over to the dealer.

QUESTIONS

1. Did the dealer act legally?
2. What recourse did Catherine have?
3. What effect did these actions have on establishing a credit rating for Catherine?

THAT OL' "DEBIL COFFEE"

Leap, Inc. was due for a government review of its affirmative action plan. Leap had the plan written and had made some effort toward implementation. The Leap Equal Employment Opportunity staff spent a lot of time preparing data in tables and figures that could be easily understood. They also carefully filled out all the required forms.

They were informed that the government review team would include an attorney from the Washington, D.C. office. Leap was not being "picked on," but Washington was spot checking the reviews to see how their own people were doing.

The Leap EEO staff had much to feel confident about; however, this was a major review so they wanted everything to go exactly right. They briefed as many people in the organization as possible to let them know that the review was coming up. The government team had asked to meet several of the top executives including Mr. Geezer, the president. Mr.

Geezer was given an hour briefing so he would know, as much as possible, what kind of data he might need and what questions to expect.

The big day finally arrived. It was decided that the review would begin with an informal get-acquainted session in a conference room. The session would include the government team, the Leap EEO staff, Mr. Geezer, and other executives who would be involved. After the get-acquainted session, the executives would return to their offices, and the government team would visit each one personally during the day.

The get-acquainted session started promptly at 9:00 A.M. Everyone was there but Mr. Geezer. The introductions began, and all was going well with a friendly, warm atmosphere. At ten minutes after 9, Mr. Geezer came rushing in. As he passed a woman standing near the door, he said to her, "Go get us all some coffee." She declined; she was the attorney from Washington.

QUESTIONS

1. Why did Mr. Geezer ask a woman standing near the door to go for coffee?

2. How could this kind of incident have been avoided?

3. What should be done now that the incident has happened — during that day? In the future?

4. How should a woman who has been treated in this way respond?

ACRES AND ACRES OF DIAMONDS RIGHT IN YOUR OWN BACK YARD

Margaret has been named coordinator of a female development program for Hoopla Electronics. This is a new position in the organization. There is no job description or precedent to follow. Margaret has a degree in business and twelve years' experience with Hoopla. But her job up until this time has been that of secretary. She begins her new assignment with enthusiasm, since it is a refreshing change from her previous routine. She also perceives it as a way to make a significant positive difference in many women's lives.

One of Hoopla's executives is friendly toward Margaret, but any time he hears anything about upgrading women, he says "Don't dangle the carrot; don't dangle the carrot!" He seems to think that if women are qualified for anything more than a secretarial position, the company will have no place for them.

The months go by and Margaret begins to feel discouraged. She can point to very few real accomplishments. When the company magazine appears each month, a page is devoted to new promotions; and month after month, all the promotions are going to men.

The chronic complaint among Hoopla's power structure is "We can't find any qualified women." Margaret begins going through the personnel files. She finds Paula with a degree in journalism and three years' experience in the same dead-end clerical position; Selma with ten years' experience in her present position; and Diana with a secretarial science degree, three years' experience teaching secretarial subjects at night at a community college, and ten years as a secretary with Hoopla. On interviewing these women, Margaret finds that Paula would like to work on Hoopla's magazine and newsletter. Selma works in a small department and her supervisor is about to retire. Over the years, Selma has learned all the functions of the department and has filled in for her supervisor when he was ill or away on business or vacation. She now wants to be promoted to her supervisor's job when he retires. Diana would like to work in Hoopla's training department. Hoopla keeps hiring outside consultants to teach their secretarial improvement courses. Diana has been teaching identical courses for three years.

All three women agree that they had informally tried to let others know what their aspirations were, but they had never been contacted to discuss their futures or had been given any indication that their qualifications or experience were under consideration for future promotions or career planning.

QUESTIONS

1.   What can Margaret do to keep from getting so discouraged?
2.   Why does the executive have a "non-carrot dangling mentality"?
3.   How should Margaret help each of the three women?
4.   What kinds of projects can Margaret plan that will make her job meaningful and set precedents for the future?

THERE ARE GOOD ONES AND BAD ONES

Laura had been in a professional position with Kweps, Inc. for ten years. Initial impressions of her were always that she was intelligent, charming, well-groomed, and had plenty of sense. However, soon after she was hired, she exhibited poor performance, disturbed others, and had a high absentee rate. She should have been terminated during her first six months with Kweps, but at the time she was hired she had influential friends who protected her. Things had been allowed to drift along year after year. Laura just couldn't seem to "get her act together." She was frequently late, would misplace papers, and was always going to the doctor. When she would come to work, all she wanted to do was talk about her previous marriages and her health problems. She cried frequently, even in front of customers, and could not meet important deadlines. When others got to know her, they realized that her personal problems were of no greater magnitude than most peoples. In many ways, others had more serious personal problems, yet they performed their jobs in a professional manner and asked for no favors.

Laura had not been promoted or been given a significant raise for several years. She had had an opportunity to work elsewhere and had been counseled to do so, but had made no effort to make the change. Over the years the work at Kweps had changed so that Laura's particular skills were of less and less value.

Somehow Laura had always been very demanding and able to get her way. Now that the company had instituted an affirmative action program, she let it be known that she had never received equal opportunity. She said that her work load was unfair. However, she was not given many of the assignments that other employees were expected to complete. She complained about her lack of promotions and merit raises. She was shown the performance records of successful employees so that there was no way she could misunderstand the evaluation process.

Morale was low among other professional women employees because of Laura. They were just beginning to see glimmers of light in terms of their own future opportunities. Laura had been a "fly in the ointment" for years, and now she was blaming lack of equal opportunity for her problems.

QUESTIONS

1. What should Kweps, Inc. do about Laura?

2. What should the other professional women do about Laura?

3. If Laura filed a complaint with the Department of Labor under the Equal Pay Act, and you were a government investigator, how would you be able to spot a "Laura"? (Remember she makes an excellent first impression.)

4. What should Kweps do in the future to protect itself against complaints from employees like Laura?

"THOSE ALSO SERVE WHO..." LEAVE US ALONE TO EARN OUR LIVING

Amy had been in a clerical position with The Beavertail Company for ten years. She had a business degree, and about six months before had been promoted to a professional position. She loved her new job, worked hard to learn all she could as quickly as possible, and was doing quite well.

One day she received an assignment that included an out-of-town trip. Herb Norris was also working on this assignment and was scheduled to make the trip. Herb had been with Beavertail for sixteen years. He was hard-working, good-natured, and well-liked by all.

Amy was pleased to be making the trip since it would allow her to tackle some duties that were new for her. She knew that she would learn a lot and be able to prove her ability. She liked Herb and knew she would work well with him.

Amy had met Herb's wife, Marlene, only briefly on two occasions — at the company picnic and in the elevator at work. Herb was there both times. About a week before the trip, Amy got a phone call from Marlene. Marlene just wanted to "visit" — what was Amy going to wear on the trip? What plane was she going to take? Where did she plan to eat while she was there? The next day Marlene called again. What were Amy's hobbies? Where did she go to school? Where did she go on her last vacation? Amy realized by the end of that conversation that Marlene was going to be a problem, but she didn't have the heart to tell Herb. She hoped the problem would just go away.

Amy took the same plane as Herb but she noticed that Marlene did not come to the airport. They had time to talk over the next day's activities on the plane. She and Herb arrived at their destination and checked into their motel about 5:30 P.M. They met for supper in the motel dining room at 6:00 P.M., finished supper at 7:00 P.M., and agreed to meet in the lobby at 8:30 A.M. to get a cab for the plant.

Amy went to her room, got ready for bed, watched TV for a while, reviewed some business papers, and went to bed. She was awakened from a sound sleep by the phone. It was 2:30 A.M. Marlene was on the phone and sounded hysterical. She wanted to speak with Herb, and when Amy told her she hadn't seen him since dinnertime, Marlene didn't believe her. Amy hung up but Marlene kept calling back. Finally, Amy called the switchboard and asked that they not put through any more calls to her room.

Amy met Herb at the appointed time. Neither of them mentioned Marlene. They successfully completed their assignment and returned home.

QUESTIONS

1. What made Marlene behave this way?

2. When Amy first realized that Marlene would be a problem, should she have asked to be taken off the assignment? If not, why?

3. Should Herb be involved? If so, when and how?

4. Should anyone else in the company be involved?

IF GIVEN THE CHANCE...

Emily had had ten years' experience with financial institutions when her big break came. She had interviewed for a position as an assistant vice-president and gotten the job. She had no illusions about her good fortune. This particular financial institution was under a consent decree to implement an affirmative action program, and she knew she had probably been hired because she was a woman. But that didn't bother her. She knew that she always gave 110% to any job so that if given the chance, within six months, she would make them wonder how they had ever gotten along without her.

This financial institution had an unusually conservative history. The officers always had been male and the clients were also male and were accustomed to dealing with the male officers. For several months Emily was treated with suspicion by the clients, but gradually she could see she was beginning to gain their confidence and acceptance. Her problem arose not with the clientele, but with her fellow officers.

For years all the officers had met for a weekly staff meeting. These meetings were important, because often information necessary to doing a competent job was presented. Emily was not invited to these meetings. Naturally she was hurt, but she could handle being hurt. What worried her most was missing the information she needed to do her job. After three months, she decided she must do something. She went to the president and told him her situation. He thought for a moment. Then, looking pleased with himself for coming up with a solution, he told her to come to his office after each staff meeting, and he would tell her what happened. She couldn't believe her ears. She was so amazed at this lack of sensitivity to professional treatment that she simply thanked him and left.

For several weeks, she appeared promptly in his office after each staff meeting. He would try to review the meeting with her but she could tell that sometimes he was not in the mood, or was in a hurry, or had his mind on something else, or found the repetition boring. Finally, after another three months, he invited her to staff meetings.

QUESTIONS

1.   What could Emily have done to get invited to staff meetings sooner?

2.   Could Emily have done anything to gain quicker acceptance by the clientele?

3.   Because of the way Emily handled her situation, how will the women who follow her be treated?

4.   Was Emily correct in accepting a job when she knew that she was probably being hired mainly because she was a woman?

WE NEED EACH OTHER

Grace Bordelon had been made a supervisor in her department. She had been with the company four years and had a good educational background. In her new position, she was responsible for three women and five men.

Grace was very pleased to have this opportunity and did not mind working longer hours to learn her new responsibilities and to get her job done. She knew that her early relationships with her employees was important and she made every effort to open communication among the nine of them in the department.

Only one employee gave her trouble—Liza Waltrip. Grace had known Liza to be a good employee in the past and she could not understand her behavior now. Liza's work was sloppy and late. She was openly hostile toward Grace and on several occasions deliberately put obstacles in the way of completing a project. Grace was disappointed in Liza's behavior and worried about the effect on her department's production. She felt an extra twinge since Liza was a "fellow woman." Grace thought Liza would have wanted to cooperate to help her prove that a woman could be successful as a supervisor, and that women can get along in a work situation.

One Saturday Grace was shopping and stopped at a department store tea room for lunch. She noticed Mercedes Cabot seated alone and she asked if she could join her. Mercedes was the administrative assistant to the company president and had worked for him for 25 years. She was always impeccably groomed and was known to be "super" efficient. Grace knew that she kept to herself at work and no one knew much about her personal life. Maybe today was a good time to become friends; now that Grace was a supervisor she and Mercedes had more in common.

Mercedes invited Grace to join her, but said that she would be leaving soon. She talked about the weather and the new styles. Every time Grace tried to get the conversation around to work, Mercedes would eat faster and talk about something unrelated. Finally, in desperation Grace told Mercedes of her problem with Liza and asked her advice. Mercedes gathered her packages, stood up, and said, "I got where I am by hard work and proving I could handle the job. Now if you can't handle your job, you should never have taken it!" And with that she left. Grace was both saddened that again a "fellow woman" had let her down and disturbed that Mercedes might tell the president that she couldn't do her job.

On Monday, an unexpected and nice thing happened. Liza asked if she could speak to Grace privately. Grace welcomed this overture since communication with Liza had been difficult, if not impossible. Liza said she wanted to apologize to Grace for her past behavior. She realized that Grace was working very hard and doing an excellent job and deserved her complete support and cooperation. Liza asked if Grace would give her a second chance with a fresh start. Grace assured her she would be delighted to work with Liza and the past was forgotten. Grace was amazed at this sudden change and was glad when Liza finally explained.

Liza said that when Grace had been named supervisor, she went home and told her family she was working for a woman. They were very upset; they continually advised her not to cooperate and to find ways to give Grace a hard time so she would quit. They felt a woman could not possibly be a good supervisor and therefore should never have been given the job. They told Liza that the department would never have any prestige or support from top management and would always be looked down on by other employees if a woman were supervisor. Liza said she finally realized that not only was none of this true but that she really admired Grace for the way she had kept trying even with the hard time she had given her. Liza was a model employee after that.

QUESTIONS

1. What kind of social conditioning (socialization or acculturation process) had caused Liza and her family to feel the way they did about "woman managers"?

2. Why didn't Mercedes want to be friends or give Grace advice?

3. What instances have you seen where women discriminate against women?

4. What could be done to change negative attitudes of women employees and "Queen Bees" toward women who receive promotions?

5. How could successful women act as mentors toward other women?

WE JUST KNEW YOU COULDN'T POSSIBLY MOVE

Jane Logan had been passed over for promotion twice, and she couldn't imagine why. Her work record was excellent; she had fine rapport with both management and other employees; and she had taken some extra training to prepare herself for the next step up.

Finally, she got her courage up and went to talk with the manager. She went over a couple of other items before she got to her question, "Why am I being passed over for promotion?" The manager looked surprised and said, "Jane, you know a promotion would mean a transfer a few months later, and we assumed that since you are married, you wouldn't want to transfer. After all, what would happen to your husband and his job?" Jane was amazed that they had not allowed her and her husband to make the decision and that they had not taken the time to get to know her family situation since that seemed to be the deciding factor.

Jane's husband was a manufacturer's representative. His office was his car. As long as he had a car and a telephone, he didn't care where they lived. After Jane explained her husband's situation to her manager, he apologized for the misunderstanding. Three months later Jane was promoted, and after six months, the Logans were packing to move. As she was carrying boxes in one day, a neighbor who worked for the same company came over to congratulate her on the promotion and to wish them happiness in their new home. As he was leaving he said, "And we sure do hope your husband will be OK."

Jane realized again that people assumed he would suffer. Jane loved her husband very much and realized that good husbands "don't grow on trees." She was very family oriented and took pride in the fact that she and her husband took good care of one another as well as other family members. The thoughtful things they did for one another were not based on the plane of a man or a woman groveling at the feet of a member of the opposite sex. They were based on the plane of a husband and wife who had formed a loving family.

QUESTIONS

1. Should managers allow any employee to have the choice of turning down a transfer based on the employee's family decision?

2. Describe situations you know of where males or females have either taken or turned down transfers based on family decisions.

3. Is a transfer always the road to a promotion?

4. Describe any unusual life styles that you know a family has adopted because the spouses work in different locations.

Appendix B

Annotated Bibliography

Ahrons, Constance R., "Counselors' Perceptions of Career Images of Women," *Journal of Vocational Behavior*, Vol. 8, No. 2 (1976), 197-207.

> A semantic differential type questionnaire was completed by 204 male and 85 female public school counselors. Counselors perceived more similarity among the male social and vocational role concepts and less similarity among the female role concepts. These subjects seem to hold a traditional view of women's roles, which incorporates a home-career conflict.

Almquist, Elizabeth M., "Attitudes of College Men Toward Working Wives, *The Vocational Guidance Quarterly*, Vol. 23, No. 2 (1974), 115-21.

> Questionnaires concerning career expectations, occupational choice processes, and adult life-style aspirations were completed by 60 male and 81 female undergraduates. Overall, there was greater similarity than difference in responses by the two groups. About 40% of the women were strongly career-oriented while 30% of the males are willing to have their wives work under any circumstances. College males seem to have more liberal attitudes toward working wives than has been generally assumed.

Almquist, Elizabeth M., "Sex Stereotypes in Occupational Choice: The Case for College Women," *Journal of Vocational Behavior*, Vol. 5, No. 1 (1974), 13-21.

> Questionnaires were given to 110 graduating seniors. Masculine (pioneering) occupations were chosen by 44 women and feminine (traditional) occupations were chosen by 66 women. The groups differed in familial influence, work values, work experience, role model influence, and some collegiate activities. They did not differ in sociability experiences or parental relationships, so that pioneer women do not stem from social isolation, rejection, or lack of appropriate feminine socialization.

Ash, Philip, "Job Satisfaction Differences Among Women of Different Ethnic Groups," *Journal of Vocational Behavior*, Vol. 2, No. 4 (1972), 495-507.

> A Science Research Associates Attitude Survey was completed by 112 white, 63 Spanish surname, and 47 black female clerical and pro-

duction workers. The Job Description Index was completed by 56 white and 14 black female university clerical employees. Black women were more dissatisfied than whites. Workers with Spanish surnames were generally more satisfied than blacks but less than whites.

Athanassiades, John C., "An Investigation of Some Communication Patterns of Female Subordinates in Hierarchical Organizations," *Human Relations*, Vol. 27, No. 3 (1974), 195-209.

A battery of questionnaires was administered to 75 female and 25 male employees. Both sexes seemed clearly aware of female job discrimination. Women in managerial positions feel less autonomous and independent than men in similar positions. They show an inverse relationship between perceived autonomy and the distortion of upward communication by female subordinates. There was no significant relationship between the female subordinate's perception of discrimination, autonomy, and her self-image.

Bartol, Kathryn M., "Male Versus Female Leaders: The Effect of Leader Need for Dominance on Follower Satisfaction," *Academy of Management Journal*, Vol. 17, No. 2 (1974), 225-33.

Several behavioral scales were given to 100 students divided into four- and five-member teams. The teams played *The Executive Game* as part of a beginning management course. In the area of satisfaction with team interaction, male follower groups were significantly more satisfied with high-need-for-dominance female leaders than with low-need-for-dominance female leaders.

Bartol, Kathryn M., "The Effect of Male Versus Female Leaders on Follower Satisfaction and Performance," *Journal of Business Research*, Vol. 3, No. 1 (1975), 31-42.

The Executive Game was played by twenty-four four-member and five-member teams (73 males, 27 females). Members and leaders were chosen randomly and divided among four types: (1) male leader, male followers; (2) male leader, mixed (male and female) followers; (3) female leader, male followers; and (4) female leader, mixed followers. Fiedler's Group Atmosphere scale was used and four other scales were developed to measure satisfaction with task structure, team leader, group atmosphere, team interaction, and task conceptualization. Satisfaction appeared unrelated to leader type or group composition on all dimensions but task structure. Male leaders appear to adversely affect task structure satisfaction for female group members while female leaders have a mildly positive effect on task situations for female followers in mixed groups.

Bartol, Kathryn M., "Expectancy Theory As a Predictor of Female Occupational Choice and Attitude Toward Business," *Academy of Management Journal*, Vol. 19, No. 4 (1976), 669-75.

A questionnaire based on the Mitchell and Knudsen (1973) research was completed by 61 female psychology and 56 female business majors. The data showed that expectancy theory can be used to predict both occupational choice and attitude toward business for female psychology and business majors. However, the model appears to be a weaker predictor of attitude toward business for females than for males. The expectancy theory model includes expectations of family and peers as well as motivation to comply.

Bartol, Kathryn M., "Relationship of Sex and Professional Training Area to Job Orientation," *Journal of Applied Psychology*, Vol. 61, No. 3 (1976), 368-70.

A questionnaire was completed by 175 students, including male and female business majors and female psychology majors. Female business majors scored significantly higher than males on dimensions related to a comfortable working environment and pleasant interpersonal relationships. These two groups did not differ significantly on dimensions related to career aspirations and intrinsic job aspects. Male and female business majors differed significantly from female psychology majors on all the dimensions, giving higher ratings to career aspirations, working environment, and interpersonal relationships; and lower ratings to intrinsic job aspects.

Bartol, Kathryn M., and D. Anthony Butterfield, "Sex Effects in Evaluating Leaders," *Journal of Applied Psychology*, Vol. 61, No. 4 (1976), 446-54.

Two versions of a questionnaire containing four stories based on different leadership style dimensions were completed by 225 male and 57 female management students. Male and female manager names were used on the two versions. Female managers received more positive scores on consideration style, and male managers were valued more highly when using initiating structure behavior. No differences between males and females were found related to the production emphasis and tolerance for freedom styles.

Bartol, Kathryn M., and Max S. Wortman, "Male Versus Female Leaders; Effects on Perceived Leader Behavior and Satisfaction in a Hospital," *Personnel Psychology*, Vol. 28, No. 4 (1975), 533-47.

The Ohio State Leader Behavior Description Questionnaire and the Cornell Job Description Index were given to 60 female and 124 male employees in a large, government-operated psychiatric hospital. From subordinates' point of view, the sex of the leader has little effect on perceived leader behavior, job satisfaction, or the relationship between perceived leader behavior and satisfaction with supervision. Subordinate's sex may be important when assessing both subordinate job satisfaction and leader behavior perceptions.

Bass, Bernard M., Judith Krusell, and Ralph A. Alexander, "Male Managers' Attitudes Toward Working Women," *American Behavioral Scientist*, Vol. 15, No. 2 (1971), 221-36.

A 56-item questionnaire was constructed to examine attitudes toward women. Respondents were 174 male managers. The male managers indicated their feelings that people want male managers, that they themselves would be uncomfortable with a female supervisor, and that women are not dependable. Men who did not work with women had more positive regard than those who did.

Bedeian, Arthur G., and Achilles A. Armenakis, "Male-Female Correlates of Perceived Organizational Legitimacy," *Academy of Management Proceedings* (1975), 457-59.

> The Schein-Ott Legitimacy of Organizational Influence Questionnaire was completed by 58 women managers. A comparative male sample was obtained for analysis. There were considerable areas of agreement between the behavioral attitudes and values of the male and female managers surveyed.

Bedeian, Arthur G., Achilles A. Armenakis, and B. Wayne Kemp, "Relationship of Sex to Perceived Legitimacy of Organizational Influence," *The Journal of Psychology*, Vol. 94, No. 1 (1976), 93-99.

> The Schein-Ott Legitimacy of Organizational Influence Questionnaire was given to 108 male and 145 female managers. Findings that factors other than sex play a major role in employee response patterns to the legitimacy of various organizational influences throw doubt on the findings of other studies that differences exist between male and female organization behavior patterns.

Bem, Sandra L., and Daryl J. Bem, "Does Sex-biased Job Advertising 'Aid and Abet' Sex Discrimination?" *Journal of Applied Social Psychology*, Vol. 3, No. 1 (1973), 6-18.

> The same four jobs were presented in three different formats: sex-biased, sex-unbiased, and sex-reversed "affirmative action." Eight other jobs were worded in sex-unbiased format and remained constant. Sixty male and sixty female high school students were asked to rate the jobs on a six-point scale from "very uninterested" to "very interested." Data indicated that sex-biased job advertisements discourage men and women from applying for "opposite-sex" jobs. Then 52 women attending Carnegie Melon were asked to rate 16 jobs in a "Jobs-Male Interest" column and 16 jobs in a "Jobs-Female Interest" column on a six-point scale from "definitely unwilling" to "definitely willing" to apply for the job. Data indicate that sex-segregated want ads discourage women from seriously considering those jobs which appear in a "male interest" column.

Bingham, William C., and Elaine W. House, "Counselors View Women and Work: Accuracy of Information," *Vocational Guidance Quarterly*, Vol. 21, No. 4 (1973), 262-68.

> A questionnaire was constructed to measure facts and attitudes related to the employment of women. Usable questionnaires came from 67 male and 59 female secondary school counselors. Both groups were misinformed as to the increasing discrepancy between men's and women's income and the probability that women will advance to leadership positions in the foreseeable future. Males were less accurately informed than females as to: women's needed occupational alternatives, their ability to be both homemaker and wife, and their general ability; whether women are clearly discriminated against; the number of jobs that cannot be performed equally well by women and men; the length of time women work; and the fact that many companies do give women fringe benefits.

Blum, Stuart H., "The Desire for Security in Vocation Choice; A Comparison of Men and Women," *Journal of Psychology*, Vol. 91, No. 2 (1975), 277-81.

> A 40-item inventory to measure emphasis placed on job security in choosing a job was completed by 102 men and 91 women. The mean security scores between the two groups were not significantly different. However, when a subsample of 26 men and 22 women oriented toward business was compared with a subsample of 25 men and 21 women oriented toward education, the mean scores were statistically different. Results imply that job security considerations are appropriate to vocational decisions rather than sex differences.

Brief, Arthur P., and Richard L. Oliver, "Male-Female Differences in Work Attitudes Among Retail Sales Managers," *Journal of Applied Psychology*, Vol. 61, No. 4 (1976), 526-28.

> Motivational perceptions of 25 job outcomes were scaled by 52 male and 53 female retail sales managers. No significant pattern of differences were found, indicating that extreme caution should be used when making generalizations about sex differences in work attitudes.

Burkhead, Marie, "Underrepresentation of Women in University-Sponsored Management Development Programs," *Journal of Business Education*, Vol. 48, No. 3 (1972), 109-10.

> Fifty-six AACSB (American Assembly of Collegiate Schools of Business) members reported having management development programs of from 1 to 13 weeks. In 1969, 4,287 people attended these programs; 270 (6.2%) were women. In 1970, 4,183 people attended; 269 (6.4%) were women. The lack of participation by women in the existing executive development programs appears to indicate one of the most subtle and perhaps most effective means of discrimination against women in the managerial professions.

Cecil, Earl A., Robert J. Paul, and Robert A. Olins, "Perceived Importance of Selected Variables Used to Evaluate Male and Female Job Applicants," *Personnel Psychology*, Vol. 26, No. 3 (1973), 397-404.

> A list of 50 variables were used to evaluate the way an interviewer would look at a male and a female job candidate. The subjects were 118 graduate and undergraduate management students. Females were perceived as clerical employees and males as administrative management employees. It would appear that each group would find difficulty being employed in the other's area of employment.

Chapman, J. Brad, "Comparison of Male and Female Leadership Styles," *Academy of Management Journal*, Vol. 18, No. 3 (1975), 645-50.

> Fiedler's Least Preferred Co-worker questionnaire was distributed to 146 male and 60 female military personnel and 49 male and 28 female company personnel. Results show that although there may be differences in leadership behaviors between male and female leaders, there are no differences in style. "Practicing female managers do not have a significantly higher need for fostering good interpersonal relationships than do their male colleagues." Females studied were not significantly more task-oriented.

Cohen, Stephen L., and Kerry A. Bunker, "Subtle Effects of Sex Role Stereotypes on Recruiters' Hiring Decisions," *Journal of Applied Psychology*, Vol. 60,
No. 5 (1975), 566-72.

> Evaluations on one hypothetical job applicant (male or female) for
> either a male-oriented (personnel technician) or female-oriented (edi-
> torial assistant) job were made by 150 job recruiters. Hiring decisions
> were influenced by the interaction of sex and position. Significantly
> more females were recommended for editorial assistant and signifi-
> cantly more males were recommended for personnel technician.

Courtney, Alice E., and Sarah Wernick Lockeretz, "A Woman's Place: An Analysis of the Roles Portrayed by Women in Magazine Advertisements," *Journal of
Marketing Research*, Vol. 8, No. 1 (1971), 92-95.

> The April 1970 issues of seven general-interest magazines were
> analyzed to determine the roles portrayed by women in advertise-
> ments. The data suggest that advertisements do not present a full
> view of the roles women actually play in American society. Images of
> women's intelligence and personality reflected in the advertisements
> need more thorough analysis.

Day, David R., and Ralph M. Stogdill, "Leader Behavior of Male and Female
Supervisors: A Comparative Study," *Personnel Psychology*, Vol. 25, No. 2 (1972),
353-60.

> The Leader Behavior Description Questionnaire and a 9-point "repu-
> tational" scale were used by subordinates to describe 37 male and 36
> female supervisors. Biographical data were obtained from personnel
> records. Results indicated that male and female supervisors who
> occupy parallel positions and perform similar functions exhibit simi-
> lar leader behavior patterns and levels of effectiveness when des-
> cribed and evaluated by their immediate subordinates.

Deaux, Kay, and Tim Emswiller, "Explanations of Successful Performance on
Sex-Linked Tasks: What is Skill for the Male is Luck for the Female," *Journal of
Personality and Social Psychology*, Vol. 29, No. 1 (1974), 80-85.

> The subjects (55 male and 75 female undergraduate psychology stu-
> dents) evaluated the performance of a male or female who performed
> in an above-average manner on either a male- or female-related task.
> Male performance on a masculine task was attributed to skill while
> female equivalent performance on the same task was attributed to
> luck. The reverse was not true for performance on a feminine task.
> Males were seen to be more skillful overall.

DiMarco, Nicholas, and Susan E. Whitsitt, "A Comparison of Female Supervisors
in Business and Government Organizations," *Journal of Vocational Behavior*, Vol.
6, No. 2 (1975), 185-96.

> The Life Style Orientation Questionnaire and the Organizational
> Structure Questionnaire were given to 24 female government and 27
> female business supervisors. The government supervisors had a
> significantly higher formalistic and lower sociocentric and personalis-
> tic life-style orientation; showed lower needs for expressed control,

affection, and wanted inclusion, and a higher need for wanted control; were lower on consideration and higher on structure leader dimensions; and perceived their organization as being more bureaucratic and less collaborative and coordinate than the business group.

Dipboye, Robert L., Howard L. Fromkin, and Kent Wibeck, "Relative Importance of Applicant Sex, Attractiveness, and Scholastic Standing in Evaluation of Job Applicant Resumes," *Journal of Applied Psychology*, Vol. 60, No. 1 (1975), 39-43.

Bogus resumes, which systematically varied applicant's sex, physical attractiveness, and scholastic standing, were rated by 30 college students and 30 professional interviewers on suitability for a managerial position. Both groups preferred males to females, attractive applicants to unattractive applicants, and applicants of high scholastic standing.

Dominick, Joseph R., and Gail E. Rauch, "The Image of Women in Network TV Commercials," *Journal of Broadcasting*, Vol. 16, No. 3 (1972), 259-65.

Trained coders viewed ads on prime time for two weeks. The unit of analysis was adult females who appeared for at least three seconds and had one line of dialogue. Professional women were not seen. Women were seen as housewives selling kitchen or bathroom products. They were also seen in service roles as stewardess or secretary. Older females were less visible than their male counterparts. The most frequent role recorded was sex object/decoration.

Driscoll, Jeanne Baker, and H. Richard Hess, "The Recruiter: Women's Friend or Foe?" *Journal of College Placement*, Vol. 34, No. 4 (1974), 42-48.

A questionnaire was completed by 38 women interviewed by recruiters at Pennsylvania State University during 1972-73. The 38 women had taken a total of 247 interviews. The responses were compared with those of 17 men who had taken 195 interviews. Interviewers spent time discussing family plans with women but not with men. Women did perceive sex bias in the interview. Both groups believed female recruiters were at least equal to, or better than, male recruiters.

Feild, Hubert S., "Effects of Sex of Investigator on Mail Survey Response Rates and Response Bias," *Journal of Applied Psychology*, Vol. 60, No. 6 (1975), 772-73.

The Attitudes Toward Women Scale was returned by 215 out of 305 randomly selected university faculty members. No significant differences were found due to the investigator's sex for questionnaire return rates or for expressed attitudes toward women.

Goodale, James G., and Douglas T. Hall, "Inheriting a Career: The Influence of Sex, Values, and Parents," *Journal of Vocational Behavior*, Vol. 8, No. 1 (1976), 19-30.

A questionnaire was completed by 437 high-school sophomores. Parental background was linked to occupational plans for boys but did not enter for girls. "Girls perceived less parental interest and pressure regarding their schoolwork than did boys."

Gordon, Francine E., and Douglas T. Hall, "Self-Image and Stereotypes of Femininity: Their Relationship to Women's Role Conflicts and Coping," *Journal of Applied Psychology,* Vol. 59, No. 2 (1974), 241-43.

> A questionnaire was developed and completed by 229 college-educated married women. The best predictor of conflicts experienced was the woman's perception of the male's stereotype of femininity. Her self-image was associated with her style of coping with conflict and her satisfaction and happiness.

Hagen, Randi L., and Arnold Kahn, "Discrimination Against Competent Women," *Journal of Applied Social Psychology,* Vol. 5, No. 4 (1975), 362-76.

> Sixty male and sixty female introductory psychology students either competed with, cooperated with, or observed two female or two male others. One of the others was reported to have performed at a highly competent level and one, very poorly. Males only like competent women when they observe them and are not in competition with them. Both sexes were more likely to exclude a competent woman than a competent man and include an incompetent woman than an incompetent man. Competent women were not discriminated against on leadership but an atmosphere conducive to low performance was established.

Hall, Francine S., and Douglas T. Hall, "Effects of Job Incumbents' Race and Sex on Evaluations of Managerial Performance," *Academy of Management Journal,* Vol. 19, No. 3 (1976), 476-81.

> A sample of 290 undergraduate students were presented with a case history and asked to complete an anonymous questionnaire as part of a study to "determine how management students view administrators." The results suggest that race and sex of job incumbents do not affect performance appraisal.

Hamner, W. Clay, Jay S. Kim, Lloyd Baird, and William J. Bigoness, "Race and Sex as Determinants of Ratings By Potential Employers in a Simulated Work-Sampling Task," *Journal of Applied Psychology,* Vol. 59, No. 6 (1974), 705-11.

> Thirty-six undergraduate students volunteered to assume manager's roles in rating eight combinations of male-female and black-white performers on a simulated work-sampling task. Results indicated that sex-race stereotypes do influence ratings even when objective measures are defined.

Helmich, Donald L., and Paul E. Erzen, "Leadership Style and Leader Needs," *Academy of Management Journal,* Vol. 18, No. 2 (1975), 397-402.

> Questionnaires measuring leadership style and need fulfillment were completed by 44 female corporate presidents listed in Marquis's *Who's Who in American Women.* A positive relationship was found between a task-oriented leadership style and a lack of fulfillment of the leader's personal needs; most specifically in the lack of opportunity to develop close friendships.

Herrick, John S., "Work Motives of Female Executives," *Public Personnel Management*, Vol. 2, No. 5 (1973), 380-87.

> Questionnaires were completed by 762 federal executives and 173 state executives. Federal: 719 male, 40 female; state: 160 male, 13 female. Males and females appear to perceive very little difference in the importance of their needs. Women seemed to favor intrinsic rewards over money and to depress the value assigned to esteem. The questions were classified into a Maslow-type need hierarchy.

Heshusius-Gilsdorf, Lous T., and Dale L. Gilsdorf, "Girls Are Females, Boys Are Males: A Content Analysis of Career Materials," *Personnel and Guidance Journal*, Vol. 54, No. 4 (1975), 206-11.

> Two career-orientation textbooks were coded for numerical presentation of working persons by sex and of jobs by sex. Both presented males and females in traditional occupational sex roles. Males are told to be bright, independent, strong, and productive so that they can hold difficult, high-level, and leading positions. Females are told that their futures are relatively unimportant, nonproductive, and service-oriented, and that they require an attractive appearance, which is often viewed as incompatible with intelligence.

Hoffer, Stefan N., "Private Rates of Return to Higher Education for Women," *Review of Economics and Statistics*, Vol. 55, No. 4 (1973), 482-86.

> Wage data were taken from the 1967 *Survey of Economic Opportunities* and compared with life styles. A college degree for women is a profitable investment under most alternative patterns of lifetime labor force behavior considered. In most cases, the investment in 1-3 years of college is unprofitable.

Hunt, John W., and Peter N. Saul, "The Relationship of Age, Tenure, and Job Satisfaction in Males and Females," *Academy of Management Journal*, Vol. 18, No. 4 (1975), 690-702.

> An attitude survey was completed by 3,338 male and 579 female white college workers. Respondents were asked how much of 16 job factors they were currently experiencing. Overall job satisfaction was found to be more strongly associated with age than with tenure for males; the opposite held for females. There was no evidence of a significant relationship of any kind between age and overall job satisfaction for females.

Jacobson, Dan, "Rejection of the Retiree Role: A Study of Female Industrial Workers in Their 50's," *Human Relations*, Vol. 27, No. 5 (1974), 477-92.

> Fairly rigidly structured personal interviews were conducted with 145 male and 70 female semi-skilled factory operatives. Females are less likely to be positively oriented toward retirement than males. Females are less likely to be positively oriented toward retirement than males. The reluctance of both groups was tied to expected extrinsic deprivations. However, among women, work-based social ties was the main reason.

Jacobson, Marsha B., and Joan Effertz, "Sex Roles and Leadership: Perceptions of the Leaders and the Led," *Organizational Behavior and Human Performance*, Vol. 12, No. 3 (1974), 383-96.

> The subjects were 36 male and 36 female introductory psychology student volunteers. They were divided into groups of three (MMM, FFF, FMM, MFF) and a leader and followers were designated. They completed a task and a questionnaire. Males are judged more harshly than females when they are leaders and more leniently as followers. There was no significant difference in how males and females enjoyed leadership.

Kaniuga, Nancy, Scott Thomas, and Eldon Gade, "Working Women Portrayed on Evening Television Programs," *The Vocational Guidance Quarterly*, Vol. 23, No. 2 (1974), 134-37.

> Principal adult characters were analyzed for their occupational representation during October and November 1972, in 44 evening TV programs on the three major networks between 6:30 and 10:00 P.M. CST. Women characters represented only 21.4% of the TV work force compared with 37.8% of the actual work force. Only 10% were employed and married compared with 60% in actuality. Only 4 TV characters were in pioneer types of work (17%) while 83% were in traditional female work roles.

Karol, Barbara L., and Richard J. Klimoski, "Worker Performance and Evaluation of a Supervisor as a Function of Subordinate Sex, Supervisor Sex, and Leadership Style," *Academy of Management Proceedings '76*, 99-103.

> A task under the direction of either a male or female supervisor exhibiting a set of behaviors labeled "consideration" or "structure" was completed by 44 male and 44 female subordinates. The participants were students meeting an introductory psychology course requirement. When the subordinate has direct experience with the supervisor, it appears that evaluations focus more on supervisor's behavior than on sex alone. "Considerate supervisors were preferred to those using the structuring style for all measured dimensions of effectiveness."

Kavanagh, Michael J., and Michael Halpern, "The Impact of Job Level and Sex Differences on the Relationship Between Life and Job Satisfaction," *Academy of Management Journal*, Vol. 20, No. 1 (1977), 66-73.

> Four scales measuring job satisfaction and situation and life satisfaction and situation were completed by 198 males and 213 females in three levels of university employment. Contrary to a 1957 study, there was a strong relationship between life and job satisfaction for females at all levels. The same strong relationship was evident for males in both this and the 1957 study. The relationship is lowest between life and job satisfaction for both males and females at the highest job level.

Kimmel, Ellen, "Women As Job Changers," *American Psychologist*, Vol. 29, No. 7 (1974), 536-39.

> A questionnaire was completed by 72 female and 74 male members of the Southeastern Psychological Association. There was no significant

difference in their job mobility. The apparent "myth" that women are poor risks may be due to their moving for family-related reasons, which is less socially acceptable than a male's moving for career advancement.

Klemmack, David L., and John N. Edwards, "Women's Acquisition of Stereotyped Occupational Aspirations," *Sociology and Social Research*, Vol. 57, No. 4 (1973), 510-25.

Questionnaire data were obtained from 300 female university students. Father's occupational status, mother's work, and family size were significantly related to the type of occupational aspirations. Approximately 77% wanted to work after graduation; 99% intended to marry; and 53% preferred traditionally stereotyped nonfeminine occupations.

Knotts, Rose E., "Manifest Needs of Professional Female Workers in Business-Related Occupations," *Journal of Business Research*, Vol. 3, (1975), 267-75.

The Edwards Personal Preference Schedule was used to measure personality characteristics reflecting "manifest needs." Subjects came from professional organizations and women faculty members in business administration at four-year universities. "Support for the hypothesis that professional female workers have significant personality differences from adult women in general is provided by evidence on EPPS scores for Achievement, Order, Affiliation, Succorance, Dominance, Abasement, Nurturance, and Heterosexuality."

Larwood, Laurie, David Zalkind, and Jeanne Legault, "The Bank Job: A Field Study of Sexually Discriminatory Performance on a Neutral-Role Task," *Journal of Applied Social Psychology*, Vol. 5, No. 1 (1975), 68-74.

Four male and four female undergraduate psychology students cashed 64 checks from a low of $2.50 to a high of $6.50. A male customer with a female teller was processed three times more rapidly than a female customer with a male teller. Tellers more often initiated conversation with customers of the opposite sex. Male tellers processed customers more slowly than female tellers.

Lawlis, G. Frank, and Jim D. Crawford, "Cognitive Differentiation in Women and Pioneer-Traditional Vocational Choices," *Journal of Vocational Behavior*, Vol. 6, No. 2 (1975), 263-67.

A modified version of Bodden's vocational cognitive-complexity grid measure was given to 50 females with traditional majors and 33 females with pioneer male-dominated majors. All were seniors. Pioneering women seem to have a wide perception of roles and, therefore, a less restrictive choice of vocational goals.

Levinson, Richard M., "Sex Discrimination and Employment Practices: An Experiment with Unconventional Job Inquiries," *Social Problems*, Vol. 22, No. 4 (1975), 533-43.

Teams of one male and one female undergraduate sociology students responded to 256 different classified ads. Clearcut discrimination was found in 28% of female inquiries for "male" jobs and 44% of male inquiries for "female" jobs. Ambiguous discrimination was felt by

31.5% females and 22% males. The study documents continuing sex discrimination and segregation in employment practices.

Levitin, Teresa, Robert P. Quinn, and Graham L. Staines, "Sex Discrimination Against the American Working Woman," *American Behavioral Scientist*, Vol. 15, No. 2 (1971), 237-54.

Interviews were conducted with 351 women and 695 men. Most women received far less income than they should. Although there was evidence of objective discrimination against about 95% of women workers, only 7.9% reported any. Discrimination in income was greatest among white-collar workers; professional employees including managers; those in trade services, finance, insurance, and real estate; non-union employees; and those in establishments with less than 500 employees.

Lublin, Joann S., "Discrimination Against Women in Newsrooms: Fact or Fantasy?" *Journalism Quarterly*, Vol. 49, No. 2 (1972), 357-61.

A Sex Stereotype Scale was completed by 80 news executives and the Perceived Discrimination Index was completed by 152 women journalists. Over half the news executives agreed that comparably qualified women would neither advance as quickly nor earn as many top positions as men. Nearly half the women news executives on the news executives' papers worked as women's section editors.

Mackie, Marlene, "Students' Perceptions of Female Professors," *Journal of Vocational Behavior*, Vol. 8, No. 3 (1976), 337-48.

An occupational prestige ranking instrument and 21 semantic differential scales were used by 94 females and 87 males to evaluate male and female professors. Females were perceived as more competent both in task and socio-emotional competence. Males were not evaluated significantly higher in prestige. Female professors were regarded more favorably by female students than by male students.

Malkiel, Burton, and Judith A. Malkiel, "Male-Female Pay Differentials in Professional Employment," *The American Economic Review*, Vol. 63, No. 4 (1973), 693-705.

Salary differentials between 159 male and 113 female technical/scientific employees were analyzed. "Experience, education, and productivity variables are able to explain over three-quarters of the variance in salaries for both men and women over several years." Men and women in equal job levels with the same characteristics get equal pay. However, women with the same training, experience, etc. as men tend to be assigned to lower job levels.

Manes, Audrey L., and Paul Melnyk, "Televised Models of Female Achievement," *Journal of Social Psychology*, Vol. 4, No. 4 (1974), 365-74.

Two males and two females gathered data on 62 female TV characters at four levels of achievement. Only those at the lowest level were depicted as having successful male social relationships. However, overall working women at all levels were depicted as unmarried or unsuccessfully married. A second study gathered data on both male and female characters. Females were depicted as less likely to be married and more likely to be unsuccessfully married than males. Ten times as many employed married females as housewives were shown to have unsuccessful marriages.

Manhardt, Philip J., "Job Orientation of Male and Female College Graduates in Business," *Personnel Psychology*, Vol. 25, No. 2 (1972), 361-68.

A questionnaire that included 25 job characteristics to be rated on a 5-point scale of importance was completed by 365 male and 301 female college graduates recently appointed to similar jobs. "Men rated characteristics contained in an advancement/responsibility factor related to long-range career success significantly higher than women who gave higher ratings to characteristics contained in a work environment factor. Only small and mixed sex differences were found in a third factor containing characteristics closely related to job content."

Manley, T. Roger, Robert J. Lucas, and Charles W. Bartholomew, "Personal Value Systems and Career Objectives of Men and Women Managers," *Decision Sciences Education and Applications, Northeast Region Proceedings*, (1974), 114-18.

A questionnaire that included 77 value concepts and 39 career objectives was completed by 307 female and 323 male Air Force managers (officers) in ten different career fields. Results indicated that both groups are motivated by important, challenging work and value consistent, intelligent personnel policies and the ability to exercise some control over their careers. "Conventional 'truths' about working women cannot be supported."

Martin, Claude R., Jr., "Support for Women's Lib: Management Performance," *The Southern Journal of Business*, Vol. 7, No. 1 (1972), 17-28.

Interviews were conducted with 60 male and 77 female professional buyers. Major differences for males and females were noted in demographic characteristics, rate of pay, and decision-making discretion. No significant differences were found in either their self-evaluation or their actual execution of buying responsibilities and activities.

Mayer, Steven E., and Anita I. Bell, "Sexism in Ratings of Personality Traits," *Personnel Psychology*, Vol. 28, No. 2 (1975), 239-49.

A sampling from the "Checklist for Describing Job Applicants" was rated by 75 male and 75 female introductory psychology students. Male and female job applicant backgrounds were exactly the same but they called to mind different stereotypes for male and female raters. Females see males and females as more similar than males do. The notion of competence depends on the sex of the ratee and rater. Males have more complex stereotypes of males and females than do females.

Meir, Elchanan I., "Relationship Between Intrinsic Needs and Women's Persistence at Work," *Journal of Applied Psychology*, Vol. 56, No. 4 (1972), 293-96.

The subjects (288 women dentists, 31 registered nurses, 20 policemen, 30 social workers, and 35 youth counselors in Israel) were asked to mark a list of needs according to the effect they had on their occupational choice. All correlations between job persistence and intrinsic needs were positive. Both positive and negative correlations were found between extrinsic needs and job persistence.

Mennerick, Lewis A. "Organizational Structuring of Sex Roles in a Non-Stereotyped Industry," *Administrative Science Quarterly*, Vol. 20, No. 4 (1975), 570-86.

Personnel data were gathered from 446 New York City travel agencies. Six measures provided data on sex structuring among agencies. Men predominated both in management and in more prestigious agencies. Women were most frequently in sales and in less prestigious agencies. Female top managers employed women in both management and sales. Male top managers employed males in management and females in sales.

Miller, Susan H., "The Content of News Photos: Women's and Men's Roles," *Journalism Quarterly*, Vol. 52, No. 1 (1975), 70-75.

Data came from 2,168 photos appearing in the *Washington Post* and *Los Angeles Times*. Coverage is dominated by male photos. Women are primarily pictured as spouses or socialites. Coverage of women's sports, activism, or professional activities is negligible compared to that of men in similar activities.

Miner, John B., "Motivation to Manage Among Women," *Journal of Vocational Behavior*, Vol. 5, No. 2 (1974), 241-50.

The Miner Sentence Completion Scale was given to 46 male and 97 female undergraduate education students, 99 male and 42 female graduate education students, 944 male and 107 female undergraduate business students, and 29 male and 47 female undergraduate liberal arts majors. Differences in motivation to manage were not found among education majors. Business administration and liberal arts females did prove to have lower managerial motivation scores than their male counterparts.

Miner, John B. "Motivation to Manage Among Women: Studies of Business Managers and Educational Administrators," *Journal of Vocational Behavior*, Vol. 5, No. 2 (1974), 197-208.

The Miner Sentence Completion Scale was given to 44 female and 26 male business managers and 25 female and 194 male school administrators. Managerial motivation was related to managerial success among females but was not a factor differentiating male and female managers. The data gave no reason to assume that female managers will be any less effective.

Mischel, Harriet N., "Sex Bias in the Evaluation of Professional Achievements," *Journal of Educational Psychology*, Vol. 66, No. 2 (1974), 157-66.

Current articles from professional literature on law, city planning, primary education, and dietetics, were combined into booklets. Half the booklets had a male author's name and half had a matched female author's name. Each booklet had two "male-authored" articles and two "female-authored" articles. The booklets were evaluated by 14 male and 14 female high school students and a like number of college students. Evaluations based on sex appeared to be a function of the occupational field of work being judged and the evaluator's educational level. Two other studies are also included in this article.

Moore, Kathryn McDaniel, "The Cooling Out of Two -Year College Women," *Personnel and Guidance Journal,* Vol. 53, No. 8 (1975), 578-83.

The data came from interviews with 62 women in three two-year colleges. *Cooling out* was defined as rechanneling student aspirations in line with their abilities to avoid disappointment and failure (Clark). Parents, uncontrollable circumstances, counselors, and the two-year institution functioned to cool women out of straightforward, unblocked, and open pursuit of their career choices and life plans. Data indicated that women were rechanneled because they were women.

Morrison, Robert F., and Maria-Luise Sebald, "Personal Characteristics Differentiating Female Executive From Female Nonexecutive Personnel," *Journal of Applied Psychology,* Vol. 59, No. 5 (1974), 656-59.

Several instruments were completed by 39 pairs of subjects matched on age, education, work site, length of employment, etc. Organization status and policy contribution differentiated the executive group, which was significantly higher in (a) self-esteem component of need for achievement, (b) the need for power, and (c) mental ability.

Moses, Joseph L., and Virginia B. Boehm, "Relationship of Assessment-Center Performance to Management Progress of Women," *Journal of Applied Psychology,* Vol. 60, No. 4 (1975), 527-29.

Performance of 4,846 women at the AT&T assessment center between 1963 and 1971 was strongly related to promotion and advancement in management. The distribution of male and female assessment ratings was very similar. Assessment-center methods appear valid for selecting women managers and do not result in proportionately fewer promotions.

Norton, Steven D., David P. Gustafson, and Charles E. Foster, "Assessment for Management Potential: Scales Design and Development, Training Effects and Rater/Ratee Sex Effects," *Academy of Management Journal,* Vol. 20, No. 1 (1977), 117-31.

Six behaviorally based bipolar scales to assess management potential were completed by 2,827 male and 434 female managers. Participants were given male and female versions of one case to rate. Training was given on the rating scale system. Then male and female versions of another case were rated.

After training, managers rated more consistently and less leniently. Female raters were less lenient than males before the training and even less lenient after training. Female case subjects were rated higher on "initiative" than males.

Oliver, Laurel W., "Achievement and Affiliation Motivation In Career-Oriented and Homemaking-Oriented College Women," *Journal of Vocational Behavior,* Vol. 4, No. 3 (1974), 275-81.

> The Adjective Check List was obtained for 250 female college students on one study and 257 college women in a replication. They were classified as career- or homemaking-oriented based on post-college plans. No significant difference was found on achievement and affiliation for the two groups but a significant interaction did occur between the two variables.

Osborn, Richard N., and William N. Vicars, "Sex Stereotypes: An Artifact in Leader Behavior and Subordinate Satisfaction Analysis?" *Academy of Management Journal,* Vol. 19, No. 3 (1976), 439-49.

> Sample leaders and employees from two organizations completed the Leader Behavior Description Questionnaire and the Job Description Index. (Organization I, N = 34; II, N = 39.) "Leader sex does not appear to have a consistent influence on either leader behavior or subordinate satisfaction, either by itself or in interaction with leader demographics, subordinate demographics, leader behavior, and subordinate sex.

Petty, M. M., and Gordon K. Lee, Jr., "Moderating Effects of Sex of Supervisor and Subordinate on Relationships Between Supervisory Behavior and Subordinate Satisfaction," *Journal of Applied Psychology,* Vol. 60, No. 5 (1975), 624-28.

> The Job Description Index was completed by 165 academic institution employees. All group subordinates displayed greater work satisfaction with supervisors who were higher in consideration. "This relationship was significantly higher for subordinates with female supervisors." Although not significant, there was some tendency for male subordinates to have lower satisfaction with female supervisors who were higher in structure.

Petty, M. M., and Robert H. Miles, "Leader Sex-Role Stereotyping in Social Service Organizations," *Academy of Management Proceedings '76,* 467-71.

> Several scientifically developed behavioral scales were completed by 226 professional-level subordinates in 51 county-level social service organizations. Participants described their agency director's leadership behaviors as well as outcomes they experienced on the job. The results indicated that leader sex moderated relationships between leader behaviors and both subordinate job satisfaction and work motivation and between initiating structure and consideration.

Piacente, Beth Stearns, Louis A. Penner, and Harold L. Hawkins, "Evaluation of the Performance of Experimenters as a Function of Their Sex and Competence," *Journal of Applied Psychology,* Vol. 4, No. 4 (1974), 321-29.

> Subjects were 214 male and female introductory psychology students who were shown one of eight videotapes. A 20-item semantic differential was then used to rate the experimenters shown on the tape. Competent females were judged equal to competent males. Incompetent females were judged less competent than incompetent males. Competent females were perceived as less feminine than incompetent females.

Rand, Lorraine M., and Anna Louise Miller, "A Developmental Cross-Sectioning of Women's Careers and Marriage Attitudes and Life Plans," *Journal of Vocational Behavior*, Vol. 2, No. 3 (1972), 317-31.

> A questionnaire to assess differences, attitudes, and future plans was completed by 60 females in junior high, senior high, and college. As young women develop they become more liberal in their attitudes and desires about work. By adulthood the biological surge for early marriage had been passed or fulfilled and career emerged as part of a life pattern.

Reagan, Barbara, "Two Supply Curves for Economists? Implications of Mobility and Career Attachment of Women," *American Economic Review*, Vol. 65, No. 2 (1975), 100-107.

> Preliminary data are presented from the Committee on the Status of Women in the Economics Profession survey. Seven hundred and ten questionnaires were returned by 55% of the women economists registered with CSWEP and the first 264 male economists in matched cohorts. The supply curve is steeper for women because of nonpecuniary returns from employers perceived by women. Men's attitudes are seen as barriers to full career development and wages. Women's will to bargain is reduced due to perceptions of previous societal conditioning. Twenty-eight percent of women Ph.D.'s felt they were paid less and had lower level jobs due to their sex.

Rosen, Benson, and Thomas H. Jerdee, "Effects of Applicant's Sex and Difficulty of Job on Evaluations of Candidates for Managerial Positions," *Journal of Applied Psychology*, Vol. 59, No. 4 (1974), 511-12.

> A personnel selection exercise was completed by 235 undergraduate business students. Male applicants were evaluated more favorably on general suitability, long service potential and potential for fitting in the organization well than were equally qualified females. Job demands also had differential effects on evaluations. "Lowest acceptance rates and poorest evaluations were given female applicants for 'demanding' managerial positions."

Rosen, Benson, and Thomas H. Jerdee, "Effects of Employee's Sex and Threatening Versus Pleading Appeals on Managerial Evaluations of Grievances," *Journal of Applied Psychology*, Vol. 60, No. 4 (1975), 442-45.

> Two grievances written in four forms to manipulate appellant's sex and type of appeal were evaluated by 101 bank managers. A male appellant with a polite, pleading appeal was very favorably received and with an aggressive, threatening appeal was fairly well received. A female appellant with an aggressive, threatening appeal was quite favorably received and with a polite, pleading appeal was much less well received.

Rosen, Benson, and Thomas H. Jerdee, "The Influence of Sex-Role Stereotypes on Evaluations of Male and Female Supervisory Behavior," *Journal of Applied Psychology*, Vol. 57, No. 1 (1973), 44-48.

> Undergraduate students (134 male, 24 female) and bank supervisors (83 male, 15 female) were asked to read one of six versions of a supervisory problem (with either a male or female supervisor and with

either male, female, or mixed subordinates) and to evaluate the effectiveness of four supervisory styles. Sex-role stereotypes did influence evaluations of supervisory effectiveness for some, but not all of the supervisory styles.

Rosen, Benson, and Thomas H. Jerdee, "Influence on Sex-Role Stereotypes on Personnel Decisions," *Journal of Applied Psychology*, Vol. 59, No. 1 (1974), 9-14.

An in-basket exercise in which an employee's sex and other situational attributes were manipulated was completed by 95 bank supervisors. Results showed that male administrators tend to discriminate against female employees in personnel decisions involving promotion, development, and supervision. Male employees were discriminated against in decisions involving competing role demands stemming from family circumstances.

Rosenbach, William E., Robert C. Dailey, and Cyril P. Morgan, "Differences Among Women in Perceptions of Their Jobs," *Academy of Management Proceedings '76*, 472-76.

Several scientifically developed behavioral scales were completed by 13 buyers and 21 clerical assistants. Buyers (higher positions) perceived their jobs to have greater skill variety, task identity, significance, autonomy, feedback, and total motivation potential than did clerical assistants. "The results suggest that hierarchical level affects women's perception of their job in the same way it affects men's perception."

Roussell, Cecile, "Relationship of Sex of Department Head to Department Climate," *Administrative Science Quarterly*, Vol. 19, No. 2 (1974), 211-20.

The Organizational Climate Description Questionnaire and some other measures were given to 205 teachers and 40 department heads in 10 senior high schools. Sex of the department head does appear to affect teacher behavior. It seems important for morale that teachers perceive a high level of influence for their subordinates.

Sawhill, Isabel V., "The Economics of Discrimination Against Women: Some New Findings," *The Journal of Human Resources*, Vol. 8, No. 3 (1973), 383-96.

Data on 32,997 individuals were taken from the *1967 Current Population Survey*. There remains a 43% differential between men and women who are similar with respect to age, education, race, region, hours, and weeks worked, and time spent in the labor force. Reduced training opportunities for women is a major source of the sex differential.

Schein, Virginia Ellen, "The Relationship Between Sex Role Stereotypes and Requisite Management Characteristics," *Journal of Applied Psychology*, Vol. 57, No. 2 (1973), 95-100.

Three hundred male middle managers rated either women in general, men in general, or successful middle managers on 92 descriptive terms. Successful middle managers were perceived to possess characteristics, attitudes, and temperaments more commonly ascribed to men in general than women in general.

Schein, Virginia Ellen, "Relationships Between Sex Role Stereotypes and Requisite Management Characteristics Among Female Managers," *Journal of Applied Psychology*, Vol. 60, No. 3 (1975), 340-44.

A previous study on male managers was replicated by having 167 female middle managers rate either women in general, men in general, or successful middle managers on 92 descriptive terms. As in the male sample, successful middle managers were perceived to possess characteristics, attitudes, and temperaments more commonly ascribed to men in general than to women. Female managers with limited managerial experience perceived the sex role stereotype and perceived the requisite management characteristics relationship most strongly.

Schermerhorn, John R., Ann L. Snelson, and Gerald C. Leader, "Women in Management: The MBA Students' Perspective," *Academy of Management Proceedings* (1975), 451-53.

A semantic differential scale was completed by 221 male and 56 female MBA candidates. "Both males and females implicitly stereotyped MBA students of the opposite sex negatively from the perspective of the effective manager concept." Males view the concept as essentially "masculine"; females view it in effectively "neuter" terms.

Schuler, Randall S., "Sex, Organizational Level, and Outcome Importance: Where the Differences Are," *Personnel Psychology*, Vol. 28, No. 3 (1975), 365-75.

A questionnaire was completed by 331 employees of a large manufacturing organization. There were 157 low-level, 76 middle-level, and 98 upper-level employees including 35 females at the low level and 15 at the middle level. No differences across organization levels were found on the importance of intrinsic job outcomes. Neither age nor education influenced job outcome importance. Other findings were consonant with other occupational role stereotyping literature.

Shapiro, H. Jack, and Louis W. Stern, "Job Satisfaction: Male and Female Professional and Non-Professional Workers," *Personnel Journal*, Vol. 54, No. 7 (1975), 388-89, 406-407.

The Job Description Index was given to 77 male and 57 female nonprofessional and 23 male and 45 female professional workers. Total job satisfaction is appreciably higher for non-professional females than males, while the professional male's total job satisfaction is appreciably higher than for females.

Shepherd, William G., and Sharon G. Levin, "Managerial Discrimination in Large Firms," *Review of Economics and Statistics*, Vol. 55, No. 4 (1973), 412-22.

Data were collected from 231 large manufacturing firms. Comparisons were made between 1966 and 1970. Women were essentially at token levels, and their managerial participation has not been rising.

Shinar, Eva H., "Sexual Stereotypes of Occupations," *Journal of Vocational Behavior*, Vol. 7, No. 1 (1975), 99-111.

A list of 129 occupations was ranked to examine the nature of occupation sex stereotypes as perceived by 60 male and 60 female undergraduate introductory psychology students. Both groups seem to clearly define and agree on sex stereotypes of occupations. Occupation sex labeling seems deeply ingrained, self-perpetuating, and self-promoting in that the proportion of men and women in various occupations matches traditional beliefs about sex-related attributes required to perform the job.

Singer, Jack N., "Sex and College Class Differences in Attitudes Toward Autonomy in Work," *Human Relations,* Vol. 27, No. 5 (1974), 493-99.

A scale of attitude toward autonomy in work and attitude toward the women's liberation movement was constructed. Subjects were 17 male freshmen, 17 male seniors, 17 female freshmen, and 19 female seniors. There were no significant male-female differences in attitudes toward autonomy in work. Seniors displayed significantly more positive attitudes than freshmen. Students' attitudes toward autonomy in work were significantly and positively correlated with their attitudes toward the women's liberation movement.

Singer, Jack N., "Sex Differences—Similarities in Job Preference Factors," *Journal of Vocational Behavior,* Vol. 5, No. 3 (1974), 357-65.

A total of 55 female and 75 male undergraduate psychology students ranked 25 job preference items according to how important they would be to them. The differences were not stereotypically male or female. Both groups want jobs where they can learn, accomplish something worthwhile, and work with friendly and congenial co-workers. A company's demonstrated broad social concern is not among the most important criteria used by students when making their decisions. There were strong male preferences for salary and security and female preferences for advancement opportunities and work recognition.

Standley, Kay, and Bradley Soule, "Women in Male-Dominated Professions: Contrasts in their Personal and Vocational Histories," *Journal of Vocational Behavior,* Vol. 4, No. 2 (1974), 245 – 58.

Questionnaires were completed by 27 women architects, 27 lawyers, 27 physicians, and 71 psychologists. The psychologists described experiences and career patterns less in conflict with stereotypic female roles than the other three groups.

Taylor, Marilyn L., Marianne Odgagoo, and Eileen Morley, "Experiences of American Professional Women in Overseas Business Assignments," *Academy of Management Proceedings* (1975), 454-56.

Interviews were conducted with 34 women who had undertaken international assignments. They indicated overwhelming satisfaction and cited verbal approval from superiors, promotions, and later assignments, which reinforced their feelings.

Terborg, James R., and Daniel R. Ilgen, "A Theoretical Approach to Sex Discrimination in Traditionally Masculine Occupations," *Organizational Behavior and Human Performance,* Vol. 13, No. 3 (1975), 352-76.

An in-basket exercise was completed by 36 male and 7 female undergraduate personnel administration students. Identically qualified males and females were hired as often; however, the female was offered a significantly lower starting salary. She was more frequently assigned to routine tasks and her second-year salary offer increased the initial salary discrepancy.

Terborg, James R., Lawrence H. Peters, Daniel R. Ilgen, and Frank Smith, "Organizational and Personal Correlates of Attitudes Toward Women as Managers," *Academy of Management Journal,* Vol. 20, No. 1 (1977), 89-100.

The Women as Managers Scale was completed by 180 male and 100 female employees of an international distributing company. Validation procedures were used with positive results. Highly educated females tend to have the most favorable attitudes toward women as managers, which may refute the "queen bee syndrome." There was no evidence of a negative relationship between organizational level and favorable attitudes toward women as managers for the male sample. (Also see Appendix D, "Research Tools.")

Tinker, Irene, "Nonacademic Professional Political Scientists," *American Behavioral Scientist,* Vol. 15, No. 2 (1971), 206-12.

Members of a professional government association were sent forms to assess the opinions and positions of women in a variety of extra-academic positions. Sixty forms were returned. Women admit to professional discrimination and underutilization while denying personal discrimination. Evidence indicates such lack of difficulties may be self-delusion.

Tolor, Alexander, Bryan R. Kelly, and Charles A. Stebbins, "Assertiveness, Sex-Role Stereotyping, and Self-Concept," *The Journal of Psychology,* Vol. 93, No. 1 (1976), 157-64.

Responses to the Rathus Assertiveness Schedule, College Self-Expression Scale, list of stereotypic items, and Tennessee Self Concept Scale were given by 61 male and 73 female undergraduate students. There was a positive relationship between assertiveness and favorableness of self-concept for both sexes. Women low in sex-role stereotyping were significantly more assertive and had more positive self-concepts than men low in sex-role stereotyping.

Touhey, John C., "Effects of Additional Men on Prestige and Desirability of Occupations Typically Performed by Women," *Journal of Applied Social Psychology,* Vol. 4, No. 4 (1974), 330-35.

Subjects were 100 males and 100 females enrolled in several introductory social science courses. They rated the prestige and desirability of one of five occupations following information that the proportion of male practitioners was increasing or unchanging. Twelve semantic differential scales were used. Attributes connected to occupations admitting additional men included increased prestige, desirability, and activity; security, usefulness, success, and wealth.

Touhey, John C., "Effects of Additional Women Professionals on Ratings of Occupational Prestige and Desirability," *Journal of Personality and Social Psychology*, Vol. 29, No. 1 (1974), 86-89.

> The subjects were 114 male and 86 female introductory psychology students. They were asked to rate five high-status professions on prestige, desirability, and several other attributes after receiving information that the proportion of women practitioners was increasing or unchanging. On four of the five professions, prestige and desirability decreased for both male and female raters when increased proportions of women were anticipated. Other attributes given to occupations that admitted more women were increased passiveness, insecurity, and uselessness, and decreased success.

Valentine, Debbie, Nancy Ellinger, and Martha Williams, "Sex-Role Attitudes and the Career Choices of Male and Female Graduate Students," *The Vocational Guidance Quarterly*, Vol. 24, No. 1 (1975), 48-53.

> The Attitude Toward Women Scale was administered to 224 male and female graduate students in four professional schools. Students in the schools of Social Work and Library Science were termed as the traditionally feminine occupational group. Students in the School of Law and Graduate School of Business were termed as representing traditionally masculine occupations. The graduate women were much more nontraditional in their attitudes toward women's roles than were the men. Individuals choosing a typically opposite-sex profession seem more liberal in their attitudes toward sex roles than individuals choosing a typically same-sex profession. Men in feminine professions and women in masculine professions had higher proportions of working mothers than students who chose traditional occupations. See Appendix D.

Veiga, John F., and John N. Yanouzas, "What Women in Management Want: The Ideal Vs. The Real," *Academy of Management Journal*, Vol. 19, No. 1 (1976), 137-43.

> The "Disillusionment Index," a shortened version of the Mahoney, Jerdee, Carroll Management Activities Survey, was given to 40 women managers. Salary level, marital status, and education level had no effect on management disillusionment. Women below 35 were far more disillusioned with their overall management position than those over 35.

Wagner, Louis C., and Janis B. Banos, "A Woman's Place: A Follow-Up Analysis of the Roles Portrayed by Women in Magazine Advertisements," *Journal of Marketing Research*, Vol. 10, No. 2, (1973), 213-14.

> The January 1972 issues of seven general-interest magazines were analyzed to determine the roles portrayed by women. The percentage of advertisements portraying women in a working role has more than doubled since April 1970. Because of known advance planning for advertising, this finding represents substantial improvement over a short period of time.

Wahba, Susanne Patterson, "Job Satisfaction of Librarians: A Comparison Between Men and Women," *College and Research Libraries*, Vol. 36, No. 1 (1975), 45-51.

> The Need Satisfaction Questionnaire was completed by 202 men and women librarians from twenty-three college and university libraries. Both groups attached the same importance to security, social, and self-esteem needs. Women were more dissatisfied in security, esteem, autonomy, and self-actualization. Social needs and satisfaction were similar for both groups.

Weaver, Charles N., and Sandra L. Holmes, "A Comparative Study of the Work-Satisfaction of Females with Full-Time Employment and Full-Time Housekeeping," *Journal of Applied Psychology*, Vol. 60, No. 1 (1975), 117-18.

> Questionnaires were completed by 629 white females. Those who reported being very satisfied with their work included 52% of those employed full-time and 53% of those who keep house full-time. These results cast doubt that females who are employed full-time are less satisfied with their work than those who keep house full-time.

Wortzel, Lawrence H., and John M. Frisbie, "Women's Role Portrayal Preferences in Advertisements: An Empirical Study," *Journal of Marketing*, Vol. 38, No. 4 (1974), 41-46.

> A convenient sample of 100 women were asked to design ads by placing a picture of a product with a picture of a woman portrayed in each of five roles—neutral, family, career, sex object, and fashion object. They also completed a scale to determine their attitude toward the women's movement. Both groups tend to select role preferences on the basis of product function rather than feelings about the women's movement.

Appendix C

Glossary

affirmative action — making additional efforts to recruit, employ, and promote qualified members of groups formerly excluded, even if that exclusion cannot be traced to particular discriminatory actions on the part of the employer. Unless positive action is undertaken to overcome the effects of systemic institutional forms of exclusion and discrimination, a benign neutrality in employment practices will tend to perpetuate the status quo ante indefinitely. See U.S. Department of Health, Education and Welfare, Office for Civil Rights, *Higher Education Guidelines*, Executive Order 11246, p. 3.

BFOQ — bona fide occupational qualification reasonably necessary to normal business operation. See Judith B. Ittig, "A Title VII Primer," *Survey of Business* (May-June 1975), p. 13.

concentration — more of a particular group (females, males, Spanish surnamed or black males/females, etc.) in a job category or department than would reasonably be expected by their presence in the work force. See *Affirmative Action and Equal Employment*, Vol. 1, U.S. Equal Opportunity Commission, Washington, D.C. 20506, January 1974.

consciousness raising — making people aware of the sexist nature of many of the things that affect our lives every day so that they will avoid discriminatory practices.

famrat — family rationalization: employers are "naturally" reluctant to hire and promote women who "naturally" take time out or resign because of family obligations. See Gertrude Ezorsky, "The Fight Over University Women," *The New York Review of Books*, Vol. XXI, No. 8 (May 16, 1974), p. 33.

goals — projected levels of achievement resulting from an analysis of the employer's deficiencies based on the availability of qualified minorities and women and the expected turnover in its work force. Does *not* require hiring workers when there are no vacancies or hiring unqualified persons. See U.S. Department of Health, Education and Welfare, Office for Civil Rights, *Higher Education Guidelines*, Executive Order 11246, p. 3.

Queen-Bee syndrome—a woman who likes to be the lone female in a male world. She is unmoved by feminist causes. After all, if she made it without equal employment opportunity legislation, why can't they? See Jacqueline Thompson, "Patrons, Rabbis, Mentors—Whatever You Call Them, Women Need Them Too," *MBA* (February 1976), p. 36.

quota—an assigned share. *Quota* is a term often used by those resisting affirmative action efforts. However, "quotas are neither required nor permitted" by Executive Order 11246, p. 4, which imposes equal employment opportunity requirements on federal contractors.

sexism—any arbitrary stereotyping of males and females on the basis of their gender. See "Guidelines for Equal Treatment of the Sexes in McGraw-Hill Book Co. Publications," McGraw-Hill Book Co., 1221 Avenue of the Americas, New York, N.Y. 10020.

underutilization—having fewer women or minorities in a particular job than would reasonably be expected by their availability. See U.S. Department of Health, Education and Welfare, Office for Civil Rights, *Higher Education Guidelines*, Executive Order 11246, p. 3.

Appendix D

Research Tools

"Bem Sex Role Inventory" (BSRI)—A highly developed instrument that contains 20 feminine, 20 masculine, and 20 neutral personality characteristics. Subjects are classified as "masculine," "feminine," "androgynous," or "undifferentiated." Psychological androgyny denotes the integration of both masculine and feminine traits within a single individual. Research has shown that an androgynous view of oneself seems to accompany some very positive attributes—maturity in moral judgments, higher level of self-esteem, and high levels of "masculine" independence and "feminine" nurturance when the situation calls for it. Dr. Bem has several fine publications concerning her research in developing the BSRI. Her "Revised Scoring Packet for the Bem Sex Role Inventory" contains both an SPSS computer scoring program and a hand-scoring method. For more information, write: Dr. Sandra L. Bem, Department of Psychology, Stanford University, Stanford, California 94305.

"Women As Managers Scale" (WAMS)—See Lawrence H. Peters, James R. Terborg, and Janet Taynor, "Women As Managers Scale (WAMS): A Measure of Attitudes Toward Women in Management Positions," *JSAS Document No. 585*, American Psychological Association (1974), 44 pp. Describes the development of a 21-item attitude toward Women as Managers Scale. Normative data for 345 male and 196 female college students are presented. The entire WAMS is reproduced and possible uses as either a dependent or an independent variable in applied research are discussed. More research has been done by Peters and Terborg with Daniel R. Ilgen and Frank Smith. See Terborg et al (1977) in Appendix B, "Annotated Bibliography." For more information, write: Dr. James R. Terborg, Department of Psychology, University of Illinois, Champaign, Illinois 61820.

"The Attitudes Toward Women Scale"—Contains 25 items on the role of women. Subjects are asked to indicate how strongly they agree or disagree with the statements on a four-point scale. See Valentine et al. (1975), Appendix B. See also J. R. Spence and R. Helmrich, "The Attitudes Toward Women Scale: An Objective Instrument to Measure Attitudes Toward the Rights and Roles of Women in Contemporary Society," *JSAS Catalog of Selected Documents in Psychology*, No. 153 (1972).

"Rathus Assertiveness Schedule" — Subjects are asked to indicate how characteristic or descriptive of themselves each of 30 statements is, by using a six-point coding system. See S. A. Rathus, "A 30-Item Schedule for Assessing Assertive Behavior," *Behavior Therapy* Vol. 4 (1973), pp. 398 – 406.

"The Attitude Toward Women as Managers Scale" — Contains 36 items to predict the relationship between superiors and subordinates in managerial situations. "The ATWAM Scale: A Forced Choice Scale for Measuring Attitudes Toward Women as Managers," is a technical report that "describes the need for, and development of, an unbiased measure of attitudes toward women as managers." For more information, write: Edward B. Yost, Instructor in Business Administration, Franklin University, Columbus, Ohio 43215 and Theodore T. Herbert, Associate Professor of Management, The University of Akron, Akron, Ohio 44325.

Appendix E

The Laws

BRIEF HIGHLIGHTS OF MAJOR FEDERAL LAWS AND ORDER ON SEX DISCRIMINATION

Equal Pay Act of 1963 (generally effective June 11, 1964)

As an amendment to the Fair Labor Standards Act (FLSA), this act requires the same pay for men and women doing equal work, requiring equal skill, effort, and responsibility under similar working conditions in the same establishment. Its provisions apply to "wages in the sense of remuneration for employment (including overtime) and employer contributions for most fringe benefits. Where discrimination exists, pay rates of the lower paid sex must be raised to equal those of the higher paid sex. In a landmark decision, a Federal court rejected a claim that the jobs of men and women have to be identical for them to receive equal pay and asserted that they need only be "substantially equal."

The act, which is enforced by the Labor Department's Wage and Hour Division, permits wage differentials based on a bona fide seniority or merit system or a system that measures earnings by quantity or quality of production or any other factor other than sex. It specifically prohibits discharging or discriminating against any employee who files a complaint. Also, it prohibits labor organizations from causing or attempting to cause employers to violate the act.

As of July 1, 1972, the protection of the Equal Pay Act was extended to executive, administrative, and professional employees and to outside sales personnel. As of May 1, 1974, the act was further extended to most employees of Federal, State, and local governments. Among the few categories still unprotected are employees in some small retail or service establishments.

Women's Bureau, Employment Standards Administration, U.S. Department of Labor, 1974.

Further information on the Equal Pay Act and other provisions of the FLSA, as well as the Federal law against age discrimination in employment, is available from the field offices of the Wage and Hour Division or from:

Wage and Hour Division
Employment Standards Administration
U.S. Department of Labor
Washington, D.C.   20210

Title VII of the Civil Rights Act of 1964, as amended by the Equal Employment Opportunity Act of 1972

Title VII prohibits discrimination in employment based on sex, as well as on race, color, religion, and national origin, by employers of 15 or more employees, public and private employment agencies, labor organizations with 15 or more members, and labor-management apprenticeship programs. State and local government agencies and public and private educational institutions are covered, but religious educational institutions or associations are exempt with respect to the employment of individuals of a particular religion. Employers excluded from coverage are Federal and District of Columbia agencies (other than the Federal-State employment service system), federally owned corporations, and Indian tribes. Specifically excluded from the definition of "employee" are State and local elected officials and their personal staff and policymaking appointees.

Discrimination based on race, color, sex, religion, or national origin is unlawful in hiring or firing; wages; fringe benefits; classifying, referring, assigning, or promoting employees; extending or assigning use of facilities; training, retraining, or apprenticeships; or any other terms, conditions, or privileges of employment.

The Equal Employment Opportunity Commission (EEOC), which enforces title VII, has issued "Guidelines on Discrimination Because of Sex." The guidelines, which were last revised April 5, 1972, bar hiring based on stereotyped characterization of the sexes, classification or labeling of "men's jobs" and "women's jobs," or advertising under male or female headings. They specify that the bona fide occupational qualification exemption should be interpreted narrowly, and that State laws which prohibit or limit the employment of women—in certain occupations, or in jobs that require lifting or carrying weights in excess of prescribed limits, during certain hours of the night, for more than a specified number of hours per day or per week, or for certain periods before and after childbirth—conflict with and are superseded by title VII. Accordingly, these "protective" labor laws cannot be used as a reason for refusing to employ women.

The guidelines state that, where State laws require minimum wage and overtime pay for women only, an employer not only may not refuse to hire female applicants to avoid this payment but must provide the same benefits for male employees. Similar provisions apply to rest and meal periods and physical facilities, although if an employer can prove that business necessity precludes providing these benefits to both men and women, the employer need not provide them to members of either sex.

Also, the guidelines prohibit excluding from employment an applicant or employee because of pregnancy. They state, among other things, that disabilities caused or contributed to by pregnancy, miscarriage, abortion, childbirth, and recovery therefrom are, for all job-related purposes, temporary disabilities and should be treated as such under any health or temporary disability insurance or sick leave plan available in connection with employment. Accrual of seniority, reinstatement, and payment under such insurance or plan should therefore be applied to disability due to pregnancy or childbirth as to other temporary disabilities. Where the employer does not have a leave plan, the Women's Bureau suggests that the EEOC be contacted.

Further information is available from regional offices of the EEOC or from:

Equal Employment Opportunity Commission
1800 G Street NW.
Washington, D.C.   20506

Executive Order 11246,
as amended (effective October 14, 1968)

This order prohibits employment discrimination based on sex, as well as on race, color, religion, or national origin, by Federal contractors or subcontractors and contractors who perform work under a federally assisted construction contract exceeding $10,000. Coverage includes all facilities of the contractor, regardless of whether they are involved in the performance of the Federal contract. The order does not exempt specific kinds of employment or employees.

To ensure nondiscrimination in employment, contractors must take affirmative action in such areas as recruitment and recruitment advertising; hiring, upgrading, demotion, and transfer; layoff or termination; rates of pay or other compensation; and selection for training, including apprenticeship.

The Labor Department's Office of Federal Contract Compliance (OFCC), which enforces the order, has issued "Sex Discrimination Guidelines." The guidelines state, among other things, that contractors may not advertise under male and female classifications, base seniority lists on sex, deny a person a job because of State "protective" labor laws, make distinctions between married and unmarried persons of one sex only, or penalize women in their terms and conditions of employment because they require leave for childbearing. The guidelines also specifically require the granting of a leave of absence to an employee for childbearing and reinstatement to her original job or to a position of like status and pay, without loss of service credits. A proposed revision of these guidelines appeared in the Federal Register of December 27, 1973. No final action has been taken as of June 1, 1974.

Nonconstruction contractors who have 50 or more employees and a contract of $50,000 or more are required by OFCC's Revised Order No. 4 (effective December 4, 1971) to develop written affirmative action programs which must establish acceptable goals and timetables for including more minorities and women in job categories where they have been underutilized.

Further information is available from:

Office of Federal Contract Compliance
Employment Standards Administration
U.S. Department of Labor
Washington, D.C.   20210